Sliced Iguana

ISABELLA TREE

Sliced Iguana

TRAVELS IN UNKNOWN MEXICO

HAMISH HAMILTON

LONDON

HAMISH HAMILTON LTD

Published by the Penguin Group
Penguin Books Ltd, 27 Wrights Lane, London w8 5TZ, England
Penguin Putnam Inc., 375 Hudson Street, New York, New York 10014, USA
Penguin Books Australia Ltd, Ringwood, Victoria, Australia
Penguin Books Canada Ltd, 10 Alcorn Avenue, Toronto, Ontario, Canada M4V 3B2
Penguin Books India (P) Ltd, 11 Community Centre,
Panchsheel Park, New Delhi – 110 017, India
Penguin Books (NZ) Ltd, Cnr Rosedale and Airborne Roads,
Albany, Auckland, New Zealand
Penguin Books (South Africa) (Pty) Ltd, 5 Watkins Street,
Denver Ext 4, Johannesburg 2094, South Africa

Penguin Books Ltd, Registered Offices: Harmondsworth, Middlesex, England

First published 2001

1

Set in 11.5/14.5pt Monotype Sabon
Typeset by Rowland Phototypesetting Ltd, Bury St Edmunds, Suffolk
Printed in Great Britain by Clays Ltd, St Ives plc

A CIP catalogue record for this book is available from the British Library

ISBN 0-241-14051-X

For my father, Michael (1921–1999),
and my mother, Anne,
for infecting me – on top of everything –
with their love of travel

The repertory of our urban insufficiencies, of our own version of Western culture, awaits us silently in the Indian world, which has become the secret repository of all that we have forgotten and disdained: ritual intensity, mythic imagination, caring for nature, the relationship with death, communal ties, the capacity for self-government.

– Carlos Fuentes, *A New Time for Mexico*, 1994

And to me the men in Mexico are like trees, forests that the white men felled in their coming. But the roots of the trees are deep and alive and forever sending up new shoots.

– D. H. Lawrence, *Mornings in Mexico*, 1927

Contents

Acknowledgements

I am deeply indebted to good friends in Mexico – Humberto Fernández Borja, Laureana Toledo, Natalia Toledo and Luis Miguel López Alanís – for taking me into their confidence and introducing me to worlds which would have remained closed to me on my own. I would particularly like to thank my Purépecha hosts on Lake Pátzcuaro and the Huichol of the northern Sierra Madre for their wonderful hospitality, their openness and generosity. They know who they are, though some names and places have been changed in order to protect them from unnecessary glare from the outside world. In Chiapas, I was put in the picture by several courageously outspoken women. Again it would be unwise to mention them by name but their help and instruction are profoundly appreciated.

Many other friends contributed to this book in other ways, as travelling companions, editors, advisers and as all-round help and inspiration. I would like to thank especially Guy Ogilvy, Jessica and Wendy Gottfried, Elisa Ramirez, Lucy MacDermot, Harriet Melhuish, Sasha Hails, Laurence Tardan, Tom Owen Edmunds, Francisco Corcuera, Michael Calderwood, Gillian Graham, Katie Hickman, Carmen Parra, Bob Somerlott, Chloë Sayer, Josceline and Jane Wheatley, Fiona MacDonald, Nan and Ian MacDonald, John and Sarah Wiseman, Sophie Fiennes, Enrice Badalesco, Damion Fraser, Alejandro Vilchis, Lisette and Pablo Span, Alejandro Vilchis, Colby Nolan Ristow, Veronika Bennholdt-Thomsen, Senator Adolfo Aguilar Zinser, Michael Zinser and Roger Whitehead.

I would also like to thank my agent, Gillon Aitken, and his assistant, Lesley Shaw, my publisher and editor, Simon Prosser, and my copy-editor, Martin Bryant.

And lastly, I would like to thank Charlie Burrell, my life's travelling companion, and Nancy and Ned for climbing so many pyramids, and enjoying it.

Author's Note

Many indigenous Mexican words can be hard to pronounce as they follow different pronunciation rules. The following are some of the more common problematic ones as they occur in the book.

Tenochtitlán – pronounced with a 'ch' as in 'loch'
Mexica – 'Mesheeka'
Xochimilco – pronounced 'Sotchimilco'
pulque – 'pullkay'
Juchitán – 'Hoocheetan'
Oaxaca – 'Wahacka'
muxe – 'mooshay'
cacique – 'kaseekay'
mole – 'molay'
Huichol – 'Witchol'
Huiricuta – 'Wirikuta'
xiriki – 'shiriki'
uxa – 'ooshah'
téiwari – 'taywari'
tequino – 'tehwino'

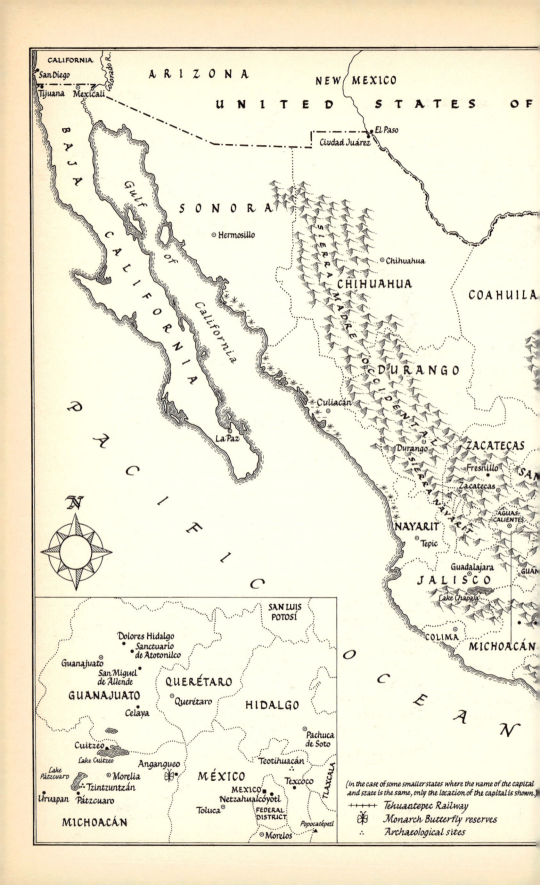

CALIFORNIA
San Diego
Tijuana Mexicali

Colorado R.

A R I Z O N A

NEW MEXICO

U N I T E D   S T A T E S   O F

El Paso
Ciudad Juárez

B A J A   C A L I F O R N I A

Gulf of California

S O N O R A

Hermosillo

Chihuahua

CHIHUAHUA

COAHUILA

SIERRA MADRE OCCIDENTAL

DURANGO

Culiacán

Durango

ZACATECAS

Fresnillo

Zacatecas

SAN

AGUAS CALIENTES

SIERRA NAYARIT

NAYARIT

Tepic

La Paz

P A C I F I C

Guadalajara

GUAN

JALISCO

Lake Chapala

COLIMA

MICHOACÁN

O C E A N

SAN LUIS POTOSÍ

Dolores Hidalgo
Sanctuario
de Atotonilco

Guanajuato

San Miguel
de Allende

QUERÉTARO

GUANAJUATO

Celaya

Querétaro

HIDALGO

Cuitzeo

Lake Cuitzeo

Angangueo

Pachuca
de Soto

Lake
Pátzcuaro

Morelia

Teotihuacán

Uruapan Tzintzuntzán
Pátzcuaro

MÉXICO

Texcoco

TLAXCALA

MEXICO
Netzahualcóyotl

MICHOACÁN

Toluca

FEDERAL
DISTRICT

Popocatépetl

Morelos

(In the case of some smaller states where the name of the capital
and state is the same, only the location of the capital is shown.)

+++++ Tehuantepec Railway
🏵 Monarch Butterfly reserves
∴ Archaeological sites

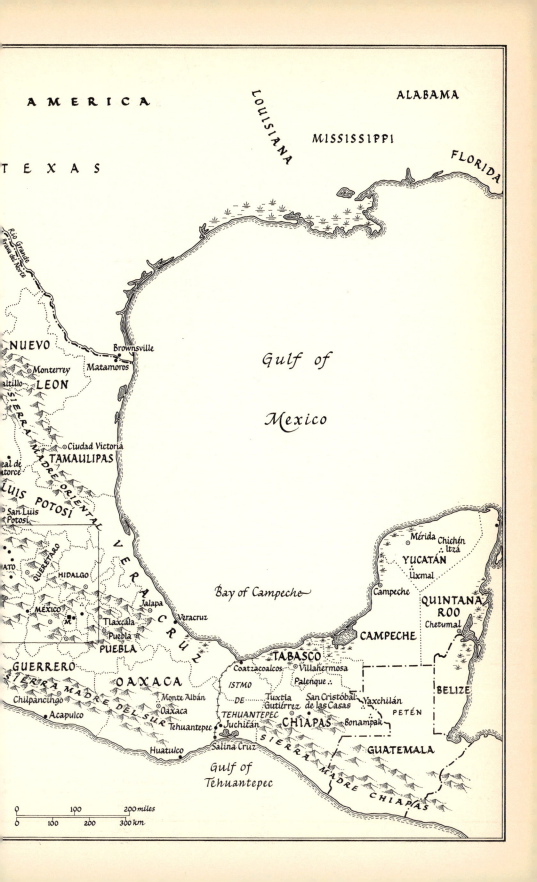

Urban Leviathan
Mexico City

This city has no history
only martyrology.
Country of pain,
capital of suffering,
the broken centre
of the great, unending disaster.

José Emilio Pacheco, 'City of Memory' 1986

. . . men build their cultures by huddling together,
nervously loquacious, at the edge of the abyss.

Kenneth Burke, Permanence and Change:
An Anatomy of Purpose, *1984*

From several thousand feet up in a jumbo jet Mexico City looks like the capital of another planet. It is monstrous, so incomprehensible in scale that it drains the mind like the concept of infinity. It stretches on for ever, a mindless concrete desert, the stuff of science fiction – something from *Blade Runner* or *Star Wars*. From up here, buildings that must be landmarks on the ground are reduced to anonymous blips; office blocks have become tiny components on the surface of an immense microchip. A macrochip.

It looks inhuman, uninhabitable, and yet it houses one of the largest populations – if not the largest – of any city on earth. Somehow, down there, are over 25 million people, more than the populations of Australia and New Zealand put together. It is a terrifying thought. All those lives, the dozens of hearts that must be stopping at this very minute, the hundreds convulsing in their very first tick. I'm struck by a sudden stirring of adrenalin, by the parachutist's second thoughts. I feel as insignificant as a microbe, a flea about to hop down and fight its way through the labyrinth of Knossos.

A small, dark woman across the aisle is saying her rosary in preparation for the descent, kissing her fingertips and crossing herself in miniature, praying for our souls, as if she's been reading my mind. It's enough to stir up the old antipathies of a convent school upbringing and resuscitate a little sang-froid. Was this how Cortés had felt, I berate myself, when he stood on the threshold of Mexico City five hundred years ago – vertiginous, betrayed by doubt, with a sudden longing to be home in bed in his favourite pyjamas?

My anxiety is fuelled, I know, by the vastness of the land that lies beneath me and my incomprehension of it. But this is my very reason for coming. Ever since my friend Guy suddenly moved here on a mad 'shamanic quest' two years ago, I'd been musing – all his friends had – about the nature of Mexico as a destination. Not that I was tempted to join him. Guy had disappeared somewhere into the northern Mexican desert after announcing he'd married a white witch who'd convinced him that Mexico was the ordained place to survive the impending apocalypse and start a 'new tribe'. For the first time, though, the idea of Mexico raised its head in my subconscious and began to mew there appealingly. And, typically, the more I began to think about Mexico, the more people I met who had Mexican connections, who struck another spark of life into the subject.

I discovered that, as a family, we had our own link with Mexico. It was there flamboyantly displayed in the coat of arms chosen by my husband's great-great-grandfather when he was given his title in 1917. Originally a Yorkshire engineer who made a name for himself building the Blackwall Tunnel under the Thames and the docks at Dover, Weetman Pearson landed his real fortune in Mexico. His coat of arms was designed to draw attention to the two agents of his success: on one side is a diver in a glistening wet diver's suit and boots, with a helmet under his arm; on the other – with the heraldic shield between them – stands a Mexican labourer in woollen poncho, sandals and sombrero. They stand on a ribbon bearing the 1st Viscount Cowdray's motto: 'Do It With Thy Might'. My husband's cousins had stone statues of the diver and the Mexican by their swimming-pool in Sussex. We hung our wet swimming costumes over them in the summer.

Working under the auspices of the Mexican dictator, Porfirio Díaz, Pearson had been responsible for creating much of modern Mexico's infrastructure. He'd built Mexico's main industrial harbour at Vera Cruz on the Gulf Coast, plumbing and electrifying the port and building a new railway terminal in the process. He'd constructed the extraordinary Trans-Isthmus Tehuantepec Railway, 'the most difficult and serious business' he ever undertook, connecting the Gulf Coast and the Pacific through some of the most difficult terrain in Mexico in order to provide the country – and the world – with an alternative to the Panama Canal. At either end of the Tehuantepec Railway he'd built two ports from scratch, providing deep-water harbours for a new influx of international cargo ships. And, eventually, he'd struck oil. The Pearson empire – Lazard's (the merchant bank), the *Financial Times*, and even (fortuitously) Penguin books – had its roots in a country on the other side of the world.

I learnt that my great-great-grandfather's brother had brought Mexico into my side of the family, too, although not quite so beneficently. He'd fought in the American invasion of Mexico in 1846. My father showed me fragments of Arthur Tree's letters written from the front. They were falling to pieces, ink-stained, sweat-stained, mosquito-splattered, in a tattered pouch among the family papers. They described 'dashing against the Mexicans', the horses seeming 'to snuff the war from afar', the impenetrable 'Mesquite and Chaparral bushes' on the banks of the Rio Grande, the 'musicians striking up the Yankee doodle' and 'the universal shout' as a squadron of Tree's regiment 'up to their necks in water, huzzaring and in gallant style, reached the opposite bank'.

But apart from an aside on the merits of Mexican cooking and the addictive nature of the 'Peppers which they put in everything', I was none the wiser about the country Arthur Tree had been attacking, or its people.

Of modern Mexico I was almost completely ignorant. The vague stereotype persisted in my mind that Mexico was a) covered in pyramids b) Mesoamerica's answer to the Costa del Sol c) populated by Mexican peons dozing in the shade under sombreros. There was little in the press to contradict this idea bar the odd piece in *Newsweek* on corruption or drugs trafficking. But sleepless nights with a second new baby hot on the heels of the first had given me an insomniac's addiction to the BBC World Service and occasionally I caught a news bulletin about the turning political tide in Mexico, the crumbling of an old dictatorial regime and the stirrings of democracy. Mexico was clearly a country on the move.

On the economic side, I heard over the midnight air-waves, Mexico was having to battle with the Pandora's box of globalization after signing the North American Free Trade Agreement (NAFTA) with Canada and the United States in 1994 – a marriage, as one reporter described it, between two giants and a midget. My British predilection for an underdog sneaked into play.

I was given a more descriptive image of the Mexican landscape by a friend who'd just been offered a post working for the British Council in Mexico City. He'd been travelling around the country as a consultant on a reforestation programme. He was nuts about the place, biologically speaking, and had come back to London to collect his wife and child for a two-year post out there. 'Mexico's the third most biologically diverse nation in the world,' he enthused. 'In fact UNESCO has classified it a "country of megadiversity". It's got more reptiles than any other country in the world; it's got the second largest number of mammal species; and the fourth largest number of amphibians. It's got more than 30,000 species of plants – over half of them found nowhere else on earth. It's got 1000 species of ferns. There are more than 135 species of oak, and forty-nine species of pine – that's half of all the pine species in the world. No one thinks of Mexico like this. But it's got every environment you could think of, including twelve of the World Wildlife Fund's 200 Global Eco-regions, from snow-capped volcanoes to mangroves to alpine meadows to lakes to rainforest.' He was as passionate about Mexico as he was knowledgeable – David Attenborough's answer to Indiana Jones. His pockets still

4

contained crumbs of pumice from a recent encounter with an erupting volcano.

One of the reasons Mexico was neglected, he suggested, was that it defied definition. It was a place of extremes, made up of different landscapes, different peoples, different cultures. 'It's like India,' he said. 'You think of it as a single country until you get to know it.' Mexico, he said, was still trying to identify itself. 'Its history has been like a teenager trying on different outfits from other people's wardrobes,' he went on, 'it's still looking for something that fits.'

But I wondered if there couldn't be another reason for the psychological blank, that our – the world's – view of Mexico had been dimmed by the perspective of the United States. When I'd travelled to the States, antennae twitching, in the last few years, I'd come home none the wiser about its next-door neighbour. There it was, this giant, the most powerful country in the world, sharing a border over 2000 miles long with what it neurotically insisted was a mad, bad and dangerous place to go. US foreign policy, tourism, and international relations at every level were magnetically drawn in an Atlantic or Asiatic direction. The compass rarely seemed to swing south. Judging from media coverage in the States, Mexico might be on the dark side of the moon.

There was a saying in Mexico, my British Council friend had told me, that having a neighbour like the United States was like a mouse sharing a bed with an elephant. There was the constant threat that the mouse would be crushed in its sleep. Every time the elephant sneezed, the mouse got blown out of the room. And yet, I thought, weren't elephants famously, ridiculously, frightened of mice? Couldn't the boot be on the other foot?

A proper look at the map inflated my notion of Mexico like a balloon. The 'Estados Unidos de Mexicanos', as it was correctly labelled, was enormous – not at all the quirky little country I'd supposed. It wasn't part of Central America as I'd always thought – some quaint little Somerset Maugham-ish backwater – but a massive chunk of the North American continent. Its total land area was 756,198 square miles – equal to France, Spain, Britain, Germany and Italy combined – making it the fourteenth largest country in the world. There were 1178 miles separating Mexico City from Ciudad Juárez, a town halfway along the North American border. Another 744 miles separated Mexico City from Ciudad Cuauhtémoc, the nearest town on the Guatemalan border. And it had once been double this size, until Arthur Tree and his regiment invaded and US President Polk appropriated California, Texas, New Mexico, Arizona and parts of Colorado, Nevada and Utah – illegally – for the gringos in 1848.

The official census in 1995 put Mexico's population at 91.2 million, and most of these, my guidebook told me, were of mixed blood – *mestizos*. But there were at least 7 million indigenous *Indios*, possibly – if you counted those of predominantly Indian ancestry – as many as 25 million. There were fifty-six distinct indian peoples in Mexico; with thirteen out of Mexico's thirty-one states regarded as 'eminently indigenous'. The remotest Mexican Indians still lived traditionally, as tribes, and hadn't yet learnt Spanish, the national language. This was what was becoming known as 'México Profundo', 'Deep Mexico' – the world of *los indígenas* and disadvantaged *mestizos* living, almost invisibly, in the remote sierras and deserts and the lost cities of ancient empires. And this is what began to intrigue me the most. But at the same time, as I pondered these figures, I was unnerved to realize I'd never knowingly met a Mexican.

It's a thought that returns to me uncomfortably as the plane wheels about and joins the stacking system over the city. Through the scratched double-perspex I can see the cones of volcanoes, lightly dusted with snow, and plumes of mist (or could it be steam or smoke?) wafting from their peaks. The whole valley is enclosed, like a fortress – the flipside of Shangri-La. The rest is hazy. A rusty fog squats over the city. It engulfs all the smaller ridges and the mini craters inside the basin, stopping only at the outer ring of volcanoes where it laps their bases, restlessly, as if trying to escape from a trap. Here and there, though, a canal straight as an arrow – courtesy of Weetman Pearson – glints like a mirror.

The British Airways flight attendant is giggling through an announcement. The Mexican stewardesses have bet him that he can't say 'Popocatépetl' correctly three times in a row.

'Ladies and Gentlemen, we will shortly be landing in Mexico City. As is customary, the Captain has enquired from Air Traffic Control about the status of . . . Popocatépetl . . . a live volcano located thirty-five miles to the south of the city. And I am happy to announce that . . . Popocatépetl . . . has not been active over the past few days and it doesn't look like any emissions from . . . Popocatépetl . . . will adversely affect landings for some days to come.'

The cabin bursts into applause and then one of the stewardesses repeats the announcement in Spanish to show how it should be done, rattling off the ancient tongue-twisting Náhuatl name for the famous 'Smoking Mountain' as easily as if it were her own.

She announces our descent as we pass down into the smog, the notorious *niebla tóxica* – the toxic cloud – that makes the Valley of Mexico one of the most polluted places on earth. At this time of year, early spring, the valley is still prone to wintertime thermal inversions which, combined with the high altitude – Mexico City is 7350 feet above sea level – produce such high ozone levels that migrating Canadian starlings flying through it plummet dead from the sky. Despite excellent weather conditions, the flight attendant informs us, visibility is down to 800 metres – the landing visibility limit for our jumbo jet. But this, she assures us, is quite normal for Mexico City at this time of year.

The world looks fuzzier now, not dimmer exactly, but slightly out of focus, as if I'm seeing it through net curtains, or someone else's spectacles.

It's chaos in Arrivals. There's a hyped-up episode of a Mexican soap on TV and all the arrivals monitors are relaying an amorous death scene instead of flight information. A crowd twenty people thick is blocking the exit. Some of them are glued to the melodrama; the rest are looking anxious and confused, accosting arriving passengers to find out which planes have landed.

Outside the terminal it is a hazy, warm evening. The air has a vaguely sulphurous taste to it, slightly fizzy. It reminds me of inhaling the fumes from igniting match-heads – something we used to resort to at school when we couldn't get cigarettes. When I'm surprised by a coughing fit in the back of my taxi, the driver winds up his window and reaches for his packet of Viceroy. '¡Carajo!' he swears, lighting up, 'Jesus! The pollution – it's terrible.'

We crawl over a flyover with tailbacks in both directions, brake lights looking beautiful against the sunset. It's the evening rush hour. Giant packets of cigarettes light up the sky. There's a building-size advertisement for Trojan, a Mexican brand of condoms – odd for a Catholic country, I think. And one for Palacio de Hierro, a Mexico City department store, with the slogan 'All women do, is cry and buy shoes'.

Scarcely have we accelerated beyond walking pace than we're pulled over by a police car which has been waiting predator-like on the hard shoulder. The cop – the *tira* – leans his elbows inside the driver's window, chews gum and appraises the contents of the car as if he had all the time in the world. Unable to find anything out of order with the driver's papers he nods at me. 'She's not wearing a seat-belt.' I begin to blurt apologies in broken Spanish, I'm English, just arrived, I didn't know, never again officer. 'Five hundred pesos,' he says to the driver who looks, for the first time, unnerved. 'Fifty dollars,' he adds for my benefit, 'I'm doing you a favour. If you like, you can come to the station – both of you – but they'll charge you a hundred dollars there.'

I hand over a fifty-dollar bill looking as shirty as I dare and the taxi driver lets out a whistle as we pull away – I'm not sure whether of outrage or relief. '¡Cabrón! Bastard!' he says. 'You shouldn't have let him know you'd just arrived. That's why he asked for so much. They think gringos are a gold mine. That's a week's wages for me. Lucky for me you paid. He would've taken my licence.' He kisses a small crucifix hanging round his neck. Then he looks back at me in the rear-view mirror where a furry troll is jiggling about beside a plastic Virgin Mary, and his face bursts into a grin. 'So what do you think of Mexico City?'

Five hundred years ago Mexico City was one of the most beautiful places on earth. Europeans, when they discovered it, were dumbfounded. It was spectacular, massive, one of the biggest human settlements in the world, even then. It was certainly bigger than any city on the other side of the Atlantic where the conquistadors had come from. It was twice the size of Seville, way bigger than Naples or Constantinople. It was a bustling, thriving, well-organized metropolis, home to more than 200,000 people, seat of the Aztec Empire.

By the time they reached Mexico City, or Tenochtitlán as it was then called, the band of 400 Spanish conquistadors might have felt themselves inured to wondrous surprises. They'd spent seven months battling their way from the Gulf Coast, arduously forcing their way inland towards the central mountains where rumour pointed to a mythical city. They'd seen plenty of impressive towns on the way. They'd been entertained by Indian chiefs; wooed with gifts of gold and silver ornaments (not much, it must be said, but enough to dangle before them the promise of treasure ahead); and been hospitably bedded by numerous Indian slave-girls and princesses. The first generation of mixed race *mestizos* was already months into gestation. They'd also, thanks to several disgruntled subject dominions who'd seized this chance to rebel against their powerful Aztec overlords, been able to swell their army with 20,000 native recruits.

The Spaniards had become familiar with Mexico's extraordinary wildlife – jaguars, pumas, armadillos, howler-monkeys, tapirs and hairless dogs; hummingbirds, long-tailed quetzals, toucans, trogons and turkeys – most of which they'd been invited to eat. They'd drunk a strange, frothy aromatic drink made from cacao beans called *chocolatl* and they'd smoked tobacco. They'd fought battles with other, hostile tribes – mostly allies loyal to the Aztecs – who'd been dressed very effectively in padded cotton armour but who, though expert with sling and stone, arrows and spears, had fortunately been intimidated by the Spanish musket and cannon and the terrifying appearance of horses.

But most of all, the Spaniards had been stunned by ceremonies they'd encountered where human beings – slaves captured in battle – were put to the knife, dozens at a time, and then ritually eaten. Wherever they'd seen a pyramid or temple, or come across yet another stinking priest with matted, blood-soaked hair, the motley band of Spanish adventurers had set up an altar to Christ and tried to instil in these strange, civilized barbarians – forcefully if it came to it – a grain of Christian decency. They must have thought they'd seen it all.

But when, in that early November of 1519, Cortés and his fellows finally breached the high pass between the peaks of Popocatépetl and its sister volcano, Ixtaccíhuatl, they descended into a landscape unlike any they had so far encountered. The valley floor was a network of broad, shallow lakes which had been connected to each other by man-made canals. Most of the lake edges were laced with settlements and small cultivated fields, with here and there a substantial town. There were many different peoples living in the valley who spoke dialects of the same language – Náhuatl – but over the past hundred years the Valley of Mexico and all the outlying areas had become subject to a powerful Triple Alliance comprising the three dominant tribes – the Texcocans, the Tacubans and the Mexica. Of these, the most powerful by far were the Mexica, or Aztecs. The Triple Alliance formed the corner-stone of the Aztec Empire, an empire that reached west to the Pacific coast, east to the Gulf and south towards Mesoamerica.

It was the magnificent city of the Mexica that floated Venice-like in the biggest lake, and that dominated the Valley of Mexico. From their vantage point on the high pass, the Spanish could see it was densely built. There were palaces two storeys high with inner courtyards and gardens; streets and squares and canals full of canoes; people bustling along the footpaths or tending gardens on the rooftops. And in the centre, a city within the city, was a shimmering mass of skyscraping towers and pyramids, vividly stuccoed in blood-red, ochre and blue.

Reflected in the water of the lake and reaching for the clouds, the great city of México-Tenochtitlán seemed to hover between this world and the next. There were three branching causeways, each two or more leagues long and thirty feet wide, tethering it to the land. It looked so fantastic, it was as if the eye was playing tricks, projecting the surrounding volcanoes, perhaps, into some extraordinary mirror-image – a gigantic, melting mirage.

The conquistadors could hardly believe it was real. 'When we saw all those cities and villages built in the water, and other great towns on dry land', reported Bernal Díaz, 'and that straight and level causeway leading to Mexico, we were astonished. These great towns and pyramids and buildings rising from the water, all made of stone, seemed like an enchanted vision from the tale of Amadis. Indeed, some of our soldiers asked whether it was not all a dream.'

When the Spaniards penetrated the city nucleus at last and were hospitably received, stinking from their long march, into the perfumed bowers of the great Aztec ruler, Moctezuma, they tried to make sense of what they saw around them. Cortés struggled to give some idea of scale in his reports to King Charles back in Spain so that the king might appreciate the priceless jewel about to be added to his crown. The pyramids, or 'towers' as he described them, rose higher than the cathedral at Seville. Moctezuma himself lived in a palace 'so marvellous that it seems to me impossible to describe its excellence and grandeur . . . in Spain there is nothing to compare with it'. The Aztec Emperor was, Cortés explained, 'so feared there could be no ruler in the world more so'.

The exoticism of the city reminded the Spaniards of the Moors. Some referred to the temple pyramids as *mesquitas*, or mosques. The palaces were airy and spacious, built of 'magnificent stone, cedar wood, and the wood of other sweet-smelling trees', with great rooms and courts shaded from the sun by awnings of woven cotton. There were orchards and gardens. 'I was never tired of noticing the diversity of trees and the various scents given off by each', described Bernal Díaz, 'and the paths choked with roses and other flowers, and the many local fruit-trees and rose-bushes, and the pond of fresh water . . . large canoes could come into the garden from the lake, through a channel they had cut, and their crews did not have to disembark. Everything was shining with lime and decorated with different kinds of stonework and paintings which were a marvel to gaze on.'

For the Spaniards, used to the medieval squalor and grime of European cities, the stench of rotting rubbish, open drains and smoke, one of the greatest wonders of Tenochtitlán was its cleanness and the sparkling clarity of the air. Yet, though they admired the great city and were let in on a great many of the organizational secrets behind it, it was – ultimately – beyond them; it was not of their ken. Like ancient Britons faced with the fantastic innovations of Roman civilization, they would not understand, could not let themselves be seduced. Pride, arrogance and envy were all to play a part in the overthrow of Tenochtitlán and the founding in its place of what was to become one of the most ridiculously inappropriate and badly designed capitals of the world. The logistical and ecological nightmare of modern Mexico City began here, though even then, it seemed, the Spaniards had some inkling of foreboding and regret.

'I say again', reflected Bernal Díaz as an old man, revisiting the moment when he was a reckless young conquistador poised on the threshold of Mexico City, 'I stood looking at it and thought that no land like it would ever be discovered in the whole world . . . But today all that I then saw is overthrown and destroyed; nothing is left standing.'

My hotel was a very cheap, rather seedy, four-storeyed colonial building a convenient stone's throw from the Zócalo – the central plaza – once the centre of Tenochtitlán. I chose it partly because the guidebook called it 'comfy' (which it wasn't) and said it had a laundry service (which it didn't). But it was also called 'Isabel' and so I fancied there was a ring of destiny about it.

There was an imposing portrait of Isabel La Católica on the wall in the lobby. She'd been the Queen of Spain at the time of the conquest, and a religious fanatic. My room was enormous with the high ceilings and full-length windows of the original colonial structure. But the toilet didn't work and sometimes nor did the shower. A much-vaunted 'air-con' contraption leaked dirty water on to the floor and used most of its energy making a noise like a washing machine on spin cycle. So when the room got hot, as it did by midday, I thought of opening the window. But then I was faced with another dilemma: was it better to be breathing hot stale air or breezy pollution? Usually the noise factor tipped the balance and, though the windows were far from double-glazed, the racket of engines, car-horns and pneumatic drills was slightly less intrusive with the windows closed and air-con rattling.

The hotel telephone system operated from a 1950s switchboard with the only outside line downstairs in reception. The receptionists had mastered an air of obsequious attentiveness while being of no help at all. They were particularly merciless about telephone messages. Sometimes they never passed them on. So, to be sure of getting them, I had to spend most of my first few days waiting for various contacts and friends of friends to return my call, sitting in the lobby of the Hotel Isabel, watching the comings and goings of travelling salesmen and prostitutes.

The hotel was also a standard favourite with backpackers, charging only $15 a night, and one morning, when the phone rang, the receptionist called me over. 'Someone calling from the UK,' he said, 'but she doesn't know who she wants to talk to. Can you speak, please?' Puzzled, I picked up the receiver. 'BBC Radio One here,' came the voice on the line, 'have you got a minute? We're researching a travel programme about backpackers going to far-flung places, what their immediate impressions are, that sort of thing. We're looking for someone who's just arrived in Mexico City. Would you mind talking to us for a couple of minutes about your first impressions, you know, something that conjures up a bit of atmosphere?'

I was beginning to feel important and adventurous, authoritative even, and was just warming to my subject when the interviewer interrupted. 'Sorry, can I stop you there? Do you mind telling me how old you are?' 'Thirty-three.' 'Oh, I'm sorry, we're really looking for someone young, you know, someone who can give us more of an up-beat kind of outlook, something fresh and zany, someone with a bit more appeal for our Radio One listeners.'

I went back to my chair feeling dejected and decrepit. I'd come all the way to Mexico to be confronted with a brutal home-truth. No matter that I considered myself spiritually Kiss FM. I was no longer cool, no longer with it; I was no longer part of the new generation. I was mainstream Radio Two.

The Zócalo, more properly the Plaza de la Constitución, is a vast, paved open square and a psychological breathing-space in the turmoil of downtown Mexico City. Covering an area roughly 57,600 square metres, it's the second largest city square in the world after Moscow's Red Square, and symbolically it's every bit as powerful. With the imposing Catedral Metropolitana – the largest church in Mexico – at one end; the Presidential Palacio Nacional, with a façade 205 metres long, standing to attention down one side; and a gigantic national flag flying from a pole in the centre, there's a similar dictatorial feel about it. This is the heart of political Mexico, a place designed to intimidate and impress the masses, to keep them in line.

The square takes its name from the Náhuatl word for a plinth. A lofty monument to Independence had once been planned for the centre of the square by one of Mexico's most unscrupulous revolutionaries (which is saying something) – General Santa Anna. Like most of his plans, this went astray and only the plinth was ever erected. Following the example of the capital, most of the squares in Mexico's principal cities also adopted the name of Zócalo, thereby extending the echo of empty political promise around the country for ever.

It's no coincidence that, within the country itself, the capital is referred to simply as 'México' – though Mexico City dwellers, or *chilangos*, refer to it as 'el D. F.' after 'México, Distrito Federal', the federal district of Mexico. It's an endless source of confusion for foreigners. But to Mexicans, the country itself is 'La República' or, in political speeches, 'La Patria'. Only abroad is the country called 'Mexico'.

Behind the capital's honorary title is the popular conviction that *Lo que ocurre en la República, ocurre en México*: 'What happens in Mexico, happens in Mexico City'. The city, Mexicans feel, represents the entire country in microcosm.

But it would be just as true to extend this principle further – to suggest that *Lo que ocurre en la República, ocurre en el Zócalo*, since this ancient square, once the heart of the Aztec Empire, is still the social and political heart of the country. The Zócalo is the seat of Mexico's collective unconscious. This is where the layering of Mexican culture is at its most forceful and dramatic, stacked, one level on top of another, like a pyramid. What goes on, on the surface, today, is inextricably part of the past; it is structured and shaped by it. If you want to try to understand Mexico, I'd been advised, start here, at its very core.

I was surprised, straightaway, at how thin, how transparent, the membranes of history were. The plaza itself was paved with volcanic stones that had been torn down from the various pyramids of Teocalli, the Aztec ceremonial centre that had once stood here, at the heart of Tenochtitlán.

In one corner of the square were excavations of the base of the Templo Mayor, the Great Pyramid where the Aztecs had, over 150 years, sacrificed thousands of human victims. The Aztecs, originally a nomadic tribe from the north, had been drawn to the Valley of Mexico, so legend had it, by a prophecy that they would found a great city where they saw an eagle devouring a snake. The Templo Mayor, according to their own myth, was built on that very site where they ended their journey, on an island in a lake in the middle of the Valley of Mexico, on the very spot where they'd seen an eagle sitting on a nopal cactus with a snake in its talons. This was the symbol that was fluttering larger than life on the national flag in the centre of the square.

Barely a stone's throw from the Templo Mayor was the Teo-calli's Christian replacement, the monolithic cathedral standing side by side with the parish church: the one made of grey stone and basalt; the other, of *tezontle*, porous volcanic stone the colour of dried blood.

In the small apron between the Templo and the church, a band of *concheros* wearing pheasant-feather headdresses, loincloths and shell anklets were beating drums and dancing about like whirling dervishes. They were Mexico's answer to Morris dancers, sort of ethnic New Agers communing with the Pre-Columbian spirit. They'd generated a crowd of credulous tourists, all holding tight to their handbags, and Mexican passers-by who were less taken in.

In front of the cathedral, along the railings, were stalls ranging through every aspect of modern Mexico: there were students selling protest posters; aid workers appealing for donations; Zapatistas from the war-torn southern state of Chiapas wearing black bala-clavas – despite the heat – and T-shirts depicting their rebel leader, Subcomandante Marcos; junk stalls laden with arts and crafts and cheap plastic tat imported from Asia; enigmatic Lacandón Indians with woodwork from the rainforest; even a few Huichols from the northern sierras selling psychedelic beadwork. Milling around them were the cripples and beggars, rickshaw boys, lottery-ticket sellers and unemployed plumbers, electricians and mechanics touting for work with boxes of scavenged tools. *Ambulantes*, or street-hawkers, were selling *alegría* or 'happiness' – little amaranth seed cakes that had been sold in this same spot for a thousand years.

Outside the Palacio Nacional, a row of coaches was disgorging sightseers – their object, the patriotic propaganda of Diego Rivera's gigantic murals which covered Mexican history all the way from conquest to independence to revolution, from Moctezuma through José María Morelos to Karl Marx.

It's from a balcony in the Palacio Nacional overlooking crowds of thousands in the Zócalo that the President of Mexico issues the famous *grito* – the cry (which, in practice, is a kind of lupine howl) for Independence. It's a tradition that happens every 16 September – Independence Day and echoes the original battle-cry of a village priest, Father Hidalgo, in the northern central highlands, in 1810. Father Hidalgo's *grito* launched the War of Independence, the struggle to release Mexico from colonial government. Though the war finally severed the umbilical cord with Spain, the separation was not clean-cut. The War for Independence lasted ten years and spawned a century of further bloodshed, infectious class wars and rebellions – culminating in the Mexican Revolution of 1910 – and an identity crisis from which Mexico is only just beginning to recover.

Despite the hustle, the tooting horns and the impact of a hundred glancing aspects of Mexico's cultural prism hitting you in the face all at once, it seemed there was, overall, a dreamlike quality to the Zócalo – something ponderous, suspended, unnerving. I tried to put my finger on it as I walked across the vast expanse in the middle of the square. There was an almost agoraphobic sensation of space – an illusion enhanced no doubt by the midday haze of suspended particles. But it was more than that. I had the feeling as I crossed the Zócalo that I was walking on the deck of a ship; that it was tilting me slightly at an angle and I was having to walk lopsided to compensate. There was a vague anxiety out there in the middle, that there was nothing to hold on to should the ground gape open and swallow me up.

Only when I tripped absentmindedly against a paving-stone did the illusion make itself manifest. The square was out of kilter, imperceptibly moving. The ground was buckling, the buildings around me were subsiding. Everything was at the wrong angle. The National Palace was tilting one way; the hotels and shops and colonnades on the opposite side, the other. The Cathedral, face on, looked like it was having a theological set-to with its neighbour, the parish church, and doing its utmost to put daylight between them. Looking down at the ruins of the Templo Mayor pyramid, 20 feet below the level of the pavement, I could see it pitching at a scary 30 degrees. The entire Zócalo was at a level 34 feet lower than when Cortés arrived.

Inside the Cathedral, the effect was even more dramatic. The gloomy, sunless interior was a maze of scaffolding. Bolts had been riveted into the walls; weights and wires were straining to heave the colossus back to the upright. A plumb-line hanging from the dome above the central nave looked crazily diagonal. The floor was so uneven that engineers had made a topographical map of it to work from. The building felt like a sinking ship. Along aisles of undulating marble, statues of martyred saints lay in glass coffins like bodies waiting to be consigned to the deep. But as I slipped into a pew to contemplate the unnerving proximity of Judgement Day, I had particular reason for feeling on shaky ground. The predicament of the Cathedral, the bizarre buckling of the whole of Mexico City come to that, pointed, like an extenuating crack, a creeping indictment, to those glinting canals I had seen from the plane and, in the intricate web of cause and effect, the reason my grandmother-in-law's grandfather came to Mexico in the first place.

It was Pearson's tunnelling expertise and, above all, his understanding of the mechanics of water, that brought him to Mexico City and that contributed to the chain of events behind the dramatic subsidence that had tripped me up in the Zócalo. Pearson had received a desperate request from Porfirio Díaz, the Mexican President, de facto dictator for thirty-three years. Díaz had dispatched an envoy to the English engineer in New York in December 1890 asking him to come and assess the major logistical problem that afflicted his city. The capital was prone to dangerous floods, a phenomenon that had plagued it ever since the overthrow of Tenochtitlán. Attempts by Mexican engineers to construct a drainage ditch leading out of the valley fortress had ended in defeat. Díaz was at his wits' end. He was driven by an overwhelming desire for Mexico to become a first-world power, with technology and infrastructure to rival any country in the world. He dreamed of seeing Mexico City on a par with the great cities of Europe or the United States. Securing the safety, and sanitation, of the capital was crucial for his own, as well as his country's, reputation.

The gruff, unassuming Yorkshireman had received this invitation from Díaz years before, and declined it. But this time Díaz caught him at an opportune – or inopportune – moment. Pearson had been working on the hazardous Hudson River tunnel – a project that defeated him in the end – and was suffering from a severe attack of the bends. He'd invented a decompression chamber that had significantly reduced the death toll of his workforce, but it was not infallible. He'd been paralysed from the waist down for several weeks after visiting a high pressure section of the site and had missed the ship that was due to take him and his wife back to England for Christmas. Still unable to walk and in considerable pain, he was bundled aboard a train and headed south, to Mexico City, for some desperately needed R&R, as the guest of the President. It was a decision that was to change his life. Not only would it cement his engineering reputation and make him a colossal fortune, it would make him best friends with a Mexican dictator and a plethora of enemies in the United States.

Pearson was my age, thirty-three, and a year younger than Cortés when he arrived in Mexico City. He would be coming here, on and off, traversing the Atlantic over and over again, with yet another engineering problem to crack, until his fifties when the Mexican Revolution stopped the clock. But his very first conundrum, in Mexico City, was the problem that had crippled the capital from colonial times. Water had obsessed the Aztecs and terrified the Spanish, and water has become the overriding issue in the present day.

In Pearson's time, it was thought the main problem was that there was too much of it. No river flowed in – or out of – the Valley of Mexico but every time it rained during the wet season, with torrential storms, water gushed down the mountainsides and filled the lakes to overflowing. Mexico City often had to be evacuated, the sewage-filled streets proving a dangerous hazard to health – not to mention the noxious damage it was doing to the ambitious President's public relations.

Pearson's solution – a 30-mile, 72-feet deep drainage ditch extending from downtown Mexico City across the state of Mexico, and then out of the valley through a tunnel near the town of Tequixquiac – was hailed by Díaz as a symbol of Mexico's entry into the modern world. It was completed in March 1900 at a cost of US$16 million. The canal (which is still the capital's main sewage and flood conductor) marked the demise, finally, of Lake Texcoco, the last of the five great lakes that had once covered 736 square miles – a fifth of the entire Valley of Mexico.

In fact, the Gran Canal was not the overwhelming success it had at first seemed. Shortly after its completion, and to the great alarm of the city's inhabitants, Mexico began to crack up. Fissures that could, previously, have been put down to earth tremors, or the odd geological fault, began to appear everywhere. Roads and pavements began to buckle, buildings began to subside, water pipes snapped – the entire capital seemed to be toppling, *Titanic*-like, into the marshy lake-bed. And, as the city collapsed below the level of Pearson's canal, it was disabled, once again, by serious floods. Far from saving Mexico City from disaster, the Gran Canal seemed, somehow, to be precipitating it.

What was happening to Mexico City, it turned out, was as much a result of too little water as too much. As the Gran Canal drained the last of the great lakes from the valley, the sopping sponge on which the capital had been sitting for centuries began to dry out. Dozens of wells which had to be sunk into the subterranean aquifer in an effort to provide the burgeoning population of Mexico City with fresh drinking water compounded the drying-out effect. The consequence was dramatic. The city began to sink, as much as eighteen inches in one year; and as it sank, the flow of the Gran

Canal began to reverse. Pumping stations had to be built to keep the waste-water going in the right direction.

Pearson's success, it turned out, had exacerbated, as well as relieved, the city's problems. He had bailed out the vessel only to help it sink even faster. But this was a dichotomy that was, by now, well beyond the scope of human ingenuity. What was happening to Mexico City stemmed from the Spaniards' destruction of Tenocht-itlán and their hubristic determination to build a European-style city in its place. The weight of nearly five centuries of human abuse and interference had compounded the inherent instabilities of the Valley of Mexico until the valley could take it no more. This was nemesis finally catching up with the galloping outriders of conquest.

There's only one place left where you can get a flavour of the paradise the Valley of Mexico once was. I was taken there one sultry, unforgettable Sunday by Humberto Fernández Borja, and his travel agent wife, Laurence, together with a few of their Mexican friends. Humberto was director of Conservación Humana, an organization dedicated to protecting the culture, land and sacred sites of the Huichol Indians of the northern Sierra Madre.

Humberto and Laurence's apartment was on the fourth floor of an art deco building called 'Edificio Ritzy'. It looked straight out of Poirot except that there was nothing straight about it. The floor of the marble lobby tilted at an angle and the lift often failed because one side scraped the lift shaft. Humberto opened the door looking bedraggled and unshaven. '¡Híjole! – Hell! The pollution's bad today. Tequila,' he commanded, 'we need tequila. One for the road.' And he brought out an elegant, thin bottle, unscrewing the cap like Aladdin rubbing his lamp, and sloshed some into tumblers. The brand was 'Chamucos', or 'Devils', and the label had wailing, vampire-like creatures flapping across it. There was a picture of a young girl asleep at the bottom and it looked like the devils were trying to wake her up. Underneath the inscription 'Agave 100%' was the legend *Si amanece nos vamos* – 'if dawn comes, we go'. It was eleven in the morning and, though we were due for an early start, the other guests had not yet arrived. 'Lubrication for the soul,'

Humberto declared, lifting his glass. '¡Salud!' He lit a Marlboro and took a deep drag. 'That's better.'

Humberto was my age. He'd been working on Huichol conservation projects for over ten years and met his first Huichol in 1983, when he was still a student, a 'long-haired layabout pretending to be a communist'. The Huichol, named Ramón, had taken part in an exhibition put on by the University of Anthropology in Mexico City. He'd put up a display of amazing beadwork and yarn paintings. It was raining and Ramón had nowhere to sleep so Humberto invited him to stay in his parents' house. Humberto's family were amazed. It was unheard of to have an Indian as a guest in one's house. Ramón stayed for weeks. He taught Humberto Huichol – together they planned to write the first Huichol/Spanish dictionary – and Humberto played Ramón Pink Floyd. When Ramón decided it was time to head back home, he took Humberto with him and, back in the remote mountains of the Sierra Nayarit, introduced him to his own family and to the important *mara'akames*, the shaman-leaders, of his village.

Ramón also took Humberto to the sacred valley of Huiricuta, near the old mining town of Real de Catorce in the State of San Luis Potosí, where he initiated him into the wonders of the rare hallucinogenic peyote cactus, a plant sacred to the Huichol and key to their ritual and visionary relationship with the spirit-world.

Humberto's friendship with the Huichol intensified and when, in 1994, they appealed to him for help to prevent a road being built through the Huiricuta valley, he dropped everything to organize the protest and, shortly afterwards, Conservación Humana was born.

Humberto had no regrets about giving up his job as a commodity broker buying and selling avocados and mangoes for a life dedicated to helping the Huichol and their environment. 'You only have to see the *mara'akames* in the desert, with their white eagle-feather headdresses fluttering in the wind, carrying all their secret bags and charms and prayer-sticks, to know that something different, something strange and mysterious is going on here,' he told me, 'that these are not dirty Indians in need of a wash and a job, like most people in Mexico seem to think. The Huichol are aristocratic to look at, like lords or princes. And they behave like royalty, because they're proud and self-confident. They know they're the true Mexicans, that they've never been conquered.'

Humberto was encouraged by my interest in the 'Hidden Mexico', as he described it, and promised not only to introduce me next time he had some Huichol friends to stay, but to take me up to the sierras where they live and induct me into their extraordinary culture. 'You'll never be the same again,' he laughed; and he raised his glass again, 'to the sierra!' A lot was to happen, though, before Humberto and I finally made it to the Huichol Sierra as we'd planned.

By the time the others arrived I was in danger of forgetting my own name, let alone registering someone else's. Laurence, a petite, fiery blonde of French descent, had been whirling round the kitchen decanting the whisky I'd brought her from England into a couple of flasks. 'Quick, before Corcuera comes,' she said. 'If we tell him it's tequila he might not drink it. But if he knows we've got Scotch . . .' The prospect clearly didn't bear thinking about. Francisco Corcuera came with a serious health warning.

Francisco burst through the door, moments later, wearing a Bill-and-Ben hat and carrying a smoked turkey like a baby in the crook of his arm. He took out a set of joke false teeth to kiss my hand. 'Encantado,' he said, 'delighted to meet you. Anyone got any whisky?' Laurence and Humberto looked evasive. 'How wonderful to be lunching with the English,' he rallied when a cold bottle of Bohemia beer was thrust into his hand, 'I went to Oxford myself. No doubt my punting skills will come in handy today.' Laurence raised her eyes to heaven. 'What he doesn't tell people is that it was a crammer he went to not an Oxford college. Some-times, Corcuera, I think you believe your stories yourself.' Corcuera put his teeth back in and gave her a mischievous leer, 'Laurence, come to Grandma, my dear, and let me show you what a big bite I have.'

Sean O'Hea and his Spanish wife, Mar, arrived shortly after. Sean's Irish grandfather had come to Mexico in 1905 as a tutor to a Mexican family but then, when the Mexican Revolution broke out, was nominated consul by several foreign nations and went through the thick of the fighting in the north of the country coolly trying to protect property and negotiate the safe passage of the nationals under his protection. Remarkably, Sean's grandfather had befriended the roughest of generals on both sides, including the notorious bandito, Pancho Villa. He'd written a spirited account of his adventures in a book called *Reminiscences of the Mexican Revolution.*

Unmistakably, Sean had the build, the wide-apart eyes and the surreptitious drinking capacity of his grandfather's genes. 'The Irish have a great affinity for Mexico,' he told me, his eyes twinkling. 'There must be something crazy about us,' he said. *Patricios* (Patricks) as they were known, had fought in almost every skirmish in modern Mexican history. Only recently the President had unveiled a memorial to all the Irish who died fighting on the Mexican side in the war against the Americans. The Mexico City phone book, I'd noticed with surprise, was full of O'Gradys and O'Learys and O'Reillys.

The last to arrive was vital to the occasion because we could go nowhere without him. Pedro was a mountain bike guide and he'd borrowed the company minibus for the outing. Pedro was tall, dark and disconcertingly good-looking, and represented yet another strand in the extraordinary racial weave of modern Mexico. Both sets of his grandparents had come to Mexico as traders from the Lebanon.

Pedro had a typically Mexican wild look in his eye as well. Humberto had once taken Pedro to Real de Catorce and the consequences had been legendary. He'd taken a dozen peyote 'buttons' in one go, ripped off all his clothes down to his underpants and wandered naked around the desert for a night and a day howling like a wolf. It was true, Pedro interjected, when Humberto began to tell me the story, he'd seen in the dark: plants, insects, animals, rocks, earth, dust, soil – everything was glowing and alive, and though he'd been wandering through scorpion-infested mesquite bushes and spiny agaves there'd been hardly a scratch on him when he came round and had to make a mad scramble for his spare clothes in the car.

At last we descended from the apartment, in several shifts, rattling in the lift, and piled into the bicycle van. Pedro took the wheel. 'Vámonos,' he cried, taking a swig from Laurence's flask and swerved the van into the maelstrom of Avenida de los Insurgentes.

Xochimilco is a suburb of Mexico City, fifteen miles south of the Zócalo. An offshoot of the now vanished Lago de Texcoco, the Lago de Xochimilco was the fruit and vegetable basket of the Aztec capital. It was here that the Aztecs had their extraordinary island gardens, or *chinampas*, made out of piles of silt and vegetable matter, which fed the population of Tenochtitlán. In Aztec times, the *chinampas* were so productive they produced 100 million pounds of maize every year. Over time these artificial islands overtook the shallow lake of Xochimilco until the area became a network of raised fields dissected by canals. Canoes from a fleet of 200,000 that serviced Tenochtitlán would carry the produce all the way from Xochimilco to the heart of the city, right into the Zócalo.

Today, Xochimilco, though much reduced in size, is an ecological haven in the urban jungle that has enveloped the valley floor. Its *chinampas* are little changed, still farmed as they were a thousand years ago; still producing a bumper crop of fruit and vegetables for the city, though this is now a drop in the ocean for the millions of mouths there are to feed. But it's Xochimilco's rarer commodities of water, fresh air and greenery that draw *chilangos* here, particularly on Sundays, so they can revive themselves like canaries from a coal-mine.

There was a fiesta atmosphere at the quayside. Hundreds of brightly coloured barques, or *trajineras*, were bumping together along the *embarcadero*, their gondoliers shouting for trade. This was Kashmir in Mexico. The boats were called 'Lupita', 'María', 'Diana' and – a sudden popular favourite – 'Mónica'. Between the *trajineras* slipped canoes selling everything you could want for a grand day out – corn on the cob, roast pork and crackling, tortillas, buckets of bottled beer on ice, sticky sweets, plywood models of *trajineras*, toy guitars, souvenir photographs, red roses. And above the dithyrambic patter of trade lapped waves of music from floating mariachi bands. The peal of passing trumpets sent a thrill through the gut. Some parties, already well into the post-prandial phase, were dancing on the sloping prows of their boats, or snaking around their table and chairs in a drunken conga. The gondoliers looked passively on, negotiating the log-jam with barely a knock.

Fortified with buckets of Bohemia we floated our *trajinera* away from the crowds, up over a lock and into the peace and quiet of the ecological zone. 'Ahhhh,' sighed Humberto, inhaling deeply, 'the lungs of the city.' On either side, up six foot banks, were fields of cabbage, cauliflower and herbs. There were acres and acres of seedlings under stands of casuarina and eucalyptus. Inspired by the sight of such incongruous intruders, Humberto and the boatman launched into a patriotic tirade against the introduction of ugly, greedy, foreign arboreal species when Mexico had the best and most beautiful trees in the world and the ones best suited to the environment. 'But that's the story of Mexico for you,' railed Humberto. The rest of the party groaned and Humberto laughed. 'I can't help it,' he said, 'this place always makes me think this way.'

The canals opened up into lagoons and lazily we drifted across them, lulled into a restful harmony. On a clear day, Laurence pointed out, you'd see the peaks of the volcanoes. But even like this, with the distance rubbed out, Xochimilco was an enchanted place. Swallows dipped and dived above the water; fish jumped; water-rails slipped among the skirts of overhanging willows; the odd canoe paddled past loaded with plants.

As we floated dreamily along it seemed incredible that the Spaniards had so ruthlessly, so determinedly, pitted themselves against this magical environment. Xochimilco had survived almost by accident, the grocery shop on the corner – a quaint, still marginally useful anachronism. Had the Spaniards had their way, they would have drained and transformed the whole valley, Xochimilco included; destroyed the entire aquatic landscape in one fell swoop, when they dismantled Tenochtitlán.

But the gulf that separated the Spaniards from the world they were engaged in conquering in the first half of the sixteenth century was unfathomable. Their world-view was entirely Eurocentric, and dominated by myth and superstition. It was only in 1483 that the French writer, Pierre d'Ailly, published a convincing argument in *Imago Mundi* that the world was round. Before that, it was taken for granted, by the Spaniards and everyone else in Europe, that the world was flat, with Europe at the centre of it.

Only at the turn of the sixteenth century had Europeans become conscious of the opportunities for increased wealth that overseas discovery offered and started pushing out beyond their continental boundaries. In 1514 the Portuguese ventured into India, presenting Leo X, on their return, with an elephant from Goa and so much treasure it took three hundred mules to carry it. A new age of empire building and of conquest had begun.

The Europeans were particularly eager to find new sources of precious metals but they were consumed, above all, by a passion for gold. The religious revival which sparked off the Reformation also encouraged Europeans to regard the task of opening sea routes to the pagans of distant countries as a duty, in order to show them the way to heaven. Returning home to decorate the churches and cathedrals of Europe with gold from afar not only glorified God and made manifest the power of the Church, it was proof of the spread of Christianity elsewhere in the world. The search for gold and the saving of souls became almost inseparable.

Of all the countries in Europe, though, it was Portugal and Spain that were best placed for exploratory travel, having already been drawn into naval expeditions along the shores of Africa. And when, in 1492, inspired by *Imago Mundi*, Christopher Columbus set off to see if he could reach India by sailing west, and discovered first Cuba, then the rest of the West Indies, and then, on his third voyage, landed on the coast of South America, he attracted a wave of young Castilian adventurers in his wake who dreamed of performing similar feats of valour, of becoming knights of the ocean, heroes whose exploits would echo the tales of Homer, or the 'golden years' of El Cid.

The courage of these seafaring conquistadors in search of gold and new lands is almost inconceivable. Even the most sanguine of men would have been troubled by thoughts of dragons and monsters, of mythic cities and strange peoples, haunted by tales of creatures that were half-human, half-beast. To sixteenth-century Europeans the world was made uncompromisingly of light and dark. They were terrified of the power of the unknown, of sorcery, and of their own weaknesses. Everything foreign, unfamiliar or inexplicable, however beautiful and benign looking, must be regarded as suspicious and potentially life-threatening, something to be tamed and exorcized, brought within the boundaries of European experience before it could be fully trusted and made use of. For the New World to cease to be a threat, both physically and spiritually, it had to be civilized, to be made European.

When the renegade privateer Hernán Cortés landed on the Gulf Coast of Mexico in 1519, deliberately scuppering his boats so there was no turning back, he was venturing into a world glittering with the promise of gold and unimaginable riches; but also inhabited by forces of darkness. Bringing the landscape under control, making it look and work as much like Europe as possible, was a form of exorcism in itself.

The Spaniards' antipathy to the lakes stemmed partly from their predilection for extensive agriculture – with land-greedy cattle and sheep and cereal crops. They were not used to intensive farming, were puzzled by the island gardens, the *chinampas*, and – crucially – saw no need for them. Unlike Europe, Mexico, to the conquistadors, was a land of infinite riches, a Garden of Eden, a harvest ripe for the picking. The very map of Mexico, colonists would discover when they'd finally plotted all her contours, was shaped like a cornucopia – the horn of plenty. It seemed the resources of the New World were, unlike those of the Old, boundless. They had – understandably perhaps, considering we're still dogged with environmental hubris today – no appreciation of the particular demands of the locality, of the limit of Mexico's natural resources, no idea of the ecological sword of Damocles hanging over their heads. But they also had a completely different worldview: while the Aztec religion stressed man's vulnerability against the forces of nature, the Spaniards believed the opposite – that nature had been created by God to serve man.

The Spaniards also had a very different attitude to water. They were fearful of lakes which they regarded, like Hippocrates – the ancient Greek physician and their only authority on the subject – as dangerous and unhealthy and harbingers of disease. The only good water, they considered, was running water. But in Mexico there is hardly any running water at all. There are no significant navigable rivers and no glacier systems. Much of the land is semi-desert, its species evolved to withstand long periods of drought and scorching sun. Apart from the rainforests in the far south and the humid zone along the Gulf Coast, Mexico's water reserves rely solely on underground aquifers or the systems of shallow lakes which geology had trapped between her central mountain ranges.

Water was one of the main reasons the Aztecs migrated down from the north and settled here in the first place. To them, as to all the indigenous peoples of Mexico, water was – and still is – the most sacred of gifts. The Aztecs had a profound respect for its wilful transience. Much of their ritual life revolved around appeasing the rain gods and ensuring the arrival of the right amount of water at the right time.

Unlike the Spaniards, the Aztecs realized, when they settled in the Valley of Mexico, that they'd arrived in a place with a highly complex and sensitive water system; that there could be no funda-mental tampering with it; that survival here depended on the natural ebb and flow of rainwater and glacier-melt from the sur-rounding volcanoes through the marshes and lakes and freshwater springs. But in the one hundred and fifty years or so that they'd dominated the valley, they discovered ingenious ways to woo their watery home under some sort of control. By the time the Spanish arrived, they'd evolved an amphibian lifestyle and built a city of staggering hydraulic ingenuity. There were dykes to separate the freshwater and salt-water lakes; a gigantic dyke seven miles long across Lake Texcoco to control the level of water affecting Tenoch-titlán; and a system of causeways and canals criss-crossing the city that also helped reduce the risk of flooding. Two stone aqueducts brought fresh drinking water from a spring on Chapultepec hill straight to a fountain in the main square of Tenochtitlán.

The Aztecs also built very few heavy structures on the islands because they realized the spongy soil was highly unstable and could only take a certain weight before beginning to sink. Pyramids and temples apart, only the grandest of citizens could have a house higher than a single storey. Expansion beyond the two islands forming Tenochtitlán was made possible by driving piles into the shallows, and raising the houses on platforms above the water. There was a municipal rubbish collection several times a day with vegetable matter and human sewage being paddled away by canoe to fertilize the *chinampas* in Xochimilco.

The Spaniards, on the other hand, never very clued up about the disposal of sewage, and disdainful of eating freshwater fish or anything else that came out of the lakes, treated the water around them as a dumping ground. Human waste flowed through the canals creating algae blooms and covering everything in green slime. On the islands land for burial was hard to come by so the corpses of Indians, dogs and horses were perfunctorily tossed into the water. In no time at all the Spaniards had confirmed their own prejudices and the lakes of the Valley of Mexico had become fetid and life-threatening and the city had begun to smell like home. Drainage, to their minds, became an urgent priority.

Wholesale deforestation in the surrounding hills didn't help. It made the water pollution worse and the phenomenon of the winter rains a terrifying experience. Twenty-five thousand trees were cut down each year to build the new Spanish city. Sheep and cows were put out to graze on the cleared land, which destabilized the soil even further. When torrential rains came, the topsoil was washed straight off the mountainsides into the lakes, raising the water levels and causing devastating flash-floods.

Forty years after the Spaniards founded Mexico City, the periodic flooding that had confronted the Aztecs had become a perennial reality. Some floods were so terrifying that the whole population had to be evacuated. Houses collapsed and for weeks at a time the city wallowed under water like an indecisive Atlantis. Yet the Spanish clung on, determined to site the nucleus of their New World exactly where the Aztecs had had their seat of power.

Normally I would have felt reticent about laying claim to kinship with the Englishman who had drained the last of the great lakes out of the Valley of Mexico. Xochimilco, especially, didn't seem the right place to mention it. But cascades of beer and tequila and exhaustive attempts to get the knack of a Spanish wine-skin had loosened my tongue and I found myself confessing to a link with the foreign capitalist who was alleged to have taken more silver out of Mexico than Cortés; who had offered the dictator, Díaz, one of his West Sussex estates when he was forced into exile, and gave him – and his son – a pension for the rest of their lives. I even spilled the beans about the 1st Viscountess's legendary bicycle, made out of solid silver from the Mexican mines, which she used to ride from one wing of their colossal Scottish pile to the other. But I needn't have worried. 'Weetman Pearson!' Corcuera exclaimed, clasping me by the hand like a long-lost relative, 'my great-great-grandfather was his lawyer.'

A lake seemed a strange place to embark on a discussion about the city's water crisis but it was, perhaps, a timely reminder to avoid face-value judgements about anything in Mexico. It was not pollution – the demon that everyone obsesses about and that slaps you in the face every morning – but lack of water, that unseen, immeasurable factor, that was threatening the survival of the capital. There was only an estimated twenty years to go, Humberto said, before the aquifer supplying the city dried up. All the nearby lakes and rivers had already been emptied. Distant reservoirs supplied a third of the city's water but piping it into the city was hideously expensive (an amazing 10 per cent of Mexico's total energy output went into the basic task of pumping drinking water into the capital and pumping waste water out). Yet no one, except the civil authorities, had any notion that the capital was so close to extinction.

Crazy ideas were being bandied about, he went on – such as sending rockets up into rain clouds, artificially creating H_2O, using giant fans to blow cold air into the valley – but none seemed as crazy as the one solution that was being taken seriously. With Mexico City consuming 60 cubic metres of water every second of every day, the nearest existing source of water with the volume to meet the capital's needs, was the ocean. But the Gulf Coast was 400 miles away and the water would have to be desalinated and pumped over the tail end of the Sierra Madre Oriental and the new volcanic ranges in between – up a total vertical distance of one and a half miles.

'Where's Pearson when you need him?' Humberto smiled. Even

Pearson, I imagined, would have thrown down his silver pencil in despair.

As the sun began to dip behind the trees we made our way to the lock and back to the party. 'There's one thing we must have before we leave,' Humberto announced dramatically, 'it's crucial to your induction into the soul of Mexico.' He tipped the boatman a nod and we slid into the back canals like outlaws. Rats swished through the flotsam and water weeds. It was growing dark when the boatman found the house he was after. It was little more than a shack with a back garden full of geraniums. He tied up the boat and disappeared inside. Moments later he re-emerged carrying a large glazed terracotta bowl. In it swilled a slimey green liquid: *pulque*, the drink of the gods.

Fermented from the sap of the maguey cactus, *pulque* was as common to pre-Columbian Mesoamerica as Coca-Cola is today, enjoyed by men, women and children. It was also given to captives to inebriate them in preparation for sacrifice. But it was outlawed by the Spanish because of its ritual and spiritual connotations. Today it's rarely found in the cities but still drunk by country people at home, bought from *pulquerías* like this. It's so nutritious, brimming with every imaginable vitamin and mineral, that it's often given to children even though it's alcoholic and, in large quantities, gives you a giggly high. In Xochimilco though, the boatman told us, the Coca-Cola and beer-selling mafiosi have elbowed the *pulque* sellers from the main canals and you can only buy it at the back door, in secret. Times have changed and now it's economic rather than cultural forces exerting the muscle.

The bowl was treated with great reverence and handed round like a chalice. The liquid looked and smelled like celery soup and clung to the sides of the bowl like ectoplasm. And though it tasted fresh and green and disconcertingly alive, it was the consistency I found hard to swallow. There was an enzymy quality to it which, together with the ambient temperature and glutinousness, made it feel like drinking saliva.

Getting home was a bleary experience but in a dim kind of way I was relieved to be beyond worrying about Pedro's driving and the wailing car horns that seemed to pursue us wherever we went.

Unexpectedly, I thought of Pearson again that evening when I was caught in my hotel shower with shampoo in my hair and no water to wash it out. There could have been a number of reasons for the sudden coughing and spluttering of the shower-head and abrupt cessation of water: a crumpled water main (30 per cent of the city's costly water, Humberto had told me, is lost in leaks); pump failure; or just the municipal water authorities deciding to activate one of their frequent emergency water bans. But as I dressed, stickily, irate, and in the early stages of a monumental hangover, and stumbled downstairs to the restaurant to buy a crate of mineral water with which to rinse my hair, I found myself cursing Pearson, President Díaz, Cortés, the King of Spain, everyone I could think of, for not being better plumbers; and the Aztecs, or at least that importunate eagle, for positioning their city in a bog in the first place.

The receptionist raised a dubious eyebrow the following afternoon when I asked him to reserve me a table for two at the San Ángel Inn, a grand ex-colonial hacienda that had once been the nucleus of an estate in deep countryside and was now perhaps the poshest restaurant in town. 'It's smart,' he warned, looking me up and down.

'I know,' I snapped. It had been a bad day. I'd been woken by a knock on the door and a man wearing a gas mask, protective clothing and a pesticide canister had pushed into the room. He'd come to fumigate it. I took the invasion – and the assumption behind it – personally. And watched in dismay with a sheet clamped over my nose and mouth as the room filled up with gas and became as noxious as the atmosphere brewing up to its midday peak outside.

Later that morning, nursing a headache like the clashing rocks of Scylla, I felt my first earth tremor. There are at least six hundred tremors in Mexico City a year but occasionally the capital is rocked by a big quake and the results are cataclysmic. *El Temblor*, the earthquake of 19 September 1985, is still vivid in the memory of all Mexicans. It registered eight on the Richter scale and brought down thousands of buildings, including the grand old Hotel del

Prado on the Alameda containing one of Diego Rivera's most famous murals, *Sunday Afternoon in Alameda Park*, and numerous shoddily built modern housing tenements. Officially 10,000 people died; but many were unaccounted for and some estimates put the death toll as high as 20,000. Up to 100,000 people were made homeless. Even now, nearly fifteen years later, there are conspicuous gaps in streets in downtown Mexico City where the earthquake reduced buildings to rubble in a matter of seconds, causing over US$4 billion worth of damage.

The tragedy was compounded by the appallingly chaotic and uncoordinated response of the capital's emergency services. It took days for the government to respond effectively to the disaster and mobilize troops to help with clearance work, and to provide sources of clean drinking water and medical supplies. During that time hundreds of people died who were trapped but should have been saved. The citizens of Mexico City rose up and took control. Humberto and Pedro remembered commandeering a bulldozer to help clear a path through the rubble, and scrabbling about through the debris trying to reach the victims, the *damnificados*.

This was the moment, many people are convinced, that Mexico's fledgling civil society, or *sociedad civil*, was born: a coalition of ordinary men and women, workers' cooperatives, human rights groups, students and non-governmental organizations who banded together to achieve a common aim; who were united in exposing the failings of the institutional government and who, for the first time, dared to take the situation into their own hands. The *damnificado* movement set a precedent for other protest organizations in Mexico City and across the country. The 1985 earthquake, it soon became clear, had triggered off rumblings of democracy; a drone that many people across Mexico sensed would soon become a roar.

The tremor that shook the Hotel Isabel would hardly have wobbled the Richter needle, but it was unnerving nonetheless. There was a shuddering through my room as if a massive pantechnicon had thundered down the street outside and rammed into the building. I waited for the shock-wave to reverberate as I'd been warned it often did, passing through the marshy subsoil before hitting the wall of volcanoes and coming back again. But the pneumatic drill started up again outside my window and I wouldn't have been able to tell if the hotel had begun to fall down.

Beyond my clanging head and the irritation these disturbances were heaping on me, there was something new in my reaction, I realized; something Mexican that I assumed had rubbed off from my day in Xochimilco. Instead of paracetamol or a week's dose of cleansing *ginkgo biloba*, the San Ángel Inn had sprung to mind. It served reputedly the best margarita in the whole of Mexico and I found myself dreaming of swimming-pool portions.

There was anyway, I excused myself, cause for celebration. My English friend Guy Ogilvy had just turned up in Mexico City. His sojourn in the northern sierra had finally come to an end. He'd parted with the white witch and her growing commune of devotees, spent nearly a year on his own in a cave 'doing the mad hermit thing' with only a bat and a cat for company and the occasional use of a burro he called 'Donkey Hotey', and at last felt it was time to return to the world. He brushed up pretty well for the occasion in a crumpled linen jacket not worn since he'd left England and cowboy boots that had accidentally been polished half black, half brown by a Mexico City street shoeshine. His waist-length curly hair had sprung into life after an hour or more with a bottle of conditioner and now rivalled Nicole Kidman's. A new moustache and goatee, neatly trimmed, gave him the air of a cavalier in the reign of King Charles, and I felt heads turn when we walked in the street.

With the air of a couple out for a night at the opera, we squeezed into the back of a typical green VW taxi with the front seat taken out and the passenger door on a string so the driver could slam it shut. We had no idea we were dicing with death. No one takes a street cab in Mexico City if they can help it. Every inhabitant of this great crime mecca of the world has some story about being robbed at knife-point, beaten up, driven around to all the names in their address book so their friends could be ripped off, too; the occasional murder. Mexico City must be the only city in the world where it's safer to take the Metro – especially at night – than a taxi. The doorman at the hotel saw us hail the cab and hurriedly took down the licence plate number – so he admonished me later – in case we were kidnapped.

The ride was safe but not uneventful. Mexican taxi drivers proved to have less nous than New York cabbies, yet they were dealing with a city twenty times the size. And usually with no maps. The problem was compounded by there being dozens of streets with the same names. Each *colonia* – some of them once towns in their own right and now absorbed into the great *mancha urbana*, the great 'urban stain' – boasted a Las Palmas, Cinco de Mayo, Hidalgo or Allende. We headed immediately in the opposite direction of *colonia* San Ángel, to the south-east of the city.

And landed in millionaire's row, a Mexican Beverly Hills, a tutti-frutti of Gothic castles and Spanish haciendas, Palladio rubbing shoulders with Le Corbusier, mini fortresses with lock-up garages, electric gates, CCTV, Alsatians and armed guards; walled gardens with secret fountains and luscious lawns; a place of privilege and paranoia, hush money and Swiss bank accounts.

Dispirited, we turned back, only to be sucked once again into the arterial coagulation of the capital's ring road, the *Periférico*. Our eyes began to itch, our throats began to burn, our noses to stream and occasionally there was a crazy, gas-induced inclination to burst into giggles. We were beginning to look, Guy observed, like rabbits with myxomatosis.

At each main traffic junction, there were kids trying to wash the windscreen or foist plastic toys upon us, or newspapers, comics, dish-cloths, anything they'd got their hands on. Some were so small they had to stand on tip-toe to appear at the window. They would have spent the whole day barely inches above exhaust-pipe level. Some looked dazed and close to defeat. Occasionally, unable to muster themselves, they had to be goaded into action by an elder brother or sister. I watched miserably as a small boy, barely older than my own son, sat on his bucket and cried.

Often there were ragged little acrobats, wearing clown noses or rubber masks of ex-Presidents, wearily assembling into a human totem pole or throwing somersaults. Once Moctezuma's court had been full of stilt-walkers, clowns and dancers like these. Their skills would have been the toast of the nobility. But today, bored drivers barely gave them a glance.

And there were the fire-eaters, *tragafuegos*, who would swig from a plastic bottle of kerosene and exhale over a lighted fire-brand, the blast for a split second matching the hue from the stream of amber brake lights. The city was overrun with human blow-torches like these. Charity-run detox clinics were full of young men and boys who'd lost their sense of taste and smell, burnt their faces, scorched their lungs and fried their brains because it made just a little more money than doing nothing at all. That margarita was as tantalizing as ever but I knew now that when – if – we ever got our hands on it, however icy and delicious and intoxicating, however many we had, it wouldn't be strong enough to still that sulphurous taste of guilt and injustice searing the back of my throat. I'd begun to feel like a *zopilote* spiralling around with the affluent few over the rubbish-tips of the poor.

The *tragafuegos* haunted me. More than all the other *chavos* from the *barrios* – *los olvidados*, the 'forgotten ones', who wandered the streets downtown. Perhaps it was because they were doing something that was so clearly destroying them: they were trying to dig themselves out of a hole only to make it collapse in on top of them.

I did, gradually, get used to the pollution, however. Even, dare I say, to enjoy it. The newspapers published levels of ozone, hydrocarbon, sulphur dioxide, nitrogen dioxide, carbon monoxide and suspended particles every day, with anticipated highs for noon, when traffic and industry were at their most active and the sun would turn the city into a pressure cooker. Most days the summary was simply 'unsatisfactory'; but on some it was quoted as positively 'dangerous'. Then schools were advised to close, or for children, at least, to be kept indoors. The old, the infirm and asthmatics battened down the hatches and burrowed for cover. And sometimes, *in extremis*, factory production was cut by 30 per cent to give the city a break from their emissions. The regular 'Hoy No Circula' pro-gramme which prevented cars from being driven on one particular day every week would be cranked up to 'Doble Hoy No Circula' status, taking about 40 per cent of the vehicles off the streets. Still, just breathing in Mexico City, even with traffic restrictions, was estimated to be equivalent to smoking forty cigarettes a day.

There was an added hazard in the toxic cocktail, though, that was not published in the press and that I learnt about from a nurse who worked for Cruz Roja, the Red Cross. She was shaking a collection box past the café where Guy and I were sitting and joined us for a coffee break. 'You've noticed the winds?' she asked. 'We always get them, this time of year, in the spring, the dry season. We call them *tolvaneras* – dust storms. They come in from the fields outside the city, from the salt pans. That's where they spread the sewage. There's too much sewage for the drains to get rid of, so people use it – untreated – to fertilize their crops; or else it's just dumped and left to dry out. The *tolvaneras* pick up the dust and blow it into the city. We've had the first cases on record, in Mexico City, of people contracting cholera just from breathing the air.'

There was a certain satisfaction as she said this, an element of pride, that a few days ago, perhaps, I wouldn't have understood. But now I was beginning to feel part of the great *niebla tóxica*, I'd begun to take a sort of masochistic pleasure in it – enjoying the we-can-take-anything-the-city-throws-at-us attitude that *chilangos* seemed to thrive on. The nurse offered me a cigarette and though I didn't usually smoke, I took it. I'd given up trying to fight the pollution. No one's body can be a temple in Mexico City. Dozens of vitamin C tablets consumed in my first few days in an effort to isolate the free radicals running riot in my system, had done nothing to assuage the daily toxic hangover. I still woke every morning feeling that my body had been encased in lead, with a lethargy that surpassed even my teenage years. I decided to take the homeopathic approach and fight like with like. I said goodbye to the nurse and went off to buy my first packet of cigarettes in fifteen years. If smoking didn't smother the effects of my sore throat, at least I could take pleasure in making it worse. Perhaps, I thought, this was what the *tragafuegos* had taken to an extreme – if they couldn't escape their fate, at least they were still free to precipitate it.

*

Perhaps because of its size the Museum of the Templo Mayor on the Zócalo held more appeal for me than the Museum of Anthropology which, though arguably the greatest museum of its kind in the world, dazed one with the magnitude and scope of its contents. The Templo Mayor was also well within my stamping ground. I didn't need to risk life and limb getting a street cab to and from it, and there was the added attraction of my favourite pit-stop on the 7th floor of the Hotel Majestic with a fine view over the entire Zócalo on the way. At my most lethargic I found I was having to bribe myself around the city.

But the site of the Templo Mayor also added a powerful frisson to the normal distractions of sightseeing. This had been the seat of Aztec power, the centre of their universe and it seemed to conduct a charge of historical electricity unlike any other site in the capital. This, after all, had been the largest of all the temple pyramids in the Teocalli, the ceremonial centre of Tenochtitlán. It had stood 40 metres high, casting its shadow over the heart of the city. And it was here that the Aztecs had carried out their biggest and bloodiest sacrifices.

Walking around the excavation site, bizarrely now below street level, you can see the Temple's extraordinary multiple construction, each layer encapsulating the last, like a Russian doll. There were eight pyramids here, inside each other. Every time a new layer was added, the temple was re-dedicated to the gods. For the last reconstruction, completed in 1487, thirty-two years before the Spaniards' arrival, the Aztecs had orchestrated a massive human sacrifice. Some sources quote the terrible figure of 80,400 victims. Though this is quite likely an exaggeration, the numbers did probably run into tens of thousands.

The victims on this occasion were Huaxtecs from the northern Gulf Coast who'd been captured and brought back to Tenochtitlán after an unsuccessful revolt against the Aztec, Texcocan and Tacuban Imperial Triple Alliance. Queues of Huaxtec warriors, linked by cords through perforations in their septums, Huaxtec 'maidens', and little boys still too young to have had their noses pierced, secured by yokes around their necks, were herded, bewildered and terrified, through the great city, wailing a pitiful lament. In four long, shuffling lines, the captives, ritually prepared for death, converged on the Temple, from north, south, east and west, and were led up the steps to the sacrificial stones.

The Templo Mayor was dedicated to the two most powerful gods in the Aztec pantheon: Huitzilopochtli, or 'Hummingbird Wizard', the warrior god and god of the sun; and Tlaloc, god of rain. Twin staircases led up the front of the pyramid to their temples, the altars of which have recently been unearthed by the excavations. They stand there, side by side, surrounded by fading frescoes, casual monuments to holocaust.

One by one, the captives were brought here and laid on the stones, which were specially shaped to push the victim's chest upwards, with four men holding his limbs, and one man holding him down by the throat. The king himself dispatched the first of the victims, plunging his flint blade into the man's chest and extracting his pulsing heart. The heart was burnt in a ceremonial urn, while the body, with seconds still to live, was kicked down the precipitous temple steps. The pile of captives' bodies at the bottom was claimed by their 'owners' – by the warriors who'd captured them in battle – and taken away to be butchered, and cooked and shared out in a ritual cannibalistic feast. When the king and the great chiefs were physically exhausted by the killing, dozens of priests took over. The massacre for the 1487 consecration was said to have lasted four days. Blood flowed down the walls of the temple, across the floor, and down the pyramid steps.

Just three decades later, the stench of human sacrifice in similar, lavish ceremonies under the aegis of Moctezuma II and lords of neighbouring states, struck Bernal Díaz as being 'worse than any slaughter-house in Spain'. The conquistadors were horrified by the sight of the high priests with their long, matted locks dripping in gore; their ears, noses and tongues torn to shreds by ritual self-mutilations; the captives – men, women and children – cowering in their cages waiting to be sacrificed. Cortés was so outraged when he came across the Teocalli's main *tzompantli* – the rack displaying the skulls of sacrificial victims (Cortés counted 136,000 in all) – that he claimed this site for the metropolitan cathedral in order to cleanse it of the devil's works.

It is hard to see the methodical, unrelenting mass murder of fellow human beings as a noble preoccupation – there is nothing to help explain it to us in the modern world, and certainly nothing the conquistadors could have compared it with – but this was anything but straightforward, gratuitous cruelty. Bloody, brutal and terrifying as these ceremonies were, the lives of the victims were honoured and valued, the rituals performed with consummate gravitas. The more appalling the torture and the more violent and painful the death, the more valuable the sacrifice to the gods. Sometimes, if we're to believe the Aztec accounts, the captives believed themselves to be the chosen children of the gods, their deaths the acts of heroes, and they went to their deaths, if not willingly, then acquiescent. It's a bewildering image, but it becomes explicable in context – when it's set against the black cloud of imminent catastrophe under which the Aztecs lived.

The Aztecs lived in a land dotted with the ruins of past civilizations. Only 30 miles to the north-east of Mexico City, the great city of Teotihuacán, with its gigantic pyramids and two-and-a-half-mile-long Avenue of the Dead, had been inexplicably and long ago abandoned. Its inhabitants had apparently disappeared into mid-air. And the great city of Tula, 40 miles away to the north, had been left to crumble into insignificance after the fall of the Toltecs in the early thirteenth century. The Aztecs were haunted by the evidence of the disappeared around them and it fuelled their collective sense of doom.

Human sacrifice was integral to the Aztec understanding of human survival. The world, they believed, was doomed to annihilation. Four worlds, the four suns, had already perished in cataclysms. The first – the world of the Tiger Sun – had ended in cold and darkness following an eclipse; the second world of the Wind Sun was ended by magic, with violent winds and men turned into monkeys; the third world of the Rain Sun collapsed in a rain of fire, and the fourth world of the Water Sun, in a deluge of water. The present world, the fifth, the world we still live in, is the world of the Sun of Movement and, according to the ancient Aztecs, is destined to end with earthquakes and hunger – a prospect that seemed all too likely to me after a week in Mexico City.

The end of the world could not be avoided, the Aztecs believed, but it could be delayed. Human sacrifice was the ultimate way of appeasing the gods and postponing that moment of cataclysm. The gods survived on human blood, that most 'precious water' that flowed from mortal bodies. They clamoured for it like children for their mother's milk. If the world was to see another day – if the sun was to rise once again, if the rains were to arrive in time to feed the crops – this would only happen with the cooperation of the gods. And the gods wouldn't work on an empty stomach.

The Museum of the Templo Mayor boasted some blood-chilling exhibits and I found myself drawn back to it obsessively time and again. Just inside the entrance there was a wall of human skulls – a *tzompantli* like the one Cortés had seen, but made of stone. And in the first room was a sinister stone eagle with a cavity in its back for collecting the hearts of sacrificial victims. Then there were the eagle-warriors made of baked clay; half-bird, half-human, they stood as tall as a man, poised as if ready to fly. Their human faces stared, tense and expectant, from inside the open beaks of their eagle heads. Every artefact seemed charged with fear and foreboding and ritual purpose. This was as far from the art of the Mediterranean civilizations as anything I had ever seen. Nothing was created for beauty's sake alone, for the sheer joy of existence, to sing the praises of man and god, to lift the earthly experience heavenward. Aztec art wasn't elevating so much as crushing.

No single piece was more alarming to my mind than the main exhibit that took pride of place in the central hall, which had been excavated by engineers laying electric cables near the site in 1978. It was a colossal volcanic stone disc, 3.25 metres in diameter, weighing 8 tons, depicting Coyolxauhqui, goddess of the moon. In the centre of the disc the goddess's bare-breasted torso was encircled and knotted with snakes. The goddess's eagle headdress and warrior ear-plugs, and the balls of down that had marked her for ritual death, seemed to shake, caught in the dynamism of terrible, annihilating violence. Her severed head and limbs, entwined with more snakes, were flying off around the circumference in bloody disarray. A human skull nestled gloatingly off-centre.

Coyolxauhqui – 'She with the Belled Cheeks' – was the daughter of Coatlicue, the Mother Goddess, deity of life and death, fount of all things. According to Aztec mythology, when Coyolxauhqui discovered her mother Coatlicue was pregnant for a second time she went into a fury. The goddess could only give birth once, to the original litter of divinity and no more. A second birth of gods was a monstrosity. Coyolxauhqui vowed to expunge the dishonour by killing her mother, rallying round her four hundred brothers to help. At the moment of truth, however, the warrior sun god Huitzilopochtli sprang fully armed from Coatlicue's womb like Athena from the head of Zeus, decapitated and dismembered his sister and threw her body down a mountain. Then he drove off the assembled army of his brothers who scattered and became stars; while the exploded, vanquished Coyolxauhqui collected herself together and limped off into space where she eventually became the moon.

As was the case with other, similar Coyolxauhqui stones, the massive disc had been unearthed at the foot of the temple, symbolizing the goddess's fall. Human sacrifice was, in part, a re-enactment of her story, as the victims were hurled down the temple steps to the ground.

I stood before this great monolith and felt chilled to the bone. It brought home as no statistics or history books could, the grim realization that human sacrifice was no mere whim on the part of the Aztecs – a last resort in periods of disaster, a desperate measure for desperate times – but a practice enshrined deep in the fundaments of their belief, cast in stone. Their very world had begun with this outrage committed against the Mother Goddess. There was no escape, no let-up in the toll of life demanded by the gods thereafter; only, inevitably, an acceleration when times became desperate and the end seemed at hand.

Which was, extraordinarily, how things had begun to look in the years leading up to the Spaniards' arrival. By the time an ominous floating mountain range – Cortés's fleet – had been spotted off the coast near the present port of Veracruz in 1519, the Aztec King, Moctezuma II, was a perplexed and jittery man. Deeply religious and prone to fits of depression and indecision, he was haunted by portents that seemed to prophesy his own death and the end of his city. Ten years earlier a comet had blazed across the sky sending the soothsayers into a spin. When they declared themselves unable to interpret the phenomenon, Moctezuma had them starved to death. Suddenly, terrifyingly, Popocatépetl, 'Smoking Mountain', the 18,000-ft volcano overlooking the Valley of Mexico, erupted.

Then Nezahualpilli, the ruler of the allied domain of Texcoco and a leader gifted with second sight, prophesied calamities that were to destroy kingdoms. So certain was he that the end was nigh, he abandoned his reign, dismissed his armies and told everyone to enjoy what little time was left. And then he suddenly died. This was only four years before the appearance of Cortés.

And there were other forbidding signs. The sanctuary of the great goddess Toci had caught fire. The water of the lake around Tenochtitlán formed gigantic waves, although there was no wind. Women's voices were heard in the night wailing about death and destruction. An enormous stone had begun to speak and proclaim the fall of Moctezuma, but defied all attempts to transport it into the city. A bird 'with a mirror in its head' had been brought before the unhappy king who had seen warriors in it.

When runners came gasping into Moctezuma's court with tales of a fair-skinned warrior who carried himself like a god approaching from the Gulf Coast, a penny dropped. This could be Quetzalcoatl, the Plumed Serpent, the god-priest destined to return from the west to begin a new world order.

The legend of Quetzalcoatl was a powerful one and had persisted from the time of the Toltecs. It had been absorbed by the Aztecs when they took over the Valley of Mexico. Quetzalcoatl was an unusual and intriguing god. He stood for learning and culture, peace and creativity and, in particular, opposition to human sacrifice. But he had engendered the jealousy of the lesser gods, especially Tezcatlipoca, or 'Smoking Mirror' – the Toltec God of Night. Bent on trouble-making, Tezcatlipoca had taken Quetzalcoatl a gift of a mirror. When he saw his human face reflected in it, Quetzalcoatl screamed and fell to the floor, terrified. That night the usually abstemious Plumed Serpent drank himself into a stupor and fornicated with his sister. The next day, mortified by his conduct, he set sail on a raft of serpents, heading away from Mexico to the east, promising only to return when it was Ce Acatl in the Indian calendar – the Day of the Reed. His return would be triumphant, the myth maintained, but the Indian universe would be shaken to its roots and the whole world would be afraid of losing its soul. To the Nahua peoples, Quetzalcoatl was referred to as the 'white hero of the break of day', the 'warrior of the dawn'.

When rumour reached Moctezuma that this new arrival, Cortés, was armed to the teeth and pitching himself against the practice of human sacrifice and all the other ancient bloodthirsty rituals he encountered, it seemed the time was up. The newcomer was described as looking exactly, though not flatteringly, like Quetzalcoatl – fair-skinned, ugly, bearded and with an elongated head. And, like the Toltec god – who was also closely associated with the skills of smelting and metallurgy – this strange apparition had an inordinate affection for silver and gold. More than this, though, it was Cortés's timing that sent the world of the Mexica into a spin. The Spanish conquistador had landed on the Gulf Coast on Maundy Thursday, 1519. But to the Aztecs it was Ce Acatl, Year of the Reed. By the time Cortés had reached Tenochtitlán, brushing aside all Moctezuma's messengers who tried to delay him with gifts and warnings, misinformation, roadblocks and female distractions, the great Aztec king was all but resigned to his fate.

The hot-house temperature was making its usual nightly nose-dive as I walked round with Guy for a drink at the atelier of a young French painter, Philippe Hernández, who lived just blocks from the Hotel Isabel. I'd been given his number by a Mexican make-up artist who lived in New York. Philippe opened the door as if expecting some pre-Columbian monster to come galloping in behind us. He looked haunted, monumentally exhausted with huge black shadows around his eyes, yet agitated – a sort of Serge Gainsbourg meets Mr Bean. It was 7 p.m. and he'd only just woken up.

His apartment was self-consciously at odds with the ancient, toppling colonial building of black volcanic rock in which it found itself. There was a milking stool, a chair and a shiny black psychiatrist's couch in the room where we sat, the three of us, at different heights and odd angles, drinking whisky. There were handwritten notes in different languages abstractedly pinned to the walls. 'THIS IS THE PAIN' was in English. There was no bed in the apartment and I couldn't imagine where Philippe slept. There were only two other rooms – one was knee-deep in torn-up pieces of paper; the other had a desk with a phone, and a chair made out of a supermarket trolley – nothing else. I came to the conclusion that Philippe must, perhaps appropriately, sleep on the couch. We sat for a while politely, disjointedly, chatting. Philippe's enthusiasm seemed to come and go in waves. 'Mexico is the only city that makes me comfortable,' he said, 'it's as restless and discontented as I am.' It was also, I realized, the only city I'd ever been where surrealism seemed totally at home.

Philippe was well connected in the art world and, when I told him about my interest in the unseen Mexico, the country of indigenous tradition and cultural extremes, he immediately championed Francisco Toledo, one of Mexico's best known contemporary artists and a Zapotec Indian. I'd heard of Toledo – he was described in one of the tacky tourist brochures lying about in the hotel lobby as an 'International Avant-Garden Artist'.

Philippe said: 'Forget Diego Rivera, Orozco and Siqueiros. They were bourgeois middle-class Mexicans idealizing the state of the Mexican Indian. They were Mexico's answer to Rousseau or Gauguin. They didn't really know where the Indian was coming from. They were still frightened, distrustful of Indians. Or at least, they wouldn't have wanted to have one round to dinner.

'But Toledo is an Indian. That's how he sees the world. His pictures are full of native symbolism – burros, dogs, iguanas, snakes, crickets, toads, fish, coyotes, deer, bulls, bats, you name it, skeletons and penises. They're erotic and frightening and piss-takes at the same time. They're about death and sex and Zapotec spirits and bicycles and Singer sewing-machines.'

Toledo, he told me, came from a town on the Pacific coast, on the Isthmus of Tehuantepec where the women were built like all-in wrestlers, big and fat and raunchy. The men in this town were so in awe of their women, Philippe said, they were content to play second fiddle to them; they worshipped them. A large proportion of the male population were transvestite. If you weren't born a woman, the next best thing was to act and dress like one. This was about the only place in Mexico where homosexuality was not only tolerated, it was seen as a virtue.

It sounded fantastic, especially in a country where even the mildest form of feminism was thought of as sick and unnatural, and machismo was aggressively promoted as the cultural norm. Women only got the vote here in 1954; and feminists are still thought of as *las locas* – 'crazy women'.

I'd started, for my own amusement, collecting sexist advertisements as I wandered around town. Wonderbra had some of the best. Billboards, big as office blocks, flaunted models with breasts like melons in a clamp, above the slogan, 'Give him a good reason to come home', or 'Behind every great woman are hundreds of men'. There were so many adverts of semi-naked women selling anything from cars to Coke to underwear, that Contac, the pharmaceutical cold remedy, had used the Wonderbra model for its advertisement, shivering in her black lacy D cup and sneezing into a handkerchief.

I was growing used to the bizarre, oscillating visibility and invisibility of being a female in Mexico City. Men barged in front of me in queues as if I wasn't there; waiters seemed deaf to the soprano octave, even when it shrieked at them in decibels; and yet eyes wandered lingeringly, unembarrassed, at chest height whenever I asked a man the way or bought a newspaper. Alone, I felt conspicuous, an easy, glaring target. In the company of Guy or Humberto I felt safer, more relaxed and yet also, somehow, defeated. It was hard not to slip into the back seat and let a man do the driving.

But Humberto's wife, Laurence, had been adamant – this would get me nowhere fast. 'You have to learn to be larger than life in Mexico,' she told me. 'Shout when you would usually talk; take up space, muscle your way in. If you want something from the waiter, bellow at him as if the place has just caught fire. Make it impossible to be ignored.'

I admired Laurence's furious energy, her gravelly self-confidence, but not everyone had her stamina. Paulina, a friend of hers, told me that she still felt uncomfortable when she passed the naked statue of Diana on the main drag, Paseo de la Reforma. Until recently, Diana's nakedness had been so contentious that a pair of bronze knickers had been put on her to make her respectable. Now the knickers were off, but cab drivers still made lewd or disapproving comments and Paulina would break out in treacherous blushes in the back seat.

I could see how exasperating this combination of prudishness and prurience could become and a week in a place where the tables were turned seemed irresistibly attractive. Philippe had never been to Toledo's home town but he'd introduce me to Toledo's daughter, he said. Perhaps she would take me to this oasis of female liberation.

Gradually, the outline of an itinerary began to unfold. My original plan, which was no more than a clutch of vague ideas at the start, became dotted with place names and people and pieces of good advice, with travel details and dates and unmissable fiestas. I began to pinpoint destinations in parts of the country which promised to reveal the more surprising sides of Mexico, the unseen faces of the polygon.

Thanks mostly to Humberto and Laurence, my remaining evenings in Mexico City were a whirlwind of bars and nightclubs, mezcal and margaritas, salsa and *música tropical*. Their network of friends was exhaustive and most of them had recommendations – some more practical than others – which they shouted into my ear above the drumbeats.

By day I wandered around galleries and museums, or sat in my favourite spot on the 7th floor of the Hotel Majestic reading tales of conquest and defeat, defiance and assimilation. I'd lost my fear of the city and its incomprehensible vastness; but my horizontal complacency was attended by a growing awe for the vertical perspective, for the crumbly *mille feuilles* of history. Sometimes it seemed as if I was walking on the thinnest of crusts. Every now and again it would give way and I'd find myself kicking around in the dust of the past, sending it puffing up, chokingly, into the present.

Nowhere had this sensation been more unnerving, more shocking, than in the Plaza de las Tres Culturas, barely a mile to the north-west of the Zócalo. If the Zócalo had all the hallmarks of an historical car crash, the Plaza de las Tres Culturas was a head-on fatality. High-rise housing blocks, 1960s style, surrounded a square in which an early seventeenth-century colonial church – the Templo de Santiago – sat amid Aztec temple ruins like a ship run aground on a reef.

This was once the centre of the ancient city of Tlatelolco – an island separate from Tenochtitlán which was annexed by the Aztecs in 1473. Tlatelolco had been the most important commercial and market centre in the Valley of Mexico and even after annexation retained this tradition, its people existing side by side with the Aztecs as allies rather than subjects. By the time the Spaniards arrived much of the swampy lake between the two islands had been filled in and built over. Cortés and his captains rode here from their quarters in one of Moctezuma's palaces and were clearly overawed by what they saw.

Cortés estimated that Tlatelolco was 'twice as big as Salamanca'. Around 60,000 people traded in the market every day – that was far more than the main market in Constantinople or Rome. This was where tributes arrived by canoe from all the subject peoples in the Aztec Empire. There were dealers in precious stones and silver, in feathers, cloaks and cottons and all types of embroidered goods. There were dealers in male and female slaves, brought in tied around their necks to poles. There were chocolate merchants and sisal sellers, and people selling the skins of jaguars and pumas, jackals and deer and ocelots. There were grocers selling beans and herbs and spices, and every known fruit and vegetable in the land; and butchers selling water-fowl, turkeys, rabbits and small dogs. There were women selling cooked food – tortillas and honey cake and tripe, and sweets like nougat. There were potters with water-jugs and cooking pots; timber merchants with boards, cradles, beams, blocks and benches; and sellers of pitch-pine for torches. There were paper, tobacco and dye merchants; sellers of salt and makers of flint knives and axes; there were fisher-women, and men who sold small cakes which tasted like cheese made from a weed that grew in the lake. And there were merchants who came with goose quills filled with grains of gold.

I took Bernal Díaz's *Conquest of New Spain* with me to the Plaza and reread his wonderful eye-witness account of the great Tlatelolco market, sitting on the tilting steps of the church overlooking the bases of the temple pyramids that had once dominated the square. Compared with his elevated description of ancient commerce and exotica, the modern Plaza de las Tres Culturas was a bleak and empty place, bereft and hollow – a place of ghosts. This had been the site of the Spaniards' first attack against the Aztecs and, a few months later, it was the site of the Aztecs' final stand. It was here that the mighty Aztec Empire finally collapsed.

It was a tragic, yet inevitable, tale. Six months into their stay in the great city, relations between the Spaniards and their Aztec hosts had reached a critical point of no return. Cortés had received reinforcements from a second fleet and official approval from the Spanish Crown sharpened his resolve. Moctezuma, still reluctant to fight a man he considered could be a god, clung to his vacillating policy of appeasement, against the council of the more bullish Aztec elite.

The turning point came during a magnificent ceremony orchestrated by Moctezuma at which Cortés was to be honoured alongside him, as an equal, a quasi-deity. All the great dignitaries and princes of the neighbouring allied states of Texcoco and Tacuba were invited to pay homage to the two leaders and there were ritual dances in celebration of the feast of Huitzilopochtli, at which 10,000 victims were sacrificed.

Somehow – and Díaz is deliberately confused in the telling of it – at the peak of the celebrations Spanish soldiers ran amok (with or without the instructions of Cortés) and murdered two hundred of the assembled Aztec nobility trapped in the square. All hell broke loose. The Spaniards took Moctezuma prisoner and in the furore he was mortally wounded – whether by Spaniards or his own people is unclear. According to Díaz, Cortés wept copiously over the body of his friend. Cacamatzin, ruler of Texcoco and the Governor of Tlatelolco, however, were unequivocally strangled by Spaniards.

The surviving Aztec leaders rallied together and hounded the Spaniards back to the palaces where they'd been living, determined at last to kill them all. But on 30 June 1520, taking advantage of a moonless night and torrential rain, the Spaniards fled. Several hundred of them, together with thousands of their Indian allies, were killed on what was to go down in colonial annals as the 'Noche Triste' – the Sad Night.

Cortés and the other 900 or so Spaniards who survived, embittered and vengeful, retreated to Tlaxcala where they mustered 100,000 troops from among the Aztecs' traditional enemies. From there they laid siege to Tenochtitlán, cutting off the food and water supplies, and building a fleet of brigantines for a water-borne assault.

In Tenochtitlán, meanwhile, Moctezuma's heir, his nephew Cuitlahuac, had died of smallpox, only recently introduced into Mexico by one of Cortés's reinforcements. He was succeeded by another nephew, the eighteen-year-old Cuauhtémoc. The siege lasted over three months with the population of Tenochtitlán suffering appallingly from famine and plague. Yet still Cuauhtémoc and his forces repeatedly resisted the Spanish attacks.

Finally, on 13 August 1521, the Spaniards broke through and the Aztecs fell back, emaciated and in a piteous state, on the plaza of Tlatelolco. They were surrounded by the Spaniards on all sides. According to the Aztec chronicler Alva Ixtlilxochitl, 'Almost all the Aztec nobility died, the only survivors being a few lords and gentlemen, mostly children or extremely young people.' Cuauhté-moc, the 'last emperor', begged Cortés to kill him on the spot but Cortés refused, dragging him off in chains instead, to imprison and torture him, and then hang him ignominiously some time later.

Just in front of where I was sitting, next to the excavated foundations of the Aztec temples, a memorial had been raised to that fateful day. The inscription read:

ON THE 13TH OF AUGUST 1521
HEROICALLY DEFENDED BY CUAUHTÉMOC,
TLATELOLCO FELL TO THE MIGHT OF HERNAN CORTÉS.
IT WAS NEITHER A TRIUMPH OR A DEFEAT.
IT WAS THE PAINFUL BIRTH OF THE COMMINGLED PEOPLE
THAT IS MEXICO TODAY.

Perhaps the fall of Tenochtitlán was inevitable. But what seemed particularly poignant, even from Bernal Díaz's swashbuckling account, which read like a tale of Homeric heroism, was the part played in its downfall by other Mexicans, by the Indian allies of Cortés, peoples who were so blinded by their hostility towards the Aztecs they failed to see that, by siding with the invader, they were sealing their own fate, too.

I sat for a little longer watching tiny white butterflies chasing each other around some nasturtiums that had begun to ramble over the old, chocolate-coloured masonry of the Aztec walls. Oddly, despite the roar of continuous traffic, I could hear birdsong coming from the towers of the church as if it were transmitted on a separate aural plane.

Just round the corner of the church was the site of another battle. Here, the Aztec scene of carnage had reassembled itself, re-evolved, transmuted through the gauze of history on to the modern stage. Here was another plaque commemorating another massacre. But this was only thirty years ago. The date was 2 October 1968. Thousands of students and intellectuals had rallied here to protest against the government's social and educational policies. It was ten days before the city was to host the ceremonial opening of the Olympic Games and, with Mexico about to be cast in the international spotlight, the authorities were desperate to suppress signs of discontent and unrest. Troops opened fire on the protesters who were trapped in the square, killing hundreds – the exact number is still not known. The site was hastily cleaned up and all mention of the incident suppressed. It was only in 1993 that the government officially acknowledged it had happened at all.

With modern housing blocks on all sides, this part of the square had the look of a children's playground. There should have been hopscotch or snakes and ladders painted across the volcanic paving stones but instead there were the silhouettes of bodies, white-outlined like in a murder case. Over time, with dozens of repaintings, the silhouettes had lost much of their definition. They'd grown blobby, like jelly babies. The paving stones were lifting and cracking here, too, as if the ghosts of centuries were wrestling around, trying to join in.

It's customary for anyone embarking on a journey in Mexico to seek the blessing of the Virgin of Guadalupe, Mexico's patron saint, 'Emperatriz de América' – Queen of the Americas. Known lovingly as 'little Guadalupe' – 'Guadalupita', ' 'Lupita', or simply 'Mi amor' – her name is echoed round the country in the Christian names of thousands of Mexicans – male and female – and the names of countless towns and villages. Her image is everywhere: in little shrines in bus stations; on posters in travel agents and hotel lobbies; on key-rings and rear-view mirrors; on car bumpers. She has a distinctive silhouette – standing on a crescent moon, draped in robes, head tilted slightly to one side – and not long after arriving in the country I'd found her shape had already etched itself on my subconscious. I began to see her randomly in everything, like the Mexicans do – in the peculiar shape of a potato chip, a pool of oil in the road, the scar on the trunk of a tree. Drivers slip cards with her picture on it into their wallets with their money and their licences; veteran travellers put her postcard in their passports. This isn't simply for good luck. There's a real chance that some corrupt official will have second thoughts when they see her face. Once in a while she hits the headlines again when there's news of another apparition. Carlos Santana, the celebrity rock musician, was one of Guadalupe's devotees to be honoured recently by a visitation.

The Basílica of Guadalupe is at the foot of a hill, the Cerro de Tepeyac, in the north of the city which was, within living memory, in open countryside and is now swallowed up in the urban sprawl along with everything else. I emerged from the Metro four miles from the Zócalo in a tide of pilgrims and vendors. The site is the spiritual Mecca of Mesoamerica – 16 million people visit it a year. It's the second most visited Christian shrine after St Paul's in Rome.

There's an animated atmosphere of expectancy in the crowd as it pushes its way up the tree-lined Calzada de Guadalupe, over the concrete flyover and into the main square of the Basílica. Both sides of the avenue are bristling with stalls selling Guadalupe trinkets and plastic statues and trays of *milagros* or 'little miracles'. These are tiny tin amulets of every imaginable body part that someone might need to have cured. There are legs, arms, hands, feet, kidneys, lungs, hearts (rather graphic, these, with severed aortae), eyes, even breasts, testicles and the odd amorphous womb. Then there are *milagros* in the shape of children and babies and, prosaically, avariciously, houses and cars. Pilgrims pin their *milagros* to the robes of different saints in churches all over Mexico, sometimes together with a passport photo or a US dollar to speed it on its way. But no saint has a greater reputation for fulfilling prayers and performing miracles than Our Lady of Guadalupe, and special boards are put up in the Basílica to accommodate the daily inundation of requests.

The buildings on the main Plaza de las Américas exhibit the same crazy drunkenness of those on the Zócalo and the Plaza de las Tres Culturas. The soil here is particularly soft and the original Basílica, a heavy yellow-domed baroque edifice built around 1700, has a massive crack down one side of it and one corner is shored up completely by hydraulic jacks. Its windows have been sealed with breeze-blocks and the clock has stopped permanently, ridiculously, at ten past five.

It is overshadowed by the new Basílica, a monstrous concrete big top designed to accommodate 10,000 worshippers at a time. It was built in the 1970s – by which time even the most fervently devout were having second thoughts about entering the old one. The architect, Pedro Ramírez Vásquez, also designed Mexico City's Anthropological Museum and Azteca Stadium. He should have stuck to Mayan frescoes and football. Looking more like a Soviet gymnasium from the Cold War era than the 'Villa' of the Mother of Christ, Vásquez's basilica is singularly uninspiring and godless. There is nothing indigenous or Mexican about it; no sense of the extraordinary influence of this home-grown Virgin, or the hopes and prayers an entire continent have invested here. It's completely at odds with the purpose for which it was built: to house one of the holiest, and supposedly most mysterious relics in the world, and one that belongs uniquely, specifically, to the Americas. The image of the Virgin of Guadalupe was the New World's answer to the shroud of Turin: a portrait of the Mother of God herself, 'miraculously made manifest' five centuries ago, on a piece of hempen cloth. Famously, she is dark-skinned – like an Indian. On top of the Basílica's domed big top is an icon that's meant to be a mitred crucifix but that looks unfortunately like the golden arches of McDonald's.

As they near the big-top Basílica, most of the pilgrims fall to the pavement and shuffle the last twenty yards or so, including a flight of steps, on their knees. There are no histrionics, no wailing or gnashing of teeth, but faces etched with concentration and the dignified, respectful containment of deep emotion. Some of them slip into the pews beneath the gigantic, gaudy, coppered dome and begin muttering prayers. Others find their way to the upper balcony where mass is said round the clock in any of seven chapels. But most head straight for the image itself which hangs behind bullet-proof glass above the main altar and can be seen from an electronic walkway that passes underneath it, backstage.

There's a typical Mexican muddle over the conveyor when I get there because some of the pilgrims are trying to eke out their moment of glory by walking backwards and hogging the spot underneath the picture. People are tripping over each other, getting bags stuck, patiently and politely snagging themselves up. But I do notice one particular man in the jostle – a grey-haired Indian with a weathered face who holds his sombrero to his chest and gazes up steadily at his queen. He brushes the tears from his cheeks with the sleeve of his coat and quietly, demurely, slips away.

Juan Diego was fifty-seven, so the legend goes, when he saw a vision of the Virgin Mary on Tepeyac Hill. It was 1531, just eleven years after México-Tenochtitlán had fallen to the Spaniards. Juan Diego and his uncle had been among the first Indians in the region to be baptized. They lived together in the village of Tolpetlac, nine miles from the fledgling city of the Europeans. It was 9 December, the feast of the Immaculate Conception, and Juan Diego was making his way over the rough, undulating terrain in the freezing cold to celebrate mass at the new Franciscan church where the great temple-pyramid of Tlatelolco had stood barely a decade before – the church where I'd sat watching butterflies and reading Bernal Díaz.

Juan Diego was crossing the shoulder of Tepeyac Hill when he heard heavenly music and a woman's voice softly and affectionately calling him. She spoke to him in Náhuatl. Following the voice he climbed to the top of the hill and found himself face to face with a vision of a beautiful young woman, whose radiance suffused the surrounding rocks and mesquite bushes and prickly pears with a shimmering golden light.

She introduced herself as the 'perfect and perpetual Virgin Mary, Mother of the True God, through whom everything lives'. 'I am your merciful Mother,' she said, 'the Mother of all who live united in this land, and of all mankind, of all those who love me, of those who cry to me, of those who have confidence in me. Here I will hear their weeping and their sorrows, and will remedy and alleviate their sufferings, necessities and misfortunes.' She asked him to go to the house of the Bishop. 'Tell him,' she said, 'that I have sent you and that it is my desire to have a *teocalli* – a temple – built here in my honour.'

Juan Diego sought an audience with the Bishop several times before he was admitted. Juan de Zumárraga, the second Viceroy and the first Archbishop of Mexico City, was dismissive of the humble little Indian standing in front of him. Incredulous, he sent him away, demanding proof of his extravagant story. So Juan Diego returned to the summit of Tepeyac and the Virgin appeared again. She instructed him to return the following day to receive a sign. But when Juan Diego got home he discovered his uncle desperately ill, dying from the plague. He nursed him for two days, unable to fulfil his promise to the Virgin to return.

But when Juan Diego's uncle begged his nephew to fetch a priest from Tlatelolco so he could make his last confession, Juan Diego found himself crossing Tepeyac Hill once again and once again the Virgin appeared to him. To his surprise, she spoke to him not in words of chastisement but encouragingly, with the affection of a mother for her child. At that very moment, she told him, his uncle was cured.

Then the Virgin reminded Juan Diego of the sign she wanted

him to take to the Bishop and instructed him to gather armfuls of
Castilian roses that were blooming miraculously around them in
the frozen soil. She told him to use his *tilma* – his homespun tunic
– like an apron to carry them. When Juan Diego received his
audience with the doubting Bishop once again, he let go of the hem
of his tunic and the roses tumbled on to the floor, casting a
wonderful scent about the room. And there on the cloth where the
roses had been, was a perfect imprint of the vision Juan Diego had
seen at the top of the hill – a young woman in a celestial blue
mantle studded with stars, hands clasped in prayer, surrounded by
a shimmer of golden light.

The image of the Virgin, barely 5 feet 6 inches by 3 feet 4 inches,
is beautiful in a sense, serene and gentle – no Bellini or Da Vinci –
but touching in the way that most madonnas are touching, with a
countenance that captures a mournful, thoughtful kindliness. What
surprises me, though, is the image's conventionality, its lack of
dramatic impact. It looks like any other portrait of the Virgin
Mary. There's certainly nothing murky or timeless about her as
there is, at least, in the spectral image on the shroud of Turin; no
suggestion of 'otherness', that some divine force might have had a
part in creating it, or that it was originally part of a peasant's shirt.
This picture is as conventional and unextraordinary as any in a
gallery.

There's nothing overtly indigenous or Mexican about Guadalupe, either. She wears a regal gown of red and gold, trimmed with
ermine, and a sky-blue silk cape covered in stars. Though her skin
is dark, her features are Caucasian, not Indian as I'd come to
expect. And at her neck a gold brooch bears the same black
cross that was carried on the banners and helmets of the Spanish
conquistadors.

I find the lack of ambiguity, her lack of Mexicanness, startling.
The Virgin of Guadalupe looks as Spanish as the conquest itself;
as Minerva was to imperial Rome. Even her name betrays her.
Guadalupe is the name of a Marian shrine in eastern Spain, in the
sierra of the Extremadura, the region most of the conquistadors
came from. It was where Columbus prayed before he set sail, and

it was the name he gave one of the islands of the West Indies after he was saved from shipwreck on his journey home. The Virgin of Guadalupe in Extremadura had been a powerful symbol of Hispanic Christianity in its struggle against the Moors. She became, by association, the conquistadors' standard against the pagans of the New World.

Given the Virgin's strong Spanish identity and the abhorrent political context in which she manifested herself, it seems, at first sight, extraordinary that Guadalupe should have become the object of such veneration in the Americas; that she should have come to represent the downtrodden Indian and the rootless *mestizo*; that she should promise salvation to the people of the New World, instead of religious and cultural domination.

The origins of the Virgin of Guadalupe are deliberately obscure. As the cult around the image grew, so the tale expanded. Originally it was said that the painting had miraculously appeared among the rocks on Tepeyac Hill. Eventually the legend became what it is today – that the Virgin, herself, appeared and that the picture was her image miraculously transferred on to an Indian's cloak.

So fervently is this myth believed, and so actively is it supported by the Vatican, which is desperate to secure the Catholic hold over Mexico against an advancing tide of evangelism all over Latin America, that questioning its origins is seen as malevolent and disloyal. Few objective experts have ever been allowed access to the painting. Catholic bookshops in Mexico City are stuffed with pseudo-scientific 'proofs' of the uniqueness of the image and its miraculous properties.

But historians are less convinced. According to Jacques Lafaye, the cult of Guadalupe as a distinctly Mexican phenomenon began with the Creole class – the mixed, coffee-coloured race that was being spawned by the conquistadors even before they reached Tenochtitlán. Neither Indian, or Spanish, the Creoles had more need than any other stratum of society in the New World to conceive a Mexican patroness and a spiritual focus of their own.

The earliest references to the Mexican Virgin of Guadalupe talk of a statue, not a painting. It was a life-size replica of the Virgin of Guadalupe in Extremadura in Spain, brought to the New World by Cortés. But some time after conquest (Lafaye puts it at forty to fifty years) the Creoles, in an effort to distance themselves from the overbearing patronage of Spain, commissioned a portrait (there are several mentions of a new Guadalupe being painted by a famous Indian artist of the 1560s called 'Marcos') of another Madonna which they placed instead of the conquistadors' statue in Guadalupe's chapel on Tepeyac Hill. What they did with the original is still a mystery.

One of the Creoles' main grievances was that, if they continued to worship an image of the Extremadura Guadalupe, even in replica, all legacies and donations given to that image were duty-bound to be returned to her church in Spain. By establishing their own Madonna, the Creoles were asserting their right to keep their alms.

But the Tepeyac Madonna was also a symbol of independence in a broader, psychological sense. It was an icon of nascent nationalism. The Virgin was not Indian; she was typically Creole – the first Mexican mestizo – a dark-skinned Caucasian in Spanish dress. Unlike her namesake in Extremadura, the Creole Madonna carried no child – she was *inmaculada*. Her feast day was moved from the Extremadura Guadalupe's date in September to 12 December – another significant departure that distanced Mexico from the original. The name Guadalupe – unfortunately for the Creoles perhaps – persisted, but the split had been made. They had their own patroness, their own mother, at last.

The Virgin's popularity among the Indians was slower to evolve. The pioneer missionaries of New Spain – the Franciscans – discouraged the cult of Guadalupe among the *indígenas* because they believed it confused the Virgin Mary with the powerful Indian Earth Goddess on whose sacred site the shrine to Guadalupe had been built.

The Cerro de Tepeyac had been a sacred site long before the Spaniards arrived. It was already established as a place of pilgrimage and miracles. It was the dwelling-place of Tonantzin, the powerful Earth Goddess, a manifestation of Coatlicue, Mother of all Gods. Her impressive *teocalli*, or temple-pyramid, was razed to the ground by Cortés shortly after the fall of México-Tenochtitlán.

It was no coincidence that a temple to the Virgin Mary was built on this spot. With all the precision of a smart bomb, the Catholic Church identified one of the most powerful seats of indigenous belief in the vicinity and dropped its own religious structure in its place in an effort to eradicate what had gone before. But the Franciscans knew this was a risky business, that indigenous belief was dangerously powerful and tended to bubble back up with the slightest encouragement; that, in the end, the Church might not be establishing the Mother of God in Mexico so much as conceiving a bastard.

The Mexican Earth Goddess had not been the kindliest of deities. She was omnipotent, all-embracing and terrifying, both creator and destroyer, a kind of Aztec Kali. A famous figure of Coatlicue, or 'Serpent Skirt', as she was sometimes known, dominates the Aztec Hall in the Museum of Anthropology. She is massive, awful, monolithic. Her great bulk is the body of the earth itself. Her neck is severed by her moon daughter's attempted matricide and from it spout twin jets of blood that form the serpent heads of her face. She wears a necklace of human hearts and hands, and a skirt of snakes, animal paws and talons. She is a mother but she has aged, withered breasts. It's clearly not with her milk that she feeds mankind, but with blood – her own, which gushes from her neck, and the blood of human sacrifice derived from the hearts of her own children hanging round her neck. She is a tyrant, wailing in the darkness, demanding blood like an insatiable, inconsolable child. She embodies all the violence and bloodshed the Mexica believed was necessary to sustain agricultural fertility and human life.

Deprived of their worship of the Earth Goddess, the indigenous Mexicans found themselves orphaned, lacking the powerful goddess figure in their midst, that quintessential female force that was, to their eyes, the fount of all things. They desperately needed a spiritual constant in the anarchy that the Spaniards had unleashed upon their world. The Spaniards were systematically dismantling the infrastructure of the Mexica culture and religion, smashing down temples, and executing priests.

They must also have begun to feel that their gods had abandoned them. Forbidden to propitiate them with the requisite rituals of human sacrifice and blood-letting, it was hardly surprising that the world had turned upside down, that the balance of nature was rocking from its very core. The years of conquest were terrible times. Exacerbated by the ignorance and vandalism of the Spaniards, the twin harpies of drought and flood were wreaking their havoc at will; the old systems of agriculture were in collapse; hunger was rife. By the 1530s vast numbers of sheep and cattle roamed the plains; by the 1570s many cattle herds contained 150,000 animals. Sheep in the Mezquital Valley alone – home of the Otomí, just north of the Valley of Mexico – numbered two million.

The damage caused by overgrazing in the central highlands was compounded by the use of animal-drawn ploughs which replaced traditional Indian digging sticks and added to the erosion of topsoil. It wasn't long before the Náhuatl word for exposed hardpan, *tepetate*, had entered the Spanish language. Widespread deforestation accelerated the process of desertification. Extensive stands of highland forest around new mine sites were felled for the construction of shafts and the production of charcoal for the smelting process. In 1543, Indians around Taxco in present-day Guerrero complained that the mines had left not a single tree standing. Meanwhile, tropical forests were cleared in the upland valleys of Veracruz and the interior lowlands of Morelos to make way for sugar-cane, and to power the mills.

The degraded and ailing ecosystem of the New World was a propitious environment for the spread of Old World weeds like dandelions, nettles, clover and grasses, whose seeds were carried into the country stuck to clothing or fur, or in animal dung. By 1600, entire meadows were largely devoid of native plants and thousands of indigenous plant species had been wiped out.

But more terrifying and catastrophic than flood, famine or the environmental apocalypse, were the demons of disease – vengeful, pitiless scourges that were scything down the native populations thousands at a time. Smallpox, mumps, measles, influenza, and bubonic plague were doing more to secure the New World for Spain than the Bible and the sword combined. Epidemics raged almost continuously with notable outbreaks in the years 1545–8,

1581–6 and 1629–31. Terrifyingly, the Indian population of Nueva España fell from an estimated 25 million at conquest to little over a million by 1605.

Compared to Europe, the Americas were a welcome mat for infectious disease. The only human diseases in the New World were the ones brought by migrants who had crossed the Bering Strait from the continent of Asia in various waves beginning 30,000 years earlier. These earliest colonists had passed slowly through an icy climate in small groups, a process which itself had reduced the transference of illnesses to the Americas to a minimum. Only hepatitis, polio, intestinal parasites and perhaps syphilis existed. On the other hand, Europe was a steaming, jostling Petri-dish of pathogens. By the fifteenth century its population had been exposed to hundreds of epidemics spread mostly by vigorous trade with tropical Africa and Asia; and the surviving population had developed immunities. In this sense at least the conquistadors were accidental agents of destruction.

It wasn't just the old and infirm like the Indian Juan Diego's uncle who were victims of these new plagues. The young and healthy and strong fell like flies. The appearance of a new goddess in Coatlicue's place must have seemed prophetic; the Virgin of Guadalupe a light in the darkness. The Indians were always ready to take on new permutations in their pantheon, to pour old wine into new bottles, and there were uncanny similarities between the old Earth Goddess and the new Catholic saint, which made the transference relatively easy. The very names of Coatlicue and Guadalupe were similar. Guadalupe was the Mother of God, just as Coatlicue, or Tonantzin, was mother of all gods. Both myths involved immaculate conception, bloodshed and torture and the sacrifice of children. The angels of the Christian church, Mary's attendants, were not so very different, with their bird wings and human bodies, from polymorphic gods like the feathered serpent. Even the Christian cross was an established Totonac symbol.

Dominican and Franciscan monks began arriving from Europe to harvest the newly discovered souls in New Spain in 1523. Many of them were compassionate and brave men and distinguished themselves by protecting the Indians from the conquistadors' and colonists' worst excesses. Their mass conversions were spectacular but largely superficial. It was the arrival of the Jesuits in the 1570s that positively encouraged the Indians' affection for religious syncretism and sank the roots of Christianity into the Mexican soil. The Jesuits were far more lenient than the Franciscans and Dominicans and under their influence the cult of Guadalupe blossomed. This bright, new manifestation of the Earth Mother, the Jesuits taught, was no longer bloodthirsty and tyrannical, but merciful, kind and empathetic. She had tamed the wrathful, vengeful gods of the past. She offered hope and comfort and affection. She was the champion of the poor and the sick and defeated. She had risen to meet the needs of a Mexico that in the space of a few decades had been utterly and terrifyingly transformed. Her message of love and compassion and, above all, forbearance, would show her people a way to live with the new conqueror. The Virgin of Guadalupe, the Jesuits instructed the Indians, made submission a dignified, heroic and perpetual state of being.

It was around this time, half a century after conquest, that the popular Indian myth of Guadalupe's apparition to Juan Diego came into being, a legend in retrospect, evolved to coincide with the detonation of conquest. 'Listen and let it penetrate your heart, my little son,' the gentle Guadalupe told Juan Diego, 'do not be troubled or weighed down with grief. Do not fear any illness or vexation, anxiety or pain. Am I not here who am your Mother? Are you not under my shadow and protection? Am I not your fountain of life? Are you not in the folds of my mantle? In the crossing of my arms? Is there anything else you need?'

The Virgin's words to Juan Diego were inscribed in an angular 1950s-style script in bronze above the doors of the modern Basílica of Guadalupe at Tepeyac. They made me wretchedly, inexplicably, sad. I wandered away from the mêlée of pilgrims, through a civic rock garden, a kind of Virgin-themed Disney park that has replaced the original woodland and cactus scrub, towards the top of the hill. A waterfall smelling of chlorine had replaced the freshwater spring, which has long since dried up. There were carts of paper flowers beneath the jacarandas; plastic purple and orange arum lilies in the flower-beds alongside some real but rather ropy roses and azaleas; and a bizarre image of the Virgin, looking like Terry Jones, being pulled by a pantomime horse. A family of Indians was looking on admiringly. 'See,' the mother was telling her child, 'the Virgin sends us beautiful flowers just like she did for Juan Diego.'

The view from the top of the hill was dizzying. The great *mancha urbana* stretched out below in a tannic haze. Another Indian family was waiting at the gate of the Panteón del Tepeyac, a cemetery said to be founded on the site of the apparition. The Indians had walked in from one of the poorest barrios in the concrete desert below. They had filthy, ragged clothes and matted, sheenless hair. A priest appeared and, using a real red rose dipped in a bowl, sloshed some holy water over their heads and gave them the Virgin's blessing.

I wandered around the hilltop for a bit and then started back down towards the Basílica. I felt suddenly exhausted. It was hot. My head was thumping. The taste of sulphur was stronger than ever and my eyes were stinging. Far away below me one and then two police sirens wailed. I sat down to take stock for a moment. Out of the corner of my eye, just inches away, I noticed a colourful little offering secreted deep in the foliage of a shrub. It was just like the ones Humberto had shown me in his apartment – a tiny yarn painting made with colourful wools pressed into beeswax. There were stains of sacrificial blood on it – from a bull or a deer, perhaps. I sat contemplating it for a while, this beautiful gesture, and my spirits began to rise a little. It was comforting, somehow, to know that Huichols had been here; that they had journeyed all the way from the northern Sierra Madre to Tepeyac to honour not a godhead that had been imposed on them by conquest, but their own traditional deities; that the undercurrents of indigenous belief, the force that the Franciscans and Dominicans were so afraid of, still surged beneath the foundations of the Catholic Church.

Senator Adolfo Aguilar Zinser was like a terrier on to a scent. He was in the middle of unravelling yet another saga of corruption. I was flattered he'd agreed to see me at all. The phone rang constantly and secretaries flitted about with incoming faxes and e-mails.

'I'm trying to nail a high-ranking official,' Zinser explained excitedly, 'someone close to my own constituency – a *cacique* of sorts.' He used the Náhuatl word *cacique* as if he was spitting out a bullet. It was the ancient Aztec term for a chief but it had come to mean an abuser of power – a provincial warlord or a corrupt political strong-man. 'I've been trying to get him for years. It looks like he won't survive this one.'

He motioned me to a chair next to his desk. There was more on Senator Zinser's mind than simply flooring a political opponent. The political temperature was hotting up in Mexico and Zinser was one of the key figures fanning the flames. The *cacique* was another high profile component in Zinser's efforts to bring down the government. There was a palpable zing in the politician's normally cool delivery.

Senator Zinser was still the only independent in the House of Senators. He'd been elected on an environmental and anti-corruption ticket by one of the most rebellious constituencies in Mexico. Though only in his early forties he was considered by many to be a serious future presidential contender. His constituency, the Nahua Indian town of Tepoztlán, 40 miles south of the capital, was well known for its resistance to the ruling institutional party of Mexico – the Partido Revolucionario Instituciónal, PRI, or simply 'El Pree' for short.

The PRI was the direct descendant of the ruling party instated by the Revolution in 1929. It had become the world's oldest political dynasty acquiring, over its seven decades at the helm, megalithic power and status. Over those seventy years the PRI had trapped the country in an increasingly vice-like embrace, exacting loyalty and dependence in every quarter through a combination of coercion, co-option and corruption. The Peruvian novelist Mario Vargas Llosa, risking his life by speaking out against the PRI on Mexican television in 1991, described it as 'the perfect dictatorship', which 'maintains the appearance of democracy but suppresses it by all means, even the worst, whenever criticism threatens its perpetuation in power'. Under such circumstances, people had come to accept that dissent was either impossible or pointless. The 1968 student massacre at Tlatelolco, in the Plaza de las Tres

Culturas in Mexico City – Mexico's Tiananmen Square – had been proof of that.

But it was in Tepoztlán, and thanks largely to Senator Zinser, that one of the largest cracks responsible for undermining the ruling party's defences first manifested itself. In July 1996 – two years ago – the people of Tepoztlán rose up against the customary PRI candidate and Zinser became Mexico's first independently elected senator. There were examples of resistance, now, all over the country, and for the first time in seventy years Mexico was undergoing political revolution, coming closer than it ever had before to breaking down the old one-party state and replacing it with what Zinser and his allies hoped would one day be a genuine democracy.

'These are exciting times,' Zinser said, after fielding yet another phone call, 'it's not unlike the situation just before the collapse of the Berlin Wall. I see the country like a giant apple tree. In some places, like Tepoztlán, the apple is ripe and it is falling to the ground. But in other places, they aren't ready yet and the PRI retains its hold.'

Recently, though, events had begun to catch up with the PRI. The infamous 'neo-liberal project', the so-called 'globalization of Mexico', masterminded by Carlos Salinas, President from 1988 to December 1994, had included cultural assaults that went beyond any of the numerous outrageous measures enacted by seventy years of corrupt, self-serving, PRI-perpetuating Presidents. Salinas's revision of Constitutional Article 27, ending the policy of land reform and promoting the sale of communally owned *ejido* land to private capital and agribusiness struck at the very heart of Mexico: it ruled against the very principle of the Mexican Revolution in which between 1.5 and 2 million had died trying to redress the colonial imbalance by securing 'Land and Liberty' for the people. Without the constitutional promise of land redistribution many of the country's poorest people were left without hope – and felt they had nothing left to lose.

But Salinas's measures struck at the middle class as well as peasant ethos. Suddenly, great national institutions, the pride of Mexico, were up for grabs: the state banks were privatized, and the national airline, the national telephone company, and the mobile phone franchise, with foreign companies invited in to buy them up. There were even rumours that Pemex, the national oil company and Mexico's golden goose, would be next in the sales catalogue.

There had been talk of a new Mexican 'miracle' as growth leapt to 7 per cent. But the miracle proved only skin-deep. While an estimated US$60 billion in foreign investment poured into the Mexican stock market, social services continued to be slashed and the federal deficit of US$17 billion remained the same. *Forbes* magazine listed Mexico fourth in the world for billionaires, after the US, Japan and Germany, with twenty-three out of Mexico's twenty-four billionaires created under Salinas's presidency. In 1990 *Fortune* magazine declared Salinas 'Man of the Year'. And yet at the same time, between 1980 and 1990, according to the United Nations, the number of Mexicans living in 'extreme poverty' rose from 13 to 18 million.

The final straw was the signing in January 1994 of the North American Free Trade Agreement, or NAFTA. To Mexicans, opening the gates to this monstrous Trojan Horse was the ultimate betrayal, tantamount to economic, environmental and cultural suicide: it was opening the borders to the mighty Canadian and American multi-national corporations, to a herd of elephants, who would trample pitilessly over Mexican mice. Mexico was still largely a subsistence economy; a nation of small local businesses who would be unable to stand up to American competition within her very doors.

When the economy subsequently nose-dived, plunging Mexico into the worst depression since the 1930s, the popular reaction was overwhelming. By the beginning of 1996, Mexico's total foreign debt had risen to US$162 billion, interest rates hovered around 50 per cent and more than 2 million people had lost their jobs. The tremors of social upheaval were moving up the Richter scale.

The election result of July 1997 heralded the first real blow for democracy in the history of Mexico. Despite the usual coercions and attempted vote-rigging on the part of the PRI, opposition candidates swept aside the PRI majority in the Chamber of Deputies, winning 261 out of the 500 seats and ceding only 39 per cent of the overall vote to the ruling institutional party.

Senator Zinser was jubilant but also wary. This was an extraordinary chance for Mexico, he believed, but it was also fraught with dangers. 'If you travelled through Eastern Europe as I did, twenty years ago in a car,' he was saying, 'you couldn't have anticipated the breakdown that has happened since the Soviet Union moved away. The same thing is happening here with the breakdown of the PRI. All sorts of differences are emerging – regional, social and cultural differences. Look at the Zapatistas in Chiapas, look at the Zapotecs in Juchitán. And the situation between all these different interests is becoming very adversarial.

'Under the PRI, their rule was compelling. Mexico felt all her differences had disappeared. In a sense, unpleasant and unjust though it was, it gave us some sort of national identity, or *Mexicanidad* – our Mexicanness. And now that it's breaking down, and since we haven't found anything that holds the country together in its place, everyone is running in opposite directions.'

There was an uncharacteristic moment of silence. We were near the top of a skyscraper, encapsulated behind glass, floating high above the cacophony of the street like a thought bubble. The Senator gazed ruefully across to the National Lottery Building towering beside us as if uncomfortably reminded that the future depended on a great deal of luck. I remembered Octavio Paz's famous allegation that the only two unifying forces in Mexico, the only things Mexicans always had faith in, were the Virgin of Guadalupe and the National Lottery.

'What we need, most of all,' the Senator said, returning to the subject with a determined note of optimism, 'is to regenerate a sense of belonging, to recover our national identity alongside all these different emerging regional identities. We need to rediscover what it means to be Mexican in the modern world.'

Zinser had been so busy smashing down the PRI over the last decade, indicting the ruling elite for corruption, trying to dismantle the engines of political coercion, that he seemed suddenly overawed, now he had the chance to stand back and look, at the chasms that were being opened up – much like the empty spaces in Mexico's streets, left there since the 1985 earthquake because nobody could think, or agree on, what to do with them. The question in Senator Zinser's mind was whether democracy was going to be strong enough, or big enough, to replace the almighty monolith of the PRI.

But Adolfo Zinser was clearly a courageous and a determined man. If anyone was up to the challenges of Mexico's future, he was. He'd first gained international recognition appearing on the CBS investigative documentary programme *Sixty Minutes*, in the run-up to the elections the year before. Zinser was heading the country's first ever congressional inquiry into corruption, and his allegations, that President Carlos Salinas was implicated in the massive fraud carried out by his brother, Raúl Salinas, earned him several threats on his life.

Zinser's campaign had been successful. Following the catastrophic failure of the President's economic policies, his brother's imprisonment for murder and embezzlement of over US$300 million, and allegations of his own murky business deals, Carlos Salinas had retreated, tail between his legs, into self-imposed exile in Southern Ireland. No sooner was the new President, Ernesto Zedillo, in office than Zinser was probing him for corruption, too.

The telephone buzzed again and the Senator was diverted by the intrigue currently unravelling at his fingertips. The latest incident with the *cacique* in question involved a typically tangled web of corruption – millionaire businessmen, kidnappings, bodies in car boots, drugs cartels, double-dealing, double crossing, knives in the back, police investigators in the pocket of Mr Big.

By now the interruptions were making it difficult to pursue a single line of thought, let alone a conversation. And the Senator was due to leave the capital for his constituency for the Easter break. The traffic of everyone leaving Mexico City for Semana Santa was going to be terrible, he said. He was keen to get out ahead of the hordes. I left him throwing a few last-minute punches and returned to the cracking pavements of a fragmenting Mexico City. I was ready to leave for the country, too.

2

Holy Week
San Miguel de Allende

Poor Mexico – so far from God
and so close to the United States

attributed to Porfirio Díaz,
Mexican dictator 1884–1911

Easter in Mexico is legendary. For well over a week – the entire stretch of Semana Santa with weekends at either end, normal daily life slams shut like a clam. Wealthy *chilangos* evacuate the city for expensive Pacific resorts, Cancún or the family villa on the shores of Lake Pátzcuaro or Valle de Bravo. Every bus is splitting at the seams as young and old hit the road, families drawn back together like iron filings to a magnet, for this, the biggest holiday of the year.

I picked San Miguel de Allende because it was the antithesis of Mexico City: clean, quiet, safe, pretty and small. I was exhausted. All I wanted was to sit on a park bench somewhere and close my eyes and take stock, to slow the world down for a minute. It felt like I'd hit the ground running and the pace hadn't slackened since I'd arrived.

What drew me to San Miguel de Allende had been attracting other gringos for decades. San Miguel had become, on one level, a retirement village for arty Americans, a kind of satellite Santa Fe. This was a phenomenon of modern Mexico. Many of Mexico's most picturesque colonial towns were being re-colonized by *norte-americanos*. Oaxaca, Puebla, Pátzcuaro, and the old silver-mining town of Real de Catorce in San Luis Potosí were already host to large ex-pat communities of artists, New Agers or OAPs. In many ways, this influx was revitalizing the old towns, whose beautiful historic buildings were in sore need of restoration; and tourism was a welcome source of revenue in areas where agriculture and jobs traditionally dependent on farming had collapsed. But some Mexicans felt these towns were being prettified out of all recognition; that they were losing their Mexicanness.

The cultural battle – if that's what it was – was far from over in San Miguel de Allende, however. The confrontation of two completely different world views would be as dramatic here as anywhere on the Mexican/American border, Laurence and Humberto told me, particularly in Holy Week, when the Mexican genie, bottled up most of the rest of the year, comes bursting to the surface and repossesses the town.

'The United States has a presence, in some way, in every town in Mexico,' Humberto had said, 'because Mexican migrants bring the US home with them when they come back full of American jargon and ideas, and laden down with American goods; or because of satellite TV – which is everywhere now. Almost everyone gets to see American soaps and movies and commercials – we've become addicted. But in San Miguel you've got Mexicans who want to be Americans and Americans who are trying to be Mexican. It's crazy, and of course neither can ever really succeed.

'We have this love-hate relationship with the States,' he elaborated, 'we long to be like the States, to be as powerful, to have the same lifestyle, to have American cars and Nike trainers and Marlboro and Coca-Cola and little suburban houses with barbecues in the back yard. But we also despise it. No Mexican can forget that nearly a third of the States once belonged to us. And we can't forgive the States for continuing to treat us like their poor cousin. Politically and economically, and even culturally, we're always seen as the dirty little kid on the corner. The US will throw us a few scraps every now and again but you get the feeling it's still doing everything in its power to keep us in our place.'

With or without gringos, Laurence had recommended San Miguel as a good place to spend Easter. In the state of Guanajuato 175 miles north-west of Mexico City – four hours' drive away – San Miguel de Allende was in the geographical heart of Mexico.

Easter here was full-on, passionate and typical of Mexico's pecu-liar, idiosyncratic style of Catholicism. The Mexican inhabitants of the town were famously pious and San Miguel boasted ten times the national average of churches. Mexico City had about 1000 of the country's 30,000 Catholic churches. But in San Miguel, a municipality of less than 600 square miles, there were nearly 300 churches – an area one tenth of 1 per cent of the size of Mexico accounting for 1 per cent of Mexico's religious structures. This was where Catholicism had put down its deepest, earliest roots.

All over Latin America, Catholics were being won over by new charismatic evangelical churches. Brazil was now, amazingly, 40 per cent Protestant. Mexico alone was still, defiantly, Catholic. Protestant movements were chipping away at the state of Chiapas, far away to the Mesoamerican south, but in the rest of Mexico, the Holy Trinity, the Virgin Mother and the pantheon of Catholic saints remained inviolate. Ninety per cent of Mexicans still claimed to be Catholic. San Miguel was at the very heart of this spiritual constancy and Semana Santa here was famous for its penitential religious fervour. 'Don't forget to pack a hair-shirt with your fanny-pack and sun-visor,' Humberto had said when I rang them to say goodbye.

It was a relief to be able to put away my pack of Camel and eye-drops. The dawn air outside the saucepan of Mexico City was crystal clear, the world and everything in it, razor-sharp. It was like going to the oculist and coming out with the correct prescription of contact lenses. Shanty towns gave way to ridges of pine forest; then opened up into expansive farmland – sorghum and bean fields, punctuated by the occasional shrinking reservoir or grain silo.

As the car began to close on San Miguel de Allende, the country-side became unmistakably Mexican, dominated by cactuses and thorn-scrub and crumbling stone walls. There were dirt tracks running away from the road, a few white oxen and the occasional hatted farm labourer. It was still early morning and everything looked fawn and ochre with a tinge of pink. In the distance, the Guanajuato mountains stood out proud and royal-blue, like a crest down the back of a reptile.

The car purred up the hill towards San Miguel and then descended at last into the town. I felt I was coming down to earth. San Miguel had all the intimacy, the humanity, of a hilltop town in Italy or Spain. It was instantly understandable, accessible, welcoming to the human mind. Here the past, I hoped, would be more forgiving. It wouldn't be dominated by earthquakes and cataclysms, by all the shuddering disasters, natural and man-made, that rebounded around the Valley of Mexico. Good or bad, history would be on a more human scale.

Despite my growing, perverse affection for the capital, I realized I'd still felt somehow trapped in Mexico City. But here, the doors were open. The country seeped into town, its colours replicated in the streets, one after the other, house by house, bold and joyful, like a child's rainbow. After what felt like a lifetime's incarceration in steel and concrete grey, it was like diving into a paintbox.

The taxi-driver (there'd been no room on any of the buses from Mexico City) dropped me at the central plaza or Jardín because he couldn't figure out the labyrinthine one-way system. I suspect he was also a little resentful of the tight corners and narrow, cobblestone streets in his nearly-new Lincoln. But I was pleased to have the chance to find my park bench – an ornate iron seat painted a deep bottle-green – and collapse on it; to sit motionless for a moment, rucksack wedged between my legs, and wind down.

Gradually the sounds of the plaza began to infiltrate the noise and speed spinning in my head. It was cool in the Jardín – a small square shaded by deep, green square-clipped ficus trees in front of the town cathedral – and peaceful. Unbelievably peaceful. I began to relax my grip on the rucksack. There was the sound of someone sweeping. There were no beggars here, no loitering *muchachos*; only a newspaper boy selling the English language *Mexico City News* and a *bolero* buffing the feet of morning customers at his shoeshine stall. Nearby a barefoot Indian woman with a baby in a shawl on her back was selling strawberries. A minute later another walked by with a basket of fresh asparagus.

I got up at last and headed for Casa Murphy with the aid of a map that had been faxed through to me at the Hotel Isabel. All the hotels in San Miguel had been booked up by the time I'd decided to make a break from the capital and I found myself in a bizarre process of booking – and paying for – one of the last available rooms in a bed and breakfast through someone in Texas. The fax that had come with my confirmation contained five pages of instructions on how to get there, most of them complex solutions for reaching San Miguel without spending a night in the horrors of Mexico City.

I found the five-bedroom pension tucked down a quiet side-street a good ten minutes' walk from the Jardín. It was ten in the morning and the proprietress, Patricia Murphy, was in full cry. Dressed in shocking pink with matching lipstick, raptorial red nails and a bouffant lemon rinse, she was bawling out a mild-mannered Mexican who was receiving his verbal lashings like a child having his daily face-scrub.

'And don't tell me it was done yesterday 'cos there's no slip to show for it today.'

I waited to one side peering studiously out of the glass-fronted reception at the patio until Patricia had hung up her gloves. Finally she turned and addressed me, 'Well, hey, welcome to Casa Murphy.' There was no change of gear, no cascade of hostessy sweetness or wringing smile, but a full-steam-ahead, like-us-or-lump-us conspiratorial embrace. 'This is Antonio, the manager here at Casa Murphy and my best friend. Don't worry, he's used to me – aren't you Antonio? Wouldn't know how to start the day without hollering, would I?'

Antonio smiled benignly and continued shuffling for the missing slip behind the desk. Patricia launched into her new guest routine, sat me down on 'The Deacon's Bench' next to a cushion embroidered 'You can never be too rich or too thin' and began piling me up with laminated fact-sheets. 'This'll tell you everything,' she went on, '– where to go, what to see, how to use the phone, when to pick your nose, scratch your elbow – anything else just holler and Antonio or I'll come getcha.'

Patricia wasn't leaving anything to chance, however. There were little messages and instructions pinned to every inanimate object. A note on my bedroom door suggested 'To Eliminate Insects, Keep Door Closed'. The bell on the bedside table urged 'Need Anything?

Ring Bell'. The bath mat was emphatically 'For Your Feet' and the switches 'Fan', 'Lamp', or 'Heater' – which would 'Heat Up Room in 20 Mins'. There was even a switch outside my door helpfully labelled 'Nothing'.

The American exodus to San Miguel had been set in motion by the American painter and writer, Stirling Dickinson, who discovered San Miguel in the 1930s, shortly after the Mexican town was declared a national historic monument. A posse of fellow American 'intellectuals', artists and GIs battle-weary from the Second World War pursued him, and art schools began popping up all over town, including the Escuela de Bellas Artes and the Instituto Allende which was headed for years by Dickinson and is still a draw for hordes of foreign art and language students.

In 1968 Neal Cassady, the real-life hero of Jack Kerouac's beat novel *On the Road*, died here, run over by a freight train while he was walking the railway tracks out of San Miguel dazed with amphetamines. But since then the genteel, parochial atmosphere of San Miguel has attracted gringos of a less wayward or experimental disposition, drawn here precisely because the town is exotic without being dangerous, foreign without being threatening. Three thousand full-time foreign residents – most of them American and retired – now live in San Miguel. Although I was beginning to wonder how I'd survive if they were all like Patricia.

In the garden, under a wrought-iron pergola like a bandstand, the six or so other guests at Casa Murphy were still having breakfast. 'Here, this is for you, honey,' Patricia called, beckoning me to the last remaining place. She sat me down opposite a woman who looked like she'd just been pulled from a car-crash. The woman smiled brightly, putting her fingers to her face as if to stop it falling off. 'This is Marcia,' said Patricia, 'she's just had a lift.' 'Oh . . . congratulations,' I fumbled, 'looks marvellous.' I was having second-thoughts about breakfast.

Marcia beamed and raised her sunglasses to expose great buttery bruises and violet eyelids. 'Best thing I ever did,' she said. 'Imagine, I only had it done a week ago and it's looking this good. Hey, even the incisions are almost gone,' and she lifted her chin to reveal a rack of vermilion scars running under the jaw-line like smocking.

Little tails of thread stuck out like transparent pubic hairs. 'Dr Burrito's coming in an hour to take out my stitches. He's such a caring man. You know it costs $17,000 to have a full facelift in Houston? And here in Mexico it's only $4000. I'll be coming back regular at this price.'

Marcia was an air stewardess with TWA. 'I'm fifty-one,' she said pinning me down with an earnest glare . . .'there comes a time when you need to re-evaluate and concentrate on yourself. I've had the best two weeks' holiday in my life and I've hardly left Casa Murphy.' She would be going back to Texas on Good Friday before all the celebrations, she said, 'or Patricia'll be throwing me out'. 'Hell no, honey,' cried Patricia, 'you're no trouble. I tell you what a bad guest is, though. We had this one guy in here before Christmas, come for a Dr Burrito facelift, too. Well, first I caught him in the kitchen – NO ONE is allowed in my kitchen – and he blew up the microwave putting aluminium foil in it. Then I caught him in there again in the middle of the night, trying to get ice out of the freezer to make a pack for his face. Well, that was IT. I obviously hadn't got through to the son of a bitch. So I called the police and had him arrested.'

'Happy surgery' was big business in San Miguel and Patricia was a walking advertisement for it. Nip it, tuck it, liposuck it, she'd had almost everything in the book, she declared. Apart from the complicated 'full face', there were simpler 'weekend lifts', and 'annual maintenance' to remove the fat and worry lines that had crept in during the year. Then there were tummy-tucks and nose-jobs, breast enlargements and buttock-lifts, liposuction and elec-trolysis and the whole gamut of dentistry for that perfect Julia Roberts smile. Like Dr Burrito, surgeons were usually Mexican but trained and qualified in the United States, with expert bedside manners and an unerring eye for that uniquely American, Barbie interpretation of beauty.

But there was more to this phenomenon than greeted the eye. For Marcia the surgeon's incisions had gone deeper than the skin. She glowed with the self-satisfaction of youth regained. Her trip to San Miguel had been revolutionary though she'd seen nothing of Mexico at all. It had been a migration of body and soul, a miracle of nature. Like many of Dr Burrito's clients, she'd come to Mexico to shed her skin and would fly back to the States reborn, like a butterfly.

The clanging of bells reminded me there was a whole world outside Casa Murphy's walls, out of reach of needle and scalpel, with its mind on something beyond the limits of the purely physical. Though many of her guests had come specifically to see the Easter festivities, Patricia herself was boycotting them. 'All that blood and gore and weeping and beseeching. I tell ya, it ain't good for ya heart. If I wanna feel close to God I go take a shower or pop a cold beer. Ain't no good whipping yourself for all the sins of the world when the Big Cheese up there ain't gonna lift a finger to change things. Hell, I've never been religious. Wouldn't know where to start.'

As inconspicuously as I could, I excused myself, claimed my set of keys (all meticulously labelled) from Antonio and broke for the centre of town.

Shortly after the fall of Tenochtitlán and Cortés's subsequent appointment as governor of New Spain, the conquistador asked the Spanish government to send out missionaries – friars in particular – to spread the word of God in the new land. Cortés was eager to discourage the export of Spain's secular, establishment clergy – avaricious, decadent, concupiscent – Cortés knew they'd earn few converts among the Indians who'd been accustomed to the strictest chastity among their own priests. They'd also be expecting rich rewards and as Cortés had realized to his own disappointment, there was much less gold and silver around in Mexico than he'd first thought. (It was a while before the opening up of the great mines of northern Mexico that would feed the Spanish Empire for three centuries.) The missionaries Cortés needed had to be honest, courageous and hard-working if they were to play a key part in the ongoing conquest of Mexico. Friars – Franciscans, Dominicans, Augustinians, even the new Jesuit brotherhood – were what was called for.

Back in Europe the Catholic Church was lurching from crisis to crisis. Rotting from within, weakened by the loss of Henry VIII and the rise of Luther in central Europe, it was to suffer in 1529 from the added humiliation of the Ottoman Empire laying siege to Vienna. The monastic orders of friars and nuns, however, were going from strength to strength, presenting themselves as a reactionary force bent on re-establishing the religious principles of chastity, poverty and obedience.

The Franciscans were hottest off the mark in response to Cortés's request. 'Run,' they were told by their Spanish superior, 'run with two feet – love of God and love of man – to bring the news of Redemption to this new world.' The first three Franciscans arrived in Mexico from Belgium in 1523. A dozen more Franciscans – the 'Apostolic Twelve' – arrived in the newly established port of Veracruz on the Gulf Coast in 1524 and walked barefoot all the way to Mexico City where they were received with great reverence by Cortés and his followers, and captured the admiration of Cuauhtémoc and the Indian chiefs.

The Dominicans and Augustinians followed, gasping to keep up. In 1542, only two decades after Conquest, the Franciscan friar Juan de San Miguel was founding a tiny settlement on the banks of the Río Laja in the semi-desert of the north central highlands, nearly 200 miles north-west of Mexico City. He named it San Miguel de las Chichimecas after his patron saint and the dominant – and hostile – Indians of the region.

This first settlement, near what is now called San Miguel Viejo, a small rancho a mile or so beyond the outskirts of the present town, was then the most northerly Spanish outpost in central Mexico. It was little more than a cluster of huts around a small chapel made from rocks and fallen branches, its population a handful of Spaniards and friendly Tarascan (or Purépecha) and Tlaxcalan Indians brought in to help pacify the local Otomí and Chichimecs. It was soon abandoned. Prone to drought as well as flooding, and to mosquitoes and their attendant diseases, the settlement was also incessantly under attack. The move to the present site came just in time.

Legend has it that one of Friar Juan de San Miguel's hounds discovered a spring, now called El Chorro, in the south of the present town, after wandering off one day from the mission. When the friar went looking for the dog he discovered a place of breathtaking serenity on a slope overlooking the valley with the mountains of what was soon to be the silver-mining district of Guanajuato looming to the west. At 6300 feet the new site proved to be blessed with a flawless climate, cool in the summer, spring-like in winter, and free from accursed mosquitoes. But it was also much more easily defended. The new San Miguel sprang up with alacrity, nestling against its hillside like a new Jerusalem, facing the setting sun.

It's hard to imagine the courage and determination of those early missionaries to Mexico. Alone, in a strange land, venturing out to places that were days or weeks from company and comfort, ahead even of the conquistadors and their Indian foot-soldiers, they confronted death at every turn, from snake-bites and scorpions to starvation and exposure and unknown diseases. Their days were characterized by feats of extraordinary physical and mental endurance, their nights haunted by all the horrors of the known and the unknown. When they went among the barbaric tribes of the north, tribes that were still semi-nomadic and that had never come under the sway of the Aztec civilization, the unarmed, barefoot friars knew they were advancing towards the likelihood of torture and death.

But for the Franciscans, beyond all the other orders, suffering was the pivot of their faith; it was their joy, their *raison d'être*. Theirs was the suffering of the ascetic who reaches God by transcending pain; who finds spiritual release in the mortification of the body. Their inspiration was derived from their founder, St Francis of Assisi, the thirteenth-century saint who had given up a life of frivolity, of knightly exercises and ostentatious living for the deprivations of a hermit. He had renounced his patrimony, his wealth and even his clothes to devote himself, unfettered, to the needs of the poor. Of the moment of Francis's conversion, John of Ceprano wrote:

... the Lord touched his heart and it was filled with such surpassing sweetness that he could neither speak nor move, neither feel nor hear anything outside that overwhelming sweetness. And, as he himself was later to describe it, he was so detached from his corporeal senses that he

78

could not have moved from the spot even if he had been cut in pieces there.

Desperate to share the sufferings of Christ, St Francis was eventually blessed, while in the ecstasy of prayer, with the wounds of the crucifixion.

The Franciscans, following in his footsteps, were driven by the same passion. They met their trials open-armed, with masochistic relish, and the Indians were astounded. The friars' feats of physical endurance, their passion for self-flagellation and scourging of the flesh, for ritual humiliations and penance, struck a cord among indigenous Mexicans already familiar with the practices of bloodletting and sacrifice and the exquisite pains of physical torture. The legend of the crucifixion excited a particularly enthusiastic response among the converted. Motolinía, another of the first Franciscans in New Spain, describes, implicitly congratulating the work of Friar Juan, the religious diligence of the population of San Miguel Viejo when he went there in 1542:

All, men as well as women, belong to the confraternity of the Cross . . . on every Friday of the year and on three days of the week during Lent they take the discipline in the churches, the men in one part, the women in another . . . some discipline themselves with wire scourges and others with cords that do not cause less pain.

To most Mexicans, from the very beginning, Christianity meant the suffering of Christ and the sorrow of the Virgin Mary. Thanks to the Franciscans, the joys of forgiveness and the happy parables of the New Testament faded into the background next to the expurgation of sin, the graphic temptations of the Devil and the terrors of Hell.

It was a state of mind that connected particularly neatly with the perception of appeasement and human sacrifice common to the Nahua civilizations of Central Mexico. The crucifixion of the mortal son of God was easily understood by native Mexicans who regularly put humans to the knife in order to obliterate their debt to the gods – just as Christ died for the sins of man, in order to forgive him, to wipe the slate clean, so that life could start again.

The idea of penance and purgation was also familiar to many of the ancient Mexican tribes. Ritual woundings in honour of the gods were imposed on Aztec men and women throughout their lives. Only a few days after birth, priests would drill a baby boy's lower lip in preparation for the warrior lip-plug. Each year there were new markings. At the festival to honour Huitzilopochtli, the god of the sun and of war, all men, from adult males to infants on their cradleboards, were cut on the stomach, chest and arms. Girls were cut on the hip or chest to affirm their affiliation with the earth deities.

Fasting, ritual starvation and self-lacerations were enshrined already in the religions of central Mexico. The drawing forth of blood from one's own body in the presence of sacred images was a routine practice. Blood-lettings through incisions made into the ear lobe, tongue or the flesh of the thigh, were a token gesture to the gods – they could not cancel out the entire debt man owed to the deities but they were gifts of appreciation for the bounty provided by the gods for man from the earth. The more active the suppliant's suffering, the deeper his submission, the more attentive the gods would be. The tongues and ear lobes of Mexican priests were often, the conquistadors had been horrified to observe, a pulpy, bloody mess.

For the Aztecs and the other Nahua civilizations of the central Mexican plateau the ritual sado-masochistic disciplines of the Franciscans came naturally. For the unconquered Purépecha and Otomí, and the barbaric Chichimecs to the north, it was a different story. Inevitably, though, the evangelizing friars had the might of an army behind them. Indians who remained hostile to the Word of God were eventually subdued by the sword.

The peculiar, penitential strain of Franciscan Catholicism took deepest root where it was first planted, in the remote outposts on the twilight borders of the new world. The Franciscans took pious Náhuatl-speaking Indian converts with them to help establish their churches in the wilderness and to spread the new religion to outlying tribes. These little colonies became hot-beds of religious fervour. It came as no surprise to learn that the Holy Week celebrations in San Miguel would focus almost entirely on the sufferings of Mary and on Christ's physical and mental agonies, culminating in his sacrifice on Good Friday; and that Easter Sunday and the joyful Resurrection would be virtually ignored.

The streets outside Casa Murphy were festooned with ribbons and bunting and balloons, all white and lilac – the same colour as the jacarandas which were dropping their flowers in light drifts on the cobbles. It hardly seemed the right colour for mourning – more like the theme for an early May ball. Streamers fluttered from lamp-post to lamp-post like Tibetan prayer-flags, light-hearted and optimistic. There were palm-fronds over doorways and strings of delicate cut-outs in lilac tissue-paper depicting the last days of Christ like scenes from a fairytale.

Outside the Temple of San Juan de Dios, a block from Casa Murphy, women were selling steaming tamales and corn-cobs. Children squealed after each other around the courtyard. Old men in white sombreros chatted amiably on park benches.

But inside the temple they were gearing up for death. It was cool and dark and musty, and nearly half full, the aisles buzzing with the discordant murmur of private prayer. I slipped into a pew near the front, surprising myself at how naturally, almost automatically, I had genuflected and crossed myself. It had been twenty years since I'd last dipped my fingers in holy water. My career as a Protestant pupil in a Catholic convent had ended at the age of fourteen after a series of unpardonable sins culminated in the accidental decapitation of a statue of Our Lady while practising my tennis serve inside the classroom. I was allowed to stay on – 'suffered' was how Sister Ursula, our RE teacher, put it – until the end of 'O' levels and was then called to Reverend Mother's study to be summarily dismissed. I'm not sure who was more thankful – the nuns who had relieved themselves of another troublesome, pubescent Prot, or me, leaving the convent drive for the last time, free as a bird.

They were troubling, ambivalent memories that came wafting back on the smell of incense and old vase-water. There was, over all, the unassailable nostalgia of ritual, so sweetly seductive it was tempting to imagine this homage to a Mexican church was some kind of homecoming instead of a passing visit from a place of exile. It was a nostalgia, I assumed, that had been forged by teenage longings – an almost sexual fixation on the body of Christ; the lingering relish of Our Lady's grief; the savouring of disgusting-sounding phrases like 'flesh of my flesh', 'cleave unto his wife' so 'they shall be one flesh', and 'Blessed is the fruit of thy womb' as they rolled fulsomely off the tongue; that lip-smacking revulsion at the altar-rail as I steadied myself for a slurp of blood. But I was surprised, now, by how little these feelings had altered in the intervening years. They were all still there, the perverse, excitable threads of self-doubt, embalmed in a web of religious sanctity.

Up at the altar a woman and a boy were washing a statue of Christ with small sponges. It was mesmerizing to watch. The plaster on Christ's shoulders seemed to glow like skin as last year's layers of dust were consigned to a pail of water. The woman was gently directing the boy, pointing out little secret crevices with the knowledge and perfectionism of a mother, or a lover. It felt wrong to be watching such intimacy. But the rest of the congregation were following the performance with the eyes of the bereaved, not those of a voyeur, like mine. Many were simply staring at the statue, faces awash with tears.

It was no ordinary figure of Christ – if any of them can be called ordinary in the Mexican church. This was a famous miracle-worker, the 'Lord of the Column', so called because it depicts Christ bending over a strange urn-shaped pilaster, being flagellated. It's not a pretty sight. His back is shredded, dripping gore. There is blood running in rivulets down his chest and arms and legs. His face is grey, twisted in pain, staring stoically, glassy-eyed, at a spot on the ground in front of him. His hair hangs in sweat-soaked tails. There's a purple cord around his neck like a leash.

The woman was taking special care over his wounds, dabbing them gently enough to avoid removing any blood. It seemed strange that she should be taking such care, such tenderness, to keep him bleeding. There must be times, I thought, when the signs of blood need to be freshened up a little; when someone forces a crimson paintbrush into the gashes to keep them alive.

The Lord of the Column is not always here. For most of the year it resides in the Sanctuary of Atotonilco, a place of penitence, nine miles away to the north-west. But every Easter it is carried on a stretcher to San Miguel in a slow, arduous torch-lit procession that lasts the whole night of Palm Sunday, to take part in the festivities. The statue works hard during its stay in the Temple of San Juan de Dios. For two weeks, he is asked to perform miracles by an endless stream of supplicants. Three wooden shafts of light are slotted into his head to signify the sanctity of this period, as if the statue has been activated.

I left the Temple of San Juan de Dios feeling spiritually sore. It wasn't just Our Lord of the Column whose wounds were being reopened. All over town, similar rituals were taking place in every church; other saints were having their lacerations spring-cleaned; congregations would be feasting afresh on the imminent horrors of the cross, laying their souls on the sacrificial altar, baring their hearts, preparing themselves for another self-imposed crucifixion.

As I pounded up the hill away from the church towards the central plaza I felt the welcome pull of profligacy. It was time to take a leaf out of Humberto's book and adjust my perspective with an ice-cold beer.

There's little left of San Miguel that pre-dates the eighteenth century. Its narrow streets, once the province of friars, traders, manufacturers and rough-shod pioneers, are dominated by splendid mansions built by the grandest Spanish families in Mexico. Barely a decade after Friar Juan de San Miguel established his modest little colony, silver was discovered in Zacatecas 250 miles to the north. A road was hurriedly pushed through from Mexico all the way to the mine and San Miguel was transformed virtually overnight from evangelical outpost to garrison town protecting shipments of silver on its way to the capital. A mandate issued by Viceroy Don Luis de Velasco in 1555 decreed 'in order to avoid the killings and robberies which the Chichimecs have carried out on the road to Zacatecas, let there be founded at the village of San Miguel a Spanish city for the security of that road'.

Soon after the great mine of Zacatecas was opened (a mine that by the end of the eighteenth century was to have produced one fifth of all the world's silver), massive silver seams were discovered in Guanajuato, only 50 miles from San Miguel, and then again in San Luis Potosí, 110 miles away. Wealth rained down on San Miguel and the rich built their houses and rebuilt their churches in escalating grandeur until what you see now, at every turn, on every corner, are the ebullient fripperies of a prodigal age, a far cry from the original Franciscan values.

There are wrought-iron balconies snarling with fantastical creatures, long elegant windows, grand portals with Corinthian columns, stone pediments embossed with medallions and crests and knightly shields. Houses that are not built of the most expensive, rose-coloured stone are painted ochre or umber, magenta or burnt sienna so their very tones resonate with the riches of the velvet-lined purse. From the street, carved wooden doors give on to cool patios with arches and balustrades, splashing fountains and flashes of baroque.

Just before the central Plaza on Calle Allende I passed the house where San Miguel's most famous son was born. San Miguel had been centre-stage in Mexico's War of Independence, and it was José Ignacio María de Allende y Unzaga, a local landowner, fanatical bull-fighter and independence hero – who gave the town the second part of its name. 'Hic natus ubique notus' reads an inscription in Latin below the cornice, 'Born here, but known everywhere'. An additional plaque acerbically comments that the more famous independence hero, the country priest, Miguel Hidalgo, only joined the movement after being introduced to it by San Miguel's Ignacio Allende.

The façade of the Casa de Allende was as grand and elaborate as any I'd already passed, featuring an elegant curved pediment supported by double-spiral scrolls and sprouting ornamental vases. The windows and balconies were festooned with hanging cut-paper ornaments in stone. The tradition was Renaissance but the detail churrigueresque, that uniquely Mexican style, highly ornamental and decorative, that was so beloved of Indian stonemasons. It's from one of these balconies that the mayor of San Miguel issues his own mini-*grito* (cry for Independence) on Independence Day.

The façade of the Casa de Allende, naturalistically engraved with leaves and flowers and shells, seemed to spell out Ignacio Allende's story, to describe the driving force behind the class that produced Mexico's legendary freedom fighter. Here, between Spanish convention and indigenous art, rose the aspirations of the Creole class, wealthy, educated, born of the New World with no memory or loyalty to Spain, and a fierce love for everything Mexican. Constantly dictated to by the arrogant and patronizing pure-blood Spaniards who held the reins of power, it was only a matter of time before the Creoles rose up and demanded government by themselves. Creole self-assertiveness seemed to be crying out from every finely chiselled corner-stone, every inventive architrave adorning the streets of San Miguel de Allende.

Just around the corner I came again to the Jardín. The square was dominated by the apotheosis of San Miguel's architectural philandering – a sort of pseudo-Gothic fantasy with pointed, pink candy-floss spires that is, amazingly, the Parroquia or parish church. Appropriately, since with its feathered pinnacles the building seems to be trying to fly, the church is dedicated to San Miguel Arcángel. It was designed by a local Indian mason, Zeferino Gutiérrez, who was inspired in the 1880s, it is said, by postcards of French cathedrals. He instructed his illiterate builders by scratching his drawings in the sand with a stick. Up in the tower eight bells commemorate the beneficence of San Miguel's wealthiest patrons; the largest, 'La Luz', cast in 1732, still calls the faithful to prayer, its clear tones a resonant blend of bronze melted with pure gold.

The Parroquia has plenty of showy paintings and statues to boast of; the great and the good are buried in its vaults, including heroes of Independence and twice-President Anastasio Bustamante, who spent his last years in San Miguel. But the church's real treasure is much older than the church itself; it's a dark, unassuming figure of the crucified Christ – El Señor de la Conquista, Lord of the Conquest. The figure is made from a paste of corn-pith and orchid bulbs – a technique similar to papier mâché, invented by the Tarascans, or Purépecha, famous artist Indians of Lake Pátzcuaro in Michoacán.

Many of the earliest religious saints in Mexico were made like this, by indigenous craftsmen, from *caña de maíz*. The images were delicate and lifelike, beautiful, like this one, and extremely light – easy for the barefoot friars to carry with them. But they were also perishable and few of the corn-pith figures survived the rigours of time. This one was rescued in the 1580s by the townspeople of San Miguel from an arroyo near Chamacuero, a few miles from town. It was found shielded by the bodies of two friars, Francisco Doneel and Pedro de Burgos, who had been killed 'with much cruelty' by the arrows of the Chichimecs. There are still traces of their blood on the figure – no paint needed here.

Sitting back, on La Terrazza overlooking the Parroquia, it struck me that the gingerbread confection in front of me was a parody of Mexico. It was a triumph of lightheartedness, a buoyant statement that in San Miguel 'El Grande' the profligate had the puritan on the run; the *caballero*, the mounted nobleman, had outstripped the barefoot friar and humble *campesino*.

At Easter, though, this spirit of frippery and self-indulgence has to change and, for a while at least, San Miguel's old standards fly from the mast. The church doors are thrown open and the spirits of the martyrs sally forth to reclaim the streets for the sackcloth and ashes. As I guiltily contemplated another bottle of Bohemia, a couple of Indian women passed by my table selling calla lilies. They were wearing little plates tied over their foreheads to preserve the thumb-marks made by the priest nearly forty days ago on Ash Wednesday. Their faces were worn and lugubrious, funereal. Even the balloon seller across the way in the Jardín looked doleful.

I wandered away from the Parroquia and all its contradictions and almost instantly found myself at a tempting-looking restaurant, just opened, barely a block from the Jardín. Deciding to side with the libertines while I still had the chance, I settled down for a long lunch. The restaurant was called Hoja Santa, 'holy leaf', after a type of local medicinal herb and the menu featured 'traditional ingredients of Mexico'. There were the inevitable beef steaks and chicken 'a la parilla', on the grill, for American clientele with one hand on the Pepto Bismol, but most of the dishes were a fanfare for things Mexican. There was chopped cactus-leaf salad (or *nopalitos*), pumpkin flower soup, local sausage, goat's cheese, indigenous tropical fruit like *chirimoya, maracuyá, jícama, pita-haya, mamey, guineo* and *guanábana*, and an instructive, if bewildering, list of chillies: *chile de árbol* (dried red chilli pepper); *chile habañero* (very hot, red or green chilli); *chile Pekin* (small, green, very hot); *chile rubio* (a 'very hot, white chilli') or *chile serrano* (a 'very hot, thin green chilli') or *jalapeños*('not so hot'); and chilli sauces: *chipotle* sauce ('hot'); *guajillo* ('never very hot'); *pasilla* ('not hot') and *morita* ('hotter than *pasilla*, less hot than *chipotle*). I chose my sauce carefully, remembering Father Joseph de Acosta's warnings in his *Natural History of the Indies*, published in 1590: chilli, which is the 'principal source of all dishes' in the New World, the obese friar observed, 'burns, going in or out'.

There was natural justice in this. The Europeans had been looking for spice, after all, when they discovered the Americas, and they found it – with a vengeance. It was gratifying to think of those early pioneers taken unawares, hoisting their robes and howling behind a cactus.

I was disappointed to notice a slightly effete, nouvelle cuisine touch to the dishes when they arrived at the table – a far cry from the earthy, peasant favourites like *cabeza* (pig's head), *criadillas* (bulls' testicles), *chicharrón* (pork crackling), *manitas de cerdo* (pig's trotters), or *pancita* (tripe). But there were two ingredients that were exciting to find – *huitlacoche* and *huanzontle*. The first was a tiny mushroom-like filament that grows on the maize plant; the second was 'amaranth', an indigenous seed which is often mixed with honey and baked into little cakes of the sort I'd seen being sold in the Zócalo. Here it had been made into a delicious, nutty-flavoured ice-cream.

Both *huitlacoche* and amaranth had been banned under the Spanish for their 'satanic' associations – they were the 'devil's food' and 'poisoners of the soul'. To the Aztecs and other tribes of Mexico, though, they were as sacred and as close to the gods as maize itself. *Huitlacoche*, perhaps because it grew on divine maize, was known as 'food for the gods'. But to the Spaniards, it was a mushroom like any other – like *nanacatl* or *teonanacatl*, the bitter little fungi used by indigenous priests to induce visions. The conquerors had been appalled by the Aztecs' and all the other indigenous Mexicans' use of hallucinogens in their rituals. To the Mexicans, mind-altering mushrooms, pulque, peyote, morning glory seeds, datura, tobacco, and even some hallucinogenic insects, were a key part of their religion, a means of communicating with the divine, a spiritual gift. To the Spaniards the practice was degenerate and in their ignorance they included *huitlacoche* on their list of banned substances, which included a number of harmless, nutritious foods.

Amaranth was always a feature of ritual feasts, and at sacrifices was mixed with human blood and moulded into little effigies as offerings to the gods and eaten with great reverence. This was too much for the Europeans who saw these little amaranth figures as a satanic parody of the Eucharistic host. They were genuinely afraid of the power of amaranth and punished any Indian who continued to grow it against the orders of the Crown. So successful were the Spanish in their campaign against the crop that they virtually eradicated it. Only now is it scientifically acclaimed as one of the most nutritious grains known to man, uncommonly high in protein and amino acids.

It seemed faintly sacrilegious to be eating amaranth in an American-style ice-cream but there was a thrill, too, of having some saporous connection with blood-splattered Aztec priests five centuries ago. I followed my ice-cream with a cup of foaming hot chocolate and here, too, history tumbled unfettered on to the tongue. Cortés had shared cups of chocolate with Moctezuma but it was two centuries before Europeans could open their minds to the bitter poison. Then, consecrated as a social beverage by Louis XV at Versailles, it became the rage, an indulgent pleasure once again, a foretaste of the addiction that would one day conquer the world.

I reflected, over a final glass of Chilean Chardonnay, on the swings and roundabouts of food and taste; how the conquistadors had brought chickens, sheep, pigs, plums, melons, cherries, grapes, peaches and grain to Mexico in the bellies of their caravels; and taken back to Europe corn, tomatoes, chillies, avocados, cacao, vanilla and turkeys. It was conquest and counter-conquest; sensory seduction by osmosis. The modern colonial bogey, of course, was not Europe but the United States. Yet if Mexico were to be judged by culinary influence alone, it wasn't doing too badly in the conquest stakes. Already it had recolonized most of the southern United States where Taco Bell was overtaking KFC and McDonald's. In a bloodless coup in 1992, salsa outsold ketchup in the US for the first time. *Burritos* and *fajitas* were becoming common parlance in middle America, as homely as apple pie.

Paying for my Aztec lunch with twentieth-century plastic, I got up from the table and left. Outside, the late afternoon sun was throwing a coppery sheen on everything. The first of the many Easter processions – the Via Crucis, or Way of the Cross – had just left the Oratorio, the domed, early eighteenth-century church a few blocks to the north-east of the main square. People were gathering on the pavements, waiting. As the procession rounded the corner, men doffed their sombreros and held them over their hearts. There was a strange weighty solemnity in the air as if the sun was melting and thickening things. The procession seemed to take an age coming. I stood in the shade of a doorway and watched. A few pigeons flapped up on to a roof. Swallows wheeled about in the sky. A car alarm went off a few streets away. Slowly the procession advanced, and the spectators around me started to cross themselves. At the front came an angel leading a group of young girls in virginal white with purple sashes, tossing armfuls of wild camomile on to the road. Next came women veiled in black carrying the symbols of the crucifixion: a piece of sheet with a crude portrait of Christ painted on it (his funeral shroud); a nasty-looking steel crown of thorns on a crimson cushion; a hammer and some nails; a lance. Then came the saints and Our Lady of Sorrows carried on heavy palanquins on the shoulders of the mourners. Then a statue of Christ staggering under his cross. This was Nuestro Señor del Golpe (unsatisfactorily translated as 'Our Lord of the Slap') after a blow Christ received, according to St John, from one of the centurions: 'And when he had thus spoken, one of the officers which stood by struck Jesus with the palm of his hand, saying, "Answerest thou the high priest so?"' (John 18:22)

The bearers – women for Mary and the saints, men for Christ – were struggling under their load. Every few hundred yards the procession stopped to pay homage to one of the fourteen Stations of the Cross. The bearers stood rock still while the Hail Marys were said, like mules waiting for the whip. The Stations of the Cross were little altars or crosses set into walls. They were draped with the purple cloth of penance; bitter oranges for Mary's anguish and Christ's bitter cup; and little pots of wheat, blanched gold through being starved of light, like the self-effacement of the penitent dedicating himself behind closed doors.

The procession moved inexorably from the Palace of Pontius Pilate winding through the streets of San Miguel until it reached the chapel of Calvary at the top of Calle San Francisco. It was almost dusk. The last of the sunshine pierced the length of the street on the horizontal, white light bouncing off the windows. The Cross of the Oratorio glinted sword-like above the heads of the crowd. Quietly, sombrely, the mourners dispersed, leaving behind them the delicate scent of crushed camomile.

The Way of the Cross wasn't always so tranquil in San Miguel. Only fifteen years ago many of the mourners still walked the stations on their knees, grinding their kneecaps against the cobbles, organ cactuses strapped to their backs. Old women, to save themselves the humiliation of not being able to complete the journey, took an old bit of carpet to kneel on, painstakingly picking it up and placing it down in front of them again and again and again. Even children crawled their way to Calvary, shredding skin. The Americans were appalled, so was the Vatican, and the municipal authorities, keen for San Miguel to be seen as a modern, progressive town, discouraged the practice.

But it was a hard habit to kick. The Via Crucis had been established as a penance for the townspeople of San Miguel two hundred and fifty years ago by a friar whose passion for self-torture made the ritual humiliations of Friar Juan de San Miguel look like summer camp. Two centuries after his fellow Franciscan founded San Miguel, Friar Luis Felipe Neri de Alfaro was doing his utmost to restore some discipline to the town. Born in Mexico City, Father Alfaro was a home-grown phenomenon, a Mexican through and through, with a burning ambition to purge his country of the decadent influences of the wealthy Spanish and Creole classes. He added a church, Nuestra Señora de la Salud, to the end of the

Colegio de San Francisco de Sales in San Miguel itself. But he is best known for establishing a centre dedicated purely to penance out in the countryside, a short remove from the temptations of town. Its very name sounded like a resounding slap: El Santuario de Atotonilco.

It was the morning of Maundy Thursday and San Miguel had assumed a temporary air of sanity, a respite before the storm. Most Mexicans were at home indoors decorating their family altars, or putting the finishing touches to the Easter displays in church. Tonight the priest would wash the feet of twelve 'disciples' in the Parroquia and the townspeople would pay their respects to as many churches as they could visit in one evening. Then the real performance could begin.

I headed out to the countryside for breathing space and a long soak in a hot spring. With the world and his wife wrapped up in the goings-on in San Miguel, this was also the perfect moment to visit Atotonilco.

The town gave out suddenly just beyond the railroad station. My taxi-driver was unfazed by the transfer from street to dirt track and we lurched from pothole to pothole, dust seeping through the closed windows, as if we were heading out on safari. We made a detour to the tiny church of San Miguel Viejo, not the original chapel founded by Friar Juan de San Miguel and then abandoned, but a later version, built near the site around 1720.

It still looked like a pioneer, out on its own, a sturdy little standard-bearer for the faith. We got to it through the backyards of an adobe village, an organized chaos of cactus fences, pig pens, stray bits of tin and tackle, and squawking chickens, probably not too unlike the first settlement. In front of the church was a large open courtyard, the holding pen for an indigenous flock too numerous or too fearful to enter the house of God itself.

Even in the 1700s, one remove from the protection of town, this was a challenging place for a priest to be. There were still a few rogue bands of Chichimecs, the Mexican Apaches, the last of their race, at large and with a grudge to bear; and lawless brigands after the silver trains who were not averse to murdering the odd priest for a chalice.

Above the door, the stone architrave was carved naively, Indian-style, with a row of cherubs, a face of Christ looking a little like a Mexican Confucius and segmented circles that might have represented flowers, but looked like bulbs of the hallucinogenic peyote cactus. Directly over the lintel a pair of flying angels in boots held a box – presumably containing the blessed sacrament – from which radiated shafts of light.

The carvings were touchingly simple in design: fresh, joyful, and full of light. They seemed to suggest the best of two worlds, a place where the fusion of two faiths was not all anger and bloodshed, betrayal and despair. As the first rays of the morning sun tipped up over the courtyard wall, dappled light played through the willows on to the portal, bringing it to life. There was character – humanity – in these little stone faces, a calm, benign humorousness. I couldn't help feeling that the Indians who carved them derived some comfort from the new Christianity; from the thought of heaven and angels, perhaps, or of redemption, that the world was organized by a benign – rather than hostile and bloodthirsty – God; or that, at very least, they found some consolation in the physical presence of this church among hostile tribes in the wilderness.

Away from the river the willows and maize fields gave way to ranch land dominated by thorn-brush and cacti. The mountains in the distance looked as barren as the Sinai. For the past five centuries, sheep and goats had grazed here as if they'd colluded in the mission to make the *municipio* of San Miguel a replica of the Holy Land. Loggers felling trees for the silver mines of Guanajuato and clearing land for cattle had done their bit, too, over time, and now there was nothing left of the pre-Columbian forests that had stood here, the soil was too poor to sustain reasonable crops and many of the *campesinos*, unable to feed themselves any longer, were now moving to the cities to find jobs. Two thousand migrants a day arrive in Mexico City alone from desertified areas of the country just like this. All around San Miguel, adobe houses are crumbling into the dust from whence they came. Only the stone churches and chapels, like San Miguel de Viejo, remain.

The hot spring was one of many in the area, halfway up a hill near another small church. There was a restaurant, closed at this early hour, with some well-used barbecues, and only one or two other bathers, throwing a frisbee to each other on the lawn. The boiling, sulphurous water fed into a purpose-built swimming-pool with a stunning panoramic view over the empty countryside. While my taxi-driver took a surreptitious snooze, I plunged about and rinsed the dust from my hair and then lay there watching the swallows and a few spiralling *zopilotes*, turkey buzzards, weightless and elated and at peace with the world.

Too comfortable by half. This was the kind of mindless sensual indulgence that would have sent the good Father Luis Felipe Neri de Alfaro apoplectic with rage. 'This spot has been a place of lawlessness and sensuality,' he railed in the 1740s when he visited a similar hot spring at Atotonilco just a couple of miles away. 'Under the pretext of healthful bathing there have been contests, music, feasts, games, and other sins.' The hot springs of Atotonilco were the perfect site, he decided, for a penitentiary. Like building a lighthouse on rocks, Father Alfaro established his church where he perceived there was the greatest danger of sin.

The Sanctuary of Atotonilco was set back a mile or so off the main road to Dolores Hidalgo and marked the entrance to a poor, dusty hamlet. It was an impressive configuration – the eighteenth-century church with its cloisters and outbuildings and grain-stores, and the long, low single-storey penitentiary attached. Outside a row of stalls was selling portraits and plastic figurines of Our Lady of Guadalupe, skeins of rosaries and little postcards of the saints.

There were boxes of *milagros*, too – the tiny tin body parts that I'd seen being sold outside the Basílica of Guadalupe in Mexico. But here there was a rural emphasis. There were *milagros* of dogs, chickens, goats, turkeys, pigs and cows – the health of the suppliant being inextricably linked to the health of his livestock; and snakes and scorpions for those suffering from venomous bites; and some *milagros* that echoed pre-Columbian offerings to the gods: fish for fishermen who wanted to secure a good catch; maize and chillies for good crops; and cormorants for finding lost objects. There were no cars or houses.

And then, peculiar to Atotonilco, there was the stall selling crowns of thorns and *disciplinas*, or penitential whips. The stall holder was grinning at me with the playful good humour of a lunatic. 'Want to buy one, Señora?' He picked out a *disciplina* for demonstration, lightly switching it around his back and grimacing in mock agony. The soles of his boots had come away from their uppers Charlie Chaplin-style so his toes poked out and there was something funny going on around the waistband of his trousers – perhaps they were belted with string or he'd missed a fly-button. There was the look of a flasher about him. He was thrilled to have a customer.

'Good *disciplina*,' he was saying, 'very strong, very good, buy one from Alfredo.' His Spanish was thickly accented, a world away from his native Náhuatl. He was leaping into the sacerdotal jungle of his stall and re-emerging with dozens of crucifixes and rosaries around his neck and armfuls of *disciplinas*. They looked oddly fresh and unused – a bundle of ropes bound together to make a handle, with the loose ends twisted into rows of knots. There seemed to be a standard size of about one-foot long but there was also one double that length which Alfredo was tossing over his shoulders like hair. 'Ouch, ouch,' he cried, bursting into giggles.

I asked him if he'd ever used one in earnest. 'Of course, many times,' he said, sobering a little, 'when I do penance, especially now, at Easter. And in there.' He nodded at the penitentiary block opposite, the door of which was firmly closed. 'In there you use the *disciplina* every day, only you don't have to use it hard all the time. Some men only tap lightly with it – like this – so it feels like nothing, not even a fly. And others – ayee, ayee, they cry, whipping themselves too much and the priest has to make them stop. It's the same with the crowns of thorns. You can choose one, like this, with hardly any thorn on the inside (and he picked out a small loop of prickly briar) or one like this (and here was a larger one, made from the slender branch of thorn tree, which was covered in spikes) and you can ram it on your head until the blood runs down your face, into your eyes.'

I could imagine Alfredo five hundred years ago, pulling a cactus spine through his tongue with equal gusto. I asked him what the week in the penitentiary consisted of. 'We get up at six,' he said, like a child running through his school routine, 'we sleep in bunks, hundreds to a room, say four hundred and twenty – no –' his face furrowed to pin down the difficult number '– four thousand two hundred penitents, all of us together. Then you start meditations and prayer at night; then there is talk by the priest; then breakfast at ten; more prayers and meditation; lunch at two. Then on Tuesday and Thursday there's recreation when you can go and rest or wash or something. And in the evening, every evening, there are the Stations of the Cross, which you can do kneeling, or walking and hitting yourself with the *disciplina* – you can choose. You have a cord around your neck like this one, like the Franciscan monks, and you can put a cross on it like this one, only if you don't have so much money, you have a wooden one like this.'

I remarked that it must have been a very difficult week. 'No, it's not difficult,' he said, adamantly, burning with enthusiasm, 'what is difficult is when you don't understand. It's a very spiritual practice, it brings you very close to God, but it has to come from your heart. The first five days up to Friday is penance and then Saturday is *pureza* – purification. The flagellation is not difficult, it's not even painful because your mind is somewhere else.'

I asked if it was expensive, and if anyone could go. 'Not too expensive,' he said, 'if you sleep on the floor you pay ninety pesos ($9) for the week. But if you want the more comfortable version, you pay a hundred and fifty pesos and you get a bed and better food. But a hundred and fifty pesos isn't so good for your soul. People can eat until their bellies are full – some eat more than they do at home. Others, who want to get closer to God, choose to fast. Sometimes the priest or the holy sisters have to tell you to eat enough or you will faint when you take the *disciplina*.'

The penitentiary was open to anyone who wanted to go, Alfredo said. If you were not yet baptized, the priest would baptize you there, in the very hot springs against which Father Alfaro had waged his holy war. There were even special months for women. He would love to go again and do penance, he added, but he hadn't the money. Just going once had made him at peace in this world. The experience had been a *gran consuelo* – a great consolation; a boundless source of comfort and relief. Since going there he felt he could die a happy and contented man, in the arms of God.

I asked if it was possible to see the penitentiary. 'Once the week has started,' he said, 'no one can go in, no one can go out. But if you come back on Sunday you can see it while they clean for the next week. The church is open now though. It's very beautiful, full of beautiful paintings by a man who lived long ago. He was called Miguel Angel, because he painted like one of God's angels.'

I thanked Alfredo and, feeling a bit of a moral cheapskate, bought a tiny souvenir *disciplina* for the rear-view mirror of my Volkswagen Golf back at home. Perhaps it would keep the car, if not its owner, on the straight and narrow.

In 1996 World Monuments Watch placed Father Alfaro's church at Atotonilco on its list of the world's hundred most important buildings in danger of destruction and in need of restoration. Yet it's still one of Mexico's closest secrets. The 'shrine of Jesus the Nazarene' gets only the most perfunctory of mentions in the guidebooks. San Miguel de Allende has treasures enough to keep most tourists occupied and though the occasional tour bus rocks up for a twenty-minute pit-stop, Atotonilco's more common visitors are local historians and special interest groups already in the know. The building that shares its status (according to the World Monument Watch top one hundred list) with the Taj Mahal, is virtually unheard of in the rest of Mexico.

The frescoes inside the church which, Giotto-like, vault the ceilings and smother the walls, are not, as Alfredo claimed, by the great Italian Renaissance master 'Miguel Angel', but it is easy to see how the misconception arose; how the Chinese whispers of the ill-informed had, in the face of such wondrous and fantastical work, to point the finger at a world-famous genius. In fact the artist was Miguel Antonio Martínez de Posangre, a local Indian, who has melted, like so many of Mexico's indigenous virtuosos, into the historical void.

But Posangre's contribution to Alfaro's vision is fathomless. It was his art that spoke to the illiterate; his colours that tempted and seduced the curious; his graphic portraits of Heaven and Hell that reminded the baptized of their continuing condition of sin; that provided – as it still does today – the inspiration for penance and remorse.

Once, the outside walls were covered with frescoes three metres high and the church must have seemed like an ark of colour, a mirage almost, against the median tones of surrounding scrub. As it drew the eye, so it would have attracted the souls of the penitent like moths to the flame. But centuries of blazing sun have bleached the paintings to nothing. All that remains is the ghost of an image of Christ carrying his cross, sheltering behind a buttress like a refugee.

Inside, though, is a different story. The place is bursting with angels and archangels, devils and martyrs; pillars and archways and beams entangled with leaves and flowers and fruits; the walls a world of action and costume drama interspersed with salutary verses and sermons composed by Father Alfaro himself.

The painting is typically Indian – simple, natural and naive. Like the stonework at San Miguel Viejo, it lends a lightness to what is here intended as a salutary, terrifying message. From the first step inside the church, Posangre's playful brushstrokes are designed to instil a sense of dread and guilt in the eyes of the beholder. The panels of the inner door greet the sinner with a colourful lesson in the punishment of vice and the reward of virtue. Just inside the door the Devil is awaiting the moment of death in the hopes of claiming another soul. He appeals to all the weaknesses of the psyche and the flesh, tempting man with offers of power, honour, riches and food.

In the main body of the church with its six small adjoining chapels, the frescoes running around the walls in the upper frame begin the narrative of the Passion with the disciples falling asleep in the Garden of Gethsemane – a scene that trumpets the failings of Christ's best friends. The weakness of man is reiterated in every subsequent scene; culminating in the betrayal of Judas, the barbarous and graphic nailing of Christ, the taunts of the crowd, the temptation of Christ himself, his pathetic descent from the cross.

In the lower frame there are scenes from the contemporary

world, from Africa and Asia and a very Spanish-looking Europe, that are whimsical yet also solemn, as if to signify that the fount of human knowledge and experience, every aspect of every life in every corner of the globe, is as nothing next to the testimony of human failing, this humiliation hovering above our heads all the time.

Yet even Father Alfaro couldn't resist a gloat of triumph in his designs. In the vault of one cupola, in the Capella del Rosario, next to a painting of the Virgin's sacred house in Loreto, Italy, is a splendid scene of the naval battle of Lepanto (a miracle of translation considering that Posangre would never have seen the sea, let alone a battleship). It shows a Christian – mainly Spanish – armada defeating the Muslim Ottoman fleet off the coast of Greece. The Spanish had fought so well in this engagement that the Pope, who orchestrated the Christian forces from Genoa, is said to have relieved them ever afterwards from fasting obligations.

Not that Father Alfaro would have seen this as a mercy. Alfaro, who wore a hair shirt night and day and slept in a coffin, positively revelled in starvation. He observed such a spartan diet that he was almost permanently fasting, his mind and soul so loosened by deprivation that they could wander ever further from the body and ever closer to God. It was part of the standard of penance he expected from his followers.

As was the practice of carrying a heavy wooden cross on the Easter processions, answering to the letter Christ's figurative exhortation to 'Take up your cross and follow me'. In one chapel, decorated with scenes of the martyrdom suffered by the Apostles, is the plinth where Father Alfaro's cross usually stands, a testament to dozens of arduous barefoot Good Friday processions down the long road from Atotonilco to San Miguel and then at the head of the Via Crucis procession where it used to lead Father Alfaro's kneeling, bleeding congregation around the streets of town. But the cross isn't here. It's in San Miguel waiting to play its part in the drama of Good Friday.

There were other even more excessive tortures that the Franciscan inflicted upon himself in private, particularly during Easter, and that were only revealed to his adoring flock after his death. In his funeral oration, Alfaro's confessor and biographer, D. Juan Benito Díaz de Gamarra y Davalos addressed an enormous crowd of mourners:

'You residents of San Miguel, you have been witnesses of the public penance of Father Luis on Good Fridays. You have seen him with a rope around his neck, a crown of penetrating thorns bathing his face with blood, carrying the heavy wood, falling three times in memory of the falls of Christ in the street of bitterness. He paid a strong man to trip him so that he would fall heavily to the ground and drive the thorns more deeply into his head.

  'But you did not see everything. You did not see the interior armature that tormented his whole body, or the insoles or templates that he affixed to his legs and feet so that the penance would be even more severe.'

Father Alfaro's body is interred in a wall near Jesus the Nazarene, the figure he had placed above the altar in 1748 and before which he prayed for nearly thirty years. Nearby, on the right aisle, the glass case of Our Lord of the Column, the Christ of the flagellation which I'd seen visiting the church near Patricia's pension, also stood empty. It was as if the statue had left of its own accord to continue Father Alfaro's traditions, to stand for his example, in his stead, in the Easter Processions in San Miguel.

The present day may be neglecting Atotonilco but Mexican history didn't pass it by. Thirty-four years after the death of Father Alfaro in 1776 another priest stopped here on his way to San Miguel from the town of Dolores, eighteen miles to the north. He was Father Miguel Hidalgo y Costilla, the sixty-year-old parish priest of Dolores, who had just uttered the famous *grito*, his rallying-cry for Independence that has echoed down the ages, growing in volume, reiterated by every subsequent President from the balcony of the Palacio Nacional, until it's become to the modern ear a proclamation, urgent and insistent, of Mexican sovereignty.

  Father Hidalgo, the humble padre, was leading a barely controllable rabble of *campesinos*, mestizos and Indians. Armed with clubs and slings, axes, knives and machetes, they were marching on the bastions of Spanish colonialism, starting with San Miguel. Hidalgo entered the sanctuary of Atotonilco, fell to his knees in prayer, then snatched up a picture of the Virgin of Guadalupe from one of the altars. Fastening it to a pole, he held it above his head, in that one simple moment making the saintly patroness of indigenous converts and Creoles the eternal icon of Mexican liberation. The Virgin Mary of the New World was free for once and for all from any colonial associations that had lingered around her. From then on Our Lady of Guadalupe would represent Mexicans. She would become the national symbol, far more powerful than any anthem or flag, or any head of state or hero embossed on Mexican coins. She would brand her image on the collective unconscious, the one figure that would connect all Mexicans together; Mexico's guardian angel, her spirit-guide, her Athena. A century later, she would be raised aloft again, as the standard of Emiliano Zapata, leader of the peasant armies of the Revolution; and nearly a century after that, at the turn of the second millennium, her banner would be held up as the standard of democracy by an opposition leader bent on dismantling the corrupt and dictatorial government of the PRI.

With Hidalgo that day in 1810 was San Miguel's homespun hero of Independence, José Ignacio Allende – whose house I'd passed on the corner of the Jardín – leading the well-heeled Creole contingent. Allende had been married in the church at Atotonilco only eight years earlier. Now he came to it on the warpath. Allende had been one of the prime movers in a conspiracy that was based in Querétaro, 35 miles to the south-east of San Miguel. The conspirators had set their date for an armed uprising against the Spanish Crown for 8 December. When the plan was discovered on 13 September, a messenger rushed to San Miguel and gave the news to Juan de Aldama, another conspirator. Aldama sped north to Dolores where he found Allende at the house of Miguel Hidalgo.

It was a few hours later, shortly after dawn, that Hidalgo sent up the cry of rebellion from the steps of his church. Mid-morning found the rebels at Atotonilco and by that evening the town of San Miguel was in their hands, the portrait of the Virgin of Guadalupe raised aloft in front of the Parroquia. A ground-swell of local

Creoles and mestizos spontaneously joined forces with the regiment from Dolores. They locked up the Spanish population and went on the rampage. Allende, the Creole, was appalled at the vengeful harpies he had unleashed on his home town and spent most of the night trying to put a stop to the looting.

From San Miguel, Hidalgo and Allende marched on Celaya and Guanajuato, north to Zacatecas, south almost to Mexico City and west to Guadalajara. But after their initial successes, the Spanish finally caught up with them in Chihuahua. Allende was executed almost immediately, Hidalgo was tortured and then shot by firing-squad several months later. In a symbolic display of hatred and contempt, Spanish regimental officers had the image of the Virgin of Guadalupe shot by firing-squad, too.

Allende and Hidalgo's decapitated heads were returned to the silver city of Guanajuato where their army had scored its first major victory, and hung in cages along with the heads of Aldama and another leader called Jiménez, on an outer corner of the huge central grain-store – the Alhóndiga de Granaditas – for ten years. The gruesome spectacle was supposed to intimidate other would-be rebels but instead it kept the flame of insurgency alive, a burning reminder of heroic, close to saintly, martyrdom. Politics apart, theirs was an end of which Father Alfaro would surely have been envious.

It was a beautiful evening for the Thursday perambulation back in San Miguel. The town was out in force. Families with toddlers in pushchairs and babies in arms were making their tour of the major churches of San Miguel, starting with the Oratory to the north of the main square.

It was a tradition that recalled in miniature the pilgrimage of Philip Neri, the sixteenth-century Florentine saint and founder of the first oratory in Rome. Saint Philip had been appalled at the 'vanity, pride and concupiscence' that had taken hold of the citizens of Rome and had instigated a penitential pilgrimage starting with a visit to Saint Peter's Basilica where he apologized to Christ in the Blessed Sacrament for the city's excesses. From there he set out for six other churches outside the capital. It was Philip Neri's name that Father Alfaro adopted as his own a century later, no doubt fancying he was doing for the wealthy of San Miguel what his patron saint had done for Rome.

The churches were decked out with massive displays of fresh flowers. There was wild camomile on the marble floors and everywhere bunches of salvia, or the 'little rope of Jesus', its delicate blue flowers strung out along the stem like knots of a *disciplina*. All the saints had been freshly made-up, coiffeured, washed and blow-dried. Each was sponsored by a local patron, their wigs made from their patron's hair. Wayward curls had been brushed and disciplined with a generous application of hairspray. Fresh underclothes had been put on, discreetly; satin robes gleamed anew in the refracted light filtering through the stained-glass windows.

But the focus of the excitement were the figures of Christ himself. Each church had its own saviour contorted in agony, each statue or painting more gruesome, it seemed, than the last. There was the 'Cristo de la Espina' (Christ of the Thorn'); Señor de la Conquista (Lord of the Conquest); Señor Ecce Homo (a black Christ worshipped by the blacks and mulattos who had been brought to San Miguel to replace the dwindling, plague-ridden workforce of indigenous Indians); Christ of the Passion with His wrists and neck bound with cords; Señor de la Expiración – Christ breathing his last on the Cross; Christ, the Fountain of Life, with blood gushing from his side into a basin where the saints could gather to drink.

This evening was a rare chance to see the famous Octagonal Chapel behind the Santa Casa de Loreto at the Oratorio which was normally closed to the public. The Santa Casa de Loreto was extraordinary. A lavishly decorated chapel in the west transept of the Oratory, it purports to be an exact copy of the 'home in which the Son of God was conceived'. According to this bizarre and anachronistic tale, when the infidels captured the Holy Land, the house of the Virgin Mary in Nazareth fell into their hands. The angels were so infuriated that, under the command of Saint Michael, they moved the house to Loreto in Italy.

There'd been a picture of the Virgin's house in Loreto in the church at Atotonilco. But this reconstruction of the house itself was commissioned in the 1730s by the wealthiest family in San Miguel at the time, the Canal family, at a cost of 35,000 pesos, a staggering sum even for the heady days of San Miguel's golden age. On the walls and floors were tiles from Puebla, Valencia and China; there were gilded cloth hangings and behind the main altar, on which stood a venerated image of the Virgin in a glass case edged in silver, and six further altars, all elaborately gilded, one of which was said to contain the bones of San Columbano.

The myth of the Virgin's house was as extravagant and anachronistic as the myth of the Virgin of Guadalupe herself, as bizarre and distorted as the idea that Michelangelo had painted the church at Atotonilco. But such was the nature of religion, it seemed to me, and the human capacity – desire even – for self-deception, and the urge to rewrite history, that myths such as these proved far more resilient, and certainly more seductive, than fact. I was quite sure that many of the people trailing humble and hatless into the Casa de Loreto were convinced this, or at least somewhere like it, was where the Virgin had lived.

I remembered how we'd been banned from using the words 'when', 'where', 'why' and 'how' in RE lessons at the convent – 'You don't ask questions if you have faith' Sister Ursula used to hiss at my back as I left the classroom to spend another forty minutes in a draughty corridor. My adult life, I felt, had begun with resistance to the Siren-like call of make believe, with the struggle to distinguish fantasy from reality, to read the Bible as metaphor, not Gospel, as the nuns did. In San Miguel I felt drawn by the same magnetic earth-pull of invention and superstition.

But here, perhaps because I wasn't in my own country; because I was a foreigner; because I was coasting along as a passenger, an observer, the sensation wasn't as unnerving or threatening. I was overwhelmed, instead, by the power of the human imagination over physical reality. Drawing a demarcation line between the two seemed less relevant here, where myth and fantasy were food for the soul, religion a release as much as a means of control.

Behind the Casa de Loreto, the sumptuous Octagonal Chapel was drawing crowds. A tailback stretched down the nave of the Oratory itself where the queue of visitors was overshadowed by a series of thirty-three salutary paintings on the life of Saint Philip Neri. Inside, eventually, the Octagonal Chapel was a jewellery box of baroque extravagance. The walls gleamed with gold and all around, carved in niches and highlighted by golden rays, were purple hearts, as realistic as the hearts of oxen on the slab of one of San Miguel's butcher shops. It was a bizarre detail of the kind that seems natural in Mexico where the saintly and ornamental are inextricably bound up with the violent and visceral.

There was a handsome painting of Aurora in her horse-drawn chariot galloping over the town of Nazareth – which looked more like a Renaissance town in Italy, perfectly in keeping with the Virgin's house next door. The floor in front of the altar was thick with crushed camomile and Christ's bitter oranges spray-painted gold.

I shuffled through the chapel, sandwiched in the crowd, and re-emerged in the Garden of Gethsemane – a little courtyard of orange trees where the stage was set for Christ's betrayal. There was a plastic rooster on a branch and the – by now – familiar figure of Christ in agony. But the children around me were far more taken with a tiny model of Judas hanging from a branch which moved an arm mechanically as if it was waving merrily in the throes of death, shaking the oranges as it did so.

Further down the street from the Oratorio, next to the public library, the Iglesia de Santa Ana was providing another attraction. A dramatic recumbent figure of Christ was lying at the foot of the altar. There was a queue to kiss his shredded knees, the gory hole in his side, his nailed hands and feet. I sank on to a pew in the choir and tried to make sense of all this ritual morbidity around me. One by one babies and children were carried forward to kiss Christ's brow; old women and men touched his knees and crossed themselves, genuflecting on their own arthritic joints; others stroked his face as if they were wiping away the tears of a child.

It was a moving and emotional scene, full of unexpected tenderness. The caresses were as intimate and loving, and as pitiful, as the embraces of the newly bereaved. Infant mortality was still frighteningly high in Mexico, poverty claimed the young and the weak and the old, violence was a way of life. Here was an outlet for that tide of grief, the tragedy of the poor unfolding into the arms of God.

There was also something fetishistic, I felt, as I watched this outpouring of human emotion over what was, in effect, a life-size doll. At what point in history, I wondered, does mankind no longer have a role for idolatry? I was beginning to believe that in Mexico it was more than just a question of wealth and well-being; or even superstition and myth. Here, it seemed, the graphic statues of Christ and the Catholic martyrs still answered an important need. They made possible the transfer of personal trauma and pain on to something benign yet impersonal and remote. It was a way of making sense of the human condition, of understanding and accepting it. To devout Mexicans, God was still the centre of man's existence, of human feeling.

Europe had moved on, in religious terms, since the medieval age. Our spiritual axis had shifted completely. Man, rather than God, had become centre stage. Since the arrival of Shakespeare religion had been banished to the side-lines. But Shakespeare was almost a century too late for the New World. The medieval Church had transplanted itself to the Americas a full fifty years before Shakespeare was born and had remained, to a great extent, isolated on this side of the Atlantic ever since. In Mexico, Christian belief was still largely unaffected by the great eighteenth-century revelation of egocentricity and the individual.

The image of Christ lying stretched out before me was as real to the people worshipping him as a human corpse. His body lay there, transfixed by the projections of each person's individual sorrow and pain as they came forward to caress him. His wounds were graphic and gory and realistic because they had to be. They were made by Mexicans who had seen it all – slavery, the Inquisition, genocide, fratricide, suicide. They were intimate with broken bodies and the hallmarks of torture. But as terrible as was the suffering of the Mexican peons, Christ's suffering had to be worse, if it was to command their admiration and allegiance. Easter was the song of Mexico's history, the thorn driven through the breast, the syrupy, exaltant trilling of a nation's tragedy. It was as natural to the Mexican psyche as it was alien to the immigrant Americans, those ultimate individuals, who were, at this very moment, recoiling from this blessed unction in the sanity of their retirement homes, quietly nursing a sense of moral indignation.

While the mestizo and peasant population of San Miguel thronged the churches, the expat community had taken to the hills. I found some of them later that evening walking their spaniels and red-setters in the Jardín Botánico 'El Charco del Ingenio', a cactus park on an exposed hilltop a mile to the north-east of the town centre. Newly built condominiums were stacked up the hillsides overlooking the park and the town below. Painted in the lively colours of a Casa Mexicana coffee-table book, there was something stark and displaced about them, out of kilter with this Mexican Jerusalem.

Sunset was breaking over the mountains, a fresh evening breeze ruffling the silky coats of the dogs as they sniffed about for rabbits and desert shrews. The light filtered through the cacti-spines like a halo through crowns of thorns. Despite the loud gringo voices carried on the wind, the United States seemed a million miles away.

The spark ignited by Allende and Hidalgo in their quest for Mexican Independence set fire to 120 years of bloody chaos. The War of Independence ended in 1824 with the drawing up of a constitution and the establishment of the federal Mexican Republic, comprising nineteen states and four territories. But this was only after a royalist general, who had first defected to the rebel cause and then set himself up as Emperor, had been deposed. This was just the beginning. It set the trend for what was to follow in the mad, dog-eat-dog power struggle that characterized the evolution of Mexican self-rule. Opportunist soldiers rebelled against elected presidents; constitutionally elected presidents were murdered; counter-presidents emerged and disappeared; Constitutional Parties, Reform Parties, Agrarian Parties, Liberals and Conservatives allied with each other, split, and then realigned on opposite sides; the Church and the landowners and the Creoles and foreign investors bullied and bribed their way round the labyrinth of power. In the twenty-two years between 1833 and 1855 alone, the presidency changed hands thirty-six times. There was even a brief period of renewed colonialism under an Austrian archduke, Maximilian of Hapsburg, after a French invasion instigated by Napoleon III. But mostly the nineteenth and early twentieth centuries were dominated by a bewildering spectrum of liberators and reformers and maverick loose-cannon brigands, upholders of the Faith and radical idealists, all claiming they had the best interests of Mexico at heart. Armed bands supporting the different factions roamed the countryside, besieging towns, burning crops and looting villages, raping, pillaging and murdering, and generally taking out their frustrated ambitions on confused Indians and *campesinos*. There were a dozen full-blown constitutions and many more Declarations of Independence and Reform. Sometimes the general populace was drawn into the killing, sometimes not. But there was never peace. Not unless you count the 'Porfiriato' (1876–1909), thirty-three years of stability under the dictatorship of the iron-fisted modernizer, Porfirio Díaz – Weetman Pearson's employer – as breathing space.

A century of turbulent pendulum-swinging veered off into a spectacular crescendo with the Mexican Revolution in 1910 – a decade of civil war which claimed the lives of between 1.5 and 2 million people, one in eight Mexicans. Again and again, attempts to create a stable government were shattered by the treacherous in-fighting of revolutionary leaders, assassinations and endless new outbursts of fighting.

But even when all that was over, when Mexico had settled on a President and a new reformist constitution – the one that is still in force today – the volcanic fountains of bloodshed were far from spent.

As part of his large-scale land reform, President Plutarco Elías Calles clamped down on the Catholic Church – a body that still, despite endless attempts to limit its power, retained enormous wealth and political muscle, as well as a great deal of the land it had accrued under the Spanish administration. In a series of severe measures designed to cripple the Catholic Church once and for all, Calles closed the monasteries, convents and church schools, deported foreign priests and nuns and prohibited public worship and religious processions. The Catholic Church has been officially illegal in Mexico ever since: it still can't own property, priests and nuns are forbidden to wear habits outside church precincts, and the only legal marriage is a civil one.

Catholic, mainly Creole, extremists fought back against Calles's censures and 1926 saw the onset of the bloody Cristero Rebellion, a conflict which seemed likely to become a war to the death between the Church and the Revolution.

Then another genie sprang out of the bottle. 'Liberal reformists' lashed back at the conservative Catholics, persecuting congregations, torching and looting churches, hounding the faithful like the faithful had hounded the infidels those hundreds of years ago. Priests and nuns holed themselves up in secret hiding places in the houses of wealthy Catholics where they held masses, baptisms and marriages in the suffocating spaces between false walls. It was a time of suspicion and guilt and paranoia, the backdrop for Graham Greene's novel *The Power and the Glory*, written after Greene visited Mexico in the 1930s on a clandestine mission sponsored by the Vatican to report on religious persecution.

Despite its religious *raison d'être* the major battles of the Cristero War side-stepped San Miguel. It was clear, though, where the town's allegiances lay. At one point eight Cristero sympathizers were rounded up by government soldiers and six of them were shot (two escaped), their bodies hung from trees in the plaza in front of the Parroquia. The commander of the garrison installed in San Miguel to keep a lid on the situation was advised that if he arrested everyone who had a sacred image in their house or burned a votive candle, he'd have to throw the entire town in jail.

When an accord was finally bridged between the American Ambassador Dwight Morrow and Father John Burke, Secretary of the American National Council for Catholic Welfare, and President Calles, the news was greeted with an outpouring of emotion in San Miguel. On the eve of Saturday 7 July 1929, the Blessed Sacrament was taken from its hiding-place in a private house on the corner of Mesones and Reloj and returned to its place in the Parroquia. The oldest inhabitants of San Miguel still remember that procession – the rain of flowers and applause and the ringing of bells as the Host entered the atrium of the Parroquia, the tears on the faces of the crowd.

It was in the aftermath of peace that the real war broke out. More Cristeros were killed in the liberal backlash of the 1930s than before the accord. In the crypt beneath the main altar of the Parroquia, only a few steps from the tomb of President Bustamante, a flat stone commemorates the burial site of Sidrónio Muñoz, a thirty-year-old Cristero murdered just weeks after the official truce was declared. His body had been found on a hillside near the road to Celaya and was sombrely carried back home to San Miguel. In the minds of the people of San Miguel, this was another historical ricochet. Muñoz's murder echoed the fate of the two martyred Franciscan friars three and a half centuries before. Though the young soldier had been dead for eight days, people say crossing themselves, his body was incorrupt.

It was midday in the Jardín, the moment, at last, of liturgical climax. Every inch of every pavement was crammed to bursting. There were boys hanging like monkeys from the trees, toddlers on shoulders and, interspersed among the crowd, little angels in white dresses sucking ice-pops.

Earlier in the morning the angels had taken part in the first Good Friday procession circling the barrio of the Temple of San Juan de Dios, near Patricia's pension. The procession had featured the famous visiting Lord of the Column from Atotonilco, but it had also honoured San Roque, the fourteenth-century patron saint of people suffering from epidemics, an all too prominent figure in the decades following European contact. The first hospital in San Miguel had been founded at San Juan de Dios and this procession was traditionally sponsored by San Miguel's physicians. The charming little figure of San Roque had led the entourage, pointing to his ulcerated leg, with the little dog who had faithfully fed the saint throughout his illness, holding a bread roll in its jaws.

Now, child Jesuses and Judases from the same procession were mingling in the crowds in front of the Parroquia, triggering off a bizarre note of déjà vu. Tourists, cherry-picking their moment, were out in force. I was rubbing shoulders, and almost everything else because of the crush, with a woman from California. 'It's just so incredible to see so many children,' she was saying; 'where I come from we don't have them any more.'

Inside the atrium of the Parroquia, away from the crowds,

Barrabas is being freed, Pontius Pilate is washing his hands and Christ is being condemned. The trigger that fires the whole inexorable process of the tragedy has been released. From inside the church of San Raphael adjoining the Parroquia, come the first of the penitents. Three men halt at the top of the steps looking on to the Jardín. One carries the small painted standard of Father Alfaro; the other two, dressed in thick purple sackcloth, carry human skulls.

Behind them come more penitents, all of them barefoot, with the knotted cords of *disciplinas* dangling from their belts. But these are no longer instruments of self-abasement. They are only symbolic. The last decades of the twentieth century have rinsed the penitential exercise of Easter free of blood. There will be no scourging of flesh or beating of breasts in the streets of San Miguel, not before an audience that will be going home to microwaved buffalo wings and satellite TV. The penitents are wearing white linen shirts under their sackcloth to stop it chafing. They look pristine, chubby and healthy.

I think how disappointed Father Alfaro would be. 'Fill up what is lacking in the sufferings of Christ,' he urged the townspeople in his day, reiterating the words of Saint Paul to the Corinthians. Only in Atotonilco is his exhortation still obeyed.

Behind the penitents, accompanied by sturdy centurions – several on horseback – in cardboard breastplates, with whips and spears, come the two thieves and Christ in his crown of thorns. For a moment there's an almost pantomime atmosphere amongst the crowd. The boys near me are excited, not by the pathetic-looking Jews, their arms roped to heavy blocks of wood, but by the glamorous Roman soldiers surveying the scene with haughty disdain.

But when Christ comes forward, he is quite clearly struggling and the crowd lapses into a chastened silence. Christ is played by the priest of the Parroquia, and he seems almost crushed beneath the wooden cross carried two centuries ago by Father Alfaro. Has the burden of guilt grown that much heavier over the centuries, or is the representative of the Church no longer strong enough to bear it? The crowd wills him on. The good thief, a fitter, younger man, looks almost relaxed. The bad thief, on the other side, releases some of the crowd from their mesmerism by struggling melodramatically against his captors and scowling like a mad man. The boys beside me laugh and jeer, egging on the centurions to prod him with their lances.

The gaggle of penitents and the prison guard move off awkwardly, crosses scoring the ground. A heavy litter carrying the figure of Jesus the Nazarene and his cross is brought through the doors of the church and there's a sweaty moment as the whole shebang has to negotiate some overhead cables. The litter tilts and wobbles and comes close to crashing to the ground. Just in time the bearers straighten and steady themselves, clear the wires and continue, eyes fixed in concentration, down the steps to the Jardín. Every one of them is dripping in sweat.

By now the sun is blazing. Hawkers are doing a roaring trade in paper parasols and ice-lollies. A few old hands have brought umbrellas. The procession heads off round a street corner where an image of St Peter, a cockerel at his feet, mutely denies his Saviour.

Waiting for the procession's return to the Jardín, a cortège of women stands rock solid under a stretcher bearing the image of Christ's grieving mother, La Soledad. The women are dressed in crow-black, with Castilian black lace mantillas over their hair and imposing, masonic-looking scapulars. They are stocky and beefy-armed, with tortoise-like Indian faces, staring into middle distance, away from the machine-gun fire of holiday snappers. When Christ's procession meets up with them again, the women are ready, steeling themselves in the eye of fate, mothers confronting the imminent death of their son.

There is a secret mechanism in the neck of Jesus the Nazarene – a device typical of those created by the Franciscans, a theatrical special effect – that allows the statue's head to be lifted by a secret trigger. When the image of Christ approaches his mother, he raises his face for a moment, as if in recognition, and then bows back toward the ground. Though they must have seen this dozens of times – even every year of their lives – the moment of the 'Encuentro' sends a shiver through the crowd as if they were witnessing a miracle. People cross themselves and mutter prayers. Handkerchiefs flutter from pockets. There are tears streaming down the faces of most of the women in Mary's cortège. To me and to the tourists around me, this is fraud. To the believers it is an echo, a visitation from history, a living sign of almost unbearable pathos, a moment that signifies a universal and continuing agony.

That evening the final procession of the Holy Burial begins with a slow executioner's drum-beat. One thousand mourners line up behind Christ of the Expiration lying in state in His glass coffin. All of them wear strict mourning dress, or *luto rigoroso* – black suits, white shirts and black ties for the men; black dresses and mantillas and white gloves for the women. For all their piety, they look like Sicilian mafiosi at the funeral of the Godfather. A posse of priests from the Oratorio follow the glass catafalque in sumptuous black and gold vestments. Behind them come angels carrying a horrible selection of crucifixion hardware: a chalice, crown of thorns, hammer and nails, a scourge, lance, dice, the jug and basin in which Pilate washed his hands, Veronica's scarf and even a ladder used in the Descent from the Cross.

Slowly, painstakingly, the cortège inches its way around town. The coffin, with its thirty-six bearers, advances and then stops every now and again, resting briefly on metal supports, while a *saeta*, or lament, is sung from a balcony. Behind it comes Mary, her heavy crimson robes flowing over the litter, her face a lugubrious vision of sorrow; and then the images of those who stayed with Christ until his death – John, Joseph, Veronica, Mary Magdalene, Joseph of Arimathea and Nicodemus. Watching from a distance, like a pariah, is the remorseful figure of Peter. Two and a half hours later, and at a cost of over $5000, the great burial procession is over.

'You know, Mexico has everything I need to enjoy life,' Patricia said as she took an enormous appreciative bite of her burger. We had just been to a *charreada*, a local rodeo, and had adjourned for a late lunch to a restaurant that was a temple to bullfighting. Patricia was dressed like a cowgirl – jeans and denim shirt and big brass buffalo-head ear-rings. It was a relief to have a respite from religious fervour, from the spirit of self-flagellation, although it felt like I was simply swinging from one extreme to another.

On the walls were posters and photographs of *toreros* strutting their stuff, backs arched in clouds of dust and swirling crimson silk. The bulls in the pictures were pawing at the ground, or lying 'picked' and bleeding, the fatal sword poised neck down towards their heart. One or two were frozen in a moment of victory, horns glancing off a human body that was flying miraculously through the air. There seemed nowhere in Mexico that one could avoid the sight of blood, the dance of life and death.

'You see, I'm lazy,' Patricia went on, 'I don't ever want to cook a meal or make a bed again in my life. I raised five sons and all I ever did was stand at the kitchen sink. I tell you it was a bucket of shit. Here I can have people cook for me, pick up my dirty laundry from off of the floor – I ain't gotta lift a finger.'

Patricia was unloading a pharmacy of multi-vitamin horse-pills from her bag. Tipping her head back, she washed them down, one by one. 'Don't know if it makes a damn bit of difference, but I started taking all these when I was thirty-five and I sure as hell ain't gonna stop now. I gotta have the most expensive urine in San Miguel.'

I began to wonder if the Mexican and American worlds of San Miguel weren't unconnected after all. Perhaps they were different sides of a coin. To Patricia's mind, San Miguel had performed miracles. It had given her freedom, a fantastic standard of living, and it had given her back her youth. While Mexicans resorted to the *disciplina*, Patricia and her friends sought solace in the surgeon's knife. Both were incising the flesh for the good of the soul, and submitting themselves to the sweet reconstructions of forgiveness and rebirth.

I was going to miss Patricia. I wasn't sure how much of Mexico had really got under her skin – apart, quite literally, from Dr Burrito. She'd taken on the country on her own terms. But she was giving back to it on her own terms, too. With irrepressible gusto she'd helped set up a system whereby tourists could give beggars vouchers instead of cash (the tickets were redeemable at local charities for food, clothing and birth control shots, thereby, she claimed, denying alcoholic husbands the opportunity of stealing funds desperately needed by their wives and children, and also reassuring tourists that they weren't simply 'throwing their money away'). She had personally lobbied the Guanajuato Governor, Vicente Fox, for a new sewage treatment plant for San Miguel. She'd convinced local religious and public schools to institute a 'litterbug' campaign to teach children not to litter the streets. She'd delivered thousands of toys and shoes to children in remote Indian villages. And she'd personally financed at least five plastic surgery operations for children with burns or birth defects. She was well respected, even loved, in a headmistressy type of way, by local Mexicans; a warrior of good intention and generosity.

I was going to miss Patricia most, though, for her no-nonsense, straight-talking sense of humour and her infectious spirits. She was living for the moment and doing everything 'in hell's way' to make that moment last.

With her obsession for elixirs of youth, for face-lifts and pill-popping, I'd thought Patricia might, like so many of her compatriots, be frightened of dying. But she was only, reasonably, afraid of incapacity, and loss of dignity. 'I've worked out how I'm gonna end it, if it comes to it,' she said, 'I'm gonna make myself look real nice – clean underwear, fancy dress, lots of make-up, the whole enchilada – and I'm gonna sit in the car and let rip with the carbon monoxide. That's the best way to check out in my opinion.'

Her ashes, she'd instructed her son, were to be sprinkled in the garden at Casa Murphy, divided between her pots of hibiscus and jasmine, pansies and arum lilies and honeysuckle. 'Then, if the flowers die, they'll say "Hell, what's that woman up to now", and if they bloom like crazy, well, I'll take the credit.'

I couldn't sleep that night. It was the evening of the *Pésames*, the Wakes, when the whole town is supposed to keep Mary company through the watches of the night. There's mass in the Oratorio and a torchlit procession of La Soledad with the Virgin dressed this time in a long black velvet train trimmed with silver, and all the same entourage of women in mourning. There are baptisms, and blessings of holy water and the liturgy of the Eucharist, and the singing of the 'Madre Dolorosa' to music by the eighteenth-century composer Luis de la Canal – a member of the wealthy family behind the excessive Octagonal Chapel.

But I couldn't face it. Not again. I was exhausted and thought I would sleep. As soon as I hit the pillow, though, I realized it was useless. My mind was kicking with images, belting about like a bull in the ring. I saw flashes of all the statues I'd seen over the past few days, each one beseeching, intrusive, demanding attention. I thought of the Virgin I'd decapitated back at my convent school; of all the nuns I thought I'd forgotten; their fearful, blinkered outlook on life; their twisted ideas of what was healthy and wholesome for young girls; the hours spent in detention scrubbing desks with wire-wool and white spirit; Reverend Mother breaking down in tears before the whole class – 'It's SEX, SEX, SEX; that's all you care about.'

The noise in the street seemed endless but varied, as if the whole world was taking turns to keep me awake. Dogs barked. Cars rattled over cobblestones. Once or twice a mariachi band came belting its way past the pension door and disappeared up towards the Jardín. Then silence. And then a passing freight train would let out a whistle. The driver would be pushing his way through the night, on up through the desert, eating up mile after mile of track between here and the border of North America. What was he thinking? Was he Mexican, or American? I thought of Neal Cassady walking the railway out of San Miguel, run down within shouting distance of Casa Murphy. The hoot of the train lingered on mournfully.

I tossed and turned, and turned and tossed, and just before daybreak finally collapsed into a dream-tormented sleep. The last sound I remember was the metallic clanging of church bells, an echo from the mines, the vulcanic striking of underground metal, from the deep dark caverns where thousands upon thousands of Indians, rasping for air, were hammering themselves to death, striking and chipping at the silver seams for an endlessly insatiable San Miguel . . . silver that was finding its way on to the altars of every church in Mexico, on to the tables of grandees in the fabulous mansions in the capital, that silversmiths far away in sooty Sheffield were forging into fancy cutlery, that was miraculously composing itself into a bicycle for a lady in Edwardian dress and a long, long, way to go . . .

*

I was blasted awake at noon by the sound of gunfire and shelling. Outside my room Patricia was in a frenzy of annoyance, putting ear-plugs in her dog. The bombardment grew louder as I neared the Jardín. Little puffs of smoke were bursting against a deep blue sky. In the plaza, strung up along the street between the Presidencia and the Jardín, monster papier mâché Judas figures were being blown to smithereens. One by one the touch-paper was lit, people ran for cover, ducking behind walls and benches, cowering in doorways, fingers in their ears, while the Judas began to spin, round and round, faster and faster, a ghostly wheezing scream piercing the brain as the gunpowder ignited and then – BANG! – shattered bits of body showered the street.

Children ran forward, shrieking with excitement, to grab a trophy leg or head or foot. The Jardín was full of amputations, as if someone had tipped a field-hospital's waste-disposal bins out of the sky. Oddly, for the first time all week, there was no sign of blood. All the automatic telling machine booths on the Jardín were jammed with ashy-faced tourists cowering behind double doors of bullet-proof glass. The gentle, serene Sunday of Resurrection was being blasted to shreds. The risen Christ was nowhere to be seen.

My ears were still ringing, nostrils prickling from saltpetre, as I headed out from San Miguel towards Dolores Hidalgo, bags crammed in the boot of a taxi. Twelve days from now Our Lord of the Column would be making his way back home along this road, wrapped in the handkerchiefs of the faithful. His return would be as triumphant as his arrival in San Miguel: a torchlit procession setting off at midnight, arriving after dawn, another superhuman feat of endurance complete. Even after Easter Sunday, for the Catholic faithful of San Miguel, Lent and the agonies of Semana Santa would continue. In Atotonilco they were never over.

Nearing the turn-off, I decided to pay one last visit to Father Alfaro's sanctuary. I arrived just as the last batch of penitents was leaving. Tough-looking *campesinos* and jaunty young bloods were milling around waiting for the bus, hold-alls and bed-rolls at the ready. They were all wearing heavy crucifixes and *disciplinas*, the purple cords of the Franciscans and white coronas of white cotton flowers. Some of them wore the white bridal veils of initiates. Roughly shaven and thick-browed they looked like parodies of virgins, vaguely transvestite. Trails of white netting fluttered flirtatiously against their chests, many of which sported graphic T-shirt designs of the crucifixion, one, the word 'DEICIDE' written in flames.

They were in buoyant spirits after their week of flagellation and contrition, and played around for my camera. They were members of a *sindicato*, they told me, from the Colonia Jardínes de Guadalupe, a barrio of Mexico City. For many of them this was the first 'holiday' they had ever taken in their lives.

The penitentiary next to the church was being scrubbed for the next batch of holiday-makers arriving later that day. I took the opportunity of the open door to take a look inside. The stench of disinfectant assaulted the senses like a blow to the head. There was a scratching, sloshing sound of brushes on concrete. Few of the cleaners spoke Spanish. They looked slow and bewildered, a little simple perhaps, like Alfredo the *disciplina* seller.

The atmosphere inside was oppressive, overwhelming, like a sanatorium, with low ceilings, concrete corridors, and concrete stairs; stained, flea-ridden mattresses; a few concrete showers in a line like a cattle stall; open, doorless lavatories. In the kitchen there were cooking vats as big as a car; sacks and sacks of cornmeal (fortified with vitamins like cattle-feed) and a conveyor belt for the thousands of tortillas that would provide some comfort for wracked and remorseful bodies over the coming week.

In the sunless labyrinth of corridors, there was the odd little chapel, almost a grotto, with figures of tortured saints, a few vases of plastic flowers, and prayers and inscriptions from the writings of Father Alfaro in illuminated script on the walls – not that these would make much impression on the penitents, most of whom would be illiterate. The odd fingermark in blood had been left on the walls – a heart, a cross, or a slogan, phonetically misspelt: *Biba Cristo* – 'Christ lives'.

It was stiflingly claustrophobic and institutional, but the feeling was more than the sum of bad architectural design and stinking latrines. There was an intensity to the air, as if the very walls were charged with the electric energy of the hundreds of men who had just vacated them; as if their depth of feeling had refreshed the memory of centuries of religious devotion, visions of the divine and the ecstasy of self-inflicted pain.

Outside again, the morning was a picture of sanity and serenity. A Dominican nun was laying out a tray of ham rolls and cakes to sell to people coming for Sunday mass. I asked her whether she'd been in San Miguel for the festivities. No, she replied. She'd been here, as always, with the thirty-two other novice sisters of her order, at Atotonilco. The village had held their own Good Friday celebration. Three specially chosen men had dragged crosses through the village from the church, up to the top of the nearest hill. There, they'd been strung up by the other villagers and left hanging there for the best part of the afternoon – a 'living crucifixion' it was called.

'He was wonderful, the man who played Christ,' said the sister, passionately, 'so devout and so strong, so close to God, an inspiration to us all. When they roped him up, he was begging for the men to put nails in his hands. The priest stopped them, of course. Sometimes passion gets the better of us,' she smiled. I thought of Father Alfaro and agreed. I could quite easily imagine him running off helpfully for his toolbox.

I looked around for Alfredo but there was a woman – his sister perhaps – in charge of his stall. Atotonilco was very quiet. You would never have guessed it was Easter Sunday. Birds twittered in the eucalyptus. The desert beyond loomed limitless and engulfing, a place for prophets and madmen. I thought of the people who once came here happily to bathe, before Father Alfaro got loose with his whip. But in a way, not so much had changed. Father Alfaro had simply switched the focus from the physical to the spiritual, or, more properly, ignited a current between the two. Atotonilco had become a place for scrubbing the soul. It was continuing, in Catholic disguise, the ancient indigenous practices of exorcism. 'This kind of demon can only be cast out by prayer and penance,' Christ instructed the apostles when they failed to cure some wretched supplicant.

I was beginning to regard the disciplines of Father Alfaro not as an expression of self-hatred or unworthiness, as the spiritual exercises of Catholicism elsewhere seemed to be; but a healing – an elaborate, shamanic ritual. There was light at the end of the tunnel but it came not in the form of resurrection or forgiveness so much as the physical banishment of evil. No wonder Good Friday was the climax of Mexican Semana Santa. It demonstrated the innate evils, the demons, that dogged mankind; but it also showed a way to overcome and expel them. Christ's salvation lay in the transcendence of pain. Every step of the Via Crucis was an expurgation. If Good Friday was a descent into Hell, it was the attainment of Heaven at the very same time. Christ's reappearance from the tomb three days after his crucifixion was comparatively insignificant – it was proof of the pudding, a foregone conclusion.

That this medieval, puritanical mysticism found such fertile ground in Mexico, so that it persists today, says as much about the spirit of the indigenous people as it does about the founding fathers. Father Alfaro and the religious disciplinarians who came before him struck a chord with indigenous belief because they, too, saw the interrelatedness of the physical and the spiritual. There was no conceptual division between the two as evolved in modern Western perception. An impact on one, they believed, would have a direct effect on the other.

When a band of soldiers galloped into the village of Atotonilco in the early decades of the last century, lathered from some hot-blooded game of cat and mouse, they rode their horses right into the church, reining them in before a tableau of the crucifixion, and shot the statue of the bad thief to pieces. It was more than a symbolic act; it was a physical attack on an embodiment of evil – a simple, sure-fire way of eliminating the bad guy.

3

A Week of Impiety
Juchitán

The lust of the goat is the bounty of God

William Blake

It's dusk on the Pacific side of the Isthmus of Tehuantepec, and the place is screaming. The main square of Juchitán is a din of long-tailed *zanates* returning from the mangroves to roost. Their scuffles send showers of leaves and seeds down from the mimosas and add a hint of guano to the pervasive smell of cooking-oil. You have to shout to be heard.

A couple of blocks away on the basketball court the shrieks of the birds are matched by a game in progress. Two teams of transvestites wearing short skirts and crop-tops – all legs and giggles and girly hysteria – are battling it out in their weekly friendly. Tonight *Las Intrépidas* ('The Intrepid Ones') are playing *Ven a Bailar Conmigo* ('Come Dance With Me') – a team who take their name from a national TV soap opera. It's a typical tropical evening and though the players are dripping in sweat none of them wants to smudge their make-up by wiping it off.

This is an unnerving spectacle to stumble on after what I've seen so far in Mexico. In the capital and San Miguel this exhibition would have been greeted with hoots of derision or, more than likely, aggression. I steel myself for taunts from the local Rambos, shouts of *putos* or *jotos* ('poofs', 'faggots'), cat-whistles, the odd missile. I keep looking over my shoulder in case Chiclet-chewing *muchachos* in back-to-front baseball caps are collecting on the street corner or under the mango trees, checking out the gay guys like sharks circling goldfish. But there's nothing of the sort.

Slowly it sinks in that in Juchitán a ball-game is simply a ball-game and the fact that the players are wearing size-ten trainers and shaving their armpits doesn't, amazingly, call for a punch-up.

Laureana leads me over to one of the spectators' benches and we sit down to watch. I had lunch with Laureana in Mexico City shortly after my drink with Philippe, the artist on the psychiatrist's couch, and she'd agreed to bring me here, to Juchitán, her father's home town, with her half-sister, Natalia. Natalia's mother came from Juchitán, she said, and Natalia still had close family there. 'They're quite something, these Juchitec women,' Laureana had said; 'it's always good to arrive with one on your side.'

I could see immediately what Laureana meant. Sitting on a concrete bench across from us on the other side of the basketball court, were women built like Sumo wrestlers, great tauruses of womanhood, mountains of lymph and water and fat. They were wearing the traditional dress of the Juchiteca: the square, sleeveless, embroidered *huipil* blouse and great voluminous skirts; but, while their sons' hair was stylishly layered and lacquered, peroxided and permed, or coquettishly pony-tailed, theirs was parted unequivocally down the middle into two straight plaits. Their necks, also unlike their sons, who lifted their chins and posed like swans, vanished into the carapace of their backs like giant Galapagos tortoises. Their biceps bulged fat and strong as pumps.

There was something so mesmerizing about them, so powerfully magnetic, that I found myself struck by an extraordinary desire to be over there in their laps, being cradled and petted, enveloped in their enormous skirts, cushioned between their thighs. I wasn't sure if this came from some disturbing Freudian impulse on my part, or if their overwhelming eroticism, combined with a beefy maternalism, made everyone who came close to them want to be their baby, or their lover – or a bit of both. As they watched the game they held each others' hands, sometimes stroking the thigh or breast of the woman next to them, laughing with a dazzling éclat of gold- and nickel-capped teeth.

They were not women I would ever have imagined finding in Mexico. Not in a country that prides itself on a culture of *machismo*, where the ideal woman is the *mujer abnegada*, a self-sacrificing slave who suffers the iniquities of life in silence, like the Virgin herself. You wouldn't see these women walking on bleeding knees, praying for mercy, for the strength to endure their lot. Just from the way they sat together, vast, regal and uproarious, like a battalion of generals, they were telling the world they owned this place; while what men that there were – their husbands, or their other, heterosexual, sons – had taken a back seat, happy to peer at the action from behind their women's backs as inconspicuous and deferential as second lieutenants.

I found it difficult to register that this was principally an Indian place, too – not colonial or mixed-blood mestizo, like Mexico City or San Miguel. These women were native Zapotecs and most of them spoke Spanish only as a second language. Pure-blood Indians are still second-class citizens in Mexico. Liberal intellectuals and artists in the city may romanticize them, waxing lyrical about their handicrafts or their closeness to nature, but few ever come into contact with *los indígenas* or do anything to trumpet their plight. My friend Humberto was a notable exception. Commonly the prejudice persists in Mexico that Indians are backward, stupid and submissive. Thirty years ago in Chiapas Indians were forbidden to walk on the pavements. But here, I learnt, as we made our way back to the town square, you step out of the way of an oncoming Juchiteca. She sails the streets like a Spanish caravel, clipping corners with her skirts, parting the waves.

We sat down, Laureana, Natalia and I, around a table overlooking the Jardín Juárez. The main square was bustling, chaotic, untidy, well-lived in; not a place that was straitjacketed in its Sunday best for the tourist trade. Juchitán was unpretentious and unashamedly hard-working, a town boasting a population of nearly eighty thousand. It was thriving without being affluent, a modestly successful commercial and agricultural centre, a going concern. One down from the shop with luscious white-satin bridal gowns in the window was a showroom for new, bright-green John Deere tractors.

The houses in the centre of town were one-storey mostly, old but not ornate. There were none of the silver-fuelled flights of fantasy of San Miguel de Allende in the architecture here. There were colonnades and double storeys on the Jardín, a pretty nine-teenth-century church just off the main square and that was virtu-ally it. On the outskirts of Juchitán, where new barrios were springing up and the noise of hammering was almost continuous, the tarmac streets devolved into dirt-tracks, and pigs and chickens foraged through drifts of litter and blocked sewage ducts. Beyond the new *colonias* a wasteland of scrap and municipal rubbish stretched uninhibited as far as the eye could see. I hadn't seen a single tourist since we'd arrived. My white face drew puzzled stares.

The stall we'd sat down at had a limited, cholesterol-laden menu like all the rest around the Jardín: fried chicken, fried potatoes, and *garnachas* – deep-fried tortillas stuffed with ground beef, sizzling in pans of hot fat. A VW Beetle drew up, driven by a young but generous-sized Juchiteca with her middle-aged, diminutive husband in the passenger seat. They unpacked three hefty teenage daughters from the back seat. The family sat down next to us and I noticed with amazement that the woman did the ordering. I'd lost track of the times I'd been ignored by waiters in Mexico – left waiting while male customers arrived, ate, and then received their bills; my protestations deflected by a wave of insouciance or a supercilious sneer of disgust.

The man had his arm around his wife and was whispering suggestively into her ear. She roared with laughter and clouted him across the chest. He reeled back and pretended to fall out of his chair. Their daughter, who must have been twelve or thirteen, climbed on to her mother's lap. The other two daughters were eyeing up the evening strollers sauntering around the square.

Everyone, it seemed, was holding hands or hooked up to some-one else, fondling, stroking, hugging each other. Fathers carried sleeping babies in their arms; friends were laughing together, arm in arm, sharing popcorn (called, enchantingly *palomitas*, or 'little doves') or slices of sugared papaya. A young man walked by wearing a T-shirt that said in English 'Button Your Fly'. The girl on his arm had 'I LOVE MY MOTHER' on hers.

When it came to our turn to order, the proprietress was intrigued to see a foreigner. Natalia told her I'd come all the way from

England. 'Ah! You've come to learn the secrets of the Juchitecas,' she teased, nudging me with a cushiony elbow. 'Come to learn how to keep your man in order, how to make love to him like a Juchiteca? Well, what will it be, little one, some fried chicken or a nice big cock? Look at you, all skin and bones. You should fatten up a little – give your man something to hold on to at night.'

And suddenly I felt my shoulders sink a few notches; my eyebrows releasing themselves from what I recognized now had become a semi-permanent, anxious frown. I could almost feel myself swelling in size. I leant back in my chair like a film director and ordered everything she had to offer. Already I could see how insidious, how all-pervasive, the convention of sexual prejudice was in Mexico and how meek and accepting I'd become; but I was also beginning to understand that, even in Europe, I'd grown used to playing a role that was dependent on age-old perceptions of how women should be. I realized, with an inward whoop of liberation, this was going to be one hell of a week.

I'd virtually despaired of meeting up with Laureana and Natalia. There were fifteen minutes left before our plane departed Mexico City for the Pacific coastal resort of Huatulco, the nearest airport to Juchitán. I'd waited as long as I dared, before joining the queue for check-in which was crawling before me like treacle. The 'last minute passenger' queue was the longest and slowest of all.

Laureana and Natalia came flying through the automatic doors just as I reached the desk. Laureana's taxi had crashed into the back of a car and she'd had to leave it, crumpled and steaming, on the *Periférico* and look for another one – not an easy task on a three-lane motorway. She was a little bruised, she said, but seemed otherwise remarkably sanguine.

Laureana was in her late twenties. She worked as a photographer and sometimes as curator for her father's art gallery. Her Indian blood was unmistakable. She was short and slightly stocky with broad shoulders and a short, strong neck. She had long jet hair which she wore scraped back off her face with a centre parting, and lovely skin, and a smile that burst out of nowhere with a dazzle of pearly teeth. Her body, I noticed later, in the days of sharing a room together, was covered in tattoos, which had been inscribed by her younger brother, a renegade tattoo artist in Mexico City. There was one tattoo on her forearm of a dodo, which she particularly liked, she told me, for its absurdity; another, made up of coloured squares on the back of her arm, was her own design. It was an encrypted piece of poetry. Each square represented a different vowel, in sequence, of a phrase – 'let ocean grow again' – by the American poet, e e cummings.

She spoke perfect English with the faintest trace of an American accent. She'd been to school in New York for a couple of years and travelled the world in the wake of her father and his exhibitions. Her father had left Juchitán long before she was born and her mother, who was from Mexico City, had brought up Laureana and her brother mostly in the capital. But despite her cosmopolitan upbringing, Laureana was a dark horse. She had an unusual collection of international rock musician, writer and painter friends that she kept discreetly up her sleeve, as well as a strong, self-conscious sense of her own Indianness.

Natalia, on the other hand, two years older than Laureana, had grown up in Juchitán, although she now lived in Mexico City, writing poems and giving Zapotec cooking lessons to her friends. Natalia spoke Zapotec and often visited her family in Juchitán for weeks or months at a time. Not as archetypally good-looking as Laureana, she was still arrestingly attractive, despite railway tracks on her teeth which she tried to disguise with a touching flutter of her hand when she smiled. She was a woman with attitude, full of wry observations, with the tropics in her blood. Cool as a Cuban, she stood with arms crossed, one leg resting like a racehorse, and sized the world up as if she were undressing it. Young, free and single, she was as lithe as a runner-bean and hadn't yet put on the matriarchal pounds that her home town would expect of her after she'd married. As she sashayed through Departures in her short skirt, tight T-shirt and rubber wedge sandals, she took the panting gazes of Domestic Security with her.

Most of the people on our flight, who were not *chilangos* taking time out from Mexico City, were gringo tourists who had bypassed the anticipated horrors and high risks of the capital and were transferring directly to the oasis of the resort. There was an air of unreality as we spilled out of the plane an hour and a half later into the tropical humidity of 90 degrees in a fluster of Hawaiian shirts and golf-bags. Natalia was indignant. 'They probably don't know if they're on the Gulf Coast or the Pacific,' she said.

Huatulco was trying to become Mexico's latest Acapulco or Cancún. There's a new one every decade, Laureana said – another wild, pristine stretch of the coast turned into a playground, into another bit of Florida, with themed hotels, water-slides and amorphous swimming-pools, shopping-malls with freezing air-con and surround-sound *música ambiental*, and livid-green golf courses sucking up the precious freshwater supply. Huatulco was still a mess of cement mixers and treacly fresh asphalt, but it was already heading the way of the other big Mexican resorts. It had had its romantic interlude as a backpackers' paradise – palm-thatched huts and Indians selling fresh *ceviche* (raw fish salad marinated in lime juice) and garlic prawns on the beach, and now that the bulldozers and big money had arrived, Huatulco had become a haven for thieves and pickpockets and professional shysters. The razor wire was going up, and the electronic gates with sentinel guards, the street lights and lock-up garages. An ill-disguised shanty town was forming on the other side of the hill, near where all the garbage from the big hotels was being dumped. As fast as it was being created, Huatulco was destroying itself. Soon only the cheapest package tours would come here and the big money would begin to look for another 'magical setting' to develop, greasing the palms of the big politicians and the little local authorities on its way.

Thankfully, we were heading beyond the designer fantasy of Huatulco, down the coast, south, where no courtesy bus had ever been, leaving the world of manicured civic roundabouts behind us. There was no traffic on the winding mountain road and bursts of thick verdant air gusted through the windows of our hire-car bringing a sudden, overwhelming post-Mexico City euphoria. As she began to relax Laureana rubbed her neck and massaged her shoulders. 'Aaeee,' she moaned, 'that car crash has made me sore.' Gradually Natalia unfolded over the back seats, legs like telescopic tent-poles, and fell asleep.

Occasionally the road gave us glimpses of long, sandy, wind-blasted beaches where Huave Indians had put up tiny thatched fishing huts. The Huave, along with the Mixe, Zoque and Chontal Indians were the oldest inhabitants of the Isthmus of Tehuantepec but had been displaced by the more powerful Zapotecs when they moved down from the central plains of Oaxaca and colonized the area around the thirteenth century. Looked down upon by the proud and prosperous Zapotecs, the Huave eke out an existence on the margins of the Isthmus fishing and collecting turtles' eggs, illegally, to sell in the Zapotec markets.

It was several hours of hair-pin bends, dense secondary jungle and spectacular drop-offs before we began our descent to the plain of Tehuantepec, the stronghold of the coastal Zapotecs. The apron of land that stretched before us was barely 20 miles wide – a hazy patchwork of maize-fields and cattle-ranches, low thorn scrub and settlements, with the China-blue mountains of the Sierra Madre del Sur rising like battlements around it. The seaward side was fringed with salt-water lagoons, mangroves and sandspits.

Looking down on this oasis, it was easy to revive the geographical imperative that had made this stretch of land so valuable, so strategically desirable, to merchant man since he first set foot here on his nomadic peregrinations from North America. This was the only flat, traversible region in the tight continental squeeze that gives birth to Mesoamerica. Virtually all traffic passing between the two American continents, from ancient times to the turn of the twentieth century, would have found itself funnelled through this plain, an avenue that is still known today simply as *El Istmo* as if the rest of the Isthmus doesn't enter the equation. Mayans traded here. The Aztecs made every effort to secure it within the Empire, valuing not only the north–south trade it reaped, but its access to the Pacific. Cortés himself launched the first ocean-going ships in the Americas from Tehuantepec's lagoons. The enterprising, strong-willed Zapotecs who'd made this land their home were perfectly placed to make a mint, and to evolve the most remarkable market culture in America.

The same impetus that brought the Zapotecs here brought Weetman Pearson to the Isthmus in the 1890s, while he was still working on the Grand Canal in Mexico City and the country's main seaport at Veracruz. The coastal road we'd been travelling along from Huatulco met the inland road to Tehuantepec at Salina Cruz, a deep-water port and one of the most difficult Pearson had ever had to build. It was now a busy oil refinery bristling with radio antennae and holding tanks and low-cost housing for oil workers banked up on the hillsides all around.

Salina Cruz had been a punishing project. There was only a slight natural bay here, no reefs or spits to build on, and in order to provide safe harbour for the enormous cargo containers he aimed to attract Pearson had had to construct a mile of breakwaters into the Pacific Ocean. Storms repeatedly smashed up the work. One devastating hurricane cost the company half a million dollars.

But Salina Cruz was crucial for the success of President Díaz's most ambitious project – part of his grand scheme to modernize Mexico and make it a world power: the Tehuantepec Railway. Ever since Columbus and Cortés opened up the possibilities of seafaring trade around the Americas, man had become obsessed with finding a gateway between the Atlantic Ocean and the Pacific, an alternative to the long and hazardous voyage around Cape Horn. The Tehuantepec Isthmus, a narrow plug of land 190 miles across as the crow flies, was an obvious contender. As early as 1524 Cortés was sending expeditions to the Isthmus to look for the strait that many pilots believed must link the two oceans at this point. This channel was, Cortés wrote to the King of Spain, '. . . the thing I wish to meet with more than anything else in the world, for the great service that it seems to me Your Majesty would derive'.

Cortés searched in vain for the mythical passage and, finally convinced it didn't exist, consoled himself with the fact that, having obtained enormous grants of land on the Isthmus from the Spanish Crown, as well as rights over the 'still and running waters' in the region, he would eventually cut a canal, or at least a road, across it himself.

Cortés never saw his dream realized. In broken health and ruined by the cost of numerous expeditions carried out at his own expense searching for gold and silver in the north of Mexico, Cortés returned to Spain in 1540 where he accompanied King Charles V on his expedition against the Ottoman Turks in Algiers. The expedition was a catastrophic failure and it spelled the end for Cortés. Barely ten years earlier, in 1528, Cortés had been showered with honours: he was granted twenty-two towns in Mexico as *encomiendas* – land entitlements; and given the name 'Marqués del Valle de Oaxaca' by the Spanish Crown. But now the great conquistador was no longer in favour. He spent his last years in vain entreaties to his king and in 1547, disgraced and neglected like Columbus and Vasco da Gama before him, died near Seville. His last request was that his body be returned to Mexico and buried in the convent at Coyoacán – a small town, now a neighbourhood of Mexico City, that had been Cortés's base after the fall of Tenochtitlán. It was only in 1629, however, that Cortés's last wish was granted.

Not until the late eighteenth century was the subject of the Tehuantepec inter-oceanic channel seriously addressed again, but plans by pioneers such as the great scientist explorer, Alexander von Humboldt, were interrupted by uprisings for Mexican independence. Then war broke out with the United States, the American armies sweeping through the northern states of Mexico and reaching the threshold of the capital itself. An armistice was arranged in August 1847 to discuss peace terms offered by the US but to the Mexicans' disgust these included a demand for rights of free passage to American citizens and merchandise through the Isthmus of Tehuantepec. War was resumed and Mexico City fell. Peace conferences were called again and once again the Americans pressed the Tehuantepec clause. But the Mexicans held out and agreed instead to sign the treaty of 1848, granting the wild northern territories of Texas, California, New Mexico and Arizona, along with parts of Colorado, Nevada and Utah (half of the whole of Mexico) to the United States for the paltry sum of $15 million, rather than let Tehuantepec go.

By the time Porfirio Díaz came to power in 1877 all plans for a canal had been rejected as unfeasible – even by Mexican standards – and the emphasis shifted to the construction of a railway. The Americans were still desperate to be in on the action but Díaz, wounded by the United States' continuing heavy-handed and patronizing attitude towards Mexico, and his own humiliating treatment by American diplomats and big businessmen, deliberately wooed European and especially British contractors, finally awarding the concession to 'S. Pearson & Son of London and Mexico' in 1896.

The Americans were outraged and, seeing the Tehuantepec Railway as a direct threat to their own Pacific Railway, decided to enter the competition by building a canal at Panama. They bought the concession in 1902 from the French engineer De Lesseps for $40 million, over twice what they'd paid for the northern states of Mexico.

While the Americans raced to build the canal, Pearson embarked on what he realized was the 'greatest of all my undertakings to date'. The track would begin at Puerto México (later renamed Coatzacoalcos) on the Gulf Coast, a port built specifically by Pearson for the project; it would cross the turbulent Jaltapec river, penetrating swampland and rainforest, then rise through innumerable rocky chasms and canyons to the village of Rincón Antonio in the uplands where a town would be established with marshalling and repair yards, with workshops and houses for the European rail staff; then it would sweep on across the Sierra Madre ridge in two horseshoe curves before dropping back down to the town of Tehuantepec and the new port of Salina Cruz. After battling against time and geography, as well as earthquakes, floods, landslides, humidity, yellow fever and malaria, the Tehuantepec Railway was completed in just four years.

On 25 January 1907, the ageing Díaz made the triumphant journey to the Isthmus with a colourful cortège of cabinet ministers and foreign diplomats, and his friend Weetman Pearson at his side. They arrived at Salina Cruz to meet the SS *Arizonian* from Hawaii, loaded with sugar bound for Philadelphia. Díaz gave the solemn signal for one of the giant cranes to load the first bags of sugar on to the freight car, which he then sealed himself, opening the gates to the railway with golden keys.

The party rode jubilantly off for the Gulf Coast, chinking their champagne glasses, no doubt relishing the anguish of the Americans who were still thirteen years away from finishing the Panama

Canal. At Puerto México the cars were ceremoniously unsealed, the cranes set moving and the sugar loaded aboard the SS *Luckenbach* bound for Philadelphia. Pearson made a speech pronouncing this the first load of an estimated 600,000 tons of cargo a year. Díaz, the dictator, replied with fine phrases on the beauties of Progress and Friendship among nations, confidently predicting that '. . . the name of Sir Weetman Pearson will endure and be held in honour in this historic region long after the 80lb rails over which our party has glided so smoothly have been eroded by age'. A new era of global trading had begun.

Pearson's predictions (unlike that of the President) were, to begin with at least, underestimates. Twenty trains ran daily in both directions carrying well in excess of 600,000 tons. By 1911 over a million tons of cargo passed across the Isthmus. But then Díaz was toppled and Mexico plunged into Revolution.

Remarkably, while foreign businesses across the country were being forcefully appropriated, or looted, or simply burned to the ground in a nationalistic backlash against Díaz's xenophilia, Pearson continued to manage the Tehuantepec Railway unmolested. But in 1918 the Carranza government decided it had had enough. It was too galling to leave the shining success of the railway in the hands of a foreigner. It was time, as Carranza put it, 'to put an end to the tyranny exercised by Pearson in Tehuantepec'. Amazingly, considering the times, the terms of Pearson's contract were honoured and Pearson was bought out by the government. But the railway swiftly fell into disrepair, its services became erratic and untrustworthy; it began to make serious losses and, when the Panama Canal finally opened in 1920, transoceanic trade moved decisively away from Tehuantepec.

For Pearson it was a frustrating end to a remarkable achievement. The project, he considered, had never been seriously put to the test and for the rest of his life he would wonder how, given the chance, his beloved Tehuantepec Railway might have stood up to the competition of the Panama Canal.

As we cut inland from Salina Cruz past the town of Tehuantepec towards Juchitán there were unmistakable signs of the faded glory of the railway years – rusting railway sidings, a crumbling grand hotel, a nostalgic suggestion of London or Glasgow in a slipping Palladian façade. I was half-expecting to pass a peeling red pillarbox by the side of the road or someone wearing a battered bowler-hat.

Instead, as we bowled along the 'Panamericana', the vaingloriously-named Pan-American Highway, we passed yet another derelict, one-horse town. This one was called Pearson. The sign was a honeycomb of bullet-holes, as hollow as Díaz's prophecy that Pearson's name would be immortalized in Tehuantepec.

'That was my husband's great-great-grandfather,' I commented, casting aside my usual reticence about the British 'tyrant' in my gloom, 'he built a railway here.' Once again I needn't have worried. Laureana looked at me amazed through the puffs of dust billowing through the windows. 'Really?' she exclaimed, 'our great-great grandfather was his lawyer.' I began to wonder whether all the Mexicans I befriended would be descended from Pearson's legal team.

The market of Juchitán explains it all. This is where the authority of the Juchiteca is concentrated – in a palatial colonial building with Spanish-style colonnades that takes up one whole side of the town square. It's a world of exclusively female creation around which the whole economy – the whole of Juchitán – revolves. Here the vitality, sexuality and size of the Juchitecas are mirrored by what they sell – a superabundance, an animal-vegetable-mineral cornucopia.

Traffic to and from the market brings the centre of Juchitán to a standstill every day. Fastidious town-planners have been lobbying for an out-of-town site for the market for years. They want to rid the Jardín Juárez of all the burros and carts, the wheelbarrows and lorries, the medieval stench and squalor, the ebullient chaos and clamour of commerce. But the Juchitecas won't stand for it. Time and again they've held the authorities to ransom, threatening to cease trading altogether if they're moved from their rightful place in the heart of Juchitán.

Inside, the building is like a warehouse, a vast depot, with gangways be-puddled from constant sluicing, running criss-cross between the stalls. There are ropes, spurs, stirrups, harnesses;

machetes, saws, hammers, adzes; locks, hinges, latches; brooms, hammocks, buckets; glazed pots, gourd bowls, aluminium pans; sandals, shoes, shirts and skirts; and glass showcases adazzle with jewellery: gold chains and tiered earrings, gypsy hoops, bangles, fake pearls and glass beads, and necklaces made out of solid gold coins worth 4000 pesos ($400) apiece. The *centenarios* date back to the building of the railway when gold flowed through the Isthmus, and these are what the women wear, now, for fiestas. It's the only real investment they're ever likely to make: proof, as if they ever needed it, of their regal status.

But the real essence of the Juchiteca is where the food is – in the food halls and the stalls that spill outside on to the street. Despite the bustle and the grind, the carting about and cleaving and chopping, the aggressive tackle of business, the atmosphere is earthily feminine. This is the Juchitecas' power-base. The only men are sweeping up vegetable peelings or humping boxes. There are no men behind the counters, though later in the afternoon one or two may show their faces to hand over their pay-cheques or to ask for pocket-money: they spend the early, cool hours of the morning toiling in the fields or working the fishing boats, leaving the Juchitecas to preside here dominant and uncontested, goddesses of bounty, triumphing over an orgy of fare as if the groaning tables were a manifestation of their exuberance, as if these sierras of food had risen spontaneously, in celebration of the women's vitality and mass.

There are pyramids of sweet-smelling guavas, papayas, watermelons, pineapples, custard apples, lemons, limes, and avocados. There are *zapotes*, the sapodilla plums from which the Náhuatl-speaking peoples coined their word for the Zapotecs (a people properly known, in their own language, as the 'Biniza'). Then there are red onions and garlic and a multitude of different black, yellow, red and green chillies so powerful your whole body reacts as you pass them, prickling your skin and your eyes and your nose.

Then there's meat: jerked beef, dried beef, ground beef, whole heads of cows peeled of skin and covered in flies; bright yellow chicken with its egg sacs in oil; stuffed suckling pig; ropes of neon *chorizo* sausage stuffed by hand; live cockerels, partridges, turkeys, guinea pigs and rabbits.

There are sweet pastries and loaves of brown sugar and *bu 'pu* – foaming pre-Columbian hot chocolate served in clay bowls and flavoured with toasted petals of frangipani. There's refreshing *horchata de coco* made from coconut milk and rice water with sugar and cinnamon; savoury tamales bound up in banana leaves; eight types of tortilla, and gigantic oven-baked *totopos* – huge round biscuits pressed with the imprint of a hundred fat fingertips. There are fresh cheeses in baskets or frames; piles of transparent turtle eggs dug up by the Huave from the beach; fried grasshoppers; ants' eggs. Then seafood: shrimps, sea snails, mussels, blue crabs, monster prawns ten inches long, buckets of baby squid. And fish: dried fish, salt fish in boxes, conger eel, whitebait, all kinds of fresh fish on ice. And ultimately, live iguanas, the greatest delicacy of all, legs tied behind their backs and mouths sewn shut, blinking sagely in the shade like strange, primeval witnesses of history. The women carry everything on their heads. Iguana sellers arriving in the market look like Medusas with live reptiles clinging to their hair.

Turnover in the market is fast and furious. It's a far cry from the village markets up in the mountains where an Indian might sit all day in front of a little pile of tomatoes or a handful of guavas and not make a centavo. This is the Isthmus equivalent of Covent Garden and Billingsgate, Harrods and Waitrose. And these women are professionals. They are the check-out girls, the buyers, the managers, trade-union leaders, bankers and accountants rolled into one.

Naturally extrovert, vivacious and enterprising, the Zapotecs took to the Isthmus economy like turtles to the sea. They had none of the timidity or the innate distrust felt by so many of the other indigenous Indians for foreigners. On the contrary, the Zapotecs were uninhibited and adventurous and mingled joyfully with the passing traffic. Since moving from the Valley of Oaxaca high in the mountains, the coastal Zapotecs have mixed their blood with the local Mixe, Zoque, Huave and Chontal, as well as with Spaniards, French, African slaves, Chinese, Arabs, Lebanese, Syrians and Americans – every race, in short, that has ever touched down on the Isthmus. Fair hair and blue eyes are not unknown and are said to originate from Pearson's time, from the English and Irish posted here to build the railway.

Yet none of this international exposure diminished the Tehuanos' fierce sense of identity. If anything, it strengthened it. They remained Zapotec through and through, independent to the point of impudence, each separate town on the Isthmus bound together by ties of intense local nationalism, cooperation and competition, like miniature Greek city states.

Of all the Zapotecs, Juchitecos are renowned as the most ferocious and untamable of the lot. They boast an unbroken record of loyalty to the causes of democracy, equality and justice throughout the turbulent history of Mexico. But their motivation was never exactly that of the altruistic ideal. The Juchitecos fought principally for Juchitán, even if this meant changing sides mid-war, betraying allies, and fighting neighbouring Zapotecs, like the Tehuanos of Tehuantepec. All was justified in the struggle for autonomy in the Isthmus.

Neither isolated nor too close to the vortex of central government, the Isthmus Zapotecs learnt to adapt, accommodate and even profit from the periodic incursions and recessions of power in the Isthmus without being crushed by them. Their response was either rebellious or opportunistic, but it was always in the spirit of self-interest. The Aztec Empire battled to retain authority in the area but the Isthmus was on the very periphery of the Triple Alliance's zone of control. When it pleased them the Isthmus Zapotecs encouraged the Aztecs, pitting them against their enemies, and developing their own profitable trade with Tenochtitlán. When the Aztecs became unacceptably high-handed, the Zapotecs rebelled, inflicting serious defeats on the imperial army, most notably at Guiengola, an impressive Zapotec stronghold with thick defensive walls, high on a hill seven miles outside the modern town of Tehuantepec – where you can still see the remains of two pyramids, a ball court and a sixty-four-room palacio.

When the conquistadors arrived in Oaxaca in 1522 the Juchitecos, like the rest of the Zapotecs and so many other indigenous peoples in Mexico, saw a chance to free themselves from old enemies – like, as always, the Aztecs or, closer to home, the Mixtecs of highland Oaxaca. But when the new devil proved worse than the one they already knew, Juchitán and the Isthmus Zapotecs provided the Spaniards with some of the fiercest resistance they encountered in New Spain. Defeated (European diseases played their decisive part, as always, decimating the population of Tehuantepec from 24,000 tributary heads of household at the time of conquest to just over 6000 by 1550, and to under 4000 by 1580), the Isthmus Zapotecs cleverly learnt to adapt to life under colonial rule, securing for themselves a remarkable degree of autonomy in the shadow of their new masters and, crucially, retaining the monopoly of local food produce and control of the basic Isthmus economy.

By 1810, Juchitán was the stronghold of Zapotec culture in the Isthmus and spearheading the Tehuantepec contribution to the War of Independence. Then, in another about-turn, the 1850s saw Juchitecos, led by the maverick local hero, José Gregorio Meléndez, allying themselves with Mexican conservatives in exchange for promises of local autonomy. But in the 1860s, they fought with the liberals, led by Benito Juárez, against French imperialists. Later that decade they turned decisively against Juárez, a native Zapotec from the highlands and governor of Oaxaca, when he determined to bring the Isthmus and the 'unruly rascals' of Juchitán back under control. 'It would take a great deal of time to describe the state of immorality and disorder in which the residents of Juchitán have lived since very ancient times,' railed Juárez, the future President of Mexico in an address to the state of Oaxaca, 'you know well their great excesses. You are not unaware of their depredations under the colonial regime and their attacks against the agents of the Spanish government. You know that during the centralized government they mocked the armed forces that the central power sent to repress their crimes, defeating and causing damage to it, making fun of its leaders, and scorning the local authorities . . .'

This was Juchitán in a nutshell. Alone of virtually all the indigenous peoples of Mexico, the Juchitecos find themselves ambivalent to Mexico's one and only Indian President. Though their main square is named after him, Juchitecos are proud to be the only Mexican Indians to have caused the great Benito Juárez, hero of the Republic, so much trouble. Unbelievably, it was Juárez, a full-blooded Zapotec, who, in an effort to unify and modernize his wayward country, tried to deny his own birthright and Mexico's indigenous heritage: 'No hay Indios en México; somos todos Mexicanos,' he declared ('There are no Indians in Mexico; we are all Mexicans.'). And the Zapotecs never forgave him.

When Porfirio Díaz (who was also, remarkably, of Zapotec extraction and from the same town – Oaxaca – as Benito Juárez) appeared on the scene setting himself up as a young liberal fighting the Mexican corner against foreign imperialists, the Juchitecos gave him their wholehearted support. Then withdrew it, when he went over to the conservatives. Like Juárez before him, the dictator was forced into battle against this recalcitrant town, the persistent thorn in Mexico's side, only managing to subdue the Juchitecos when he levelled the forests where the guerrillas were hiding and threw the Juchitec women in jail.

The Juchitecas proved as formidable in war as their men. When the Revolution broke out in 1910 and toppled Díaz, the Juchitecas marched alongside the troops carrying their husbands' Mausers. The town contributed a thousand men and ten generals to the side of Alvaro Obregón in the war, and in 1920 the one-armed revolutionary arrived in Juchitán to thank the town for its extra-ordinary effort. 'There is no cemetery in the Republic,' he told them, 'that doesn't contain a Juchiteco who died for the cause.'

But Juchitán's belligerence wasn't to be confined comfortably to the pages of history. It erupted again only recently with spectacular effect, setting an example for anti-governmental rebellions across the rest of Mexico. In 1981 Juchitán became the first town to wrestle its autonomy back from the clutches of the PRI, electing its own mayor, leader of COCEI – the 'Coalición Obrera Campesina Estudiantil del Istmo', a leftist, Juchitán-based, worker-student-peasant coalition party – in defiance of national government. 'The Juchitecos are a bunch of no-good bums, rabble-rousers and drunkards,' declared a COCEI representative, Daniel López Nelio, at the time, 'and I am their leader.'

The Juchitecas, as usual, played their own characteristic, high-profile part in the struggle. Traditionally, they aren't involved in the day-to-day running of the town. There have rarely been women elected to local government – which is why, many anthropologists insist, Juchitán cannot be described in the strictest sense as a matriarchy. But their political clout is undeniable. It's no coincidence that the municipal offices are directly above the market. Looking up at the shuttered windows on the first floor it's impossible to imagine how any man sitting around the table in City Hall could remain unaffected by the intimidating presence of their women below, by the clamour and charisma climbing the stairs.

As the tensions mounted in Juchitán in the 1970s, it was the women who took the rebellion out of the government offices and into the streets. It was their pictures in the papers, their voices in the news. In demonstration after demonstration they marched through Juchitán in phalanxes, six abreast, in red *huipiles*, COCEI banners held high, shielding their mayor like the nucleus of an egg. Arm in arm they blocked the roads and faced the riot squads; they barricaded politicians in their offices; lay in the streets in front of the army tanks and jeeps; organized strikes; ran messengers; distributed pamphlets; negotiated face to face with angry soldiers and policemen to free their husbands and sons from jail. They became known as the 'shock troops' of COCEI. 'My blood is not hot but it boils every time I see a PRI member,' exploded one Juchiteca interviewed by the international press, despite having been incarcerated twice and having her hair shaved off with an old razor blade. 'They can fuck their mothers, but I will not leave the struggle.'

Dozens of men and women from Juchitán were killed in two decades of fighting with the PRI authorities, but eventually the government was forced to capitulate and Juchitán's David-like example sent indigenous protest movements springing up all over the country. The chink in the PRI's armour swiftly became a crack until now, some twenty years later, it's beginning to fall away altogether. In Senator Zinser's terms, Juchitán was the first apple to fall from the tree.

Laureana, Natalia and I have come to the market with a purpose. Overnight, Laureana's neck has seized up and she's in considerable discomfort, suffering, she assumes, from a mild case of whiplash.

She wants to have a *limpia*, a healing or – literally – a 'cleansing', from one of Juchitán's famous *curanderas*. 'She's remarkable, this Juchiteca. She's a grand old lady,' Laureana tells me; 'she cured my back last time I was here. You feel as if she's sucking all the bad energy out of you. The ache just left.'

There are male healers in Juchitán, too, but traditionally they're given the more practical side of things to deal with – broken bones and the like. It's the women who preside over the powerful mystical, spiritual dimension, as if, by adding this to their food-based repertoire, they can be totally responsible for keeping body and soul together. 'They see things in terms of bad spirits and devils,' Laureana expands, 'to a *curandero*, there's no such thing as an accident. There's always some malevolent force responsible.'

We find Na Marcelina caretaking her daughter's jewellery store. She's a wrinkled Mrs Tiggywinkle figure dressed from head to toe in widow's black, her grey plaits tied with black ribbons, black beads and a silver crucifix around her neck. She gives each girl an enveloping hug, face blossoming into smiles, her doughy hands clasping Natalia's all the time they're talking, catching up on gossip in Zapotec.

When Natalia introduces us Na Marce's beady black eyes give me the once-over. 'She's checking your aura,' explains Laureana.

They put me down for a *limpia*, too – I'm not surprised my aura's in need of a dust-down – and we're given a shopping-list of special ingredients to bring to her house for our appointment the next morning. Laureana writes them down: 3 lemons, 2 green chillies, 2 large bunches of basil, a red onion, some orange-blossom water and (emphatically) a duck egg each. She won't trust a chicken's egg, Na Marce says. Its shell is too brittle and often cracks under the strain.

It's a testing experience trying to execute our shopping list. To Juchitecas, food is irresistibly bound up with sex. Everything on sale seems to be an aphrodisiac, and the Juchitecas have a field day bringing blushes to the cheeks of strangers, particularly if they happen to be a wide-eyed *turista*. Nothing, it appears, is without a double meaning. 'Does your man have a sweet penis or a salty penis?' a woman roars at me as I pass by, lifting a handful of slippery pink prawns from her basket. The female butcher, the *carnicera*, joins in, screaming with laughter: 'Fancy some real meat, *gringa*?' The word for eggs is the same as 'testicles' so we get a tirade when we ask for some: 'You beating some eggs tonight, sisters?' The down on the medlar fruit, I learn in passing, is soft pubic hair. Bananas are suggestive everywhere but here it's the enormous plantains (*plátanos machos*) that are the obvious joke. You can't ask for a bunch without everyone leaping in to suggest places to stick them.

When they're not toying with their customers like cats with mice the women banter together in Zapotec. Their native tongue clearly delights them. Zapotec is far more elastic and spirited, certainly more sensuous, than the language of the conquerors. A sort of liquid sing-song, staccato yet musical, Isthmus Zapotec has been called the Italian of the Americas, yet it uses a tonal system like Chinese, relying on pitch and emphasis to change the meaning of a word. Natalia tries to give me a crash course. *Bi:ži'*, she tells me, with the first *i* long, the second high and choked, means 'bullfrog'. *Bi'ži*, with the first *i* choked, the second low in pitch means 'seed'. While *Bǐzí*, the final *i* pronounced high, is the fruit of the pitaya cactus. *Bizi'ì*, though, with the last *i* choked, then re-articulated in the lower tone, means 'handed back'; and *mbìzi'*, with a nasalized *b*, a low first *i* and a normal-pitched, choked second *i*, means 'dried up'. I'm utterly confounded, much to Natalia's glee. 'And don't say *gí* when you mean *gi*,' she laughs, 'or you'll be saying, put out the "shit" instead of the "fire".'

Its pitfalls, though, are part of Zapotec's vibrancy, part of its charm. It's a language that lends itself to puns and poetry, metaphors, witticisms and wordplay like Náhuatl and most of the indigenous languages of Mexico but unlike Spanish, which, with its Latinate taste for semantics sounds clumsy and obvious, even stupid, to the Zapotec ear. Natalia illustrates the point as we pass the fish counters by singing a few verses from one of Juchitán's most erotic songs – the *Huachinango*, or Red Snapper, song – which is sung at fiestas the morning after the wedding night. It describes a voracious 'red-hot' snapper who's bleeding because she's stuffed herself with so many plantains. It's all about bloodstains and broken hymens, fishy smells and pink urine and it underlines more than a linguistic divide since Natalia finds it sensuous and funny and I can't help finding it disgusting.

It's this blatant eroticism that gave rise, at the turn of the twentieth century, to a misleading reputation for Juchitán and its women. Visitors, enchanted by the sight of bare-breasted nymphs bathing in the rivers of the Isthmus, and hearing tantalizing tales of promiscuity, were either scandalized or fascinated, but couldn't resist comparisons with the South Sea idyll where girls would loll about Gauguin-like all day, fanning themselves and eating fruit and doing their hair, taking pleasure with any man lucky enough to come their way. The very name Juchitán – from the Náhuatl lxtacxochitlán, shortened to Xochitlán, meaning Place of White Flowers – seemed to suggest a place of bounteous ease. The mythology brought Diego Rivera here in the 1920s, who subsequently used the exotic river scenes as inspiration for his famous *The Bather of Tehuantepec*, a painting that marked a breakthrough in his art and opened the doors for his idealized Indian-based re-evaluation of the spirit of Mexico. His wife, Frida Kahlo, and many of his mistresses dressed 'á la Tehuana' at home, in Mexico City.

In the 1930s the American poet Langston Hughes came here. So did French photographer Henri Bresson, and the Italian-American actress/photographer Tina Modotti. And when Russian film-maker Sergei Eisenstein came to El Istmo he was knocked off his feet. His film *Qué Viva México* was never finished although he regarded it as the great oeuvre of his life. He filmed scenes of the Isthmus, Zapotecas naked from the waist up, swinging lasciviously in their hammocks. 'You are left with the tenacious idea that Eden was not located somewhere between the Tigris and the Euphrates,' he wrote feverishly in his diary, 'but, of course, here, somewhere between the Gulf of Mexico and Tehuantepec.'

But life is not an idyll in the Isthmus and the Juchitecos are emphatic about the hard graft it is to make ends meet. 'Juchitán is not an easy place to live,' Natalia tells me. 'It's true the Isthmus has natural advantages like the sea, the salt pans, the lagoons. The plains are fertile and there were huge forests in the old days – we had everything we needed to produce a fantastic variety of food.

But it never just dropped off the trees or fell into our baskets. It takes hard work to make all this happen.'

The climate doesn't help. El Istmo is blasted constantly either by wind, or by rain. In the wet season – late May through October – torrential storms in the mountains inundate the plain below with floodwater and silt. The rains bring waterborne diseases, fevers like *la quebradora* (dengue fever), and a plague of *sancudos* – a type of mosquito with a bite like a burro. The rest of the year – the dry season – is characterized by *El Norte*, a merciless north wind that whips up sand and dirt and sends it lashing through every crack and crevice into houses and courtyards. It brings conjunctivitis, sore throats, asthma and colds.

Juchitán has the rawest deal of all the towns on the Isthmus, Natalia insists. Juchitecos joke about it, she says. They say their patron saint Vicente Ferrer, went to great lengths to find the worst place in the region. When he found a spot deep in arid scrub, prone to flooding, where fresh water was so deep underground it couldn't be welled, where the air was thick and stultifying, he's supposed to have exclaimed, 'This is it! This is perfect. Here there are obstacles and dangers and my children will become hardworking and swift; not indolent and dispirited like people elsewhere.'

It was the rigours of life as well as its great opportunities that gave rise to the phenomenon of the Juchiteca. While the men laboured all the hours available to them in the fields or the salt-pans or the fishing-boats, the women were left to manage the market. It enabled them to keep their children out of the worst of the heat and the dust and the wind. And it catapulted them to power. While the men remained *campesinos* at heart, the women became muscular bargainers and international traders, as well as frontline defenders of Juchitec autonomy and Zapotec culture. Market life in the Isthmus expanded the Juchitecas' horizons as magnificently as it expanded their girths. They were running the show.

At last there's just one item left on our shopping list. We cross the street to buy basil. There's a cluster of flower sellers on the corner with buckets of tuberoses, agapanthus, arum lilies and hibiscus and baskets full of fresh rose petals. An old woman is threading frangipani flowers. We take some basil, whole bushes of it, roots and all, dripping from a bucket, but it's not until I hear the voice of the basil seller that I notice she's a man. She's wearing the traditional long skirts and braided hair of a Juchiteca but her hands are big and hairy and there's a prominent Adam's apple above the collar of her *huipil* blouse.

She flashes a beefy, saucy grin as she hands back my change. Natalia and Laureana laugh when they see my confusion. Peeved, I ask them if there are any straight men left in Juchitán. They can't give me statistics but they're confident that at least a third of Juchitecos must be gay, and many more have homosexual encounters but don't consider themselves gay because they take the 'active' rather than the 'passive' role. Wives are never jealous, they say, of their husbands' homosexual affairs – or vice versa.

Laureana and Natalia refer to gays as *muxes*, a Zapotec word, and, though the phenomenon is widespread across El Istmo and across much of the Tehuantepec peninsula, Juchitán, they tell me, is so famous for homosexuality it's known locally as 'Muchitán'.

Poor old Saint Vicente Ferrer is blamed for this, too. 'They say God gave San Vicente the job of cleaning up South America, told him to get rid of all the promiscuous homosexuals on the continent,' says Natalia, 'so he went around collecting them all up and putting them in his suitcase. But by the time he got to Juchitán his suitcase was so heavy he dropped it and all the *muxes* in South America fell out and they ended up here.'

Arguments abound among outsiders about whether this extraordinary sexual freedom and the prevalence of gays among the Isthmus Zapotecs is a genetic or a cultural thing – nature or nurture. Anthropologists and sociologists have tied themselves in knots over the matter. What is known is that transvestism and homosexuality were openly accepted in the indigenous cultures of Mexico when Cortés arrived. The conquistadors were outraged by the 'wicked practices' they encountered, particularly on the Gulf Coast. 'Sodomy', if we are to believe the homophobic Bernal Díaz, was rife, and there were 'boys dressed as women who practised that accursed vice for profit'.

Even among the warrior Aztecs, who were among the most sexually restrained of the Mexican civilizations, sex was not the confusing, torturous issue it was to the macho Europeans. There was no notion or rhetoric implying the sexual subordination of women. Women were seen as different, but equal in status to men. Though she could not take part in public office, an Aztec woman, like the present-day Zapotec, could be a powerful trader or merchant, and as a curer or midwife she could attain priestly status. She could achieve economic independence and was free to dispose of her own wealth as she chose, and her role as mistress of her household and of her family was formidable and respected.

Sex, even to the Aztecs, was a great pleasure – for men and women. It was natural for women to be sexually enthusiastic and to expect sexual gratification. The vagina was the 'place of joy'. Lust and eroticism and sexual playfulness were celebrated. There were none of the Christian ideas of male aggression and female submission bound up in the act of sex; no suggestion that carnal relations were sinful; that the sexual act itself was an assault – the man an invader, the woman a reluctant sexual 'conquest'. In Aztec descriptions sex was represented not as a matter of women being penetrated, but of males being depleted, their 'honey' engulfed by a voracious 'cave'.

Though there was a sharp distinction between the sexes, at least among the Nahua peoples of central Mexico, that depicted a clear ideal of male and female virtues, the Western idea of 'sexual opposites', or of a 'battle' between the sexes, did not exist in the native Mexican mind. Men and women were mutually dependent and good for each other. And there was none of the pathological fear of homosexuality displayed by the Spaniards, even among the Aztecs who discouraged and sometimes even punished the practice. In the more liberated world of the Aztec pantheon, away from the human need to adhere to strict social codes, many of the Aztec gods were androgenous, their relationships with each other sexually ambiguous.

In Juchitán, though, no one could care less about the theories or origins of promiscuity and homosexuality in their town. *Muxes* are a celebrated fact of life, almost a third sex. Traditionally *muxes* dress, like the basil seller, as Juchitecas. They are honorary women and therefore the only men allowed to sell in the market. Or they wear *pantalones* like other men, the only give-away a flamboyant handkerchief or a flower in their hair. It's only in recent years, says Natalia, that *muxes* have started modelling themselves on soap opera stars like the birds of paradise we saw preening themselves on the basketball court.

Muxes have a reputation as hard workers. They're gifted and creative, and – until they're crossed in love, at least – patient and kind. Apart from selling in the market and, most popularly, working as *cantineras* or barmaids, they become cooks, seam-stresses, hairdressers, florists, set-designers for parties and wed-dings, or they simply stay at home to mind the children and do the housework – a job that is regarded with exceptional admiration in Juchitán. They've even been known to adopt children themselves. The son of one *muxe* coined the touching, and eminently accurate name for his combination parent – 'Mampa'.

Juchitecas are generally pleased when their sons prove to be gay. Natalia remembers her family commiserating with one woman when she gave birth to yet another son. 'Never mind, perhaps this one will be a *muxe*,' they consoled her. Teenage heterosexual boys, as all mothers know, are bound to bring you heartache. They'll be disobedient, idle, wasteful, staying out all hours, endlessly looking for somewhere to 'raise their mast', getting into fights. And they're expensive. In order to get a son off your hands, to make him acceptable to prospective in-laws, you may have to set him up with some money or some animals or even some land; you'll certainly have to throw the wedding party.

There's no stigma attached to sexual preference in Juchitán, so having a homosexual son doesn't give rise to the traumatic soul-searching and sessions on the couch that the most liberal of mothers in the West have to contend with. And without the overriding prejudices of a macho population like the rest of Mexico, there's no bullying or persecution. Homosexuality is as natural and straightforward as heterosexuality; it's a physical reality. As Natalia succinctly, and unforgettably, puts it: 'God puts the heat in different holes, that's all.'

Na Marcelina's door is opened by a *muxe* maid with hairy legs, a frilly apron and fluffy slippers. 'Enter,' 'she' lisps, brandishing a duster as if it were a lace handkerchief and spinning on her heel for us to follow. We wait in a tiny internal courtyard, typical of Zapotec houses, under an *almendro* with a white-washed trunk and a simple wooden crucifix tied to it.

Moments later, Na Marce emerges, her long grey hair loose and crimped from its customary plaits. Her moon-like face breaks into a beam. Almost imperceptibly she goes about the preparations for our *limpias*, chatting as she does so in a soft, continuous burble, then moving things about and gathering them together inexorably as a lava flow. She dons a white overall with a masonic-looking symbol crudely stitched above the left breast that makes her look suddenly and disconcertingly like a Druid.

She wants to tackle me first. Laureana and Natalia are ushered away to a veranda where they swing about in hammocks and wait their turn. I'm shown to a stool in the centre of the courtyard and told to take my shirt off.

I'm uneasy about the protocol (hands clasped in prayer? head bowed? eyes open or shut?) and I'm feeling a bit self-conscious anyway in my Marks & Spencer light-support bra, so I just sit with my hands on my knees and try to look receptive. Helpfully, Na Marce closes my eyes with one of the duck eggs. Then she begins her incantations. This is more unnerving than I'd imagined. Within seconds Na Marce is shaking like someone possessed, sucking and rasping and whispering evocations to God and Jesucristo, Antonio Romero and a host of saints I've never heard of. Her breath comes in short judders and is expelled now and again in a low feverish hiss. I peek through my eyelashes and see her eyes are closed and there's a look of irritation on her face as if she's trying to untangle a knot that won't come undone. I make a concerted effort to try to relax as if that's somehow going to help her extricate the demons she's after.

Meanwhile, though, she's rubbing my head so hard with the duck egg that it's an effort not to shout 'Ow!' Then she puts the egg gently in my hands and begins scrubbing me all over with the vegetables, first the chillies and then the onion, over my head, face, eyes, neck, shoulders, arms, hands, back, buttocks, legs, feet, and concentrating – worryingly – on an area above my left breast where I imagine she's divined the start of a tumour.

146

I'm beginning to ache all over and my eyes, even though they're now clamped shut, are smarting from the juice of the bruised onion and chillies. When she finishes with the chillies she sticks them under my armpits where I squeeze them in a sweaty salute so they don't fall out. The onion goes under the ball of my left foot; and the three lemons, after they've inflicted a considerable amount of deep tissue trauma, are packed under the other foot. This is beginning to feel ridiculous and dozens of humiliating pub games come to mind. I have an overwhelming urge to open my eyes and turn round and make sure Laureana and Natalia aren't falling about laughing on the veranda. But Na Marce is still hissing as insistently as ever and I daren't do anything to break the spell – if that's indeed what it is.

Suddenly there's a resounding 'thwack' and a stinging sensation extends across the breadth of my back. Na Marce is beating me with what must be one of the switches of basil dunked into a bucket of water. Before long I'm dripping wet, smarting all over and beginning to smell like a mixed salad.

At last she takes the egg from my hands and raises me to my feet. The onion and the lemons roll to one side and the chillies fall out of my armpits. Uncertainly I open my eyes and Na Marce gestures to me to stand well away from them. Then she beats me again with what I fortify myself by calling the 'Basil Brush', before inviting me to stand on it. Gradually her incantations that had reached fever pitch a few moments before, subside into a blessing, and her robe rustles as she makes a final sign of the cross.

I realize I'm trembling and wobble towards my shoes and my shirt like a new-born lamb. My bra has turned sludge-brown and is covered in spinachy smears like grass-stains. The remains of the *limpia* lie strewn around the courtyard as if someone's shopping bag has split. Calmly, softly, as if nothing has happened, Na Marce tidies them away and brings out fresh ingredients for a repeat performance for Natalia.

I'm removed to recover in Na Marce's sitting-room and plonk myself down on one of a row of high-backed Spanish chairs ranged against the side of the wall. I feel completely stunned. At the end of the room is the family altar – a large shrine with a portrait of the Virgin of Guadalupe and next to it a mini-shrine to Jesus Christ. There are vases full of tuberoses and carnations and all the candles are lit. There's a big TV in the corner, family photos on the wall, and an old poster advertising a bullfight with the matador Vicente Marcial – Na Marce's husband. The shutters are closed but I can hear a bus sounding its horn in the street and the babble of women heading for the market. In the courtyard Na Marce takes up her sortilegious sibilation once again.

Though it is cool and dark, cavernous almost, I have the strange sensation that there's someone else here besides me and turn round to find a large picture just behind my head and the Black Christ of Esquipulas staring equivocally past me into the room. I recognize him as the Indian icon of central America, as powerful in his way as Guadalupe to the north – the patron of healers, a sorcerer of sorts, whose origins, also rooting deep beyond the Christian phase, stem from the pagan traditions of the ancient Maya. Suddenly I feel an emptying sensation, as if I'm being drawn through a plug-hole into the floor. I feel dizzy and light-headed and bruised, pulled between contradictory forces of magnetism, whirling in the vortex of the Tehuantepec bottleneck, caught up in some powerful chemistry I don't understand. Remotely, as if it's been planted there by somebody else, I feel a single hot tear rolling down my cheek.

A few days later Na Marce's son, Vicente Marcial the younger, meets us at the Casa de la Cultura – *Lidxi Guendabiaani* in Zapotec – to show us around. The Casa is a beautiful nineteenth-century mansion next to the church, its inner courtyard shaded by a gigantic silk-cotton tree. Laureana and Natalia's father converted the place in 1972 as a centre for Zapotec culture. Vicente used to be its director. Its cool airy rooms exhibit local photography and art. There's a print-making shop, an archaeology museum, a library, a stage and large rooms for conferences, classes and creative perform-ances. Tonight there's a showing of archive footage of Juchitán – part of a film taken by Miguel Covarrubias, the explorer/anthropol-ogist who travelled the Isthmus in the early 1900s. The place, Vicente says, will be packed.

The Casa has become a powerful focus for Juchitecos. Toledo, himself a COCEI activist, saw it as a way to consolidate Juchitán's interests, to sustain the culture of resistance and independence in the difficult years of the struggle against the PRI. Often, it became a political battleground itself, with the government and state authorities wrestling for control against the artists and intellectuals who ran it. At one point soldiers were posted here and the Casa used as a staging-ground for their assaults on the Juchitec demonstrators.

In Juchitán, as in the rest of Mexico, politics and art are never far from each other. A poet or a painter is, by his very nature, considered a politician at heart. A magazine, produced by Toledo's publishing company, Ediciónes Toledo, and edited by the Zapotec poet, historian and essayist Víctor de la Cruz made this abundantly clear. *Guchachi' Reza*, meaning torn or ripped iguana, became a crucial tool of Juchitec self-determination in the 1970s and 80s. It contained articles on Zapotec and COCEI politics, of course, but love poems, too, alongside translations into Zapotec of Brecht and Neruda, myth and folklore and historical documents, photographs and illustrations by Toledo and his friends. Though it was more likely to be read by intellectuals in Mexico City, anthropologists in Paris or artists in Madrid than local Zapotec peasants, *Guchachi' Reza*'s subversive potential so rattled the PRI that they burned down one of the bookstores that sold it.

Toledo's own work is a similar blend of the political and the satirical, the beautiful and erotic and mythological. Since meeting Laureana's crazy artist friend Philippe Hernández in Mexico City, I'd sought out Toledo's paintings and drawings hanging in galleries in Mexico City and in the town of Oaxaca. But it was only since coming to Juchitán that I'd begun to see where he was coming from. The Kafkaesque, metamorphic nature of Toledo's work – a bat with a man's penis, death lying in a hammock, a toad on a draughts board, a woman bull, a deer with shoes, Benito Juárez as a cricket, the 'cannon of Juchitán' poised like an erection, ready to fire – seemed to orbit around the pre-Columbian world of Juchitán's market where language itself takes flight, flicking from metaphor to metaphor, from animism to abstraction; where sex is everywhere in everything; where a ripe plum is a testicle, a prawn is a penis and a fish a deflowered virgin; where eroticism is power and power is politics. Worlds that we would separate in the West, seem integrated, interdependent, even indistinguishable in Juchitán.

'Nothing in Juchitán is as it seems,' smiled Vicente; 'you only have to look next door to see that. Where would you find a Catholic Church like ours, or a patron saint like Vicente Ferrer?'

While we'd been talking, the bells of the nineteenth-century *iglesia* had begun to peal. A mass was being said for a *muxe* known as Cuqui who'd run a *licuado* stall in the market. Though the community was cagey about the circumstances, it was well known that Cuqui had died of AIDS. *Muxes*, smartly and unconventionally dressed in black suits and ties, and a choir of girls wearing traditional white-pleated frills around their faces, had been arriving at the church carrying candles and flowers. 'Where else in Mexico would you find a priest willing to say mass for a bunch of gays?' said Vicente. 'To most Catholics homosexuality is an unpardonable sin.'

But Juchitán was hardly a model for Catholic conformity. Though aggressively evangelized by Dominicans shortly after conquest, the Juchitecos had persisted in the worship of the old gods alongside the new. Fiestas and ceremonies are still held today in honour of Coqueelaa, the god of wealth; Leraa, the god of Hell; Nohuichana, the goddess of the river and of fish; or of the Lizard; or the Plum Tree; or the protectress of pregnant women and new mothers.

When the Dominican saint, Vicente Ferrer – a pious, studious, proselytizing thirteenth-century evangelizer of Arabs and Jews – was imposed as the patron saint of Juchitán, the Juchitecos were swift to re-mould him in their image. He became a fun-loving hedonist, a liberal, a ferocious defender of Juchitec ways, the butt of jokes. Some even say he was gay. His name was evoked on the battlefield, shouted in victory, made Zapotec and Juchitecos proudly begin to call their town not Juchitán but 'Sabizende' – a corruption of 'San Vicente'.

When Porfirio Díaz's brother, '*Chato*' or 'Pug-nose' Díaz, sent an army to punish the Juchitecos for their insubordination while he was Governor of the state of Oaxaca, he became Public Enemy Number One. He captured the town, ordered prisoners executed, looted the town's treasury, but worst of all, he kidnapped the image of Vicente Ferrer and defiled it. A decade later when Porfirio staged a presidential coup against Benito Juárez, the Zapotecs hadn't forgotten his brother's outrages against them. They sided with Juárez and Díaz's rebellion failed. Everywhere the Díaz rebels were defeated and Chato made a run for the sea. Unfortunately for him, he fell into the hands of the Juchitecos. He was caught in the sand dunes of Chacalapa. The skin was stripped from the soles of his feet and he was made to run across the burning sand before being finally lynched to death to cries of 'Viva San Vicente!'

Juchitecos would never succumb to the meek, guilt-ridden, God-fearing Christian ideal, and though San Vicente became their patron, the church would never become their spiritual focus. 'They all love God,' said Vicente, as I noticed the significance of his name for the first time, 'but in their own homes, at their own altars, with their own saints. Church is for big occasions. It's not a place for personal feelings.'

The loose web of Catholicism in Juchitán has allowed other denominations to slip in through the net. Protestants, Lutherans and, most recently, Mormons, all claim to have made inroads into the town. 'They pick on the weak,' says Vicente, 'on the very poor, the alcoholics, the criminals, the narcos, people on the margins of society. The core of Juchitán remains proud and strong. You won't find them making promises to some foreign padre that they'll abstain from sex and stop drinking alcohol.'

Natalia had spotted a friend in the throng emerging from the church. She'd gone over to greet him and returned several minutes later with invitations to a *vela* that was being thrown the following night. The party was being hosted by one of the teams we'd seen playing basketball on our very first evening. The invitations were printed on pieces of card that had been made into fans. One was a picture of a fluffy kitten playing with a ball of wool; another was a flamenco dancer; the third, a high-diver in Acapulco. The message on the reverse read:

TRADITIONAL VELA OF THE GENUINE
'INTREPID ONES'
SEEKERS OF DANGER INC.
(WHERE MAGIC AND FANTASY BECOME REALITY)
COURTESY OF CAMELIA
YOUR HOST(ESS) FOR 1998

JUCHITÁN, OAX.   SALON:
NOV. 21, 22 DE 1998   CAZORLA

Vicente took one look at the invitations and roared with laughter. 'Now you're in for an experience!' The party was to celebrate the crowning of *Las Intrépidas'* new transvestite queen and while some women – friends and family of the organizers – had been invited, it was almost exclusively a gay party with 'real' men barred. It was famous among *velas* for being meticulously organized, lavishly decorated and frenziedly abandoned. While the *muxes* used the occasion to indulge their fantasies and strip, if they wished, to the barest minimum, women were expected to dress respectfully and traditionally – presumably so as not to upstage their hosts. 'I can just see you in a *huipil*,' laughed Laureana when she saw my anxious face, 'but we'll have to do something drastic with your hair!'

It's the night of the *vela* and Laureana, Natalia and I are holed up in Natalia's cousin's salon having our hair done. We're dressed to kill. Natalia and Laureana have borrowed their *huipiles* and long skirts, or *enaguas*, complete with white pleated lace underskirts, from Natalia's aunt. Being a foot taller than your average Zapotec, I'd proved more of a problem, and Natalia had taken me round to the biggest Juchiteca she could think of, a woman still a good few inches shorter than me and considerably larger around the girth. Her name was Florinda but Natalia referred to her respectfully as 'La Maestra'.

As soon as she saw me La Maestra had raised her arms in dismay. 'What's this? So skinny?' she cried. 'You should be *frondosa* like a Juchiteca – big and generous like a leafy tree.' I wondered if anorexia had ever been heard of in Juchitán. Resignedly, La Maestra ushered me into her bedroom. There was a prehistoric pedal-driven Singer sewing-machine in the corner, a favourite subject of Francisco Toledo's paintings and now I saw why. The railway days had brought a thrilling injection of ideas for the Juchitecas. Sewing-machines revolutionized traditional designs, and suddenly Juchitecas were able to order material for their *huipiles* straight from the textile mills of Manchester where bolts of cloth were made specially to sell in the Isthmus and nowhere else. Elderly Tehuanas still sigh for the good old Manchester cottons, strongly woven and colourfast. Now inferior cotton is imported from Asia. But sewing-machines still take pride of place in the Juchiteca's battery as Juchitecas continue to create more and more elaborate designs.

La Maestra led me to her wardrobe where she brought out a beautiful red and yellow embroidered *huipil* and a long colourful skirt. 'Try these on,' she said and, finding the skirt still hovered four inches above the floor, she readjusted the waist-tapes until she had them slung over my hips. With the lace underskirt hooked on even lower, the skirts at last hit the ground.

'There,' she said, 'just don't lift your arms or you'll be showing more flesh than the *muxes*.' She took them off me again and folded them into a plastic bag. 'It's not my best outfit,' she added, 'but it's the first I ever owned. I wore it for the first *vela* I went to with my husband, nearly thirty years ago. I've grown a bit since then' – she patted her spare tyres proudly – 'but it's given me good memories, this one. Yes, you'll have a good time in this.'

As if in an effort to pack a more appropriate figure inside her costume La Maestra insisted we stay to an enormous lunch – bowl after bowl of chicken soup to which we added handfuls of raw onion, avocado, raw cabbage, lime, chillies, broken tortillas, from a volley of dishes in the centre of the table. 'Just a little more,' she pressed, until I felt my stomach reach breaking point.

The conversation revolved around Laureana's work, La

Maestra's daughter studying at college in Oaxaca town, and then veered on to the subject of sex, or the lack of it. La Maestra wanted to know if Natalia had a boyfriend yet and if not, why she couldn't find a nice Juchiteco while she was here.

'Juchitec men are not for me,' said Natalia teasingly, 'they're too soft, like puppies. I can't respect a man who plays at my feet and rolls over for his food.'

'It's these feminists from the City, journalists and anthropologists and so on, who are giving us a bad name. They say the Juchitec women are strong; and therefore they think that our men must be weak,' retaliated La Maestra. 'I don't know why they have to make everything so complicated. We are strong women here, that is true. But our men are strong, too. They are the head of our households. We do things to please them – in bed, in the kitchen. We look after our men like all women should. And it's the men who always tell the women what to do.'

'Ah, but you don't have to do it,' insisted Natalia. 'That's the difference in Juchitán. The men tell the women what to do and the women go ahead and do what they planned to do anyway. It's always the woman who has the last word. If her man gets drunk he gets the door slammed in his face and has to sleep in the gutter. If he beats his wife, he'll soon have every woman in the neighbourhood after him with meat-cleavers.'

'That's as it should be,' laughed La Maestra, 'but it doesn't mean we make our men weak, that we've swallowed their balls.'

We've turned up at the beauty salon in full dress because Natalia says it will be difficult to get a *huipil* on over our hair-dos. I wonder what she has in mind. We've also come early in the evening to give the hairdressers time to concentrate on themselves. There's already a buzz of excitement around the blow-driers.

'Felina' is a close friend of Natalia's and they kiss in the air so as not to mess up Felina's face-pack. Felina's long black hair is mussily scraped back in a clasp and she prods it impatiently with blazing red fingertips. 'Oh, you've caught me out,' she wails, 'I look such a mess.' Though her arms are elegant and hairless, the muscle grouping along them is unmistakably male.

Felina's salon is a confection of sugar-pink and pistachio-green. On the wall there's a poster of Marilyn Monroe, and Felina's certificates of graduation in various courses of styling and make-up. An early one refers to her as 'El Señor Ángel Santiago Valdivieso'; subsequent diplomas record her as 'Senõrita'.

Like most *muxes* Felina is proud of the fact that she doesn't take hormones and isn't tempted by a sex-change. 'Everything you see is mine,' she says coquettishly, reaching under her slip to readjust the contents of her bra. 'Thank God for Wonderbra,' she says, 'and Kleenex.' She reminds me of the billboards on the highways in Mexico City, and I think blissfully of the irony of those advertisements here, where the women are so large they have to wear vests and the main candidates for underwired 'cleavage boosters' are men.

Felina swivels on a chair, stretching out her long sinewy legs, twirling from one mirror to the next. 'That's me, when I was queen two years ago,' she says, handing us some photos. She looks drop-dead gorgeous, hair piled on her head, balancing under her crown, in a lithesome, sequinned gown, sceptre in hand, as tearful and triumphant as Miss World. 'This year's queen is *so* ugly,' says Felina with undisguised glee, 'so *old*. And she's from Ixtepec. God knows why they chose her. She must have given the right person the blow-job.'

Other *muxes* come into the shop as we are settled into our chairs. One of them, wearing a candy-striped bodice and hot pants, is Natalia's cousin. The bitchiness cranks up a notch. These are the bad girls of town, prostitutes or sexual *servidoras*. Felina, a little flustered now, takes up her tweezer-set and begins plucking their eyebrows.

The television in the corner, meanwhile, is relaying scenes of a ticker-tape parade commemorating the Revolution live from the Zócalo in Mexico City. There are processions of gymnasts and teams carrying canoes, band-leaders and drummers twirling drum-sticks, civic dignitaries taking the salute – a remote vignette from the conventional world. From here the participants look rather silly. 'Look at his ass,' pouts one of the *muxes* as the camera zeroes in on an earnest-looking pole-vaulter. The shot cuts to the President. 'We should ask El Presidente to our party,' says another. 'Do you think he's *puto* enough for us?' They laugh at the connotations of *puto* which can mean 'gay' as well as simply 'disreputable' or 'mean'.

Felina's assistant, a bashful peroxide blonde called 'Sandy', comes up to do my hair. She's wearing a sleeveless T-shirt that reveals a whiff of deodorant and stubbly armpits when she reaches in front of me for the tray of kirby grips. She has whipped-Spaniel eyes and mauvish lipstick that makes her mouth look bruised. She's completely silent and avoids my eyes in the mirror but goes about the task of transforming my shortish hair into a luxuriant imitation of a Juchiteca with determined perfectionism.

This entails pinning a long, thick plait of real Zapotec hair to the back of my head, curling it around into a massive bun and fixing it with a huge yellow satin rosette on one side like a present. To make this construction safe she pins in a total of fifty hairgrips until my head feels like the Eiffel Tower, and applies enough hairspray to stop a palm tree rustling in a hurricane. I notice with dismay she's topped it all off by giving me a 1970s flick in the front à la Charlie's Angels.

Sandy has hardly stood back to appreciate her work before she's reaching for the make-up boxes. Alarmed, I try to protest but she's insistent. 'Muy natural,' I plead, but Sandy has more colourful visions of her own. Laureana laughs when she sees the transformation. 'Now you look like a real Juchiteca. We'll call you "Chavel-ita", Zapotec for "little Isabella".' She's not so happy with her own appearance, though. Her hair has been parted in the middle and greased back into a bun. 'I look like a gypsy from Valencia,' she groans, swinging the gold hoops in her ears. Natalia joins us. 'You think you've got problems,' she exclaims, peering distastefully in the mirror at the thin plaits looped Heidi-style over the top of her head, 'they've made me look like Frida Kahlo.'

Juchitán is famous for its obsession with parties. There's at least one big fiesta every day of the year. Juchitecos boast that no one can starve in their town because you only have to turn a corner and you run into a party going on right in the middle of the street and have plates of food thrust into your hands. Already we've been to a wedding, side-stepped a few smaller shindigs, and had a man pass out on the bonnet of our car when we drove past the inauguration of a new sector of town.

Sociologists and anthropologists like to explain this 'phenomenon' as a way that Juchitecos manage to preserve the status quo. No one can get rich or above the rest because they're always spending their money. The only time Juchitecos ever save is when they're building up for a party. Prestige in the community is not linked to wealth, it's linked to generosity and spending power. In this way, the community is bound together by the reciprocal pleasure – and cost – of throwing and attending parties.

Juchitecos, of course, don't burden themselves with the analytical detail. 'Piggy banks are for pigs,' they say. They're driven simply by the prospect of having a good time. They have a saying which Vicente had tried to explain to me. *Hay más tiempo que vida*, which translates, unhelpfully, as 'There's more time than life'. It's basically the Juchitec equivalent of *Carpe diem*, and it applies to every decision a Juchiteco makes in favour of self-indulgence. 'You don't take money with you when you die,' Vicente expanded, 'so why kill yourself trying to earn it?'

It was the philosophy, I discovered, behind Natalia's decision to get plastered when I'd accidentally parked next to a hole ten foot deep by the side of the road. Natalia had been sitting in the back seat. When she got out and discovered that our back wheels were barely two inches from the edge of a crater she declared the occasion a 'brush with death' and went straight off and downed half-a-dozen bottles of beer.

She's still in the same life-with-a-vengeance frame of mind when we arrive at the party of *Las Intrépidas*. Entrance to the *vela* is an obligatory donation of a box of beer.

There's a lorry backed up to the entrance of the music hall where the party's being held. Waiting inside to receive the guests is the owner of the hall and the sponsor, or *mayordomo*, of the *vela* – Oscar Cazorla. Short, fat and egotistical, he's a cross between Danny de Vito and Telly Savalas's brother and, apart from the waiters, the only man so far not wearing a dress. His tiny feet are packed into patent leather shoes, and a white silk shirt, already transparent with sweat, clings to his stomach like onion skin.

But the most conspicuous thing about him, an aspect that obviously excites him, is his jewellery. His fat wrists and fingers are dripping in gold *centenarios* worth, I calculate, at least 80,000 pesos. They swing around his neck like Olympic medals. It looks as if someone has emptied a box of after-dinner mints over him. He directs the flow of beer boxes by pointing his little finger, which sports a massive ruby ring, and jangling his bracelets. The waiters leap about in response like fleas around a cat.

Cazorla is joined by our hostess, Camelia, who makes a sweeping entrance in a ball-dress of rose tulle and a tiara. They embrace and survey the room together like Duke and Duchess. After a moment Camelia spots Natalia and sails over to greet us. 'So glad you could come,' she croons, head tilted like a budgerigar testing its reflection in a mirror. 'You look beautiful,' says Natalia, generously. 'Thank you,' beams Camelia, radiant. 'At least this year I can go for a piss. My last dress buttoned up to the neck and fitted like a condom. I had it sewn all over with sequins and stones – very glamorous – but it weighed twenty kilos. By the end of the evening I was so tired I could hardly stand up and I daren't have more than one beer in case I needed the toilet. It would've taken twelve people to help me get to my prick.'

More and more *muxes* arrive, teetering in, in single file, staggering exaggeratedly under their boxes of beer. Some have taken, like Camelia, the Cinderella approach; others drag sheaths of velvet like Morticia Addams. There are a few Lauren Bacalls. But many have envisaged themselves as Pretty Woman – before redemption – in spray-on Lycra mini-skirts, fish-net stockings and spangly boob-tubes. The effect makes some look as lumpish as pantomime dames; others could be on the catwalk. Felina is breathtaking. She radiates femininity and heads turn from all directions in hunger and envy. She flashes us a blissful, jubilant smile.

I search the crowd for Sandy my hairdresser, and find her at last hanging back sheepishly by the wall. She has a green Lycra dress on that clings Lolita-like to tiny tissue-balls for breasts. She has victim written all over her, an invitation to the sadist's boot perhaps, or even manacles and chains, and I feel suddenly desperately sad for her. She manages a weak smile of acknowledgement when I catch her eye.

A band on the balcony strikes up electronic salsa music and the *muxes* take en masse to the floor. The few who are dressed in trousers with prominent polka-dot handkerchiefs in their back pockets are in great demand as they circumvent the dilemma over who dances the man's part. The air becomes stultifyingly thick, redolent with pheromones and competing brands of perfume. Camelia's invitation cards come into their own and the *muxes* flap frantically as the temperature soars. Waiters rush about sweeping up empties, supplying fistfuls of fresh bottles from the ice-drums, laughing when they get their bottoms pinched. Natalia is whisked on to the floor by her cousin and I'm so engrossed in their hilarious routine, shaking their chests at each other and tossing their hair, that I fail to notice a very drunken woman with leering eyes in a polyester trouser-suit, sidling up and asking me to dance. Suddenly there's a punch on my arm. 'I said, DANCE!' she bellowed, dragging me to my feet. As we hit the dance-floor, though, the music changes tempo and I find myself clenched vice-like to her bosom. 'I speaking good English. Let's go to bed,' she yells. Frantically, I extricate myself and dodge out of her reach, looking desperately for Natalia and Laureana.

Despite liberal applications of antiperspirant, the *muxes* are beginning to sweat. As the evening wears on, their personas are starting to droop. Dresses sag; hair-dos flop; seams split; stockings ladder; breast-pads poke up above plunging necklines. The waiters begin distributing paper-napkins among the dancers for mopping up.

At last this year's queen makes her *grande entrée* to a thumping rendition of 'The Girl From Ipanema' and the crowds part to form an aisle to her throne. Felina is right. 'Diana Sheila' from Ixtepec looks like a Yiddish mama, and is totally eclipsed by her two handmaidens who are wearing G-strings and see-through body-stockings. Felina throws us an 'I-told-you-so' look of satisfaction and a complicated hand gesture which explains what the handmaidens have managed to tuck away – and where.

Soon, though, we're fighting for breathing space and, as the *muxes* grow increasingly red-eyed and predatory, I'm still having trouble with my lesbian friend. She keeps popping up next to me, putting her hand up my *huipil* and trying to stick her tongue in my ear. I decide to beat a retreat.

Outside the air is warm but at least it's oxygenated. Laureana, Natalia and I meander automatically towards the Jardín, passing on our way a wedding entourage led by bride and groom. It's a relief to have left the queenly hyperbole of *Las Intrépidas* behind. It's nearly one in the morning and we plan on having a quick bite – a fattening *garnacha* or two – before retiring to bed.

But the Jardín is thumping. The market street has been transformed into an open air dance hall. There's a floodlit stage and an electronic band of musicians, or *gruperos*, in transports of salsa-invoked delirium. There are Juchitecas dancing belly to belly, fat arms around fat shoulders, gliding about like hot-air balloons. Watching them tipsily from the sidelines, from rows of plastic chairs, are their husbands and lovers. 'This is more like it,' says Natalia.

We bump into Vicente and he steers us manfully through a gang of over-excited youths smashing bottles on the periphery. He instals us in some chairs and goes off to fetch fresh Coronitas. The floor is rattling with empty bottles and polystyrene food trays. 'It's a *vela* for Santa Cecilia,' he shouts on his return, 'the patron saint of musicians. It's turning into quite an evening.'

Younger girls are dancing together, too, in skin-tight, backless dresses and strappy high-heels, snaking about suggestively, the eyes of their *novios* fixed on them as if held in the sway of cobras. There's no hint yet of the kilos of fat that will transform them one day into stately matriarchs. One or two *muxes*, who've avoided the scene at *Las Intrépidas*, are dancing with the girls and, as they grow bolder with beer, some *novios* venture into the fray.

'They say there'll be a *rapto* before the night's out,' shouts Vicente. Natalia's brother conducted a *rapto* several years ago, abducting his girlfriend from a party like this one and seducing her, producing as evidence for his mother and the assembled matrons waiting outside his bedroom door a white T-shirt soaked in blood.

It's a practice that still persists, especially in the poorer quarters of the town, although Natalia condemns it as barbaric. A *rapto* is traditionally a prerequisite to marriage, and the boy doing the seducing must be fully committed to slipping the ring on when it's over. But it can still be alarming for the girl, with her mother-in-law-to-be knocking on the door, shouting through the key-hole to see if everything is going OK; even barging into the room to give directions or reassurance. The deflowering has to be done with a finger.

Then a napkin, or tissue, or a piece of clothing, or a sheet with the bloodstains on it is produced and placed on a tray, surrounded by flowers, for inspection. When the Juchitecas are satisfied, they take the tray to the girl's mother as proof of her daughter's deflowerment and betrothal.

The girl, meanwhile, becomes a side-show. She's confined to her boyfriend's bed like an invalid, her head bound to reduce the fever engendered by having lost her virginity and having come so close to the sexual act without actual consummation. She is visited by friends and relations, and by all the men of her boyfriend's family who are rolling drunk and wearing crowns of red tulips and hibiscus. After two weeks she's allowed to return home and, about a year later, she'll move in with her boyfriend and eventually get married.

If a successful *rapto* is a shock to the system, it's at least more welcome than an unsuccessful one, when the girl is discovered not to be a virgin, or at least fails to produce a convincing amount of blood. Then she's returned home with a symbolic broken pot to face the future as a cheap *cantinera* or a mistress of married men.

'Of course it doesn't have to be like a rape,' said Natalia archly. 'I'm quite sure my brother and his girlfriend had been at it for ages. They had a jar of chicken blood under his bed, ready for the occasion.'

The rumour of *raptos* tonight is indicative of the success of the party. The atmosphere is wired. More and more boys are joining the skirmishing on the fringes, posturing and wrangling like stags in the rut. The Juchitecas drag us on to the dance-floor and when we collapse our fists are crammed with bottles, three at a time. It takes a while to master the Juchiteca technique of holding a Coronita between each knuckle and draining them one after the other.

A man sitting next to me nudges my arm and gesticulates towards the dancers. 'That's my wife,' he says, his eyes misty with adoration and alcohol, 'and my beautiful daughters.' I find I'm losing track, though, of who's who and what's what. The *muxes* are beginning to look more like women than some of the Juchitecas, some of whom look decidedly macho. Some of the young girls could be *muxes*, so could some of the young men they're dancing with; and some *muxes*, I discover, are dressed conventionally, like me, as a Juchiteca – except that I look like a woman dressed as a man dressing up as a woman. I feel suddenly, liberatingly androgenous and sexual conventions elsewhere – the uptight social mores of the rest of Mexico, South America, or far away in England – seem ludicrously neurotic.

When it's finally over, when the musicians have surrendered and the last bottle has bitten the dust, as the street-dogs begin homing in on the debris, Laureana and I totter to our feet and head for our hotel. Behind us, the remaining Juchitecas drag their men upright, hoist them up under the arms and, swaying slightly like ships in a swell, plough home with them through the darkness. It'll be a late start for the market in the morning.

It's sad to be leaving Juchitán. We've said goodbye to Natalia who is staying for a while longer with her family. Laureana and I are both wearing dark glasses and have already finished a packet of Tylenol and several bottles of water by the time we reach Tehuantepec. Hopelessly I searched the speeding roadsides for the sign for 'Pearson'. We were going to take a photo of the two of us standing behind it. But I must have blinked and missed it. It was that sort of town.

I was little the wiser about Natalia and Laureana's ancestor, the lawyer, who'd worked for Pearson. I knew more about him, certainly, but his CV was confusing rather than elucidating. It seemed typical of the Juchitec ability to swing both ways. Jose F. Gómez – 'Che' Gómez – was a local hero and martyr to the Juchitec cause. Gómez had worked with both Pearson and Díaz. When, in

1911, Francisco 'Pancho' Villa's revolutionaries ousted Díaz, and the liberal reformer Francisco Madero (who had also worked with Díaz and Pearson) became President, Che Gómez seized the opportunity of general political mayhem to stage a separatist rebellion in Juchitán. Gómez was rebelling specifically against Juárez Maza, the governor of Oaxaca and son of the former President, Benito Juárez. On his way to discuss an armistice with Madero, however, Gómez was betrayed and assassinated by government agents.

What this didn't explain was how Gómez came to ally himself with the Mexican dictator and a foreign capitalist who was opening up the Isthmus to outside trade in the first place. Perhaps he'd seen a window of opportunity for Juchitán in all the wheeler-dealing and political indecision and leapt for it. Perhaps somewhere in some musty document, in some peeling archive, were special concessions granted to Juchitán, above and beyond all the other towns on the Isthmus – some preferential trade agreement that Che Gómez and Pearson had cooked up together. Whatever colour his cloak, I was certain the rebel Che Gómez had worn the interests of Juchitán closest to his heart.

As we sped on for Salina Cruz I made a mental effort to remember how all this looked this day. Juchitán had been buzzing before we left with rumours about the revival of the Tehuantepec passage, with six-lane rail tracks and a super-highway to service it. With the expiry of the American treaty with Panama, and the canal itself overwhelmed with shipping and underwhelmed with the water necessary to process it, all sights were once again on the potential of the Tehuantepec Isthmus. There was a real possibility that Pearson's dream might be resuscitated and a railway at last prove its worth against the Panama Canal. Using the Tehuantepec route, Pearson always maintained, would shave days off sailing time south to Panama. But modern strategists also see the trans-Isthmus project as a way to channel Asian Tiger exports through Mexico for distribution to prime consumer markets on the US east coast. Eight transportation giants, including Burlington–Santa Fe and Union-Southern, had already begun bidding for the rail-lines.

But Juchitán was, as ever, gearing up to do battle. Opening the

Isthmus to international trade on this scale would light a beacon to poor migrants from the rest of Mexico, and other desperate opportunists from across the sea in Asia. It would mean *maquiladoras*, too – the notorious processing and assembly plants that had, post-NAFTA, burgeoned on the border with the States. These were factories that ran on cheap labour, tax incentives and a blind eye to environmental degradation. If the northern border was anything to go by, the Isthmus region would become a black spot of poverty, prostitution, alcoholism, drugs trafficking, inflation, pollution and crime. A prospectus for a *maquiladora* zone on the sun-baked Tehuantepec plain claimed it would draw its power from hydro-electric dams in the Chimalapas, a 4.4 million-acre forest located on the saddle of the Isthmus – one of Mexico's last wildlife reserves and home to the 12,000-strong Zoque people, descendants of the Olmecs. The Tehuantepec plain itself, the Isthmus Zapotecs were predicting, would become a *Taiwancito*, a little Taiwan. 'The Juchitecos would never stand for it,' warned Natalia, 'there'd be revolution, you can bet on it. They'd spill their blood rather than see the Isthmus overrun.'

Not AIDS or another Huatulco on the doorstep, or the narcos and mestizo traders who were already moving in on Juchitán, seemed as dark a threat to Juchitec culture as this. I had glimpsed pre-Cortésian Mexico – not in detail, but in spirit: a place that had the vibrancy and self-confidence, the *joie de vivre* of the unconquered; somewhere where native belief systems prevailed; where indigenous language was king. I'd seen the only modern market that could compare with the great ancient trade-centre of Tlatelolco – a dynamic, exuberant, triumphant place, unfettered by the guilt and humiliations and hypocrisy of Western, Christian civilization; unbowed by the Arab/Hispanic legacy of homophobia and misogyny. How long could Juchitán and its powerful Juchitecas retain their control over the birth canal of the Isthmus, keeping the rest of the country at bay, clenched between their legs, slave to their tractive pelvic muscle? I took heart from a *corrido* folk song that commemorated Juchitán's defeat of the Austrian Archduke Maximilian's French-sponsored invasion of the Isthmus:

Listen to me, my brothers
I am going to say a few words
about the day that Señor Binu Gada had a fight
with the foreigners they call 'francés'.

Our people were shouting,
Señor San Vicente came and helped;
suddenly it grew dark
and a storm thundered there and then.

We come from Binigula'sa' origins,
we come from the Biniguenda;
some brought wood and other short machetes,
others carried slings.

As if you were tending to young maize,
put in the stone, swing it and pitch;
what good shots are the people from my village,
with every stone, they knocked down a foreigner.

Tona Taati', a woman in a wrap-around skirt,
shouted: 'Go in head on,
don't let your head pound,
that's the way to kill the foreigners.'

The tall foreigners thudded as they
fell in the mud because they were tired,
ever since then they talk about us,
they've got balls, those Tecos.

4

Secret Wars in the Cloud Forest
Chiapas

True civilization means harmony between men and the earth and between men among themselves

> Diego Rivera, *La Asamblea Primera de Mayo mural* 1923–4,
> *Secretaría de Educación Pública*

I want there to be democracy, no more inequality. I am looking for a life with dignity, freedom, just like God says

> *Zapatista guerrilla, 1994*

It was a nineteen-hour bus journey from Mexico City to Chiapas, Mexico's southernmost state. Much of the route (the Pan-American Highway was a deceptive name for it) zigzagged through the mountains like a streak of lightning. I chickened out and took the plane.

And landed, barely an hour and a half and a refreshment trolley from take-off, in a war zone. This was Tuxtla Gutiérrez, the modern-day capital of Chiapas. I was back in southern Mexico, barely 180 miles east of Juchitán, but it might have been Bosnia or Chechnya. The runway was flanked every 500 yards with sandbag bunkers and sentinels with machine-guns. Army jeeps were ready to go; tanks dozed under camouflage netting. A platoon of soldiers was hopping about like an aerobics class with rifles.

The stewardess smiled and wished us a pleasant stay in Tuxtla or, if our final destination was elsewhere in Chiapas – *Buen viaje*. I hauled my rucksack off the conveyor and hailed a taxi. There was a bullet-hole in the windscreen – the result of a brush with bandits on the road to Palenque a few months previously. The driver said he was keen to learn English, 'Like, how do you say, "you are very beautiful"?' When he leaned over to get his cigarettes out of the glove-box his hand reacted unnecessarily with my knee.

The road to San Cristóbal de las Casas surged away from the humid central valley of Tuxtla and up into the 9000-foot mountains with barely a pause for breath. Gradually we wound up our windows against the cold and the driver turned on the demister. As we gained altitude pockets of fog slowed our progress from Formula 1 to granny on a Sunday afternoon. The taxi-driver drummed impatiently on the wheel as if the weather was a personal affront to his driving prowess, and put a tape on. I gazed evasively through the fog at scraps of scenery – an unfathomable drop-off on one side; willowy maize crops and pine-scrub on the other – while somewhere in another dimension Olivia Newton-John *ooh-ooh-oohed* at John Travolta that he'd better shape up.

Occasionally figures materialized through the mist – Indians working or walking to work in the fields or quarries with hoes and pick-axes. The women were barefoot, wearing woollen wraps or *rebozos*, thick felt skirts and woven waistbands; the men, *huaraches* made from tyres or wellington boots, with loose cotton trousers and anoraks. Their clothes flagged snatches of pink and red in the white-out, like warnings. Convoy after convoy of army trucks, jeeps, armoured cars and troop carriers, telecom vans, hydroelectricity company trucks and oil tankers thundered down upon us as we cornered the hair-pin bends. Occasionally we slowed to a crawl past an army checkpoint. Once we were forced to stop when a gang of villagers demanded a *propina* at a hasty road-block. My driver thrust a ten peso bill at them, wound up his window and accelerated away before they could impose themselves further.

The forest deepened as we climbed, giving the disorientating impression that we were sinking upwards. This was a world away from the lively tropical exuberance of Juchitán. In colonial times these mountains would have been part of Guatemala. In fact Chiapas itself was originally half of Guatemala. On the map this single Mexican state is the same size as the country to which it once belonged, and equal in size to Belize and San Salvador put together.

Only after the collapse of the Mexican Empire in 1823, when the Central American federation was founded, did Chiapas choose to side with Mexico. Its people, Indians for the most part, still have more in common with the indigenous peoples of Guatemala and the isolated peninsula of the Yucatán than the rest of Mexico. This was the realm of the ancient Maya – a civilization that incorporated, at its height (between AD 250 and 900), all of present-day Chiapas, the Yucatán peninsula, Guatemala and Belize and parts of Honduras and El Salvador.

The natural boundary of the Isthmus of Tehuantepec kept the Maya spinning in a separate orbit from the Nahua civilizations of Central Mexico – the Aztecs, Toltecs and their forebears. Though they borrowed ideas and systems from each other, an elastic tension persisted between the tribes of the North American continent above the Isthmus and those of Mesoamerica below it, much like the conflictual division between Europe and the Middle East. And though they can't be separated neatly in time, the Aztec Empire was in the ascendant as the last of the great Mayan centres in the Yucatán were on the wane.

The Maya was not a civilization as such, at least not of the imperial nature of that of the Aztecs. It was more like a loose federation, an amalgamation of city-states such as existed in ancient Greece; like the market towns on the Isthmus, only on a greater scale. No two Mayan cities were alike. Each had its own astounding architectural character – from low and spacious Copán in what is now Honduras, with its broad staircases and wide plazas full of statuary; to Tikal in Guatemala, the Manhattan of the Maya, with its vertical pyramids soaring way above the trees, forerunners of the Chrysler Building.

The Mayan centres traded together, copied each other, squabbled with each other, but shared the basic affinities of race, culture and religion. Between them they spoke over twenty different but associated languages; while their aristocracy – the priests, rulers and astronomers – shared a complex hieroglyphic writing system which is only now being cracked by the experts. The Maya were an intellectual and artistic people but their culture was closely bound by the strictures of ritual and ceremony. They were as fearful of the displeasure of their gods as were the Aztecs. The famous murals of Bonampak I'd seen in the Museum of Anthropology in Mexico City were as alarming as they were beautiful, with scenes of mythical warriors with lobster-claw arms and crocodile heads; royal women jovially piercing their tongues; men in jaguar-skin tunics plunging obsidian-tipped lances into the chests of their enemies; humbled captives pleading for their lives; a decapitated head on a bed of leaves.

The Maya are most famous (if you discount the minor linguistic achievement of having given us words like 'hurricane' and 'shark') for their mathematical and astronomical genius. They invented zero – a concept obvious enough to us today, but only conceived by one other civilization in human history, the Hindus (who had either invented it themselves or inherited it from the Babylonians). Had it not been for the Arabs – who borrowed zero from the Hindus and passed it on to Europe, modern mathematics might have been held in a strait-jacket until the discovery of the New World.

The other extraordinary Mayan invention was their calendar – a complicated system using two interlocking calendars which rotated together like two different-sized cogs. The Maya recognized that the day is the fundamental building block of earthly time. Unlike the lunar or the solar months, the day does not vary and is easy to measure. So the Maya counted time in days, starting at a particular date in the past, using the second calendar wheel to help keep track of the enormous number of days that accrued. It was a system that avoided the inaccuracies we still battle with today with our uneven months and leap years; and the very same principle as the Julian Day Count used, for accuracy, by modern astronomers.

No one knows how or why the Mayan civilization went into decline. Fantastic temples and pyramids, even whole cities, evidence of their brilliance and confidence and ingenuity, are still being unearthed in the jungle in Chiapas and Guatemala and in the scrub of the Puuc hills in the Yucatán. Theories abound from the Atlantis and Lost Tribes of Israel crackpots to the ecological disaster proponents to the simple decline-and-fall-ists.

What is certain is that while the great civilization behind the famous tourist landmarks of Tikal, Copán, Palenque, Yaxchilán, Bonampak, Uxmal and Chichén-Itzá has disappeared, the Maya people lived on. Drifting away from the ancient centres, returning to the forest, or resorting to the mountains, the Maya adapted, migrated, merged with one another but to an astonishing degree maintained their original identity: their Mayan language, their spiritual beliefs, their crafts, their calendar and their concept of time. A combination of resilience and adaptability and a strong sense of cultural identity clearly marked out the Maya for survival as a distinct race into the twenty-first century but, unlike the Isthmus Zapotecs, they faced such aggressive persecution by the Spanish that collusion became the most effective part of their armour. They learnt to mask themselves, to hide their ethnicity behind the colonial façade, to disguise their nationhood behind a formula of meekness and acquiescence. They were so successful at making themselves invisible it was thought, until recently, that the Maya had disappeared altogether. In reality, though, there are estimated to be 5 million Maya speakers in south-eastern Mexico, Guatemala and Belize today, belonging to nine ethnic groups – Tzotzil, Tzeltal, Tojolabal, Chol, Mam, Zoque, Mixe, Zakchiquel and Lacandón; making them the second largest indigenous population in the western hemisphere, second only to the Quechua-speaking descendants of the Inca in the Andes. Numerous they may be, but their technique for survival makes them the most unlikely insurgents.

Chiapas's roots may be Mayan, buried deep to the south of Mexico and away to the east but it has to look north now towards the old Aztec seat for government, and the resulting impression to the uninitiated visitor is of a strange directional weightlessness, of negative gravity, as if the region is a force-field that even the magnetism of Mexico City has trouble penetrating.

Few people in the rest of Mexico dwell on the crisis in Chiapas – the guerrilla war that is being waged not simply on their doorstep, but within their very doors. No one talks about it, even though it's constantly headline news. It's as if Chiapas is a separate case, its history and geography segregating it from the real world, as if its proper place should be in the history books or in one or two designated rooms in the Museum of Anthropology.

When we finally reached it, 2100 metres up in the pine forests of Los Altos, the old colonial city of San Cristóbal, with its single-storey houses painted every colour of the rainbow, was more like something from Hans Andersen than a forum of civil war – a Beirut or Sarajevo. Mist swirled romantically around the mountains that encapsulated it within the verdant Valle de Jovel. But military opposition to the Mayan rebels, the 'Zapatistas' as they are known (after the hero of the Mexican Revolution – Emiliano Zapata) was clearly alive and kicking. There were armed government soldiers in the main plaza in front of the great yellow ochre cathedral with its great pine cross; and army jeeps patrolled the streets. Meanwhile, on the street corners Indian children were selling the traditional Mayan dolls – only now they wore black ski-masks and carried matchstick machine-guns and were named after members of the Zapatista high command.

Tourist agencies were open but keeping a wary eye on the political thermometer, ready to book their clients out at the slightest rise in temperature. The Mexican government was eager for tourism to continue in the region because it made it look like they had the lid on the situation. Between 40 and 60,000 troops had been dispatched on a permanent basis to Chiapas. That was enough, ironically, to scare most of the Americans away. The only foreigners in San Cristóbal now were students, aid-workers and missionaries, and adventurous backpackers from Europe.

My taxi-driver left me – ruefully – with the recommendation of his favourite restaurant, which served a lethal local sugarcane and maize alcohol called *pox* (pronounced, delightfully, 'posh'), and I made a bee-line for it that evening. I found El Fogón barely fifty metres from the Cathedral in the Avenida 16 de Septiembre. A typical colonial inner courtyard had been glazed over against the freezing high altitude nights. There were tables under the Spanish colonnades and someone playing a marimba rather loudly in the corner. The waiters were wearing the white pedal-pushers and belted red woollen *chuh* (like a poncho, or *sarape*, but stitched down the sides) of the Tzotzil-speaking Mayans. There were only two other customers in the restaurant.

On a table in the middle of the courtyard was a large plasticine mock-up of the Chiapan mountains. There were pitched battles being fought all over it by toy soldiers with tanks and jeeps and hand-made matchstick Zapatistas. Most of the soldiers were on their backs, and the Zapatista dolls had their arms raised, triumphant on the ridges. Swinging over them was a mobile of Airfix army helicopters on lengths of cotton thread.

The menu was a rousing combination of traditional cuisine and revolutionary cocktails: spicy local *chorizo* sausage, slow-roasted chilli pork, chicken in spicy, black chocolate *mole*; with a 'Mayan Sacrifice' or a 'Rebellion in the Ravines' to wash them down.

Rashly perhaps, I ordered '¡Viva Zapata!' recommended 'only for people with a brave heart'. A straight shot of *pox* seasoned with chilli and tabasco, it came escorted by a tiny figure of a Zapatista made out of cocktail sticks and nearly blew my head off.

The food was cooked from scratch in clay ovens and took a decade coming, so on my second or third cocktail I wandered into the back room of the restaurant and turned the light on. The walls were plastered with Zapatista propaganda: posters, the official 1994 '*Hoy decimos "¡Basta!"* . . .' ('Now we say "Enough!"') declaration, plastic sub-machine-guns, combat knives and machetes. There were the familiar photographs of the rebel leaders, the famous masked Subcomandante Marcos, and Ramona – the sturdy little Comandante in her thick felt skirt – and a few amateur snapshots of dead Zapatistas. Under one of them a typed inscription read:

> The little men of the land of Chiapas
> have had the courage and the dignity to offer the only
> thing they own in life . . .
> life itself . . .
> in exchange for the justice and democracy
> that all Mexicans yearn for.

I wandered back towards my pension. Despite the 'Viva Zapata's burning in my chest it was still hard to register that this was a war-zone. Foreign students from one of San Cristóbal's Spanish language schools were noisily embarking on a bar crawl. The bandstand café in the Zócalo was closing for the night; the balloon seller had gone, so had the children with their Marcos dolls and the stall with the black balaclavas. The sky glittered so bright and so cold it brought tears to the eyes.

For many Mexicans it's not the war that makes Chiapas unappealing. 'Why on earth do you want to go there?' exploded a banker at a party in Mexico City when I told him I was going to Chiapas. 'It's a throwback to the Dark Ages. Forget about the twentieth century, or even the nineteenth. They're still getting through the eighteenth down there.'

Which is true, in part. Most of *los indígenas* in Chiapas – the Maya Indians – still live in wattle huts, without electricity or running water, planting their maize on clifftops and mountainsides, on the poorest margins of the land. Indigenous Indians make up 90 per cent of the population in the uplands, the heartland of Chiapas – that's more than any other state in Mexico and reason enough, to their minds, for most people to continue to ignore it. Politically speaking, little has changed in Chiapas in 150 years. Indentured labour still exists on some of the big haciendas. The Mexican Revolution that brought about the redistribution of land in much of the rest of the country passed Chiapas by. There were no middle classes or mestizos here in the 1920s to push forward the reform. Today over half the land – most of what is fertile and farmable – is owned, just as it was pre-Revolution, by wealthy landowners comprising only 2 per cent of the population.

Developments in the twentieth century have stretched the inequalities even further. The state has immense natural resources. Chiapas is now the primary producer of coffee, cattle and cacao in Mexico; fourth in natural gas. It also produces 5 per cent of the country's timber and 4 per cent of its oil. But while Chiapas produces 55 per cent of Mexico's hydroelectric energy – 20 per cent of Mexico's total electricity – seven out of ten indigenous homes have no electricity. Nine out of ten have no water. Chiapas also produces 28 per cent of Mexico's meat supply. Yet of its population of 3.7 million, 66 per cent suffer from malnutrition and 90 per cent cannot afford to buy meat. Around 37 per cent of men and 63 per cent of women are illiterate; 20 per cent of people have no income; 40 per cent of farmers are paid half the minimum wage. Infant mortality is double the rate in the rest of Mexico and one third of adult deaths due to curable infectious diseases.

But while the incursion of modern industry into Chiapas over the past four decades managed to avoid bringing material improvement to the Mayan Indian, it couldn't help bringing about a psychological change. Soon after the establishment of the hydro-electric, gas and oil industries in the region, faint tremors of unrest began to emanate from the cloud forests and canyons. The ancient status quo began to wobble.

Until the Pan-American Highway reached San Cristóbal in 1950 it was easier, people used to say, to get to France or Spain from Mexico City than it was to get to Chiapas. But when roads eventually penetrated the state, the population began to move – and began to get ideas. Itinerant workers headed down from Los Altos to the hydroelectric dams along the Grijalva, to the coffee plantations of Soconosco, the oil fields of Tabasco, even as far as Mexico City itself and the United States, and returned to their villages emboldened by a different view of life.

But still the Mayan Indians, enduring by nature and by force of circumstance, held back. For most of the twentieth century the Chiapas peasants had been kept mollified by the Mexican government's promise of land reform. When, in the 1930s, President Lázaro Cárdenas redistributed thousands of hectares in Chiapas, expropriating stagnant commercial estates and turning them over to the peasants as communal *ejidos*, the Chiapas Indians' faith was, for the time being, confirmed. Though the gift was a drop in the ocean and the expropriated land by no means the best available, it gave them solid grounds for hope. Dogged and determined, encouraged by endless promises from government, they were holding out *in extremis* for further redistributions – sooner or later.

Then, in 1992, in the run-up to the signing of the North American

Free Trade Agreement and largely, most people believe, to encourage US investment interests in Mexico, President Salinas de Gortari rewrote the agrarian reform section of the Mexican Constitution. To the Maya, as for so many impoverished, landless Mexicans, this was tantamount to treason. Ending land redistribution and promoting the sale and renting of communal *ejidos* to private capital and agribusiness, Salinas reversed in one swipe much of what the Revolution had fought for.

Changing Article 27 was controversial across the whole country, but in Chiapas it had dramatic effect. The *Tierra y Libertad* cry of Emiliano Zapata had been betrayed. In the eyes of many Chiapenecos the government was no longer their ally. It had taken up the role of the large landowner and become the enemy. There was no longer any reason for waiting.

When the dam finally burst, on 1 January 1994 – the day the North American Free Trade Agreement took effect – the most extraordinary thing about the event was that it took the rest of the country by surprise. As one rebel later described it: 'When President Salinas went to bed on New Year's Eve he thought he was going to wake up a North American. Instead he woke up a Guatemalan.'

A hero of the hour, calling himself 'Subcomandante Marcos', burst on to the stage that New Year's Day with all the swashbuckling glamour of a modern day Robin Hood. His battle cry was *¡Ya basta!* – 'Enough!'; his band of Merry Men a troop of 2000 well-trained men and women, mostly Mayan Indians, dressed in rubber boots and home-made polyester army fatigues, disguised in black ski-masks and bandanas.

Marcos's timing was perfect and veiled almost a decade spent getting his act together in the jungle. His 'movement' called themselves the EZLN – Ejército Zapatista de Liberación Nacional (Zapatista Army of National Liberation) – or, less formally, 'Zapatistas', who were, they announced, taking up the banner for land and liberty first held aloft by Zapata himself in the bloody uprising of 1910.

According to the Subcomandante, the Zapatistas owed their military training to '. . . Pancho Villa, as far as regular army tactics are concerned, and Emiliano Zapata, with respect to the inter-change between guerrilla and peasant. We got the rest out of a manual of the Mexican army that fell into our hands, and a small manual from the Pentagon, and some work by a French general whose name I can't remember.'

However they'd managed to train themselves, their strategy clearly worked. The local security forces were caught napping over the New Year holiday and Marcos's guerrillas swiftly seized all the major towns in Eastern Chiapas. Ocosingo City Hall was their main objective, being the centre of bureaucratic power for the Lacandón jungle region, and Marcos had made a wooden mock-up of it in their hideaway for his gang to practise on in their long months of waiting.

But it was the rebels' seizure of the city hall in San Cristóbal de las Casas in the highlands that caused the sensation. Running through the colourful, cobbled streets of the old colonial capital, the tourist mecca visited by over a million people a year, with one-shot rifles, bayonets, home-made grenades, machetes, AK-47s and M-16s, proclaiming war on the government, army and police, the Zapatistas were markedly courteous to the startled civilians and tourists they happened upon in their rush for city hall, the radio station and strategic points of power.

Within twenty-four hours the Zapatistas had launched an attack on the Rancho Nuevo army base about six miles south-east of San Cristóbal and freed 179 prisoners from a nearby penitentiary. And they had kidnapped Absalón Castellanos Domínguez, the former governor of Chiapas, one of the largest landowners of the region and renowned for the repressive measures with which he'd defended his 15,000 hectares from encroachment by desperate *campesinos* while he was in power. The guerrillas dragged him off to the jungle to begin a life 'sentence' of hard peasant labour – a lesson, they said, designed to teach him how the other half lived.

The panic-struck Mexican government swiftly moved 12,000 troops and equipment into the region. A pitched battle ensued over Ocosingo – the only sustained fight of the war – and it went badly for the Zapatistas. They were cornered in the market-place and fifty of them were killed. With the central highlands now flooded with troops, the Zapatistas dispersed out of the army's reach into the rugged and inaccessible strongholds of the Lacandón rainforest in the eastern lowlands.

But the stage was now set for what one Mexican intellectual described as 'the first post-modern guerrilla war'. San Cristóbal, with its comfortable hotels, good restaurants, satellite links and cyber cafés, became a communications centre for hundreds of foreign and Mexican journalists. Guessing the identity of 'Subcomandante Marcos', the green-eyed idealist smoking a pipe through his black balaclava and wearing a Madonna-style headset, became a national obsession. All the rebels would admit was that his name represented the main towns in the zone of conflict: Margaritas, Altamirano, Rancho Nuevo, Comitán, Ocosingo and San Cristóbal, and that they, the Mayan Indians, had engaged Marcos – who was clearly an educated outsider – as their spokesperson because of his facility with Spanish (most of them still had trouble with the 'foreign' language), his literacy, and his knowledge of constitutional law.

The Marcos mystery baffled the world and anguished the Mexican government. The city of San Cristóbal was flooded in the following months with press releases hot off Marcos's laptop which was plugged into the lighter-socket of his jeep somewhere in the jungle, and news desks around the world received regular updates by e-mail directly from the man himself. A legend was in the making. The forgotten backwater was making waves.

When I arrived in Chiapas three years later the situation was still nowhere near resolution though things had started well. Peace talks between the Zapatistas and the PRI government had been instigated only six weeks after the storming of San Cristóbal and as a gesture of good will the Zapatistas had released their hostage, the former governor, condemning him 'to live to the end of his days with the pain and shame of having received the pardon and the good will of those he had killed, robbed, kidnapped and plundered'. Two weeks later, thirty-two tentative accords had been announced covering broad-ranging issues of political, economic and social reform. It looked like the Zapatistas had done in two months and with fewer than five hundred deaths what had taken the Salvadoran guerrillas a decade of brutal fighting.

But the Zapatistas soon became victims of their own success. The uprising had thrown the whole of Mexico into crisis. Since the rebellion of Juchitán, cracks had begun to appear in the PRI's defences. But the subsequent Chiapas insurrection, highly publicized thanks to Marcos's expertise, proved a body-blow to the old political dinosaur. It had attracted international scrutiny and thrown the old bogies of corruption, government fraud and dereliction of duty into the public arena where they were being torn to shreds.

The government, fearful that it was setting a dangerous precedent for the rest of the country, began to stall on delivery of the peace agreement; and the Zapatistas, tired of waiting and being toyed with, eventually withdrew their support for it, too, insisting on the withdrawal of the army from Chiapas before entering into talks with the government again.

Then, on 22 December 1997, forty-five defenceless villagers – twenty-one women, fifteen children and nine men were gunned down in the village of Acteal in Chiapas by government-trained paramilitaries. The dead were all members of Las Abejas, 'The Bees', a citizens' organization sponsored by the diocese of San Cristóbal and known to be sympathetic to the Zapatistas. They had been praying at a local shrine when they were attacked. This was one news bulletin that had made it into the headlines in England.

If anything, the situation in Chiapas, as I wandered the dreamy streets of San Cristóbal on a crisp, sunny morning in 1998, was more polarized and more entrenched than ever before. Marcos was, after a couple of years of low morale (there'd been rumours that he'd been murdered or paid off, or simply given up of his own accord), back in the headlines with a vengeance. In 1995 he'd been unmasked by President Zedillo whose exhaustive research had revealed the Subcomandante to be Rafael Sebastián Guillén, the son of a furniture salesman from Tampico, a former university professor, and veteran socialist activist. But subsequent attempts to smear the Subcomandante with allegations of corruption and power-grabbing at the expense of the Indian poor failed to stick. Marcos had continued to wear his disguise as a point of principle. The Zapatista command would remain symbolically anonymous, he insisted, because they represented people who were, as far as the world was concerned, invisible. This was not a publicity stunt, the Zapatistas claimed, but poetic justice. 'Below in the cities, the Mayans of Chiapas did not exist. Our lives were worth less than those of machines or animals. We were like stones, like weeds in the road. We were silenced. We were faceless.' By masking themselves the Zapatistas were forcing the world to stop ignoring their plight. 'We are the voice that arms itself to be heard,' they explained, 'the face that hides itself to be seen.'

Marcos himself, waging what the US military had begun to describe as a 'netwar', had carried the analogy of 'non-self' even further. 'My mask is a mirror,' he declared to the world at large. 'We are you. Marcos is gay in San Francisco, black in South Africa, an Asian in Europe, a Chicano in San Ysidro, an anarchist in Spain, a Palestinian in Israel, a Maya Indian in the streets of San Cristóbal, a Jew in Germany, a Gypsy in Poland, a Mohawk in Quebec, a pacifist in Bosnia, a single woman on the Metro at 10 p.m., a peasant without land, a gang member in the slums, an unemployed worker, an unhappy student and, of course, a Zapatista in the mountains.'

Marcos's message was resonating across the world. In an age of cynicism, he was daring to appeal to something beyond the intellect, to the sense of wonder and intuition that he'd found in the mountains of Chiapas. And he'd become an international new-age hero in the process. He'd been filmed by MTV; even the film director Oliver Stone had come to the jungle to sit at his feet. Benetton had asked him to pose for a corporate advert, but he'd declined. His principles, remarkably, had held firm. And in Mexico, among the indigenous poor, Marcos was now an icon of mythic, almost magical, proportions. The Zapatista propaganda stall I'd noticed outside the Cathedral in the central Zócalo in Mexico City had become a permanent fixture. Copycat rebel groups kept popping up over the country. Meanwhile, 5000 Zapatistas were still holding out in the Lacandón jungle, just a few hours away from San Cristóbal, hosting highly secretive conferences, continuing their unignorable racket about the plight of the Mayan Indian.

It was not long before I witnessed the groundswell of support for the Zapatistas myself. It was Saturday – market day – and the uncharacteristic hush around the sacks of multicoloured beans and spices, coffee and herbs and raw chocolate, the pyramids of vegetables and fruit, the buckets of flowers, was unmistakable. There was only the bare minimum of stall owners holding the fort. The mestizo shops and cafés were doing business as usual; tourists wandered the streets with their fingers in the pages of guidebooks, and queued at the automatic cashpoints; students chatted over cappuccinos. But there was, unusually, no traffic. Then, like the cry of distant birds, I heard the drifting rise and fall of people chanting.

Gradually sounds burst into shape – words like 'liberty', 'land', 'solidarity', 'Indian', 'water', 'electricity', 'hunger', 'Zapata'. Curiosity amassed a pack of *ladinos*, mestizos and gringos on the pavements as the first ribbon of *indios* threaded their way into the town square. They marched with fathomless determination as if this was a rhythm that could propel them through mountains.

They came in blocks. Four abreast. Village by village. There were men marching in the red and white striped tunics and flat, ribboned palm hats of Zinacantán; there were villagers from Comitán; women from San Andrés Larrainzar wearing highland-style *huipiles* with a distinctive design I later learnt represented the ancient Mayan concept of the cube shape of the universe. There were banks of black skirts and red sashes; solid blocks of white wool tunics and long white *pantalónes*; followed by rows and rows of white shawls with red pom-poms; then red shawls picked out with white. Dotted throughout the procession like human safety matches were men wearing Marcos's black wool balaclava; while others, too hot from marching in suffocating ski-masks, pulled cotton neckerchiefs up over their noses like *bandidos*.

Their slogans called for food, clean water, medicine, transport, roads, electricity, for an end to racism and repression, for human dignity for all. 'To be brown is to be forgotten', read a banner painted the breadth of three people, 'To be Indian in Mexico is to be lost'. The sentiments blazed with emotion but the demonstrators themselves looked as collected and non-confrontational as a congregation on its way to church. Only the front-liners seemed to be chanting.

The hundreds became thousands filing past the onlookers crushed together on the pavements – pavements that, only thirty years ago, were out of bounds for Indians. If the protesters were nervous their faces – those that weren't covered – betrayed nothing but solemn purposefulness. The army kept their distance though there were conspicuously more soldiers in town than the day before. On they threaded, still chanting, to the big open Plaza in front of the cathedral where they jostled to find spaces and then lapsed into an expectant silence.

One of the organizers stood up to address the crowd from a rostrum, in front of an amateur dramatic backdrop painted with masked gunmen. A TV crew whirled into action. Journalists and excited tourists raised their cameras. 'Today we are happy for people to take our photographs,' the speaker announced, attempting to reassure the camera-shy, 'the media is our friend. The world outside must see our faces.'

There followed a number of interminable speeches from local trade union leaders through which the Indians stood as patiently as if they were waiting for a bus. Then copies of a letter from 'Subcomandante Insurgente Marcos' were circulated through the crowd. It was dated the previous month and addressed to the 'Workers' Trade Union and the Municipality of San Cristóbal de las Casas, Chiapas'. This was characteristically more stirring:

Brothers and sisters,
    With interest and indignation we have read your letter describing the atrocities and humiliations which have been dealt you by the municipal authorities in San Cristóbal de las Casas, headed by the dissembler Rolando Villafuerte. We have also read, this time with admiration and respect, about your struggles and your commendable resistance against the injustices of government.
    It is well known that the present state and municipal authorities

are not in control of the land of Chiapas, that the work of
government is in the hands of the military, and that the civil
authorities are only concerned with appearing to govern in the
press and during festivals. This irresponsibility is reflected in the
increasing public insecurity, the deterioration in the standard of
living of the people of Chiapas (not only the indigenous people),
the total absence of any social works that don't serve some
strategic, tactical or military purpose, and the violation of the civil
rights of everyone who has raised the name of Chiapas out of the
mire in which the present government leaders have plunged it.

Your struggle is just and, for this reason alone, merits
success . . .

Farewell. Good wishes and may the dignity of the workers be
like a flag that gives shelter to everyone.

From the mountains of south-east Mexico,

(signed) Subct. Marcos

December 1996

The letter fluttered in hands the length and breadth of the Plaza
but few heads bent to study it. Unable to decipher the words the
crowds waited for the speaker to read it aloud. There was a tiny,
polite clatter of applause when he finished and then, finally, as if
suddenly succumbing to the old, familiar world weariness once
again, the assembly drifted apart, back to the buses and *colectivos*
(collective taxis) that had brought them from their villages. A few
dozing protesters in balaclavas were left stranded on benches,
exhausted by the pre-dawn start to get here.

There have been two great uprisings in Chiapas before this one
and to most minds they are linked to the same movement – tremors
predicting the present earthquake. In 1712 a young girl, María
Candelaria, saw an apparition of the Virgin. News of the miracle
spread through the province and thousands of *campesinos* flocked
to the site. But the Church refused to legitimize her vision. Six
thousand Tzeltal Indians from around San Cristóbal, led by Sebastián Gómez de la Gloria, took up arms against the Spanish.

In 1868, another young girl, Agustina Gómez Checheo, from the
township of Chamula, heard the voice of God speaking to her in

some stones. Once again the indigenous people, this time mainly Tzotzils, flocked to the speaking-stones and the oracle became a focus of indigenous discontent. Agustina was thrown into prison but a non-Indian from Mexico City, Ignacio Fernández Galindo, became leader of the protest. He promised to lead the Indians into a 'golden age' when their land would be returned to them.

Both revolts were crushed, the first by the army of the viceroy and the second by the army of the Republic, and both leaders were executed.

But Marcos's Zapatista rebellion has epoch-making resonances and is carried on a tide of local and international optimism. Though emphatically secular as an organization, the movement itself is swathed in divine and mythical portent. In March 1994, just over two months after the Zapatistas' New Year uprising, shamans representing the five Maya groups – Tzotzil, Tzeltal, Tojolabal, Chol, and Mam – convened at the Temple of the Inscriptions in Palenque, site of the tomb of Lord Pakal and the Maya Tree of Life, to conduct an important ceremony of worship. Climbing the precipitous steps to the top of the Temple, in which Lord Pakal had been entombed in AD 683, they set up a sacred shrine with multi-coloured candles, wild plants and copal incense burning in a large censer, symbolizing 'the heart of heaven and the heart of earth'. There they announced the end of the era of the Fifth Sun, the time of hunger and disease, and the dawning of the era of the Sixth Sun – a time of hope and unity for indigenous peoples everywhere.

In December that same year, as if fulfilling the shamans' prediction of the collapse of the old world order, three weeks after a new President, Ernesto Zedillo, took over from the discredited Salinas, the country suffered its severest economic crash in modern times: the peso lost half its worth, US$10 billion of capital fled the country in panic and the stock market, once the best performer in the world, became the worst. And, true to form, that national Geiger counter, the mighty Popocatépetl volcano, blew its top. The whole country, it seemed, was reacting in sympathy with the uprising of the Maya.

*

My *pensión* in San Cristóbal is a right-on, PC, ethnic jewellery and hairy jumpers, big bear-hugs and back-rubs kind of place. It's called 'Na Bolom', which is Mayan for 'House of the Jaguar' and was once the home of the Danish archaeologist Frans Blom and his Swiss wife Trudy Duby Blom, the conservationist and photographer.

Frans, a handsome, Boys' Own, Hemingway type, devoted to the whisky bottle and feats of endurance in the jungle, died in 1963 from cirrhosis of the liver; the entrance-hall immediately inside the front door, paved with the upended bottles of a hundred late nights is, unintentionally perhaps, a tribute to his excesses. He was responsible for excavating the extraordinary Mayan city of Uxmal in the Puuc hills in Yucatán, as well as several important Mayan sites in Guatemala and Chiapas. His office is just as he left it – trays of unidentified potsherds, antique typewriter, full ashtray, empty bottle.

The overflow extends to the garden at the back where pathways, criss-crossing a hillside of organic vegetables and flowers and a reforestation nursery of pine saplings, are marked out by an impressive curb of green and brown bottles. The muralist Diego Rivera and his crippled wife, the artist Frida Kahlo, might easily have downed a quantity of these staying as the Bloms' guests; so might Leon Trotsky, a close friend of Diego and secret lover of Frida. Trotsky had fled to Mexico to escape the clutches of his rival, Stalin, and enjoyed a social, more than socialist, three years in the country until an agent of Stalin's finally caught up with him and drove that famous ice-pick into his skull.

Trudy Duby Blom died in December 1993, less than a month before the Zapatista uprising, and though then in her nineties is said to have entertained Marcos and other key insurgents in the run-up to the rebellion. Certainly their strategy would have appealed to her notoriously fiery temperament and communist leanings. Ever since she arrived in Chiapas in the 1950s Trudy Duby had championed the cause of the Mayan Indian, focusing in particular on the pathetic plight of the Lacandóns – a distinctive tribe from the Lacandón rainforest who were down to barely a couple of hundred in number when she discovered them. Their elder, Chan-kin, became Trudy's closest friend – her soulmate the

Indians believed – so no one was surprised when the two died exactly a month apart.

Trudy's photographs of Chan-kin and his family, dressed in their traditional white *shikurs* – a kind of coarse, long shirt looking unfortunately like something from a lunatic asylum – cover the walls around the courtyard of Na Bolom. They are frozen in time, these Lacandóns with their straight, long hair, paddling dug-outs across misty lakes, hunting with arrows, leaping over tree trunks, playing with wooden toys around their huts deep in the rainforest. On the pin-board in reception, leaflets invite you to visit the last families still living in the forest. This is part of Trudy's legacy, a desperate attempt to provide the last of the Lacandón people with medical support and an alternative income to logging and cattle farming – the means to provide some kind of bulwark against the outside world.

Of all the Mayan peoples the Lacandón have had the sorriest time in terms of numbers surviving to the present day. Resorting to a primitive existence deep in the rainforest sometime after the collapse of the last Maya strongholds in the seventeenth century, they retained the purest relationship of all to their forebears. Unlike the Highland Maya who were enslaved by the Spanish, the Lacandón cut themselves off from the mainstream populations in the region and avoided the diluting effects of intermarriage and cultural exchange. Farming tiny gardens, familiar with more edible and medicinal species of plant than most modern botanists could name, they continued to worship the ancient gods, traipsing through the jungle to light copal in the temples of their ancestors at Palenque, Bonampak and Yaxchilán. Hidden away in their jungle villages they avoided direct confrontation with the Spanish, only to be decimated by proxy when the European diseases finally caught up with them. They were brought to the verge of extinction, it is said, without ever setting eyes on a white man.

And there they remained, isolated in the forest, their culture intact, their numbers dwindling beyond the point of no return, until the arrival of rubber-tappers, roads, ranchers, loggers, oil prospectors, archaeologists and the photographic lens of Trudy Blom brought them into the limelight.

It is difficult to believe, looking at these fading pictures, that the three hundred or so remaining Lacandón – those who have not already become converted *evangélicos* or thrown in their lot with the *rancheros* – could survive the onslaughts of the twenty-first century, galloping deforestation and the inexorable process of *mestizaje* of intermarriage and cultural dilution, particularly now Trudy and Chan-kin, the twin pillars of their tiny culture, are gone. Traditional Lacandón say the reign of the God of Creation is over: the supreme god is now the Lord of Foreigners and Commerce.

Dinner around the thirty-foot-long cedar table in Na Bolom's dining-room – the table that Frans used to thump in impassioned debate deep in his cups – is an unpredictable affair. Sometimes you find yourself sitting alone on your bench like the school reprobate staying behind for detention, shivering with cold yet uneasy about lighting the fire just for yourself and too self-conscious to ask for another glass of wine (there is a reluctance in the kitchen, stemming from Trudy's dislike of the demon drink, to be forthcoming with alcohol). Then there are other evenings, like this one, when the dining-room is suddenly stuffed to bursting, the fire has been lit – by someone else, and the chatter and clatter of knives and forks on hand-painted plates lifts the preponderant gloom close to revelry.

I find myself sitting next to an earnest and humourless Israeli, a volunteer on one of Na Bolom's conservation projects, so eager to divest himself of his problems and insecurities ('I feel closer to the Maya than my own people, especially the orthodox Jews. I think it's because I've connected with the collective unconscious. I'm a tribesman. This is my destiny. This is where I feel I belong'), that there's no chance to acknowledge, let alone engage with, the person on my right, who seems an intriguing pocket of silence in the rowdy room.

Opposite, though, it's impossible to miss the American girl from Oregon who has, over her stay here of three weeks, perfected an eye-catching imitation of Frida Kahlo – hair plaited on top of the head Zapotec-style, black embroidered *huipil*, lips thick with red, kohl-drenched eyes, and heavy earrings. Even her eyebrows are as daunting as her role-model's, like thick black caterpillars meeting in the middle; though the American has managed to avoid Frida Kahlo's moustache.

Next to her, a vegetarian couple from Switzerland, newly arrived, are nervously studying protocol. One of the local tourist guides takes the opportunity for a standard tease. 'Could you pass the monkey-meat?' he asks. A look of horror crosses their faces but it's left to one of the other foreign volunteers to explain it's a joke.

At last I escape the Israeli bombardment and can turn with relief towards my fellow diner. He's instructing his wife what to put on her plate. At first I take them for Japanese. It's not until I notice the strange guttural language between them – oddly evocative of Klingon in *Star Trek* – that I realize they're Lacandón. The man's hair is cut short and he wears an unremarkable shirt and trousers, but his profile is heart-stoppingly, miraculously, identical to a lord on a Mayan frieze. There is the broad, slanting brow; the tilted, Asian eyes; the deep, earth-red complexion; and most of all, the prominent, unmistakable nose rounded at the end, with no bridge, coming straight out from the forehead – not Neanderthal but noble – princely, intelligent. It should be adorned with jade. I find myself worrying for a moment about how, should he lose his sight in old age, he could ever wear spectacles.

We eventually fall into conversation and he shyly explains that he's on his way to Mexico City with his family to sell Lacandón wood carvings. He's been to the capital once before and was amazed how easy it was to sell everything he had. There were wads of cash in his pockets. Then he asked someone the way to the Metro and they offered him a lift. But once in the car, they put a gun to his head and drove him round for hours before taking everything he had. Now he has friends to stay with in the city and he won't be so gullible again – the man from the rainforest finding his feet in the asphalt desert.

He shakes my hand when he gets up to leave and as I watch him thread his way round the table with his family I can't help feeling that a number of mysteries that will never be solved go with him. I make a mental note that I have seen surely one of the last living profiles of the ancient Maya.

*

At the other end of the scale of Mayan survival the Tzotzil-speaking Chamulans have fared conspicuously well. Their communal lands are mountainous, eroded and over-grazed, but they cover 142 square miles – more than the sovereign nation of Grenada – and are home to 50,000 native Chamulans.

The main town – the centre – of Chamula is six miles to the north-west of San Cristóbal and is notorious for its ethnic ferocity. It features prominently in every guidebook on Mexico. Since the Revolution Chamula has banned all outsiders from living in their community centre. In the 1980s the Catholic priest was expelled after conflicts over Chamula's peculiar, home-grown Mayan brand of Catholicism. The Church of San Juan Chamula is now administered by shamans.

The church has consequently become one of Chiapas's main tourist attractions and an easy source of income for the township. But tourists are suffered rather than welcomed here and while visiting the centre are subject to Chamulan rules and the typically Chamulan manner of law enforcement. Two years ago, an Australian couple were so badly beaten for taking pictures of the church they ended up in hospital in Tuxtla Gutiérrez, and in another incident a tourist was clubbed for refusing to contribute to the collection box.

I mustered a skirt, long sleeves and my best behaviour and squeezed into a *colectivo* plying the winding road from San Cristóbal up to Chamula. As we climbed, the denuded hills of the Valle de Jovel stole back snatches of pine forest and the breeze gusting through the driver's window was clean and fresh and redolent with sap. It gave the air, already sparky with altitude, an extra thrill of elevation.

We were heading for a hanging valley, a Pre-Columbian command post, and with each new turn in the road the countryside seemed to slough off more of the Spanish influence and regain more of its Indianness. There were wattle huts by the roadside and the fields were marked by crude boundary fences of sticks plaited together with ropes of twisted grass. The maize crops were skeletal and withery and almost ready to harvest, stalks deliberately broken so the ears could dry. Here and there creeping fingers of erosion had gnawed at the topsoil, exposing ridges and fissures the colour of dried blood. We turned off the tarmac road and down a track leading to the centre of Chamula where the *colectivo* stopped, at the edge of the market-place, in full view of the church.

The principality of Chamula was once a Mayan trading centre in the Post-Classic period and, like their Tzotzil rivals in nearby Zinacantán, used to export amber, salt, quetzal feathers and animal skins to central Mesoamerica. The Aztecs never managed to gain control of these centres despite repeated attempts, although they had an enclave of their own traders in Zinacantán.

When the Spanish arrived in the region under the auspices of the conquistador Bernal Díaz, author of *The Conquest of New Spain* – hot-foot from playing his part in the fall of Tenochtitlán – they enlisted the help of the Highland Maya to subdue the warlike Chiapenecos (after whom the Europeans named Chiapas) along the Grijalva River. Like the Tabascans and the Zapotecs and all the others before them, the Chamulans took advantage of this unexpected opportunity to wipe out an old enemy and threw in their lot with the Spanish.

But when, with the Chiapenecos disposed of, Spanish soldiers started throwing their weight around in the highlands, demanding gold and tributes from their former allies, Chamula revolted. A pitched battle ensued, which might have gone the way of the Chamulans had not the ever-devious Spanish enlisted the help of Zinacantán, Chamula's nearest neighbour and oldest enemy. Despite a desperate stand in which they pelted the Spanish troops and their Tzotzil neighbours with rocks, boiling oil, rotten fish and boiling water mixed with blood, the Chamulans were overcome and the women and children and the few men who remained were dragged off down to the valley where the Spanish had set up their camp. This rude camp became the principal market for the selling of Mayan slaves, earning itself the name *Villa Viciosa* – 'Village of Vice'. This was the ignoble genesis of beautiful San Cristóbal de las Casas.

With Villa Viciosa as their base, the Spanish troops proceeded to subjugate all the surrounding Mayan communities one by one, destroying their cities, burning their hieroglyphic texts and sacred relics, and forcibly converting them to the Catholic faith. Remarkably, the Aztec prophecy of doom and the cataclysmic ending of the world of the fifth sun was mirrored in Mayan mystical texts attributed to the great priest-seer, Chilam Balam. The Mayan tradition, too, seemed to anticipate the arrival of the Europeans: 'Prepare yourselves, oh my little brothers, for the white twin of heaven has come, and he will castrate the sun, bringing one night, and sadness, and the weight of pain.'

The township of Chamula and its territory were handed over to Bernal Díaz as a reward for his efforts in the conquest of Chiapas. But if he had hopes of finding gold here at last, he was disappointed. What little gold the Chamulans had, had already been surrendered as tribute. Like many indigenous peoples they failed to see the magnetism of the stuff. They had no secret hordes, no knowledge of rich seams in the mountains or tales of rivers heavy with alluvial metal. The conquistadors' dreams of El Dorado floundered yet again.

Díaz's prospects were further squashed when a decree was carried to Chiapas from the King of Spain placing all Maya communities of the Highlands under the sole jurisdiction of the religious order of the Dominicans. Bernal Díaz and his fellow conquistadors were stripped of their titles to Maya lands. The man dispatched with the royal decree, who had solemnly pledged to convert all the Maya to Christianity, but who also, unusually, vowed to preach to them in their own language and to protect them from the depredations of the civil authorities, was the courageous and visionary Bishop Bartolomé de las Casas. Falling thankfully on his protection, the Maya converted, and the Knowledge and Love of God, the Peace that passeth all understanding, settled like a veil on the mountains of Chiapas.

It was Sunday and the market in Chamula town square was in full swing. Women in black felt skirts and red cummerbunds, with ribboned plaits, draped in shawls a universal midnight blue, were engrossed in the art of commerce. Their tables were piled with oranges, tomatoes, onions, clothes, spices, dried beans, medicinal herbs, hats, clay incense burners, bundles of resinous pine-wood kindling, little pottery animals. The men of Chamula sauntered around the periphery, hands in pockets, making their presence felt. They wore jeans, white stetsons, belted ponchos and were well-heeled, unlike the women and children who went barefoot. Most of them were drunk.

Off to one side, on benches arranged in a semicircle and facing a bust of Benito Juárez sat the *caciques*, the Lords of Chamula. They watched over the scene with eagle eyes, staves at the ready, ostentatiously arrogant like a meeting of customs officers or prison wardens. Today was the day villagers came to them to resolve their disputes. The law lords wore wide, straw, cymbal-shaped hats hung with ribbons. Underneath, their skulls were bound pirate-like with white headscarves.

At odds with this display of ethnicity, behind a phalanx of blue Mayan crosses, advertisements for Coca-Cola ran around the edge of the plaza like billboards at Brands Hatch. A few Pepsi signs were sneaking up the side-streets, getting ready to take the soft drinks war on to a fresh battleground.

The Church of San Juan Chamula billowed over the end of the plaza, bright white against the rain clouds like the sail of a Spanish galleon. From the outside, at first glance, it looked like any church in Mexico – grander and larger than most village churches, perhaps, but with the familiar façade: the stout square belly, the sloping shoulders, the neon crucifix at its peak. Beneath the bells hanging idly in their arches was the date 1522–1524 – the Spanish conquest of Chiapas.

But there were differences – signs that a more primeval, indigenous voice was ringing out from within the imposing tower of Christianity. The arches around the great oak front door were painted turquoise and moulded with arches of flowers, so it looked like you entered the church through a rainbow. In front of the door, in the courtyard – the open chapel where the first Chamulans would have converted – stood a large wooden crucifix. It was not simple and straight like the Christian cross, but carved and rounded at its three ends. This was the Mayan cross – a totem already worshipped by the Tzotzils when the Spanish arrived.

To the Maya the cross symbolizes the Tree of Life that stands at the centre of the world and supports the heavens. Seen vertically, it represents the roots, the trunk and the canopy of the tree – the underworld, the world and heaven. Horizontally, the cross is 'the eye of God' – the axis of the four directions. It features in the ancient hieroglyphs describing the celestial bodies and on the tomb of Pakal in Palenque, built eight centuries before Columbus. In the lowlands, the cross is made from *ceiba*, the sacred hardwood of the Lacandón rainforest. But up here in the Highlands it has always been made of pine, like the one Christ was nailed to in Israel, and decorated with fresh, living pine branches to symbolize happiness.

Pine or not, for the Maya the Catholic crucifix – that frame of mortal death, the key to the Resurrection, gateway to Heaven – was but a short remove from their own view of the Tree of Life. Happily or unhappily, it eased the way for their conversion.

But there were other coincidences that paved the road to synchronicity. The Mayans already practised baptism, for instance, and confirmation, and fasting, and sexual abstinence before rituals. They used incense, and dressed their idols in fresh clothes every year, just as the Spanish would one day demand they dress the statues of their saints. Aided by a complex and flexible mythology, and a talent for lateral-thinking, the Maya were able to mould their religion to fit the new clothes of Catholic dogma, much as the conquered Aztecs, and the Zapotecs had done. But, unlike the Aztecs, the Maya were fortunate in a protector, the unusual Bishop de las Casas, who saw to it that they lost as few of their traditional *costumbres* as the Church could possibly allow.

The conquistadors not only brought Christ and the Virgin to Chiapas, they brought the other subversive mainstays of their civilization with them, not least of all, their livestock – chickens, pigs, horses, cattle and sheep. The poor, rough terrain of the Highlands proved perfect for sheep and before long Chamula, long renowned for its skilful techniques of weaving with native cotton and rabbit fur, had marked itself out as the wool-making capital of the region. The church of Chamula was founded, inhabitants insist, on the very spot where St John, or San Juan – who was supposed to have brought the first flock here himself – discovered water. He touched his sheep with his crook, one by one, and they turned to blocks of stone which were used to build the foundations of his church. No Chamulan will eat mutton to this day, preferring to sell his animals, if he has to, to the neighbouring Zincantecos so they can commit this sacrilege instead.

I paused for a moment on the threshold of the church. There was that familiar reluctance, that brief shiver of hesitation I always felt before entering a place of God. Since San Miguel, my usual suspicion that someone might leap out from behind the door and clout me over the head with a Bible seemed more powerful than ever. Only here that recalcitrance proved to be justified. Just inside the dark, cavernous entrance, a Chamula 'policeman' in white woollen *chuh* was on the lookout for anyone inappropriately dressed or carrying a camera. He was tapping his club like a *mafioso* with a baseball bat. He was clearly enjoying himself in a brutish sort of way and I could see him leaping in at any opportunity to teach a tourist a lesson. He looked me over like a shepherd checking a sheep for blow-fly, then reluctantly let me pass, taking an extortionate 30 pesos off me 'for the collection box'.

I took a few steps further inside and all thoughts of the policeman vanished. I was arrested by a more profoundly unnerving sensation. I had steeled myself for the thin, rarified atmosphere of a cathedral, the aching hollowness of an empty stomach. I hadn't bargained for a blanket of heat and smell and the shimmer of thousands upon thousands of candles. The great belly of the church was brimming with a sickly, heady fog of copal seeping from hundreds of little pottery braziers. This was food for the gods, sustenance for dozens of saints who ranged the walls, wraith-like in the mist, in vertical glass coffins. The air was so thick and smothering it seemed, as I plunged deeper into the miasma, that I wasn't breathing any longer, but drowning.

There were no pews. No pulpit. No priest conducting a service. People were sitting on the floor like families at a picnic, or kneeling by themselves, cocooned in the light of their candles. The floor was covered in fresh pine needles and spent candle stubs. In front of me, an attendant was busy scraping at the floor-tiles with a hoe, but as fast as he scraped up the wax, more candles sank into oblivion and even more flickered up from the floor to replace them.

Babies cried. The sick groaned. The grieving sobbed. And beneath the staccato cacophony, from all sides, came a mumbling rhythm of prayer. It was a gut-wrenching, rending sound – unintelligible, of course, in the Tzotzil tongue – but wrung from the core, a collective anguished ululation.

Slowly, meticulously, I threaded my way round the church. Shafts of sunlight fell through the haze from somewhere near the ceiling. On my left was a row of glass boxes housing the saints – Catholic martyrs striking over-dramatic poses like mannequins in a shop window. They were all male down this side; females were opposite, on the right – or supposed to be. Oddly, a couple of saints had swapped sides, as if they'd come to life at night when no one was looking and traded places for a bit of hanky-panky. The saints in Chamula could be as mischievous as Juchitán's San Vicente Ferrer.

They were dressed, not in the gaudy satins of conventional martyrs like the saints in San Miguel, but in finely woven Mayan cloth and traditional wool tunics. They had wigs made of Indian hair. And there were mirrors hanging around their necks. The Maya, like the Aztecs and other Amerindian cultures, have always regarded mirrors as vital religious tools. Originally concave and made of polished obsidian or slate-black pyrite, mirrors symbolize reality – its surface and its depths; as well as concentrating and containing the magic or spiritual power of shamans. Mirrors were often buried with the dead to act as a portal or guide to the Underworld. Here, though, they were also talismans, protectors of the souls of people praying to the saints. Sometimes, in its fervour, a soul might become detached, transported, from its body. The mirror's reflection would remind the supplicant of time and place, of who he was; it would help keep body and soul together.

Many of the congregation, I noticed, could have done with a little extra grounding. They were swigging from bottles of *pox*, swaying drunkenly on their knees, eyes rolling blindly at the middle distance. Others were gulping down bottles of Coca-Cola and belching for all they were worth. This was the time-honoured way to expel demons. The floor around them was littered with Coca-Cola bottles. For the congregation of the Mayan church,

Coke was a godsend. It made burping easy even obligatory. Great bubbles of excess wind rolled up the oesophagus, erupting in lusty blasts as the supplicants gulped down bottle after bottle of this sacred wonder drink, this efficacious fizz-pop. I wondered if even the Mexican franchise of Coca-Cola had any idea that their product was being used as an exorcist.

The billboards round the market-place no longer seemed symbolic of global capitalism, of conquest in a modern disguise; but another case of Chamula converting the outside world.

I began to feel a bit dizzy. There were beasts in the ceiling above the altar: a mountain lion in one corner; a jaguar, or *bolom*, the messenger of God in another; then a bull, the Mayan god of rain; and an eagle with a snake. In the altar itself, a typically ornate gold affair, was a tableau of a pair of cattle. I felt I was losing my bearings. This was Christianity inverted, returning to animal roots. The distance to the door seemed endless. It felt like the church was beginning to rock. The noise of prayer, the low, mumbling hubbub began to boom inside my head.

On my way past the line of female saints, I encountered a man and a woman standing together holding hands. The woman was racked with grief. The man's lips moved robotically in prayer. There was something familiar about them. At first I took them to be husband and wife. Then the man began passing an egg over the woman's body and I realized, with sudden, foolish clarity, that this was a shaman with his patient. That the whole church, in fact, was full of shamans practising their art, teasing out demons like Na Marce had done for me, imprisoning them in the tiny, fragile orbs. The man, I realized now, had not been holding the woman's hand but feeling her pulse, telegraphing life from one world into the next like a lightning conductor. I was seeing black spots in front of my eyes and my legs felt like jelly. I burst out of the door just in time, taking great gasps of fresh air into my lungs, and sat on the church steps, head between my knees in brilliant daylight as though I had broken a spell.

Bartolomé de Las Casas, the missionary who gave his name to the capital of Chiapas and brought Christianity to the Maya, was a remarkable man by every account. His reputation has survived the vagaries of history like no other Spaniard from the times of Conquest. Even the virtuous Bishop Vasco de Quiroga of Pátzcuaro in Michoacán, land of the Purépecha, has come through the fires of contemporary criticism a little singed at the edges. But Las Casas is a case apart. Every Mexican recognizes his legacy to their country, cherishes that brave solo cry for reason in the midst of the chaos of conquest, that oasis of pity in a moral morass. He was perhaps the world's first liberation theologist.

Las Casas was seventy in 1544 when he arrived to assume the Bishopric of Chiapas, the wild new province at the fringe of the Spanish Empire. He'd had a tempestuous career, one that had earned him enemies amongst conquistadors, colonial administrators, merchants and traditionalists back in Spain, even the Spanish Court and the Catholic Church.

He'd first raised his head above the parapet shortly before the turn of the century when, following in his father's footsteps he'd crossed the Atlantic to the Caribbean as an ordinary colonist. His father had sailed with Columbus in 1492. It would have been an irony not lost on Las Casas that the town he came to minister at the end of his life was named after Columbus's patron saint, San Cristóbal.

Bartolomé was appalled by what he found in Hispaniola. Again and again he recrossed the Atlantic to lobby the king to put a stop to the persecution of the Caribbean natives by his fellow countrymen – 'the destruction of the Indies' as he called it. In 1510 he became the first priest to be ordained in the New World and his title 'Protector of the Indians' became official.

A liberal thinker like Quiroga, Las Casas, too, tried to establish Utopias in the New World, model colonies whose success might change his country's barbaric methods of colonization. But his colonies were not a success. The first, on the Venezuelan coast, was destroyed by hostile natives; the second, Verapaz (True Peace), established among the Maya of Guatemala, had some initial success but was soon sabotaged by Las Casas's compatriots.

In 1543 the Spanish king tried to persuade Las Casas to take on the Bishopric of Cuzco, the old Inca capital of Peru, but he declined.

He wanted a territory without gold and riches, something poor and unassuming, where his humanitarian hand would be most appreciated. He undoubtedly found that in Chiapas. Las Casas took on a Sisyphean task and engendered so much opposition in just three years from all the colonials, the regional administrators, the privateers and filibusters, rival preaching orders, even Indian *caciques* in the pockets of the Spanish, that he was called to answer charges of treachery before the Council of the Indies.

The debate that ensued between Las Casas and his prosecutor, Sepúlveda, a man whose beliefs put him somewhere to the right of a modern-day Milosevic, is one of the most extraordinary in history. Sepúlveda was arguing that American Indians, like Africans, could not be classed as human beings because they had no intelligence and therefore no soul and no free will. Like animals, Christianity and the laws of humanity could not be applied to them. Sepúlveda backed his argument with the famous papal bull that had granted rights of dominion in the New World to Portugal and Spain. Las Casas argued that the papal bull only decreed the responsibility of the Catholic Church to evangelize in the New World, and moreover, that it should do so without the use of force. Not only were the Indians civilized, intelligent human beings, they had the right to refuse the political hegemony of Christendom if they so wished. 'When we entered [New Spain],' he asked, 'would we have found such great unions of peoples in their towns and cities if they had lacked the order of a good way of life, peace, concord and justice?' He presented appalling estimates of the cost of conquest: fifteen million Indians had died, he said, as a result of Spain's greed. At the time this figure was viewed as ludicrous. Nowadays it appears horrifyingly accurate.

Las Casas went so far as to report one *cacique*'s statement that if the Spaniards went to heaven, the Indians would prefer hell. He even defended cannibalism, land redistribution and retribution for all the wealth Spain had plundered from the Americas.

He won the case but it was a Pyrrhic victory. By then the Arawaks, Caribs and Aztecs had been destroyed; the Maya and Inca civilizations were in tatters; and though Spain now tried to halt the runaway train of conquest, there was no putting the brakes on the plague of gold-diggers and freebooters already unleashed on the jungles of Mesoamerica and South America.

Las Casas's achievements were not inconsiderable, however – one might say they were miraculous given the times. In 1542 he pushed through laws reducing compulsory labour, and in 1550 managed to ban slavery among the Indians (although not among blacks imported from Africa).

But his greatest legacy was symbolic rather than material; it lay in the very fact of his existence. In poor rural areas like Chiapas the Las Casas precedent established a tradition of filial attachment between priests and Indians, a tradition that was to spark off flashes of rebellion from within the Catholic Church at critical points in Mexico's history. Hidalgo and Morelos, the nineteenth-century leaders of the War of Independence who had raised aloft the banner of Guadalupe, were both village priests, and their armies, in the first stages of the rebellion at least, predominantly Indian.

Today that tradition is reflected in an extraordinary historical echo, some people say a reincarnation, of Las Casas himself. A prominent standard-bearer in the human rights battle in Chiapas is Samuel Ruiz, the present Bishop of San Cristóbal de las Casas. Conscious of the historical comparison, and equally of the little that has changed in Chiapas in the intervening centuries, Bishop Ruiz held his first state-wide indigenous congress in 1974 in honour of Bartolomé de Las Casas. Only the previous year public attacks on Bishop Ruiz by the Mexican government brought over 15,000 indigenous people down from the mountains to march in his defence through San Cristóbal. It was the largest protest in the history of Chiapas – larger even than the 1992 protest against the 500th anniversary of Spanish Conquest.

Hanging on the wall of the Bishop's office in the episcopal building in San Cristóbal is a painting of Samuel Ruiz meeting his predecessor, Bartolomé de Las Casas. The two look almost identical. Samuel Ruiz is living out his last years (he, also, is now in his seventies), like Las Casas, in Chiapas, having devoted his life to raising the standard of living of the Indians and seeing them granted equal status alongside all other Mexicans. Like Las Casas, who condemned the practice of compulsory conversion, Samuel Ruiz has even supported the cause of Protestant converts in their bid to free themselves from repression by their ruthless village overlords.

It was undoubtedly Samuel Ruiz's championship of the poor in Chiapas, the fever of moral outrage that his extreme brand of liberation theology encouraged across the region, that helped bring Indian discontent to crisis point. 'These people', said the 'Red' Bishop, referring a little dismissively to the Zapatistas, 'have arrived to mount a saddled horse.'

On my wanderings around San Cristóbal I found myself constantly passing one particular street where an Indian woman was selling tiny Zapatista dolls on the pavement. We began to acknowledge each other and smile and slowly her natural reticence began to fade and we were exchanging greetings and the occasional flippant remark. One day I decided to stop and buy something and, squatting down by her mat, turning over some of the dolls in my hands, asked her where she came from. 'Chamula,' she answered, 'but now I live here, in San Cristóbal.'

I told her I'd just been to Chamula, that I'd visited the beautiful church there, that I found the place very moving, very powerful. To my surprise, the shutters came down. She looked away, busying herself with the things in her basket, muttering that she hadn't been to Chamula in nearly a year. I persisted, as gently as I could, and asked whether she didn't have family or friends still living there that she'd like to visit. I assumed she hadn't the money to spend on a *colectivo* to get there. Looking down at her mat, ostensibly rearranging her wares, she answered, in an almost imperceptible whisper, '*Soy expulsada*'.

I'd heard of *los expulsados*, the expelled ones, the exiles – tens of thousands of Chamulans who'd been expelled by the *caciques* over the last couple of decades for converting to Protestantism but I knew little about the circumstances. Try as I might, I couldn't draw her out further, but later that day I stopped by to pick up a shawl she'd promised me. She was guarded now and at first I found it difficult to engage her in any conversation at all. Only when I began to ask about her handiwork did she seem to find it easier to talk, as if we could somehow deflect the intimacy, the invasiveness of my questions by focusing them indirectly at the mat.

She showed me which of the dolls were Subcomandante Marcos, which ones Comandante Ramona and other members of the Zapatista command. Apart from Marcos, who smoked a matchstick pipe, they looked indistinguishable from each other, little rifles across their chests, black balaclavas over their faces. Only Ramona was distinct. She wore a black felt skirt and fuchsia cummerbund and had green eyes. She also had bare feet. 'Women in Chiapas are always barefoot,' my friend said. 'They cannot buy shoes. Men buy nice things for themselves – jackets and boots and always they buy alcohol – but women and children, they do the work and they go hungry.'

I was surprised by the vehemence of her words. Her voice had barely risen from its soft murmur but there was a perceptible heat behind it. 'In San Cristóbal', she continued, packing up her things to go home at last, 'things are different.' She was a Protestant now and her children were at school. They had money and new clothes and plenty of food, and a good roof over their heads. 'Jesus is merciful,' she said. 'He looks after us now.' She made no mention of her husband and I wondered if some awful fate had befallen him or if, as she seemed to suggest, he may have been part of the reason for her conversion in the first place, and her subsequent expulsion. The doll-seller gave me a sweet smile, hoisted her wares on to her back, adjusted the tumpline across her forehead, and hurried off down the street, head bowed beneath its strap, but with new shoes on her feet.

As I headed back for dinner at Na Bolom I found myself marvelling, not for the first time, how one country could foster such extremes of womanhood. There were only 200 miles but a world of difference between the big, bold Juchiteca and this tiny Mayan, and it seemed clear that misogyny was one of the benchmarks of conquest. The Spanish had come down hard on the Indians up here in the Chiapan highlands, and all the complexities of conquest, the Indians' humiliation and anger and guilt, seemed to have found a voice in a universal condemnation of woman.

Their world vision destroyed, the Maya had taken the ideal of the Catholic Virgin to heart. Women were disenfranchised within their own society, instilled with the discipline of sufferance, their old powers taken away. They learnt to be non-judgemental, ever-loving, ever-giving, as silent and as patient as the Mother of Christ, like Guadalupe herself. If men needed someone to blame, someone to hit out at for their misfortune, their lack of purpose and self-esteem, Catholicism was offering them ready-made punchbags.

It was an attitude so ingrained in the psyche of the conquered they had invented their own words for it. The verb 'to beat someone up' in Mexican Spanish is *madrear*. *Valen madres* is to be worth nothing, to be utterly useless. *Me vale madre* means 'I don't give a fuck'; *¡Qué desmadre!* – 'What a mess!'; and if you want to tell someone to piss off, you tell them *chinga tu madre* – fuck your mother.

Distrust and fear of women runs deep. Conquest brought the Indians and mestizos their own Eve to haunt them and to blame. She was the transverse of the virginal protectress Guadalupe – a promiscuous betrayer who opened her legs to the invader and condemned her country, her people, and all her descendants to the evils of the Spanish Empire.

'La Malinche' was Cortés's mistress and interpreter. She was one of twenty women awarded him by Indian *caciques* as a gift of victory after the conquistadors won their first battle on the coast of Tabasco in March 1519. The women became the first Christian converts in New Spain and mothers of the first mestizos to boot. Foremost among them, according to Bernal Díaz, was one Doña Marina, a 'most excellent woman', daughter of a *cacique* of the village of Painala, a barely pubescent virgin whose name had been Malintzin before she was baptized. She became known among the soldiers as La Malinche.

Though she didn't immediately become Cortés's mistress – Cortés gave her first to one of his captains – La Malinche was clever and charming and opportunistic. She quickly learnt Spanish and was soon making proclamations to the Mexicans on Cortés's behalf, conducting negotiations between the *caciques* and conquistadors, driving home Cortés's demands and advising him of military tactics. Without her willingness to impart her knowledge of the indigenous *costumbres*, of native vulnerabilities, of local politics and geography, without her as a mouthpiece to communicate and win allies among tribes subject to the Aztecs, Cortés's expedition might have had a very different outcome. She was by his side throughout his campaign and eventually bore him a son, Martín Cortés. The fact that La Malinche supported Cortés as an act of rebellion against the despotism of the Aztecs was soon forgotten. History rewrote her story as a 'betrayal of the fatherland' and La Malinche became a scapegoat for Mexico, a vessel for Mexicans' overall sense of betrayal, anger, rejection and humiliation.

Malinchismo, another uniquely Mexican word, has entered the language, too, thanks to her. It refers to Mexico's magpie weakness for foreign things, the kind of magnetic failing that makes the country's youth hunger for Chicago Bulls baseball caps and Nike trainers. *Malinchismo* is cultural betrayal and it underscores an inherent national insecurity: Mexico is not good enough. Nothing she produces is quite up to scratch. Mexico is not The Real Thing. *México vale madres*. Revelling in a sense of self-negation, Mexicans refer to themselves as bastards, sons of bitches, *hijos de la chingada* – literally 'children of that woman who's been fucked'; offspring, in effect, of La Malinche, the ultimate national whore.

Since the arrival of the Spanish, Indian and mestizo women have found themselves trapped between these two contradictory perceptions of womanhood: Guadalupe and La Malinche. Even if they are paragons of virtue and behave like the Virgin herself, they are still whores and betrayers at heart – the weaker vessel, never to be trusted. It's a fear that underpins the Mexican cult of machismo. A woman's sexuality is a fearful weapon. She may never be satisfied. She may turn to another man at any time, when you're least expecting it, even when she seems at her most loving and trustworthy. It makes her a dangerous creature to live with. She is the enemy within. For the sake of her children and, naturally, other men, she must be kept out of temptation's way, caged like a wild animal, her spirit crushed. 'A woman's place is in the home', goes the saying in Mexico, 'with a broken leg.' It doesn't take a psychiatrist to see that this fear stems from insecurity, from that sense of degradation and impotency instilled in the nation from the moment of conquest.

That Juchitán escaped this cultural perversion was testimony to the irrepressibility of the Zapotec character and culture, their extrovert, cosmopolitan outlook, as well as luck and geography. Yet up here in the secluded Chiapan mountains, something similar, at last, was happening, too. Comandante Ramona was showing Maya women the way. 'For five hundred years,' she protested at the outset of the Zapatista movement, 'women have not had the right to speak, to participate in assemblies, they have no right to education, nor to speak in public, nor to take *cargos* (public posts, both civil and religious) in their communities. No. The women are completely oppressed and exploited. We get up at 3 a.m. to cook corn and we don't get to rest until the evening after everyone else is asleep. And if there isn't enough food, then we give our tortillas to the children, to our husbands. We [women] demand the respect, true respect as Indians. We also have rights . . . and my message to all women who feel exploited, ignored, is take up arms as a Zapatista.'

In February 1997, risking arrest, Comandante Ramona went to Mexico City, to the Zócalo, to lead a demonstration against the army occupation of Chiapas. Crowds turned out in their thousands. The foreign media was out in force and the government had no alternative but to allow the little Mayan woman in her black, sheep-wool skirt, a platform to speak. As Ramona was still unable to speak fluent Spanish, an interpreter translated her words from Tzotzil. 'I have sixty thousand olive-green reasons for coming here,' Ramona said. It was the first time the tiny Comandante had ever left Chiapas; the first time she'd seen the capital.

My friend, the doll seller, had taken her Mayan *comadre*'s words to heart and made a bid for freedom, voting with her bare feet. So were thousands of Maya women like her. Half the fighting force of the Zapatistas were now women. Thanks largely to the mobilization of the *madres*, Chiapas was breaking its bonds.

My admiration for Chamula's 'cultural integrity' and its fiercely guarded customs had been shaken by my encounter with the doll seller, but I wasn't aware of how serious and how widespread the discontent with Chamula's famous *costumbres* was until I unearthed a video called *Blood of Chamula* in a local Protestant bookshop. I'd found the shop in a side-street and thought at first it was a stationer's. The significance of the tambourines nestling among the notebooks in the window didn't register until I'd gone inside. There were boxes of Good News Bibles open on the floor and trays of *¡Cristo Vive!* stickers by the till. Postcards of happy Indian converts were pinned to a board. *Blood of Chamula* was sandwiched on the video shelf between *Witnesses of Jehovah* and *Hope of the World.*

I watched the video in Na Bolom's lecture room where normally they show footage of Trudy and Frans' life. The acting was appalling, like a Mexican TV soap, with macho posturing, bad hair-dos, gratuitous violence and the odd rape scene. Protestants were identified by their smiles and Bibles and the happy songs they sang while they did their chores; Chamulans staggered around swigging on bottles of *pox*.

The story the film conveyed was one of systematic brutality by the lawlords of Chamula, and the persecution, even murder, of anyone who dared challenge their rules. A man was clubbed close to death for buying goods at cheaper places outside Chamula; a woman was beaten because she said she had no money to buy candles for the church and refused to go into debt; a girl gang-raped for listening to Protestant hymns on the radio. Abused, bruised and battered Chamulan villagers found refuge with Protestant pastors in San Cristóbal – their wounds were tended, they saw the light, their mournful faces burst into sunny smiles.

The video was unashamedly propagandist but it was disturbing nonetheless. It was well known that Protestantism was gaining a foothold among the Maya, but the view in Catholic Mexico was that this was evangelism by coercion – rich gringo Bible-bashers bribing native Indians away from their culture. I'd never heard it suggested that the Maya might have good reason to convert.

The following day, a Sunday, I ventured out to Nueva Esperanza – 'New Hope' – a colony in the northern suburbs where 15,000 Protestants, mostly *expulsados* from Chamula, had established themselves. I was expecting something similar to the dirty, impov-

erished barrios of Mexico City but the taxi dropped me in a
neighbourhood that the home counties would have been proud of.
The streets were pristine – no dead dogs or blocked drains or
rotting vegetables; everyone, even the children, smartly turned out;
the houses spanking new, two-storeyed, with glazed windows and
expensive doors, all newly painted brilliant white or blue or pink
or yellow. The streets themselves were called 'New Palestine',
'Gethsemane', 'St Anthony of the Mountain'.

The Church of Nueva Esperanza was the antithesis of the Church
of San Juan Chamula. It was built out of concrete and brick and
looked like an aeroplane hangar. The pastor and his associates
were greeting the congregation at the door, shaking hands and
welcoming people in; a far cry from the Chamula policeman with
his club. Inside it was light and airy, large enough to accommodate
a congregation of 3000. Conspicuously, there was no altar, no
crucifix, no bleeding saints or sorrowful Virgin, no incense, no
candles, no pulpit; just a raised platform at the far end with a
dispatch box on it and a microphone. The women were ranged in
pews on the right of the church (their older children were occupied
in Sunday school) – not hiding away at the back like in most
Catholic churches, but up front and parallel with the men. Gone
were their traditional midnight-blue shawls. Here they were
dressed in a riot of pink, green, white, purple and turquoise
rebozos. They still wore the traditional hairy black skirt bound at
the waist with a woven Mayan cummerbund, but their hair
gleamed in sleak black plaits and they all wore shoes. They laughed
and chatted with each other, where in Chamula they would have
huddled close to the floor not daring to utter a word. I looked for
my friend but couldn't see her. It was obvious, though, who among
the women were new recruits, like her; and those who had the
benefit of several years or decades of self-confidence.

The service struck up with a toe-curling teenage electric band
who clearly had rock 'n' roll ambitions but fell way short of a
talent show on a bad day. Girls in long white shifts (not dissimilar
to the Lacandón *shikur*) and purple sashes gambolled in like Pan's
People and began skipping about with ribboned tambourines. They
were joined by a handful of boys in purple waistcoats waving flags

like toreadors. The congregation leapt to their feet and started clapping and bouncing in time to the music which was relayed in overwhelming decibels from speakers up and down the walls.

At the end of the first song the pastor welcomed the congregation first in Spanish, then in Tzotzil, and, spotting me, the only white face in a sea of brown, announced, 'I see we have guests today from the United States.' 'Err – *Inglaterra*,' I corrected him, reddening as everyone turned to look. 'I don't know much English,' cried the pastor, 'but I can say *Bienvenidos* – "Welcome!"' Everyone clapped and shouted 'Amen' and the women around me shook me warmly by the hand.

A hymn sheet was handed around and I noticed with surprise that almost everyone could read it. It was printed in Spanish with a Tzotzil translation. More songs followed, an upbeat Girl Guides by the camp fire type of song followed hotly by a syrupy lament that had people who had been waving their arms in the air a few seconds ago reaching for their hankies.

Then the pastor spoke, wailing in a voice ragged with emotion, about how Christ died on the cross for us, how we killed him and tortured him, stoned him with our insults and abuse and denials, yet still he loves us all, each and every one of us, no matter how terrible our sins, he loves us, he does – Hallelujah! – more than a mother loves her children, he forgives us and welcomes us – Hallelujah! – opens his arms for us, so we can know his love and kindness like a sheep coming back into the fold after a long night lost on the mountain, like a lamb in the arms of a shepherd, so he can wipe away our tears and bring us happiness – Hallelujah! – (then falling to a whisper) O Lord, forgive us, forgive us, teach us to love you as much as you love us, save us O Lord from the darkness (voice rising as if strengthened by divine inspiration), take us into your fold, our shepherd (shouting triumphantly), O Lord, we are saved! We are SAVED! WE ARE SAVED!

It was too much for the woman next to me who screamed 'Hallelujah!' and collapsed in a heap of ecstatic sobbing. I looked around and others were trembling as if on the verge of an epileptic fit; more still were in trances, their eyes meeting with something wonderful in the ceiling.

Three hours later, emotionally drained, hands tingling and voices hoarse, the happy-clappers spilled out of the church, radiant, purged and invigorated, eager to get back to their new life. I waited behind so I could corner the pastor.

Juan Hernández Hernández, in his mid-twenties, was younger than he looked in the dispatch box. He had a sweet, kind face and a little son who ran off in his sneakers and sweatshirt to buy an ice-cream with his friends. I asked him first where all the money came from to build such an enormous church. 'We had a donation from a Swiss evangelical mission, near the beginning,' he answered, with disarming frankness, 'but that was a one-off. Most of the building has been paid for by the *expulsado* families – with donations and free labour.'

There were forty Protestant churches in San Cristóbal now, he went on – that's more than Catholic. In all, 35,000 Chamulans had been expelled from their land, nearly a third of the Chamulan population; and 15,000 from Zinacantán. Nearly all the pastors were Mexican; many were Mayan. There were very few foreign *evangélicos* now in Chiapas.

I asked him about the allegations that Protestant evangelists had been offering Indians cash and promises of employment to join their church. Juan nodded. 'There are many stories like this,' he said. 'People see that the converts have become wealthy since they left their village and they assume it must be because of bribes. They don't know any other way.'

And he began to explain the dynamics of poverty and power in Mayan villages like Chamula. It was the *caciques*, he said, who had the monopoly on shops allowed to trade there; who sold all the compulsory religious accoutrements like *pox* and *copal* at vastly inflated prices. Villagers were expected to light dozens of candles in church every week – one for every family member, every chicken, every sheep, every pig. But a candle cost 7 pesos in Chamula, compared to 5 pesos in San Cristóbal – a significant difference for an impoverished villager who couldn't afford the *colectivo* to town to buy the cheaper ones.

It was the *caciques* again, he said, who included most of Chamula's hundred shamans, who insisted on the *costumbre* of prolific *pox*-drinking – not only because they were the only ones licensed to sell it, but because it kept the adult male population, at least, in a malleable state of addiction and poverty. If you didn't drink *pox* with the boys, he said, you were branded a homosexual and hounded out of the square. It was the *caciques*, too, who had introduced Coca-Cola into the equation back in the seventies, no doubt receiving generous acknowledgements from the distributors in the process. If you got sick you had to go to a shaman for a *curación*, which was very expensive. The shamans didn't like you going to a doctor. But you needed to buy sixteen bottles of Coke for one healing, and *pox* on top of that. 'That's another advantage of being a Protestant,' Juan smiled, 'our healings cost nothing.'

Bound up with their economic stranglehold over Chamula was the *caciques'* political clout. For decades the *caciques* had been receiving 'privileges' from the PRI in return for guaranteeing the votes of their villagers. In the past this had not proved so contentious since the voting was always rigged anyway and few people were brave enough to defy the national ruling party. But now that the PRI was losing its grip and the voting procedure was being cleaned up, an individual's vote had currency again and villagers began to resent being coerced.

When Protestant *evangélicos* arrived in Chiapas many Chamulans, like Hernández's father who converted in 1974, saw the light. They saw their church for what it was – the lynchpin of the *caciques'* power; not a sanctuary or a refuge or a place of inspiration but a symbol of Chamula's way of keeping most of its population down at heel. Juan Hernández's father was beaten for possessing a Bible and for trying to teach his wife to read. The whole family was eventually expelled and Juan, who was two at the time, had never been back. He didn't even know what the famous Church of San Juan Chamula looked like.

Like all *expulsados*, Juan's father made a pledge of teetotalism and was helped to find a job. Protestant friends taught him to drive and he became a taxi-driver in San Cristóbal, eventually earning enough money to take a share in his own car. The congregation helped build a house for Juan's family on the understanding that they would help other *expulsados* establish themselves once they had found their feet. For the first time they had plenty to eat, clean water, electricity; they could buy clothes and luxuries; it was no longer a struggle just to keep clean. Juan's mother got a job doing housework; she learnt to read, and soon was teaching Bible classes herself. Eventually there was enough money to send Juan's brother and sister to college in Tuxtla Gutiérrez.

Juan's elder brothers often told him of the bad times back in Chamula, when their stomachs burned with hunger, when their father got drunk and beat their mother, spent all their money on drink and never lifted a finger to help in the fields. But more than all that, they said, they could never forget what it was to live in fear. Now they were free from the long arm of the *caciques* and their *costumbres* and they could hold their heads up high.

'That's why I became a pastor,' said Juan, 'so I can spread the Word. It's a way of thanking the Lord for giving us His Love, for showing us a life of peace and dignity. I give thanks every day that Jesus Christ came to release us from our predicament.'

'Don't you want to go back to Chamula, one day?'

'Of course,' said Juan. 'We all miss our land. It is where most of us were born, where our people came from. We're still Mayan and we're proud of that. That's why we teach in the Tzotzil language. We try to go back to Chamula all the time but we're always driven out again. Only a few months ago, some members of our congregation managed to get a small church built just inside Chamula territory. The *caciques* got to hear of it and sent men to burn it down.' His eyes blazed with passion. 'But the flames did not take. Witnesses who saw it said the petrol they were pouring on the building turned to water and their firebrands went out. It was a miracle. We'll go back there soon. Christ is merciful. He holds the Valle de Jovel in the palms of His hands. I pray that one day all the repressed Maya will know His Goodness.'

From Nueva Esperanza I crossed a stream back down to town but after wandering around the centre for an hour or so I decided to gain height again in order to try to clear my head. The narrow streets with their elevated pavements that had you jumping off to make way for oncoming pedestrians, seemed muddling even though they were neatly organized on a grid. Somehow I never had the right sense of direction or distance. I was constantly surprised by where I'd ended up.

The main square seemed to be part of the problem. There was the typical park and bandstand enclosed in a plaza of colonial mansions (one of them, the Casa de la Sirena, is said to have been built in the 1570s by the conquistador Diego de Mazariegos), but the cathedral ran along it, sideways on, its flank taking up nearly the entire length of the north side. Squeezed into the north-east corner like an afterthought, at the back end of the cathedral, the much smaller church of San Nicolás did the honours and faced the square. The cathedral itself – where Bishop Samuel Ruiz had conducted negotiations between the Mexican government and the masked Zapatista rebels – faced west, the way of the infidel, and overlooked a secondary, empty plaza.

The directional conflict of the two churches seemed to emphasize the paradox of everything I'd encountered in the past few days: the Catholic church dedicated to Mayan gods; the dichotomy of Chamulans who'd kept their faith because they had no choice, and who now faced a choice of land or liberty, but not, as in the great precept of the Mexican Revolution, both; the Protestant pastor who preached the New Testament in Tzotzil and still believed himself a Mayan; the silent, orderly Indian demonstrators whose banners screamed with centuries of pain and neglect; the Lacandón Indian learning survival in the concrete jungle; the masked university professor hiding out in the Lacandón rainforest with his laptop and AK-47.

Eventually I found my way to the giant flight of steps leading to the Church of San Cristóbal, once the site of an old hermitage chapel, high on a hill overlooking the capital. The church faced east, the way of the rising sun, towards Europe, which somehow helped to settle my swinging compass. I sat with my back to the front door, exhausted but exultant, high as an eagle, looking out over the red-tiled roofs and secret inner patios. The wind whistled nonchalantly through the pines. A thermal of *zopilotes* wheeled over the city at eye-level.

I was brought back to earth after a while by a tiny outstretched hand brushing against my knee and a little voice piping 'Cinco mil pesos, señora, cinco mil pesos,' then, 'My face is cheap, señora, take my photo.' For a moment I was stunned that a poor Indian child could really be asking for the equivalent of $500 instead of the usual *cinco pesos*. But then I realized she was talking in a currency that pre-dated the dramatic devaluation of the peso over fifteen years ago. I handed her some coins and she skipped off to show her sister, a toddler barely on her feet.

Far below, the cathedral chimed minutely in the plaza like it was battling against the ether. There was a different pace of time in Chiapas. The clock ticked slowly, taking its cue perhaps from the Mayan perspective where the past and the present were constant rivals, where the concept of infinity was familiar and undaunting; where the idea of zero was as natural as one or two, and the future lay aeons away, in the lap of the gods.

From here the colonial capital of San Cristóbal was a feudal place, magical but anachronistic, a Forbidden City, a source of mixed blessings. The Maya had avoided so many of the evils of the modern world, but at what cost? As a race they'd struck a remarkable balance in the wake of the Spanish Conquest, preserving their *costumbres* from cultural attack and grafting their spiritual beliefs on to the new Cross. Certainly they'd been fortunate in the patronage of Bishop Bartolomé de Las Casas who'd arrived just in time to snatch them back from cultural annihilation at the hands of the conquistadors, like so many of the central and northern tribes. But even the famous Protector of Indians could do nothing to save them from the enemy within.

When the Spanish made allies of local leaders, gave them gifts and privileges, taught them Spanish, used them as intermediaries between their two civilizations, they were using an age-old tactic, setting a time bomb that would shatter the traditional village structure for ever. In Chiapas, *caciques* were no longer chosen by the villagers in recognition of their leadership strengths; and the *caciques* were no longer wholly indebted to their villagers, bound to them by material necessity and a sense of duty. From that time on, village leaders would also be in league with the outside authorities, with the invader. Honest, traditional elders, the ones who only spoke Tzotzil, who adhered to the ancient customs, who had a healthy disrespect for money and foreign goods and the 'bitter tongue' of the Spanish would always be at a disadvantage; while the corrupt, the greedy and the culturally malleable, would find themselves on the fast track to positions of authority. In exactly the same way *Caciquismo* was the system exploited by the national ruling party, the PRI, four centuries later; and the means by which the 'democratically elected' government party could keep a stranglehold over the country for seventy years.

Increasingly, from the time of conquest, the primary interest of the *caciques* in places like Chamula became not that of the community as a whole, but of themselves: their main purpose had been to keep the villagers in obeisance, primarily by keeping them poor, and to keep their own pockets full. If the *caciques* could disguise this strategy as preservation of the Mayan culture, all the better. They could collaborate with the colonial authorities and deprive the villagers of material improvement – all in the name of cultural integrity.

Meanwhile another agent of Spanish dominion butted its way through the back door. Sheep swiftly took over as the mainstay of local farming. They were admitted into the Mayan scheme of things, were pronounced sacred in Chamula, and began to munch their way across the hillsides, disrupting traditional agriculture, eroding and degrading the communal land until it was unfit to support its native population. They changed the face of Chiapas as they changed the landscape around San Miguel de Allende and across the rest of Mexico. Mexico was not a place of lush green pastures. It could never support intensive grazing by ungulates as Europe could; sheep and goats irreparably impoverished the country wherever they went.

The rot spread from the inside out. The internecine struggle for power and land had begun. It would take centuries for the long-suffering Maya to say 'Enough!', to begin to recognize a Trojan horse within their walls. The cry of 'Land and Liberty' that had echoed across the rest of Mexico would be a hundred years late reaching Chiapas, and then it would be taken up not by gun-slinging banditos but by unarmed Bible-bashers and postmodern guerrillas.

I looked back over San Cristóbal, charmed and medieval looking in the last rays of evening, and saw how convincingly I'd fallen prey to the seductiveness of appearances. I'd fallen into the classic tourist trap. But Chamula had begun to lose its magic over the last few days and for that very reason, I felt I had to go back.

The day I returned to Chamula was inauspiciously dank and miserable. Fog clung stubbornly to the mountainsides much as it had on the day I'd arrived in the Highlands. The maize drooped in the fields, damp and sorry for itself, every stalk hanging its head. Overlooking Chamula, from hilltops conical like pyramids (which, in a way, they were), stood Mayan crosses, bleak and solitary in the mist, marking the shrines of Chamula's three wards. Of the Holy Trinity the crosses represented, Christ, the Rising Sun, was not doing his job. As soon as I got out of the van it began to pour with rain. Something was out of sorts, too, with Christ's other two Mayan partners – fertility and the four directions. The rain, a godsend in the spring, was pronouncing disaster coming now, just before the harvest; and the fog seemed to be doing its best to obliterate all memory of north, south, east and west.

In the town square the trestle tables were abandoned. A few figures huddled under the colonnade of Chamula's municipal building, shivering. The church looked washed out and uninviting. Every now and again one or two men would stumble out of the front door, drunkenly fumble about in their pockets and set off rockets and firecrackers to frighten away the rains. There was a searing sound, whistling up above the height of the church; and then a little smattering of debris falling back down again to fizzle on the paving stones.

The rain was doing a good deal to dampen my resolve. I'd been planning to ask for a traditional *curación* with one of Chamula's most famous shamans, Salvador Lunes, who was also, this year, head of the church. But now, fresh from my encounter with Juan Hernández, the Protestant pastor, with *Blood of Chamula* smouldering on my bedside table at Na Bolom, the prospect of a shamanic healing no longer looked quite so appealing. I was ashamed to recognize a queasy sensation in the pit of my stomach.

The road to Salvador's hut was up a steep hill directly behind the church. In the garden of every house along the way there was an altar and a pot of *copal* smoking at the base of a cross – another desperate attempt to steer away the rain. I was soaking by the time I reached the shaman's house, an unassuming concrete bunker roofed in corrugated iron. The inside was not so typical. Salvador was sitting with his mates in a fallout of empty beer bottles watching *Nightmare on Elm Street* on video. They barely looked up when I entered and it was some time before Salvador swivelled his eyes in my direction and asked why I'd come.

'I've come for a *curación*, Don Salvador,' I said. 'If this is a bad time I can come back.' The shaman struggled to his feet, a beery grin spreading across his face. 'No, now is good,' he said. 'Give me a few minutes', and he shoved his friends out of the door.

Salvador had good living, if not good taste, written all over him. He was wearing a black leather jacket, orange shirt open-necked with medallion, grey flannel trousers with a paunch, and tan cowboy boots which added a feel-good few inches to his height. His hair was oiled back to emphasize generous sideburns which gave him the look of a diminutive Engelbert Humperdinck. Incredibly, there was a gold Rolex watch – or a good imitation of one – on his wrist.

'Present from President Bush,' he said when he saw me looking at it. He may have been drunk but he didn't miss a trick. A smile of satisfaction spread across his face when he saw my look of amazement. He wasn't joking.

'That's me and the President,' he said, pointing to a picture of the two of them sitting on a sofa in the White House together. 'The Governor of Chiapas took me to see him because they thought the President had cancer. But he didn't. It was a spirit illness – something you can only get rid of with a *curación*, something only an experienced shaman like me can deal with.'

It was too good to be true, I thought, forgetting my scepticism – how perfect, how eminently satisfying that Mayan shamanism could be finding fertile soil in the United States; that a tiny town in southernmost Mexico should be turning the tables and launching such a high-flying missile of counter-evangelism! A thrill of excitement, of discovery overtook me; I was already back in London thumping out headline news. Salvador, however, was moving swiftly on. He had material matters on his mind. 'It's one thousand pesos – one hundred dollars – for a *curación*,' he said, handing me a bundle of well-thumbed photographs of other satisfied clients. There was Bob and Barbara smiling on their porch in Santa Monica; Rick in a wheelchair in Minneapolis; Rutger on a motor-bike in Holland.

Even for a shaman with Presidential connections this price was extortionate. It was more than most Mayan farmers earned in two months. Almost reluctantly I found myself protesting. 'Why's it so expensive?' I asked, 'is there a different charge for tourists?'

'Foreigners are more expensive because they're more difficult to treat,' he said, eyes glittering with irritation, 'their spirits are usually much sicker.' He was standing close to my face, accosting me with clouds of beery breath. The whites of his eyes were shot with blood vessels like road maps but the pupils still seemed capable of boring through walls. 'My price isn't for just one *curación*,' he lurched insistently, 'but for many ceremonies. I do many healings on my own, even after you tourists have gone home, to make sure you stay well. It's difficult doing long-distance *curaciónes* – it takes much time and energy.'

A flicker of suspicion crossed my mind. 'You must be busy with this lot,' I said defensively, handing back the bundle.

'Do you want a *curación* or not?' he snapped.

I bargained him down to $60, beginning to feel foolish, and took the chance while he was out of the room assembling bits and pieces, to study the trophies on his walls with a more critical eye. Next to a brochure of the Marriott Hotel in Washington, the menu from a revolving observatory restaurant and some unused air miles, was a 'Certificate of Appreciation' from the 1991 Festival of American Folklife.

Presented to
SALVADOR LUNES COLLAZO
by the Smithsonian Institution Office of Folklife Programs
in official recognition of participation in the
25th Annual Festival of American Folklife
in the National Mall in Washington DC

and in appreciation of exceptional contributions
to the increase and diffusion of knowledge
about the cultures and traditions
which enrich our nation and the world.

I turned back to the picture of the shaman with the President. There was something funny about the shadows. Why was Salvador looking so grey and the President so sunny? Slowly, stupidly, it dawned on me. Without the intimidating presence of the shaman in the room the photograph reasserted itself as what it had been all along – a tourist gimmick, the kind of jokey photo-montage that could have been done at any drugstore or corner shop. The certificate looked genuine enough and proved that Salvador had taken part in a Festival of Folklife in Washington DC, but hobnobbing with the most powerful man in the world, nudging up to him on the White House sofa, was clearly stretching the point.

Confused by the deception, I wondered why and how Salvador could get away with it. Did the Chamulans really believe he'd been treating the ex-President of the United States? Perhaps many of them did. Many of the villagers hardly ever left Chamula, and a photograph like this, crude as it was, would be impressive proof. His 'Presidential connections' might also explain Salvador's outstanding wealth, a fortune that put some of the other leading *caciques* in the shade. But even if some Chamulans did have doubts, Salvador was only, after all, exercising his shamanic prerogative by playing with the truth. As an elder and a shaman he would have a freedom of behaviour beyond that of the average villager. He'd be expected to embellish his stories. Exaggeration, even downright fabrication, would not lose an elder the respect of the community – it might even increase it.

What was disconcerting was how close I'd come to swallowing his story, when I considered myself reasonably observant and well educated – beyond this kind of trickery; how others had also given him the benefit of the doubt, and their wallets. The shaman clearly did a roaring tourist trade. Most of the foreigners who'd come to his house must have looked beyond the missing shadows in the Presidential photograph, the Rolex and the hi-fi and the video, the glaring inconsistencies and the shaman's three-inch heels, and seen only the spiritual authority, the ancient wisdom they had come for.

Salvador returned with a bottle of rose-water, an incense burner, candles, rosaries and a few bottles of *pox*, which he arranged on a large altar on the same wall as the equally impressive TV. The altar was composed of a brand-new glass cabinet with pictures of the Virgin of Guadalupe in it and a traditional Mayan cross, with branches of pine and laurel draped over the top. Pots of dying marigolds and paper roses stood in front.

Salvador sat me down on a wooden chair, put some candles into my hands and pitched into his incantations, taking a swig of *pox* whenever he drew breath. He felt my pulse, asked me to sniff the bottle of rose-water, and blew clouds of *copal* about the place. I watched him sheepishly as he continued his incantations. There was none of the kindness and warmth and conviction of Na Marce; and none of the emotion that I'd felt in the church. Had my perceptions changed so much since then, or were the performances in the church, perhaps, the genuine article, and this only a sham? There were no eggs, no Coca-Cola, no sacrificial cockerels. Salvador shook for a minute or two and then announced in a husky voice that my animal-spirit was the eagle. Despite my hesitations, I was flattered, touched by the intimacy of personal detail. The pull to believe I had an animal-spirit familiar, a Mayan guardian, was surprisingly strong. Would I have felt the same, though, if my spirit had been a rat? The *curación* was over.

There was a rather awkward silence. 'Thank you,' I said. I stood up and started rummaging for the $60 in my bag.

'It must have been a strange experience going to Washington,' I said, unwilling to leave the shaman with the last word, giving one last stab at the bubble. 'Do you think you'll ever go to the States again?'

'I've just come back,' said Salvador blithely. 'President Clinton is very depressed. He needed a *curación* very bad. His spirit is very sick. I may go back to the States in a few months' time to make sure he's OK.'

I felt as though he'd sent me sprawling face-down once again across the length of the room.

'I don't suppose you have a photograph of his *curación*?' I tried to rally.

Salvador grinned. 'Of course. It was a very special occasion. He and his wife, Doña Hillary, were very pleased with me.' And he opened a small suitcase that had been lying under the table. Out came a picture of Hill and Bill beaming into the camera and Salvador next to them, a little blurred, looking the wrong way. Underneath was the caption 'I made friends in Washington'.

Outside it was still pelting with rain. A man and woman were hurrying down the hill bent double under bundles of firewood. They slithered in the mud, the woman barefoot, several yards behind her husband; both were propelled into a trot by the impetus of their loads. At the bottom a group of Americans in Colombo raincoats were being disgorged from a coach. A guide was giving them a brief discourse on the Mayan cross as they unrolled their umbrellas and made a beeline for the church.

Uneasy and dispirited, I made a detour to the old graveyard of Chamula on my way back to the main road. It had been abandoned in the 1960s after being inauspiciously hit by an earthquake. This was where the latest Protestant victims were buried, six young men murdered by their fellow Chamulans only a few months ago. Their coffins had been paraded around the main square, brought to account before the municipal building as if the *caciques* were determined to repossess their souls. The mounds were marked with bright blue Mayan crosses to signify they were the graves of unmarried men and strewn with white and pink chrysanthemums made out of plastic so the graveyard sheep wouldn't eat them.

As I walked slowly back to the road, the rain began to abate, a thin horizon of light lifting the clouds. The tour bus splashed past me, heading for Zinacantán and the next attraction. I wasn't sure any longer what we tourists came away with from here but it was clear now what we were leaving behind: more money in the *caciques'* coffers, the church bouncer's palm well-greased, another rubber stamp on the guidebook version of 'Chamula's proud and picturesque indigenous culture', while a silent revolution raged on backstage, unnoticed.

5

Night of the Dead
Lake Pátzcuaro

For life in Mexico foresees death; it knows that death is the origin of all things. The past, the ancestors, are the source of the present. Now the craters are lakes, are cornfields; once they were boilers filled with fire. Could they be that again? Of course – just as life will come back again, because death precedes it.

Carlos Fuentes, A New Time for Mexico, *1994*

To realize the supremacy of death is not the same as to nullify the life of the present. It is to put this life in its place, to make it ride over several planes at once, to recognize the stability of the planes that make the living world a great force for balance; it is, in short, to re-establish a great harmony.

A. Artaud, Mexico and a Journey into the Country of
the Tarahumaras, *1984*

If death can fly, just for the love of flying, What might not life do, for the love of dying?

Malcolm Lowry, Under the Volcano, *1938*

Mercifully the boat ride across Lake Pátzcuaro was quieter than this time a year ago. I was sitting among islanders, mostly, who were returning from a final day's last-minute shopping in Pátzcuaro town. Shopping baskets on the floor of the boat were stuffed with long tallow candles, candy skulls and skeleton bread – but the region was yet to be crushed by the blockade of holidaymakers that had me stymied a year ago.

Lake Pátzcuaro is high in the volcanic mountains of Michoacán, 40 miles from Morelia. It's a sleepy, tranquil place most of the year. The town of Pátzcuaro, with its red-tiled roofs and whitewashed houses, its cobbled streets and small, provincial plazas, could be somewhere in the mountains of Eastern Europe. The lake is somewhere outsiders come to unwind until bucolic life once again becomes a drag and the city resumes its attraction.

But once a year Lake Pátzcuaro is transformed. Traditionally associated with a pre-Columbian cult of the dead, Pátzcuaro has become the most popular venue in all Mexico for the modern Day of the Dead fiesta. People come here from all over the country and from abroad for the festivities. Traditional celebrations conducted by Pátzcuaro's indigenous inhabitants are becoming harder and harder to find.

I was doing my utmost, though, this time, to outwit the holiday crowds, the three-mile tail-back, the spontaneous rock concert, and to find the 'authentic Purépecha Night of the Dead' that the brochures depicted but so consummately failed to deliver. To do this, I'd learnt from last year's painful experience, I had to take a different tack, veering away from the groove of the tourist mantras and against the flood of mestizos and one-stop party-goers. I decided to take a boat a day early, on 31 October, a full twenty-four hours before the Night of the Dead itself, and head for an island that no one had heard of.

Even so, there were four *juniors* on board – the Mexican equivalent of Hooray Henrys, or *hijos de papi* ('Daddy's boys') as they're sometimes called. They were the vanguard of tomorrow's invasion, bound for our first stop, the island of Janitzio, and they were yelping and bouncing about like labrador puppies and wrecking the sunset for the rest of us. The Indian women with their armfuls of magenta cockscomb looked passively out over the black water with barely a sigh of irritation.

I glowered at the boys in their designer jeans and luminous Nikes without effect. Even the cold which fell like an avalanche with the dipping sun failed to penetrate them. They charged up and down the boat tripping over our bags in the darkness, leaning over the side to splash each other with cold water, roaring at each other's jokes. A brace of duck – a rare sight on Pátzcuaro nowadays – winged their way across the flaming sky like ornaments on a wall. One of the *juniors* raised an imaginary gun and shot them down.

Memories of the year before came swooping back. Seduced by adverts and brochures and posters of candlelit graveyards, I'd headed for Pátzcuaro for what was billed as the most moving and spectacular of all the Mexican holidays.

The Day of the Dead is celebrated all over Mexico. Its roots lie in a pre-Columbian tradition common to all the indigenous cultures of Mesoamerica; a celebration that, in the Aztec calendar at least, went on for two months, instead of just two days conveniently tacked on to a weekend and a bank holiday. It was a period when past kings and their retinues, war heroes and sacrificial victims, children, mothers who had died in childbirth, parents who died in their beds – when all the souls of the departed would visit this world from the various recesses of theirs to mingle with the living and share again the earthly pleasures of food and drink and human company.

When the Spanish arrived they found the tradition too entrenched to eradicate so they merged it with the similar Christian remembrance of All Saints on 1 November and All Souls on 2 November and tried to squash the celebrations into forty-eight hours: the day of 1 November for the *angelitos*, the 'little angels' – children who died before puberty; the day of the 2nd for the adult dead; and the night in between for a traditional vigil.

Over the centuries, as pre-Columbian customs everywhere in Mexico (those that weren't simply eradicated) faded under the spotlight of Catholicism, this ancient celebration was one of the few surviving remnants of Mexico's spiritual past, a communion with the ancient gods and heroes as well as the recently dead. It established itself as one of the nation's national holidays, second only to Holy Week, and, though it had been converted by Christianity into an acceptable form and length, contained much of the colour and character and detail of the indigenous original.

The Mexican Day of the Dead has become famous the world over as the fiesta of death, with revellers dressed as skeletons, ghouls and cadavers; families feasting in the graveyards; towns consumed by a kind of Hallowe'en Mardi Gras.

But the original custom was a much quieter, deeper affair. Focusing on a night-long vigil over the graves of the dead – the *Noche de Muertos* – families would meet up with their loved ones once again, bringing them gifts of their favourite food and drink. The dead of night was a time for gentle contemplation; it was a timeless moment; a space in which the living would assemble to commune with the spirits of the past.

Now, though, influenced by modern consumerism and middle-class spiritual apathy, if a vigil for the dead is conducted at all, it's usually during the day, with portable TVs and sound-systems perched on the headstones to help while away the hours. People still go to the graveyards with baskets of food for their loved ones, especially in the countryside; but not so many of them believe the dead actually come down and consume the essence, the soul, of the food as they used to. Relatives bring flowers to decorate their family graves but now poinsettias, gladioli, arum lilies, dahlias, hydrangeas, ornamental grasses and 'baby's breath' smother the traditional scented marigolds. Few know the old purpose of the wild *cempasúchitl*: that its beautiful smell attracts the dead and shows them the way back to earth through the darkness.

In cemeteries, now, satin wreaths and family photographs and pictures of the saints, marble hymn books and stone epitaphs wrestle for attention among the flowers on tombs that are made of solid stone or concrete and exorcized by crosses. Few people are aware that the dead may be disorientated, even driven away, by daytime noise and the thump of *música estereofónica*; that traditionally souls must be guided through the still of the night, softly, sympathetically, using the delicate scent of wild marigolds and slow-burning *copal*, light from candles and the clear tones of a bell.

Now, particularly in the cities, the Day of the Dead has developed into a parody of its old self – a satire of death. The celebrations have become infected with machismo and cynicism – they are humorous, riotous and seductively irreverent, but a million miles from the gentle spiritual communion that originated with the ancients. Now it's a festival designed to make light of mortal fear and tragedy and loss. It's a mestizo battle-cry; bastard offspring of wars and revolution; a finger up at fleeting lasts and endures; a joke; a chance to bring the Great Leveller down to size.

In Mexico City, Oaxaca, Puebla and Veracruz, *calacas* – little intricate tableaux featuring figurines of skeletons a few inches high – are sold in the markets as gifts and decorations. They cover every imaginable aspect of a dead person's life, or the manner of their death. A skeletal dentist pulls a tooth from his patient's skull; a drunk skeleton falls out of an upstairs window or throws a punch in a bar-room brawl or gets run over by another skeleton behind the wheel of a truck; a dead secretary gets her bottom pinched by her dead boss; a defunct banker does a deal into his mobile phone; a wife catches her cadaverous husband in bed with his bony mistress: *El amor es una cosa esplendorosa, hasta que se entera tu esposa*, reads the caption – 'Love is a many splendoured thing, until your wife finds out'.

There's political satire, too. In the uncertain days of the Revolution and under the present totalitarian regime of the PRI, the Day of the Dead is one of the few occasions when you can ridicule politicians with impunity. Life and the rules of normality are turned on their head. In the face of Death, is the implication, even dictators and politicians have to be man enough to laugh. Before I left for Pátzcuaro, I found skeletons of the President hanging in shop doorways all over Mexico City. One had deliberately muddled President Ernesto Zedillo's name with *cerdo* – the word for a pig. 'This is how I'm waiting for family welfare' read a notice around *Zerdillo's* neck jibing at the time it's taking him to fulfil his electoral promises.

Pátzcuaro, though, is said to be one of the few places in Mexico where the old cult of the dead persists. Here, in Michoacán, in the land of the great lakes, Purépecha Indians still keep vigil by the gravesides through the watches of the *Noche de Muertos*, communing with another world, clinging to the spectre of the pre-Columbian tradition.

One of the people who'd been most moved by what he saw in Pátzcuaro was the muralist Diego Rivera who was a regular visitor to the lake in the 1920s and 30s (his wife Frida Kahlo's part-Indian grandfather had come from the region). It shaped his thoughts about the purity and integrity – the ancient dignity – of the Mexican Indian; themes he'd first been attracted to in Tehuantepec. He brought André Breton and Leon Trotsky here. Pátzcuaro inspired a set of murals called *The Offering*, which Diego painted for the Secretaría de Educación Pública in Mexico City. In them he depicted an obvious difference between celebrations for the Day of the Dead such as he saw performed by the Purépecha and the corrupt imitations by city mestizos: one scene is shown reverently, almost magically, with marigold frames and candles and Indians at their devotions, first in the graveyard and then around the table at the family dinner; the third is a crazy tableau of self-indulgence and commercialism – a jam-packed scrum of dancers in skull masks and skeletons in spurs playing guitars in a city street with Indian women serving them food. The first time I came here I'd set my hopes on the former but found only the latter. I wondered if I'd come too late.

Michoacán. The name derives from 'Michoaque' which is Náhuatl for 'Land of the Fishermen'. Five centuries ago, when the Spanish arrived, the entire state of Michoacán was a mosaic of mountains and water. There were thousands of lakes, immense and small, created by the exceptional geological conditions of the New Volcanic Axle – a ridge of adolescent volcanoes running east–west between the two older, north–south mountain ranges of the Sierra Madre Oriental and Occidental. The New Volcanic ridge had been created by the friction of three tectonic plates that began to collide sixty million years ago. As the volcanoes peaked, now and again bursting in protest and sending lava down their steep slopes, the valleys in between began to fill with rainwater like puddles in an egg carton. There was nowhere for the water to escape beyond the high valleys. Here there were no rivers, no waterfalls, just pocket after pocket of standing water gradually being silted up by topsoil washing down off the volcanoes.

It was a geologial structure similar to the one that created the great, shallow lakes in the Valley of Mexico, except that Michoacán benefited from more expansive topography. The New Volcanic Axle created a fertile oasis in a land that was hard-pressed for water and verging on desert in many areas. Michoacán's exaggerated mountain chains and valleys, creating a natural physical boundary between North and Central America, also produced a range of micro-climates and encouraged the evolution of extraordinarily rich eco-systems within short distances of each other. Thanks to the lakes, there was plenty of water, a good climate, and soil that benefited from a high mineral content. The Axle was akin to the great delta regions of the world, with all the conditions needed to incubate a great civilization.

The Michoaques, or Purépecha as they call themselves, came down to the great lakes from the north-west in the twelfth century, and flourished there from the thirteenth century until the arrival of the Spanish in the sixteenth, creating a civilization to rival any in Mexico. Like the Aztecs to the south, they quickly learnt the advantages of their watery environment and evolved a sophisticated and intensive method of agriculture involving *chinampas* of the kind that survived in Xochimilco, in the suburbs of Mexico City.

Making up for the lack of available farmland in Michoacán, the Purépecha grew an enviable variety of crops in their island nurseries. It was this region that is believed to have produced some of the very first varieties of pumpkin, beans, amaranth, tomatoes, avocados, guavas and chillies. It was probably here – crucially – that the first edible variety of maize was developed from a plant – called *cintle* in Náhuatl – that was originally no more than a grass but that would, over a 4000-year period of careful human husbandry, be encouraged to grow taller than man himself, bear huge cobs of seed and become the staple of all the Americas.

The Purépecha were very different in other respects from the Aztecs. They were artists: woodworkers, engravers, painters and lapidaries; the women were famous for their weaving. They were renowned for their distinctive ornaments and mosaics made out of feathers, and for their gigantic and extraordinarily lifelike maize-pith idols (a technique later exploited by the Franciscans for their own statues – like the early image of Christ in the Parroquia in San Miguel). Massive maize-pith figures of the deities adorned the distinctive Purépecha temple pyramids, or *yacatas*.

The Purépecha were not as flamboyant or dressy as the Aztecs.

They wore only loose cotton shirts and shaved their scalps and bodies until they were totally hairless. The Purépecha themselves claimed to have accompanied the Aztecs on their pilgrimage from lands in the north. Legend has it that when the Purépecha went to have a swim in Lake Pátzcuaro, the Aztecs stole their clothes and ran off with them. And so the Purépecha stayed in Pátzcuaro, semi-naked, cutting themselves off linguistically from their treacherous companions by evolving a different language. The Purépecha language was, indeed, completely different from Náhuatl, the language of the Aztecs and other peoples of the Mexican highlands, bearing striking similarities, instead, to Peruvian Quechua.

The Purépecha originally sacrificed only animals to their gods, although wives and servants were often buried beside their lord. By the fifteenth century, however, the Purépecha had followed the Aztec example and were sacrificing humans – to the God of Fire, Curicaveri. Perhaps because of their metal-working advantage, the Purépecha remained one of the few significant cultures existing in Mexico at the time of the Aztecs not to be conquered by them. Despite repeated attempts over the centuries the Aztecs failed to make headway into the Land of the Fishermen.

Notwithstanding their long, cantankerous history, however, the Aztecs sent desperate pleas for help to the Purépecha when the Spanish arrived. But, like the Aztec Empire, the golden age of the Purépecha was already on the wane. Their king, Tzimtzincha-Tangaxoan II was as confused and irresolute as Moctezuma. He'd already had all his brothers put to death on trumped-up charges of adultery, so anxious was he over the safety of his throne. When the Aztec messengers arrived he disappeared to consult his priests and astrologers, eventually becoming convinced that the only policy was to do nothing. He, too, was worried that these bearded white intruders might be messengers from the gods. He decided to stand back and await events while down in the Valley of Mexico Tenochtitlán fell.

Fearful of a similar fate, Tangaxoan then sent gifts and ambassadors to Cortés. The conquistador Cristóbal de Olid was dispatched by return and he rode into Michoacán placing Tangaxoan under arrest and ordering his men to smash all the idols and burn the altars on the pyramids of three great Purépechan cities – Ihuatzio, Tzintzuntzan and Pátzcuaro. His men, in blatant disregard to the instructions of Cortés, began to plunder, searching obsessively as always for caches of gold.

Even so, it seemed the Purépecha had escaped the carnage and wholesale destruction that befell the Aztec Empire. Until, that is, the infamous Nuño de Guzmán arrived on the scene in 1529, seven years later.

Ironically, Nuño de Guzmán, a nobleman and lawyer from Galicia in northern Spain, had been appointed by the Crown as president of an *audiencia* which was to punish the atrocities of Cortés and the other freebooting conquistadors and set a good example for the future government of Mexico. Spain couldn't have picked a more unsuitable candidate for the job. Before Guzmán had even reached the capital his treatment of the native Indians on the Gulf Coast made Cortés look like a saint. But it was as he headed out to conquer the west and north-west of Mexico that Guzmán's atrocities reached truly abominable proportions.

The territory Guzmán conquered was vast. It became known as Nueva Galicia (after Guzman's home province in Spain) and encompassed the present states of Colima, Jalisco, Nayarit, Aguas-calientes, Sinaloa and part of Zacatecas, Durango, Querétaro, Guanajuato and San Luis Potosí – nearly 20 per cent of present-day Mexico. The expedition began, though, with a massive assault on Tzintzuntzan, the great city on the shore of Lake Pátzcuaro, formerly capital of the Purépecha kingdom in Michoacán.

A number of friars were already busy among the Purépecha, building churches and convents and their kindly labours had almost caused the Purépecha to forget what they had suffered from the soldiers of Olid and to believe that the Spaniards had come to Mexico to bring them a higher civilization. When Guzmán arrived in Tzintzuntzan the peaceable Purépecha greeted him with great ceremony, offering to 'provide him with every service and con-venience'. Guzmán's reaction turned their whole world upside down once again.

Straightaway he summoned King Tangaxoan – known since his baptism as Don Francisco – ordered him to muster 8000 Purépecha to join the expeditionary force, and then threw him in irons, imprisoning him in an alcove between two walls, next to Guzmán's own bedroom. There Guzmán tortured and tormented the wretched king day and night for two weeks. The protestations of the friars were ignored, one of them being dragged down from his pulpit when he preached a sermon denouncing Guzmán; and the Indians who begged the friars for protection were jailed and threatened with hanging.

Guzmán was not only driven by a passion for cruelty, he was consumed by greed. Even though no conquistador had yet uncovered any trace of mineable gold, Guzmán was convinced that his El Dorado, a city 'rich in gold and inhabited only by women', lay just around the corner. He burned the feet off his Purépecha interpreters in an effort to get them to confess to the whereabouts of Tangaxoan's mythical treasure, and submitted others to the dreaded cord and water torture. Wives and daughters of the Purépecha were taken in tribute, dragged off to assuage the sex-starved Spanish soldiers and the Purépecha perhaps ironically, perhaps in an effort to salvage some shred of dignity, began to refer to the Spanish as 'brothers-in-law' or *tarascue*. The Spanish, misinterpreting their meaning, believed this to be the name the Purépecha called themselves. 'Tarascans' is the name that persists commonly today for the Purépecha people although with its shameful connotations it's a particularly distasteful misnomer.

Finally, losing his patience, Guzmán hauled the unfortunate king from his hole in the wall, ordered him dragged by a horse, then had him tied to a stake where he was burned alive and his charred limbs eventually thrown into the river.

Guzmán was getting into his stride. The expedition marched on to neighbouring Cuitzeo where it made war on the population for a week; and when the *cacique* of Cuitzeo approached them to make peace, he was thrown to the dogs because, as Guzmán's accomplice the conquistador García del Pilar later explained, 'he did not bring bearers, or gold or silver as Nuño de Guzmán demanded'. Del Pilar elaborated: 'We left [the *cacique*] bitten all over, at the doorstep of his house, then set fire to the house and the town.'

On the wrathful convoy went, looting and pillaging their way through all the major towns in Michoacán, up towards Jalisco and Tepic in Nayarit, hanging and garrotting any miserable Indians who caused them displeasure or who failed to produce some glittering reward. In direct contravention of the dictates of the Spanish Crown, Guzmán enslaved thousands of Indians who were foolish enough to surrender to him, branding them and forcing them into neck shackles. 'Everything is now done by trickery and deceit,' several of Guzmán's captains reported from their campaign in the province of Zacualpa. 'When the lord and nobles came out to us in peace we surrounded and captured them; then our Indian allies killed more than 2000 people. But the most pitiful of all were the children left to die along the way.'

Guzmán's aim was to build himself an army of miners to help him find his gold but most of them died. Out of 1200 Tlaxcalans who went with him originally as allies only 20 survived the campaign and those were kept in chains so they were unable to escape and return to their families. The sierra was dotted with the bodies of Indians who hanged themselves rather than face this tornado of butchery.

Seven years after he first set out on his bloody *entrada*, the Spanish Crown finally caught up with Nuño de Guzmán. At first, Guzmán had kept a watch over the seaports to prevent any news of his activities being carried back to Spain. Dispatches were intercepted and messengers slaughtered. But Zumarraga, the Archbishop of Mexico City, managed to have a letter smuggled across the Atlantic in a barrel of oil. Zumarraga's complaints were heeded, and a new audience had been set up in 1530, presided over by Bishop Ramírez de Fuenleal, to try this new wave of atrocities. By then, however, Guzmán had raided the royal treasury in Mexico City and was off on the rampage.

Unwilling to interfere as long as Guzmán was at least proving useful by conquering new, uncharted regions, the Spanish authorities carefully noted his crimes and waited for him to return to Mexico City.

At last, in 1536, Guzmán was dragged off to a common prison in the capital where he spent two years before being returned, penniless and anonymous, to Madrid. Two years later he met the fate of almost every other conquistador: that of dying alone and in obscurity. A respected judge and Franciscan bishop, Vasco de Quiroga, was appointed to clear up the mess in Michoacán.

Vasco de Quiroga was one of the rare individuals who, even without the flattering back-to-back contrast with a homicidal predecessor, shines out like a lightship in the tumult of Mexico's early colonial history. Like Bartolomé de Las Casas, who made his name defending the Indians of the Yucatán and Chiapas, Vasco de Quiroga was a man ahead of his time, a missionary of ideals and compassion, a man of peace, with convictions about the dignity of all humankind. This was a giant leap beyond the swashbuckling, self-seeking Homeric ideal that the conquistadors around him adhered to. He was a sophisticated, educated, yet practical man, up-to-date on the latest philosophical thinking in Europe – a far cry from most of the Europeans who had taken it upon themselves to transform the New World.

What Quiroga found in Michoacán dismayed him. He encouraged the people back down out of the mountains where they had fled and, like Las Casas, he set about creating village cooperatives based on the humanistic ideas of Thomas More's *Utopia*. 'Since,' he wrote, with fiery conviction, 'it was not in vain but in good cause and with good reason that this world here was called the New World and so it is new, not because it was recently found, but because it is in its people and in almost everything else, akin to the first Golden Age, which thanks to our malicious and greedy ways has become an age of iron and even worse.'

Quiroga promptly set about realizing his utopia among the despairing Purépecha, establishing communal property, a six-hour work day, the proscription of luxury, elective family magistrates, and equitable distribution of the fruits of labour. Towns around Lake Pátzcuaro still specialize in traditional crafts Quiroga saved from the brink of extinction 450 years ago: lacquerware in Uruapan and Pátzcuaro itself; copperware in Santa Clara del Cobre; pottery in Tzintzuntzan; wooden furniture in Quiroga; guitars in Paracho.

Appalled by the devastation, the poverty, the sight of starving orphans and people already dying from European diseases,

Quiroga set up hospitals and food centres. Just after arriving in Pátzcuaro, I'd visited Santa Fe de la Laguna, a medieval-looking village at the base of Tzirate mountain. There, on Fridays, in the grounds of the chapel, women still cook beans and tamales for the needy according to Quiroga's instructions. Next door in the Vasco de Quiroga museum, crumbling vestments and various items of heavy furniture are displayed – despite the obvious incongruities in style and age – as the original property of the great bishop. They are venerated like sacred relics. A tour guide advised me against questioning the claims made on the labels too loudly. 'The villagers can get very defensive about their "hero",' he said.

Today Quiroga is affectionately referred to by the Purépecha as 'Tata Vascu', Father Vasco, and his statue stands in almost every town square. Despite his inevitable zeal for conversion, for saving the souls of his 'children of nature' as he called them, he is almost universally celebrated as one of the most benevolent of the colonial evangelists – one who tolerated, even encouraged, Indian tradition within the Catholic Church.

Thanks to Quiroga's example, Michoacán became a deeply religious state. It was a stronghold in the reactionary 'Cristero' movement, which fought a bitter war in defence of the Church after the Revolution. Thanks also to Quiroga's early championing of human rights and communal land, the hacienda system that generated such a backlog of suffering and resentment elsewhere in the country, never took possession in Michoacán to quite the same degree as in the rest of Mexico. The revolutionaries Pancho Villa and Emiliano Zapata never became the heroes here that they were in the rest of the country. Equally unbowed, in present times, by the PRI's intimidatory tactics, Michoacán gave birth to the leftist opposition party, PRD (the Partido de la Revolución Democrática – the Democratic Revolutionary Party). On my way around the lake, I'd noticed slogans freshly painted on the whitewashed walls of Ihuatzio cemetery: ¡No más masacres de estudiantes! No más masacres de indígenas y de campesinos! (No more massacres of students! No more massacres of indigenous people and peasant farmers!).

Quiroga may have set a lasting example of social equality and philanthropy in Michoacán and put to rights some of Guzmán's wrongs, but he was no match for the other harpies unleashed on Mexico by the Europeans. Smallpox, typhoid and measles continued to spread like fire in a dry pine forest. In 1643 a plague of typhus swept through the non-Spanish in Michoacán killing five out of every six people. In four months the population of Tzintzuntzan shrivelled from 20,000 to 200. As a race, the Purépecha were scythed to just thousands in number, their spectacular civilization reduced to the realms of legend.

European farming practices had played their part, too, although in a more protracted and insidious way. As in the Valley of Mexico, the Spanish were unappreciative of the Purépecha *chinampas* and the balance they preserved in their unusual environment. One by one the settlers drained the shallow lakes and released cattle, sheep and goats to graze across the new valleys. The extraordinary wildlife, particularly the gigantic populations of water birds, was decimated. Eventually, out of the thousands of lakes that had once existed, only four remained: Cuitzeo, Chapala, Zituarén and Pátzcuaro. The Land of the Fishermen had vanished.

The *juniors* and most of the other passengers got off at the island of Janitzio. The boat felt lighter in every way. A fingernail moon was rising above the mountains with the glittering planet of Venus in attendance. There was still just enough light to see the statue of Morelos – a hideous steel and concrete monster erected in the 1930s in honour of another hero of the War for Independence – saluting us with clenched fist from the top of the island, a Gulliver in Lilliput. The restaurants down on the quayside were getting ready for tomorrow's invasion – thousands of customers who would be demanding the famous *pescado blanco* – a fish unique to Lake Pátzcuaro and now so rare that other white fish must be supplied from outside to masquerade as the real thing. In the soft twilight Janitzio looked benevolent, idyllic even, with its cobbled streets and medieval timber houses. But tomorrow it would earn a place in Hades.

I could remember my last visit here only too well. I'd walked two miles from my hotel to the lake beside a queue of impatient motorists revving their engines, chuffing out clouds of exhaust fumes. Then I'd joined the embarkation queue for Janitzio and took an hour to get to the front of it. When I'd boarded a boat there was no room to sit so I fought for space on the floor. Around 20,000 people poured off the boats on to the island of Janitzio that evening. The back streets had already begun to reek of human faeces and urine as queues for the mobile *sanitarios* lengthened and people became impatient of signs to 'Use the Toilets and Wash your Hands to Prevent the Spread of Cholera'.

Those of Janitzio's inhabitants who were not taking advantage of the business windfall were huddled in their houses watching TV. You had to pay to get from one street to another. There was a queue to cross the basketball court where a Purépecha dance group was performing the famous mask dance of *Los Viejos* – The Old Men – to a packed auditorium. It was a parody, brilliantly choreographed, of how the Spanish conquistadors looked to the Indians when they reached old age – all stooped over and shaky and incapacitated. In other circumstances it would have been wonderfully entertaining, but the crowds were restless and inattentive and there was hardly an Indian in the audience to appreciate the satire. Every once in a while a man with a microphone would yell 'Sinaloa!' or 'DF!' or 'Monterrey!' and a different corner of the crowd would stand up and cheer. People on the grandstand were trying to orchestrate a Mexican wave.

I'd passed through Janitzio's famous graveyard, scene of candlelit serenity on so many tourist posters, before realizing it. Not until the constipated sausage squeezing out of the basketball court had shunted me through some iron gates, moved me by an irresistible process of peristalsis across a patch of bare ground and spat me back into the mainstream revelry did I realize that the bumps and ridges we'd just tramped across were Janitzio's graves. That was the famous cemetery, I realized to my shame, where Princess Mintziata, daughter of Tzimtzincha-Tangaxoan, the last Purépecha king, was said to be buried. The Princess had been captured and imprisoned by Nuño de Guzmán alongside her father.

The legend the Purépecha tell their children today has all the pathos of a vanquished people trying to wrestle back the reins of history; to prove they'd really got one over on the Spanish after all; that, despite the fateful outcome of events, the Purépecha had still managed to hit their oppressors where it really hurt. When the Spanish first arrived and began to plunder the area, the story goes, the Purépecha lords put all their gold and silver, their jewels and precious ornaments into twenty canoes, paddled it all out to the middle of the lake and dumped it where Guzmán could never find it. The twenty valiant captains of the canoes were sacrificed by the king and their spirits sank to the lake-bed where they remain to this day as guardians of the hidden treasure.

The story takes a tragic turn, but here, at least, the Purépecha are agents of their own destiny; here, however unwittingly, they seal their own fate. When Mintziata's husband, the warrior chief Itzihuappa heard of his beloved's capture, he dived into the lake to try to retrieve some of the gold for her ransom. But he was overwhelmed by the guards who had been charged by the king to defend the treasure come what may, whoever tried to plunder it, and for whatever reason. Again and again Itzihuappa tried to wrestle the gold from their grasp but eventually, despite being a legendary swimmer, he drowned – and became the twenty-first guardian of the Purépecha treasure. And Princess Mintziata, for-saken, imprisoned and alone, died of a broken heart. Every *Noche de Muertos* since then Itzihuappa's spirit is said to lead the ghostly funeral cortège of Mintziata to the cemetery of Janitzio.

But there hadn't been room to squeeze a ghost into the cemetery when I'd seen it. I'd steamrollered across the grave mounds in a crush of panicking bodies as if the graveyard hadn't been there. Once Janitzio had been the centre of the Purépecha universe, a place so sacred that no human being lived here. Only one high priest and his attendants administered the island, paying tribute to the gods and communicating with the different realms of the spirit world that revolved like planets around it. Now Janitzio was just another sideshow. The spirits were being vacuumed from their home.

Thwarted and disconsolate, I'd fought my way for breathing space to the top of the island and sat at the feet of Morelos feeling as lonely and depressed as if it was New Year's Eve. '*¿Qué onda,* *mano?'* A teenager wearing hair gel and an overpowering after-shave had leant across me to pass a bottle of whisky to his friend, 'How's it going, buddy?' His friend had looked at the bottle appreciatively. *'¡Qué padre!* Hey, cool! – it's not Mexican, is it?'

Right time, right place, wrong party. This wasn't the idyll that had inspired Diego Rivera; it was his nightmare. It had been a perfect illustration of Heisenberg's Principle of Uncertainty (if one can stretch the rule of physics to the world of tourism): we'd all come to see something we thought was worth seeing, but just by coming here, just by looking at it and scrutinizing it, we'd transformed it. We'd changed what we anticipated we'd see so completely it no longer existed. Now no one seemed to know why they'd come to Janitzio in the first place.

I followed a tour group of Americans back down to the boats. Snaking their way through the crowds, terrified at the prospect of being lost in the mêlée, they were holding hands like children – the blind leading the blind.

Luis Miguel López Alanís was a godsend. Only last year I'd found him too late. In the ashtray aftermath of the morning after the night before, we'd sat in a hotel foyer while waiters swept up flowers and cigarette butts and ticker tape, and picked over last night's event. Luis told me, not without relish, that the fog had been so thick on the lake in the early hours that several of the boats laden with washed-out party-goers from Janitzio had been lost for hours trying to make it to shore.

Luis was a small, unobtrusive, intelligent-looking man; middle aged, respectable, still managing to look dapper in pressed shirt and trousers despite last night's shadows under his eyes. He spoke in a calm, measured way, double-checking grammar and syntax in his head so that an error in his English wouldn't somehow mar the effect of what he was saying. He was thankfully not, like most of his profession, a prattler. He was a tour guide with integrity and conviction. He maintained his job gave him the chance to show outsiders the real Michoacán, 'not something you get from a flyer under your hotel door, or from a tour guide from Mexico City'. *'Para los toros del Jaral,'* he twinkled in a *campesino* accent, *'los caballos de allá mesmo*' – 'For bulls from Jaral, you need horses from the same place, too.'

Luis was born in Michoacán, not far from the mountains where 30 million monarch butterflies migrate from the United States and Canada to winter. Now he lived in the capital, Morelia, with his wife who was a social-worker and their two children. Michoacán was in his blood. It was his past, his present and his future, he said. He'd had a choice, once, to leave for good, but he found he couldn't. 'I couldn't enjoy wealth without peace in my heart.'

In his early twenties Luis had, like most men in Michoacán, tried his luck *al otro lado*, on the other side, in the United States. Of all the Mexican states Michoacán is responsible for the greatest number of illegal immigrants. Most cross the border regularly, timing their visits to coincide with the harvests in California and returning home weeks or months later with hard-earned wads of greenbacks in their pockets. California represents one third of the United States' entire agricultural wealth and 90 per cent of it is harvested by Mexicans. The US Border Patrol knows about this flux. Many Mexicans say that agents of the *Migra* patrols are tipped the wink by the major American crop producers so they know how many to let across in a season – especially during times of bumper harvest. When enough have been let through, the patrols crack down again. They call the Mexicans 'tonks' because of the sound a flashlight makes when it hits them over the head.

Around 5000 Mexicans cross the border every day, but of course official US immigration figures rarely take into account the fact that most migrants return. To many Americans it's inconceivable they'd want to. The figures report the number of border crossings made but rarely the number of people making them. They don't register the common fact that one migrant may make several crossings in a year, or be caught several times before being success-ful. The swollen statistics provide a political excuse for America's unemployment figures – for, as presidential contender Ross Perot inflammatorily described it, 'that sucking sound' of jobs leaving the US for Mexico.

Illegal immigrants are a convenient scapegoat for crime and drugs and any other political bogeys the American government

finds itself needing to deflect. The result is a tide of mounting
xenophobia, mainly directed at its closest neighbour, and a paranoid belief that its southern border somehow makes the States
insupportably vulnerable, an open door, an invitation to invasion.
There are always agitators in the border states trumpeting the
building of a Berlin Wall along the 2000 miles from San Diego to
Brownsville, as if this 'tortilla curtain' would somehow block out
the reality of the poor cousin living next door. It's a fanatically
popular prejudice, particularly unsavoury in a nation so recently
born out of immigrants itself; part of the hypocrisy that moved
Carlos Fuentes to coin the delightful misnomer, the 'United States
of Amnesia'.

'Few Americans, even Congressmen I've guided around my
country', said Luis, 'realize how much Mexico contributes to the
standard of living in the United States and its economy. They just
refuse to see that there's another side to the coin.'

What the United States so conveniently chooses to forget – at
least publicly – is that Mexico is the third largest client for American goods after Canada and Japan; that 700,000 American jobs
became dependent on Mexican imports post NAFTA; and that
undocumented workers in the States spend £29 billion more on
taxes than they receive in welfare.

'It's not a pleasant situation', Luis said, 'to have to leave your
home country and your family to look for work, to face all that
racism and prejudice and hatred; to be told you're "mooching"
when you're really working your butt off. One day Mexico's
economy will be strong again and we'll be able to provide work
for our own population. But until then the States should be at least
partly grateful to have us on their doorstep supplying all these
cheap, uncomplaining manual workers, doing all the hard and
dirty work that Americans don't like doing themselves.'

It's the young men who often end up staying in the States.
Without wives and children to go back to, with the energy and
optimism to endure the hard grind and an appetite for material
wealth, they learn English quickly and graft themselves on to the
culture of the Other Side.

Luis's border crossing at El Paso was nerve-wracking. He and two friends from Michoacán hired a *coyote*, or border-runner, as their guide. Crossing the Río Bravo – or Río Grande as the Americans insist on calling it – by jumping along a dam wall, they crawled into tunnels that must have been aqueducts or sewers beneath El Paso University. They popped their heads up through a manhole at the other end like characters in a gangster movie and made a run for it while no one was looking. The *coyote* left them on a bench downtown while he went for his car. Neither Luis or his friends could speak English but Luis had brought a packet of Camel cigarettes with him, although he didn't smoke, because he thought it might make them look American.

When the police appeared they were sitting like the Three Stooges on their park bench, looking absolutely terrified and very Mexican, with Luis fumbling about trying to light a Camel. 'What fools we looked!' laughed Luis. The police ordered them in Spanish to come with them and in one voice, like parrots, the three squawked '¿A donde?' They were thrown into prison for a couple of hours, had their fingerprints taken and were sent back across the border.

The next day they tried again. They were lucky. Their *coyote* had a conscience. He caught up with them, apologized for his failure and offered to take them back again for free. They went exactly the same way again but this time they were parked on a different bench. The car arrived and took them to a safe house where they stayed for two nights while the *coyote* bought their plane tickets to Chicago. Luis had a good friend, another man from Michoacán, who'd promised to put them up.

When Luis and his friends reached the Windy City they were still dressed for Texas. It was January and they'd never imagined a place so cold. They thought their ears would fall off and shatter into tiny pieces on the ground. But their friend's apartment had central heating – a luxury none of them had ever experienced.

For weeks they tried to get work, Luis with his few words of English going to restaurants and bars and construction sites, telling the proprietors that the three of them were, euphemistically, 'looking for Joe'.

Eventually they found jobs but as Luis began to think more and more about home, his friends were being seduced by the American dream. The siren of *malinchismo* had them in her thrall. 'It was hard to see my *compañeros* begin to talk so much about material things. We were there for the money, of course, but it was to take back home and do good things with. Not to spend on all these electrical goods and clothes and things that were being pushed at us all the time. They thought they were worthless unless they had all this stuff. I kept trying to remind them of the reason they came to the US in the first place, that we were Mexican, and young, and not out-and-out capitalists, that we should remember our roots, our politics, our families, the important things in life.'

After two years Luis returned, leaving his *compañeros* to their new-found lifestyle in the United States. Back in Morelia he found work as editorial assistant, and then as editor, on newspapers with opposing political viewpoints. Painfully, he came to realize that the only way he could preserve his personal integrity was to work for himself.

'So I trained as a federal tour guide. It was a hard three years – no money coming in, and a lot of studying. But now I feel it's worth it. I meet gringos who come here from the States, nice people most of them but with all the typical preconceptions of the idle Mexican in a sombrero dozing in the shade, and I can send them back home with a different idea in their heads. It's not much, I know, but I feel like I'm providing that little grain of sand that will start them itching and make them think.'

Next year, he promised, he would take me to see a very different side of the *Noche de Muertos*, a glimpse of the old world, where there wouldn't be a *junior* or a *calavera* (skull) or a pumpkin in sight.

We disembarked and walked up a steep cobbled street, the only one on the island, extravagantly lit by new neon street lamps. There were open fields on either side. The damp, green smell of the lake seemed to cling like a pall. Just before we reached the top of the hill, where there was a basketball court and the church, we branched off for one of the houses hidden in a lee, with a loose barbed-wire fence around it to keep out the cows. Luis called out, some dogs barked and the ghostly white sombrero of Don Amador materialized in the gloom. We shook hands. '*Mucho gusto*,' he addressed me nervously, flashing two silver teeth beneath a trim moustache. 'Welcome. Please, *mi casa es su casa*. My house is your house.'

Don Amador was about fifty with a gentle, dark, walnut face and hands of polished leather. I noticed, as I followed him up the path, that he was a foot shorter than me, even with his hat on. 'We were worried you weren't coming. A little plane flew very low over the island about an hour ago,' he laughed, 'and we thought it was you.'

His house was a surprise. I'd brought a hammock, torch and sleeping-bag with me but it was clear I wouldn't be needing them. He ushered us into a brand-new concrete building comprising four rooms completely bare but for electric strip-lights, televisions and double beds made up with sheets and blankets. 'It took a while to save for my first TV,' he explained; 'then just as I got it, I won two more in the lottery.'

In the room next to mine, a kind of hallway or ante-chamber, was a simple wooden table dressed in a lace cloth with fresh orchids and marigolds. On it were trays of fruit, a sugar cat and a sugar angel, and a large plastic bottle of fizzy pop called 'LIFT'. A tiny pot of copal incense was releasing a shroud of pale-blue smoke into the room. On the window-sill a picture of the Virgin was resting against the lace curtains. 'Our altar for the dead,' said Don Amador.

He watched anxiously as I put down my bags. There were no doors to the rooms. 'Will this be all right? We have water outside if you would like to wash. Some coffee? A beer? We've bought fresh milk from Pátzcuaro. Will you drink here? Outside? In the kitchen?' Don Amador fussed about in solicitous confusion. He took Luis quietly to one side. 'What would she like to eat?' he whispered. Suddenly he bustled off in a panic about the toilet, to shovel more sawdust down the long-drop.

The kitchen was a traditional, wooden outhouse with a beaten-earth floor where the dogs and a pile of mothy kittens had retreated from the cold. It was a paragon of orderliness: stacks of baskets, saucepans, clay pitchers, ropes of onions, chillies and garlic, regiments of upturned glasses and cups with a tomato balanced on each. Don Amador's wife, Doña Estella, was warming up tortillas on a large clay oven, shunting sticks into the fire. She was half his age, with a bright, lively face, a similar pair of silver-capped teeth, and a mischievous twinkle that belied the immediate, short-lived convention of shyness. She had her hair in two straight plaits, and wore a pink apron and cardigan over the traditional pleated skirt and bare legs.

As she settled us with plates of fried whitebait and a piquant salsa freshly pounded in her volcanic-stone *molcajete*, Doña Estella was queen of her domain once again. She talked as she worked, deftly moving about the kitchen like a juggler, baby slung on her back, toddler at her heels. Don Amador watched in mute admiration, and slowly began to relax.

'There are so many stories about the *Noche de Muertos*,' she laughed, after Luis had recounted how his wife, as a little girl, had once crept down to the family altar in the middle of the night to steal some candy and been frightened witless by her brother who was doing the same thing.

'Tell us one of your stories,' Luis requested Doña Estella. 'Tonight is the night for ghost stories.'

Doña Estella picked up a chicken and began to pluck it. 'I know a good one – a true story,' she smiled teasingly, 'about a girl and boy who were to be married. But their families distracted them from each other and they ended up marrying other people.' She waited until her audience, even the cat and the two-year old, were stock still, waiting expectantly for her to go on. 'The boy became a drunk – a *borracho* – and beat up his wife. The girl was happy because she'd found a kind man who didn't drink and who loved her. She realized she'd had a lucky escape.' Luis and Don Amador exchanged a look of husbandly solidarity.

'Unfortunately, though,' Doña Estella continued, as she scalded the stubborn chicken quills in boiling water and pulled at them doggedly, 'the young girl's husband died. So did the wife of her old boyfriend. As time went on the girl became lonely. Her old boyfriend wanted to marry her but she kept saying "no". Eventually a friend persuaded her to marry him. Her life soon took a turn for the worse. Her old boyfriend drank away all their money. He beat her. He neglected their children. The girl missed her first husband more than ever, and when the time for the *Noche de Muertos* came around, she wanted to leave him some of his favourite dishes as a present. The old boyfriend refused to give her money for the offerings but secretly she put some by and bought a chicken. She spent all evening plucking it, just like I'm doing now,' said Doña Estella meaningfully, 'boiling it up and preparing it; then she laid it out on the table while she went to fetch some chillies.'

'When the old boyfriend came back home, drunk as usual,' Doña Estella continued, 'he saw the chicken, realized it was an offering for the first husband and ate the whole thing, leaving only the skeleton. The wife was distraught when she discovered the bones left on the plate and went to church in tears to see the priest. The priest told her to bring her husband to mass to make amends for what he'd done. That night she managed to persuade her husband to go to the church, but he wouldn't come inside with her. He stayed outside, watching through the door. Suddenly, even though he was no longer drunk, he saw the church full of *ánimas*, souls, all carrying the delicious offerings that were left out for them by their relatives, and they all looked so happy. All except for one wretched soul who was looking downcast and disappointed. It was his wife's former husband, carrying nothing but a plate of chicken bones. Aieeee!' Doña Estella collapsed in laughter, lifting her apron to wipe away the tears. 'That greedy good-for-nothing – he felt so guilty, he never got the sight of the poor ghost and the chicken bones out of his mind till the day he died!' Don Amador, his son on his lap, guffawed from the shadows.

After a while Doña Estella put the chicken on to boil and brought out a pot of braised fish. She put a small fish in four little bowls and carefully ladled some vegetables and broth over the top. 'For the altar,' she explained for my benefit, 'for the *angelitos*.'

Tonight was the night the little angels would come back from the world of the dead. The altar in the house was for Don Amador's son who died when he was only seven, Doña Estella said. Her voice had tightened. She found the story hard, even after nine years. 'He was the son of Don Amador's first wife. They had eleven children together,' she said, 'but when she died and I married Don Amador, I thought of the children as my own. I loved them as though they were mine. One day my "Papá" – that's what I used to call the little one who died – was looking after the cow in the field with his elder brother. The older one had to come back to the house to fetch something and he told his brother to stay close to the cow and on no account let her get into trouble. So the *pobrecito* tied himself to the cow with one end of the tether around his waist. But a bull got into the field and scared the cow and he was dragged all over the field, over the rocks and everything. When we got to him he was unconscious. We had to get a boat to Pátzcuaro and he woke up in my arms and he just kept crying and crying how much it hurt. I told him over and over again, "Little one, Papá, you will be fine, everything will be all right." But when we got to Pátzcuaro hospital they said he'd have to go to the big hospital in Morelia. They put him in the ambulance, they wouldn't let us in, and we went by ourselves, by bus, to Morelia. We waited and waited but little Papá never came. He died in the ambulance and it had turned back to Pátzcuaro.'

Doña Estella's eyes had filled with tears but she busied herself clearing away our plates and went back to the chicken. 'Tell me, Doña Estella,' I asked, 'why are there four bowls of fish for the altar?' 'In case our Papacito brings some little friends with him,' she said, as if it was the most natural thing in the world.

In the early hours of the morning I was woken by a rustling sound as Doña Estella shuffled past my doorway up to the altar. The tall church candle in the centre of the table threw her shadow across my wall. She was carrying four glasses of *atole*, a soft drink she'd been making from boiled maize-meal and honey. High on the lintel above the hall doorway was a shiny red truck I hadn't noticed before – an expensive new toy for the little boy to play with.

'Atole, Papá,' she whispered to her son as she put down the glasses. And a moment or two later, quiet as a ghost herself, she left the room.

*

Pátzcuaro town was already packed when I arrived two days ago. Holiday houses down on the lakeside had been thrown open for the long weekend, the driveways jammed with sportscars and suburbans from Morelia and Mexico City. But most of the tourists in town were American. Every hotel was full, every table in every good restaurant was *reservado*. The Plaza Vasco de Quiroga was a caravanserai of canvas stalls. Local crafts – glazed pottery, woollen *sarapes*, incense burners, copper bowls, embroidered tablecloths, painted wooden furniture – were back to back with witches' hats and plastic cats, devils' horns and Dracula teeth, satin capes and rubber bats and tubes of squirty cobwebs. The stall next to the weavers' cooperative was doing good business with rubber face-masks of Frankenstein, Quasimodo, President Nixon, Bill Clinton and Monica Lewinsky. The Hallowe'en effect was in full cry.

It's a recent phenomenon and one that reflects the not-so-subtle nationwide shift to the American way of doing things. Hollywood and US-style shopping malls have had a powerful impact, particularly on the middle classes. Films like *The Addams Family*, *The Witches of Eastwick*, *Nightmare on Elm Street*, *Scream*, *The Blair Witch Project* have all contributed to a growing taste among mestizos for horror and the trappings of Hallowe'en. Pumpkins have started appearing in graveyards. Children in the cities go trick-or-treating. Elementary schools have a hard job trying to convince pupils that blood-soaked bandages and meat cleavers through your head have nothing to do with the traditional Day of the Dead. Hallowe'en is big business. In the States it generates over $5 billion a year. In Mexico it's catching up.

I ordered a traditional Day of the Dead dish – chicken *mole* – at a popular restaurant on the second floor of a seventeenth-century mansion overlooking the square. The table next to me were asking if the kitchen could run to a couple of steaks, medium rare. The waiter shook his head regretfully and referred them back to the menu – an exotic array of Mexican specialities written in Spanish. The American lady with the salt and pepper bob peered through her steel-rimmed glasses and prodded the list, with a little trilling laugh. 'I'll have that one,' she told the waiter, 'though Heaven knows what's in it.'

Her friend had assumed siege mentality. 'I thought this was a no-smoking restaurant – *No fumar, no fumar!*' she wailed at the waiter, pointing at a young Mexican couple enjoying a post-prandial Marlboro. The waiter looked uncomprehending. The two large balcony windows were wide open and soft skeins of smoke were drifting straight out into the night. He turned up the back-ground music instead – a compilation featuring 'White Christmas' and 'As Time Goes By' – perhaps hoping it might help the *gringas* relax.

I'd just ordered some coffee and was considering lighting up, myself, for the fun of it, when an earnest-looking girl approached the table. 'Mind if I join you?' she asked, or rather demanded. 'The restaurant seems to be full.' Within minutes I'd had to withdraw my finger from the page in my book and give her my full attention. 'My brother died six months ago,' she was saying by way of introduction, 'I'm here as part of the grief process. Some friends of mine said they thought it would be good therapy. They came to Pátzcuaro last year. My brother was HIV but he never told our parents. They didn't find out till the very last few weeks. He didn't want anyone to see him at the end. He just slipped away one night in the hospital when no one was there. I didn't even get to say goodbye. It's been very hard for me to come to terms with.'

It was ambiguous whether she meant the fact that her brother was gay, that he'd died, that he'd died alone, or that he'd deprived his nearest and dearest of the drama of his final act. It was obviously a sad story but I was finding it hard to drum up a sympathetic ear. Anyone could have been on the receiving end of this dolorous, self-pitying steamroller; I just happened to be in the headlights. She began to talk about the funeral. I could see it now – a frosty, awkward affair characterized by euphemisms like 'passing on', 'laid to rest', 'casket', 'garden of rest'.

We talked a little about the Mexican tradition but she winced visibly when I mentioned the words 'death', or 'coffin', or 'grave-yard'. I wasn't sure she'd find much comfort here. The Mexicans had a lifetime of preparation for this kind of thing. Sometimes it seemed they did nothing but toy with conceptions of death. Everywhere you go in Mexico, death stares you in the face. It's in the Aztec skull racks in the Museo del Templo Mayor, receptacles for the beating hearts of sacrificial victims; it's in Mayan hieroglyphs, and the recently mummified bodies on display in Guanajuato cemetery; it's in the tortured self-portraits of Frida Kahlo; the funeral photographs of sombre fathers holding dead babies in their christening robes; it's in the Indian dances of death, in death masks, in skeletons dangling from rear-view mirrors; in the graphic, bloody martyrs in every Catholic church; in living crucifixions during Semana Santa; it's in pilgrims with grazed knees beating their breasts before the Virgin of Guadalupe, straining to catch a glimpse of heaven; it's in jokes about the Grim Reaper, bull-fights, dead dogs by the road, open coffins. The intimacy with *Santísima Muerte* (Most Holy Death) seems sometimes shocking, sometimes perverse. Over the festival of the Day of the Dead it can be positively macabre. Death is entertained, given food and drink, invited into homes; He is teased, provoked and laughed about over a *tequilito*. However perverse, Death is always the brother of Life – the flip-side of the same coin. Only in Mexico, Death can be the easier to accept.

America sees death in a different way. It doesn't see it at all. It's hidden from view, nailed down, lid on the box. There are no bodies, no smells, no spirits, no humorous or cynical observations. Death happens remotely, behind hospital doors, in the papers, to strangers. The dead are cremated, in a sudden, electronic flash – not mummified, or left to rot. In England, I felt, we're already beginning to think the same way. We, too, were coming to regard death as the humiliating failure of the body, the failure of modern medicine, of plastic surgery, the failure of one's mind to overcome matter, a failure too painful to consider. Life, for us, is survival of the fittest. It's an heroic, pathological denial of the one thing that happens irremediably to us all. The US/Mexican border is responsible for many divides, I thought, but this has to be one of the biggest.

A boy came up to our table and put a flyer under my glass advertising a Night of the Dead party, part-sponsored by a local travel agent. On it was a cartoon of a skeleton packing his suitcase. 'Death is a larger kind of going abroad' it said. I wondered if my companion, who was now leaning over and bending the ear of her compatriots, would think it appropriate – let alone funny.

Doña Estella had been up since 3.30 in the morning when she'd gone to the grinder in the village to get her maize ground ahead of the queues. She was busy stuffing tamales, wads of maize dough packed inside corn-husks. In the centre of each ball of dough she put a little piece of the cooked chicken and some chilli salsa. Then she wrapped them up and laid them aside for cooking. So far she'd made nearly a hundred. It was going to be a busy day, with relatives dropping in, and visits to be made to everyone else's houses. She'd have to make tortillas, too. And a huge vat of *ponche* – a hot sweet drink infused with tamarind, guavas, cinnamon and hibiscus flowers.

I went with Don Amador down to the family's maize field by the water's edge to cut wild marigolds and cane for the altar. It was mid-morning and the blanket of indolence that had begun to weigh upon the lake belied the fever of activity going on inside the houses on the island. Cows swished through the long grass; orange-tailed lizards posed motionless on the dry-stone walls; water-snakes glided through the reeds. Occasionally a humming-bird darted past as casually as a bee.

Over on the near side of the lake, just visible in the haze beneath a small volcano, were the twin pyramids of Ihuatzio, 'Place of Coyotes'. And beyond the mountains, up towards the north-eastern shores, were the five similar, flat-topped *yacatas* or pyramid-platforms of Tzintzuntzan, built in 1200 – once a great city, plundered by Cristóbal de Olid, decimated by Nuño de Guzmán, depopulated by smallpox and flu. It had been named after the sound made by a hummingbird, whose iridescent feathers had been such a prized component of ancient Purépecha ornaments.

The hummingbird was a magical, sacred creature in the pre-Cortésian world. Nahua civilizations believed that warriors who died in war, in honour of the warrior Sun god, were reincarnated as hummingbirds and it was these hummingbirds that pulled the chariot of the Sun out of the world of darkness every day, across the sky so he could light up the earth. Women who died in childbirth were also honoured by reincarnation as hummingbirds, because their death was considered similar in every way to a warrior's.

Not long ago a king was recovered from a tomb at Tzintzuntzan, whose entire court, including his hairdresser, had been killed and buried with him. The tomb contained highly worked obsidian lip and ear ornaments – symbols of nobility; a sacred obsidian mirror, and depilatory tweezers made of silver. A dog had been buried, too, to lead the king and his entourage through the murky realms to the Underworld. There was also food and water in the tomb to sustain them all on their journey.

The ancient Purépecha believed they lived on the doorstep of death. Legend has it that when they first arrived at Lake Pátzcuaro, as a wild tribe from the north, they searched far and wide for a good place to settle. The water in the lakes was stagnant and undrinkable and they were desperate for fresh water. They wandered through the dark oak and pine forests around the lake searching for a spring. Suddenly, they saw a stream that appeared, miraculously, to be running uphill. Following it into a clearing, they found a bubbling spring. Around it were five black stones.

According to the ancient religion of the Purépecha, the universe was divided into three great cardinal regions. There was no hell in the Christian sense. There was Avandaro where the gods and their messengers lived; Echerendo, which was the mortal dimension, here on earth; and Cumiechúcuaro, inhabited by the dead. Each had a physical entrance and all three regions were connected to each other. At the entrance to Cumiechúcuaro there were said to be five black idols.

When the wandering Purépecha found the spring, they were sure they had reached the gateway to the realm of the dead. They called the site Petátzcuaro – Place of the Black Stones – and built a huge platform 450 metres long and nearly 18 metres high in honour of it. On top of the platform they constructed great stone bases on which to erect their magnificent wooden temples. The temples were among the first to be destroyed by the conquistadors. The platform itself was too enormous to be levelled so the colonial town of what came to be called 'Pátzcuaro' was built over it, with Quiroga's huge Basílica taking pride of place on top of the platform. Few people realize as they climb the steep, cobbled streets to worship at the feet of the miraculous sixteenth-century Virgin 'Nuestra Señora de la Salud' – Our Lady of Health – that they're walking up the sides of an ancient pyramid. The Virgin is a delicate little figure made of corn-pith like the travelling saints of the Franciscans and El Señor de la Conquista in the Parroquia in San Miguel.

Today the Purépecha myth has been supplanted by Christian legend. The spring of Pátzcuaro has been renamed the 'Fountain of Miracles'. It is said to have appeared when Father Quiroga struck the ground, like San Juan in Chamula, with his staff.

Don Amador was more at ease with me this morning. He chatted about his first wife as we gathered together bundles of *cempasúch-itl*. 'She was so beautiful,' he laughed, 'that my friends would say "How did such an ugly mug like you get such a beautiful wife?"' She wasn't dark or *blanca* but *roja* – red-skinned, from the same family as Doña Estella. When she became ill, he took her to hospital in Morelia. One day she suddenly announced she felt better. 'She said to me, "Amador, go out and get me some beautiful clothes, like people who have risen wear." I thought she was tired of being an Indian, that she wanted to dress for once in her life like a mestizo.' So Don Amador borrowed some money and went out and bought the clothes and by the time he'd come back, she was dead. 'Then I realized – it was her way of saying she was about to go to heaven.'

Without her Don Amador went to pieces. Even when she was alive, with the two of them earning, it had been desperately hard to support eleven children. Sometimes there were days when they had nothing to eat. Don Amador began to drink. It was a while before he eventually took hold of himself. 'I had to change. I was drinking my way to the grave. I decided to marry again and since then my life has become so much better it's hard to believe what it was like before.'

Don Amador, too, had tried his luck in the States but after a year and still unable to fight his way through the English language, he returned to his island. Then he landed a job as nightwatchman with the Fisheries Department in Pátzcuaro and at last all his prayers were answered. He had a steady wage now and all the perks that came with being a member of a trade union. He had built a proper house; had a good wife and four more little children. Five of his children, now grown up, are working in the States. They send clothes and presents back but he won't accept money from them 'or all the aunts and cousins would be asking for some for themselves'. He didn't want his children to be burdened with supporting the entire family. 'I want them to get on, so they can make their mother happy in Heaven,' he said.

The household altar was ready to receive the rest of the spirits. Don Amador's little son had had his turn, playing and eating and drinking and laughing with his friends, in the early hours of the morning. Now it was time for older members of the family to join the party. Don Amador had built a big arch out of the cane he had cut by the lake and dressed it with the marigolds. It ran up the walls and over the ceiling of the little ante-room. More fruit, gifts from relatives, had arrived, and there were home-made loaves of *pan de muertos* in the shape of bones and bodies on the altar table. Where there had been fish there were now plates of spicy, stewed Pátzcuaro duck. They were hard to find, these days, said Don Amador, but he'd managed to shoot this pair two days ago. He'd sat in a canoe for hours in the reeds waiting for them to fly in. In the old days, the duck hunt leading up to the Day of the Dead was one of the most exciting and convivial aspects of the whole fiesta. In his grandfather's time, they still killed the duck with spears. But since the Revolution everyone seems to have guns, and the birds are no more.

It was four in the morning and a piercing chill had invaded my skeleton. I was wearing all the clothes I had with me – tights and thick socks and two pairs of trousers – and still my legs felt frigid, moulded to the cold, damp earth like blocks of marble. Doña Estella was still bare-legged. She pulled her blanket over me and I inched closer to share her warmth. Somewhere under her sarape her little boy and baby were asleep.

We were sitting by her parents' grave. The rest of the family – her sisters, brothers-in-law, nieces and nephews – were swaddled in blankets like figures in a Henry Moore bomb shelter. Some of the children were wrapped so completely, and lay so still on their reed mats, they looked like corpses.

The graves – two large, simple, unmarked mounds of earth, side by side – had been suffixed with a pair of large, elaborate cane frames, like bedheads. It had taken the whole day to make them, trimming them like Christmas trees with marigolds and apples, guavas and bananas, *pan de muertos* and sugar skulls. The mother's had a sugar angel hanging from the centre; the father's a sugar bottle of *Sol*.

The grave itself was dusted all over with marigold petals and there were tin trays and baskets of food sitting on the top, covered in embroidered tea-cloths like a picnic. Fifty tall, thick church candles bristled out of the earth mound like spines on a hedgehog. They created a deceptive warmth with a gravitational pull like a tiny solar system. Beyond our sphere were other galaxies, other families huddled around their graves, each bound up in their own orbit. Behind the graveyard walls, outside our universe, twinkled lights from the islands of Yunuen, Tecuena and Janitzio, a million light years away.

Earlier on, at dusk, even before the dancing had begun on the basketball court, a TV crew had descended to film the Night of the Dead scene in the cemetery. They had solicited the performance of a few locals to kneel by the gravesides holding candles and told them to look mournful and peasantish. The evening wind had scythed through the graveyard snuffing out every flame as soon as it was lit. The Polish film director, a bear of a man, was trying to conjure up atmosphere. He was desperately searching for that mystical image I'd seen in the posters: candlelight flickering across etched and beatific Indian faces; the glow of marigold petals; a hint of deathly visitations in the shadows. As he barked orders at his crew, an interpreter scuttled from grave to grave handing out cigarette lighters. The Indians sat trying to look passive, stifling a desire to smile. Eventually, defeated by the wind, the film crew packed up and went away. A gaggle of tourists had arrived, ambled round conspicuously, cameras flashing and then been beaten back to their boat by the cold. 'Don't worry,' said Doña Estella, 'the wind will drop around one a.m. It always does.'

Now the dancing was over. Mass had been said in the church and the priest had sped off to the next island. At last, at nearly two in the morning, the *arcos*, decorated cane arches, began to arrive in the graveyard. Families arrived, pushing wheelbarrows, carrying baskets and cloths of bread, bundles of flowers, and rolled-up mats, and set up their vigil. The church bell sounded every thirty seconds or so, summoning the dead. The wind had dropped as Doña Estella had predicted and thousands of candles leapt into life. The air drifted with the combined scents of marigolds, wax, copal and *ponche*. A companionable peace descended. There was laughter and the sound of voices in mid-flow, and now and then a few people wept, discreetly, on their own.

The night wore on imperceptibly. Time hung nowhere. The children fell asleep and adults began to nod off, waking with a jerk to stretch a cramp or stamp out pins and needles. Doña Estella stared blankly through her shimmering exhaustion into another world. Every now and then a hand wrestled free of the woollen *rebozo* and she crossed herself, kissing her fingertips before returning them to the warm. For her there was no doubt about the spirit world. Her parents were palpably here. She'd told me she'd prayed as she cooked earlier in the day that their favourite dishes would please them, that she'd be able to make them just the way they had liked them. In the morning the family would take the dishes back home and have their own feast. It was always extraordinary then to notice how the taste had changed, she said, how the essence of the food had been spirited away – a bit like an aeroplane meal, I imagined.

In the centre of the graveyard, clustered around the only cross, a chorus of men, drunk on *ponche* spiked with *piquete* – a sugar-cane alcohol 96 per cent proof – struck up a lament. '*Salgan, salgan, salgan* – come out, come out, all souls in pain . . .' They bayed, swaying on their feet, for souls who had no one left to remember them, for unbaptized children, for those who died young, or unexpectedly, or alone. The refrain was weighed down with Ave Marías and Our Fathers.

'Where's Don Amador?' I asked.

'He's gone home,' said Doña Estella. 'When he saw the men had started drinking, he thought it best to get out of the way. If he'd stayed, he would have had to get drunk.'

One man had peeled off and was staggering about the graveyard, tripping over graves and crashing into candles. 'Ay-aye-aye – ooh-hoo-hoo,' he wailed, laughing maniacally. Doña Estella caught her sister-in-law's eye and they smiled wryly at the folly of *los machos*. No one attempted to field him. This was predominantly the women's fiesta. They shored it up with their faith and their strength, just as they held together their families, and the ties of history, binding the living with the dead.

At seven a.m. a watery dawn at last began to gather substance. Slowly the sun picked up and the world returned to the living. Even so, people lingered by the graves, aching limbs and frozen bodies and all, reluctant to tear themselves away from their loved ones for another year.

Back at home Doña Estella put her youngest children to bed. A kind of exuberant exhaustion had overcome her but still she pressed breakfast on Luis and me, and when we declined, picked offerings off the altar for us to take home. We joined Don Amador in a last glass of *ponche* before heading down to the jetty to catch a ride to Pátzcuaro with a boatload of musicians who were off, bleary-eyed, to play in a hotel.

'*¡Adiós! Que le vaya bien.*' Don Amador shook my hand and passed on messages for my husband, my mother, my children, a family he'd never seen, in a country he still couldn't place on the map, '*¡Feliz viaje!* When you fly back to England, we'll wave at your plane. Look out for us down here!'

Doña Estella stretched up and gave me a hug. 'God be with you,' she said, and made the sign of the cross at our departing backs.

There was a mist floating around Janitzio by the time we drew past it, like dry ice on a dance floor. Boats were loading up with garbage at the quay. I was tired and, despite the splendour of the morning, out of sorts. The beauty of the scene seemed a shallow mirage. It recalled some prophetic lines from the great poet king Netzahualcoyotl (Hungry Coyote), ruler of Texcoco in the time of Moctezuma.

All the earth is a grave and nothing escapes it;
nothing is so perfect that it does not descend to its tomb.
Rivers, rivulets, fountains and waters flow,
but never return to their joyful beginnings;
anxiously they hasten on to the vast realms of the rain god.
As they widen their banks, they also fashion
the sad urn of their burial.
Filled are the bowels of the earth with pestilential dust
once flesh and bone, once animate bodies of men
who sat upon thrones, decided cases, presided in council,
commanded armies, conquered provinces, possessed treasure,
destroyed temples,
exulted in their pride, majesty, fortune, praise and power.
Vanished are these glories, just as the fearful smoke vanishes
that belches forth from the infernal fires of Popocatépetl.
Nothing recalls them but the written page.

I wondered how long it would be before tourist boats started arriving in force at Don Amador's island looking for fresh terrain; if they could be persuaded to tread more lightly than the hordes on Janitzio; or if a tourist invasion was just another of the irrevocable processes connected with the dying of the lake, and the rape of an ancient culture.

As we grew closer to the shore, floating rafts of pale purple water hyacinth, a species that had migrated here from Asia, sucked at the sides of the boat. It was the same plant that was choking Lake Victoria and the shallow lakes of Africa. A few years ago the Department of Fisheries had introduced manatees to eat the stuff but locals had been so afraid of the gentle creatures they'd killed them all. The same thing had happened when manatees were introduced several years ago into the waterways of Xochimilco.

Lake Pátzcuaro was disappearing, drying up through natural geological processes accelerated by man. More topsoil was sliding into the water now forests on the mountainsides were being felled in greater quantities to make painted furniture and curiosities for the tourists and mestizos. Even as the evaporation process gained momentum and the water grew shallower still, more and more sewage was being pumped into the lake. Levels of faecal bacteria were growing alarmingly high. Soon it would be dangerous to eat what fish remained.

Over the last fifty years, Lake Pátzcuaro has dropped 7 metres and shunting the jetties closer to the water has become a regular chore. One of the islands closest to the shore has already returned to being part of the land. You could wade, now, to several of the others. Like Cuitzeo, Chapala and Zituaren – the last of the great lakes in the Land of the Fishermen – Pátzcuaro's days are numbered.

Driving back to Morelia, Luis treated me to his favourite tape. The band, Bola Suriana, was from Michoacán. They were friends of his and had just produced their third album, called *Canto a Mi Terra* – 'Song to My Land'. One of the instrumental numbers featured a developing harmony of old and new world sounds – a Spanish guitar and a violin gradually weaving their way in among the ancient magnetic rhythm of Purépecha flutes, percussion and gourd rattles. Another, with lyrics in both Tarascan and Spanish, was a lament sung by Lake Pátzcuaro to one of its islands:

Ay, what sorrow it gives me to see you like this, my little Yunuen!
I am the lake which will die tomorrow.
Maybe, tomorrow, when the sun comes up
I'll no longer be there to reflect your beauty.

There are no more fish and the egrets have gone, my little Yunuen!
The ducks are flying away and saying their goodbyes.
Janitzio is finished which once was a poem
And on the mountain the cinnamon tree has died in flower.

You are kind, mother of all my children
What I feel in my soul is:
When I die, inevitably,
Everyone will emigrate north.

When he stopped the car outside my hotel in Morelia, Luis pressed the eject button. '*Un recuerdo*,' he said handing me the tape. 'A souvenir. Don't forget us.'

6

Visions from the Sierra
Huichol Country

Primitive people as they are, they taught me a new philosophy of life, for their ignorance is nearer to truth than our prejudice.

Carl Lumholtz, on the tribes of the Western Sierra Madre and the 'Tarascos' of Michoacán, Unknown Mexico, *1902*

For more than 99 per cent of human history, the world was enchanted and man saw himself as an integral part of it. The complete reversal of this perception in a mere four hundred years or so has destroyed the continuity of the human experience and the integrity of the human psyche. It has very nearly wrecked the planet as well. The only hope . . . lies in a re-enchantment of the world.

Morris Berman, The Re-enchantment of the World, *1982*

I did not arrive at my understanding of the fundamental laws of the universe through my rational mind.

Albert Einstein

We stood still on the ridge at last, numbed by the sudden onrush of motionlessness. The engine of our combi, adjusting to the shock of inaction after two days on the road, emitted the occasional relaxing tic. Chucho drew back his shoulders and took a deep breath. Above us *zopilotes* were making use of the last thermals of the day. A breeze sashayed through the pines. 'This,' he announced, sweeping his arm at the surrounding forest, to the rocky peaks turning pink in the dusk, and the valley where his village lay a thousand feet below us, 'is my house. You are guests of the Huichol. *Mi casa es su casa*.'

'My house is your house', that familiar expression of Mexican hospitality – a phrase I'd heard again and again during my travels, whether from the stone portals of a grand hacienda hotel or from the beaten threshold of an adobe hut. Here, though, there was a different ring to it. Chucho had used the phrase now, as our host, without irony, but he was implying something more. There are no walls where I live, he was saying. The boundaries that you're familiar with, that you Europeans, you city-dwellers, set so much store by, don't exist here. You are standing on the doorstep of the true *indígenas*, the original occupants of Mexico. Here, where the Spanish Conquest was turned away, sent packing like a delinquent, the old laws apply. You are walking into virgin territory, setting foot into a land still governed by the gods.

The Indian who stood before us, natural, assertive, grandiloquent, a trifle patronizing, was a different man to the one who'd climbed into our hire van in Mexico City. In the city he'd looked exotic, an anomaly, a walking tourist attraction. His clothes – the typical wide, white trousers and loose white Huichol tunic gathered in at the waist with a colourful sash – drew gawking stares from passers-by. His reed hat, broad-brimmed, trimmed with red wool and pom-poms with little dangling triangles of white plastic was ill-suited to the business of getting in and out of the back of a VW or jostling for space on a bus.

Even his *huaraches* seemed to have something excessive, something arrogant and promiscuous about them. Plenty of poor people made their sandals out of car tyres, but no mestizo from the Mexico City barrios would have paid such attention to the way they were cut, or threaded them with fine soft calf-leather thongs so they looked like a chic new import from Italy.

The looks Chucho got in the street, or when he came with us to a smart restaurant, ranged from curiosity to disdain. There was something in his demeanour that many found discomfiting. What would have passed for natural self-confidence in a city suit was misconstrued as threatening or untrustworthy when it was presented in Indian cotton. I was cornered, once, by a woman who had seen me with Humberto and Chucho in a café. 'Aren't some of them still cannibals?' she inquired with a little prurient thrill as we washed our hands next to each other in the Ladies. Kindnesses were edged with condescension. When Chucho was addressed directly it was often in the intimate 'tú' form, as if he were a servant or a child; or, indirectly, in the diminutive, as if he were something cute or just plain weird: 'Look at the Huicholito!'

Chucho responded to the reactions he evoked in the metropolis with a dignified silence. He watched and listened but he never made eye-contact and he hardly said a word. But unlike most *indígenas* in the city, intimidated by the might of the dominant culture, Chucho was no chameleon. He didn't try to disappear into the mestizo melting-pot. He was like a jay, dipping about the concrete jungle dextrously yet conspicuously, the flamboyant opportunist. In true Huichol fashion he switched from apprentice shaman and subsistence farmer to street-wise *vendedor ambulante*, travelling salesman, without changing his clothes.

Though he must have seemed an obvious target on the crime-ridden streets, Chucho had only once fallen victim to thugs. He'd been mugged in the subway and the *gandallas* who'd jumped him had made off with all the artefacts he'd been intending to sell. Chucho drew satisfaction over the next few days, as his stomach burned with lack of food, from the knowledge that, sooner or later, the images of the sacred deer and other gods that had been snatched from him would find a way to punish the thieves for their irreverence. Those kids would be sorry they'd ever taken sacred symbols from a Huichol, he said.

Chucho had brought similar stuff with him to sell this time. There were the fine bead necklaces and bracelets, shoulder-bags and little *jícaras* – gourd offering-bowls – and the famous Huichol psychedelic bead masks and yarn paintings inspired by visions under the influence of peyote. Some were the work of friends; others were Chucho's handiwork. They were lurid and arresting, full of colour and motion, exploding like fireworks. Passers-by were either alarmed or attracted, most likely both. I'd certainly seen nothing like them before. If you stopped, even casually, for a moment to look at the designs whirling kaleidoscopically on their mat on the pavement, they seemed to exercise an unnerving power. They drew you into them like Alice through the looking-glass. There were moons and stars and rain and lightning and fire; a searing white sun; thunderous storm clouds; there were double-headed eagles, and snakes coiled or flickering or swallowing their tails; opossums and jaguars and dogs and fireflies and crows; shamans with power-arrows, and paths of light; there was life and death, souls on their way to the sacred valley of Huiricuta, a woman giving birth to a burst of rains. And attending these visions, the magic protagonists of Huichol inspiration: deer, leaping with blazing antlers; elegant stalks of life-giving corn; and the geometric flowers of *híkuri* – the hallucinogenic peyote cactus. Deer, maize, peyote – the Huichol holy trinity.

Chucho's artefacts had sold well. He, his wife and two small children and a young nephew, based in a small room lent them by a friend, had been out on the streets around the Zócalo in Mexico City for two months. Huichol art was becoming popular, although how many people who bought it knew the first thing about Kauyu-mari, the deer god, or even the divine attributes of peyote, was doubtful to Chucho. People even assumed that the bead face masks and jaguar heads he was selling were traditional, he said. They had no idea this was a conceit created for the tourist market; that this simply bowed to the famous metaphor of Octavio Paz, repeated in every guidebook on Mexico and consequently the expectation of every foreigner, that Mexican culture is based around the use of masks because everyone in Mexico is hiding from something.

Chucho was pleased when people took an interest in his work and especially appreciated commissions. But at the same time he distrusted the avariciousness of non-Huichols, or *téiwari* – the 'neighbours' – as he called them. The story of Mota Apohua, one of the most famous of Huichol artists and from Chucho's own tribe, had become a parable of *téiwari* tightfistedness and political skulduggery. In recent years the Mexican government, while still uninterested in the plight of the Indians per se, had come to see that promoting indigenous art could be good publicity. Mota Apohua was commissioned by the Mexico City Metro to paint a gigantic mural for the entrance to the Palais Royal-Musée du

Louvre Metro Station in Paris. It was to be a gift, in effect, from Mexico to France and was unveiled on 6 October 1997 by the Mexican President, Ernesto Zedillo.

But on the same day as the unveiling, Amnesty International and other pressure groups staged a demonstration in Paris against President Zedillo's violations of indigenous rights. Mota Apohua had originally been invited to be present at the unveiling of his work, but a few days before he was due to leave Mexico, his invitation was cancelled by the President and no reason given. Most of the balance of 450,000 pesos still due to Mota Apohua and signed for by contract, has still not been paid. There was little honour in the outside world, Chucho surmised from this fiasco, and his own intimate experience confirmed the general Huichol view that there were few *téiwaris* you could trust.

It was nearing the end of the dry season in Chucho's village 500 miles away in the sierra; time to go back and prepare all the rituals needed for planting. But there was another matter pressing on Chucho's mind. It was one of the reasons he'd come to Mexico City. He wanted to approach his friend Humberto, one of the few *téiwaris* who had so far disproved the rule, for help – a matter, he insisted, of life and death; and so set in motion the chain of events that was to take me with him to the sierra.

So it was, one evening, that I was invited round to Edificio Ritzy feeling something momentous was afoot. Humberto and Laurence's apartment was periodically invaded by Huichols and this evening was typical. They'd had a whole family staying with them for nearly a week and Laurence's patience was running a little thin. There was maize boiling away in the kitchen; beer and tequila bottles spilling out of the bin; cartoons rampaging on TV; a blanketed form immobilized on the nineteenth-century French mahogany day-bed handed down from Laurence's grandmother. Laurence was making pointed comments about the men's inaccuracy in the lavatory and the disappearance of her collection of peacock feathers.

In the midst of this imbroglio, Humberto explained Chucho's predicament. Chucho's mother-in-law, Humberto told me, was desperately ill and urgently needed to make offerings at a sacred site on the Pacific Coast at San Blas. She was a *mara'akáme*, a sha-man, and it was because she had failed to fulfil obligations to her patron deities that she had fallen ill. Now she was too weak to walk and the only way for her to make the pilgrimage was by car. It was clear to everyone that if she didn't make it to San Blas she would die. But the journey could take two weeks and the family couldn't afford to hire a vehicle or pay the living costs of the expedition.

I realized, now, why I was here. 'It's an amazing opportunity,' said Humberto, 'a clear case of putting two and two together. You could drive Chucho and his family back to the sierra and then go with them on their pilgrimage. It'll be an incredible experience.' He smiled conspiratorially, 'There's a combi-hire place round the corner.'

It was only as we began unfolding maps on the floor, that I understood Humberto would not be coming with us. 'What hap-pens if the sick woman dies?' I asked nervously. '¡Hijole!' Humberto laughed, tickled by the idea. 'It won't look good – an English *turista* with a stiff in the back of her car and lots of weeping Huicholes. Bags of peyote and mescal and maybe even a calf ready for sacrifice. That'll test your Spanish.'

He decided to type up a letter on Conservación Humana-headed paper addressed 'A LA ATENCIÓN DE LAS AUTORIDADES CIVILES, JUDICIALES Y MILITARES' explaining that I was carrying out important research and, though a British citizen, would abide by Mexican law. 'Keep this with you and show it to any official who crosses your path. With any luck it'll keep you out of jail,' he smiled, enjoying himself. I said I wasn't so confident and begged him to supply me with additional moral support. With amazing ease – a single telephone call – he came up with Jessica Gottfried, a twenty-four-year-old photography and anthropology student, founding member of the board of Conservación Humana and inveterate traveller who'd been several times to the Sierra Huichol. Not for the first time I marvelled at the ease with which Mexicans can drop everything at a whiff of adventure. Jessica turned up the next day with a small ethnic bag, some sachets of soy sauce and a Walkman. I was immeasurably relieved.

*

Of all the indigenous peoples Nuño de Guzmán and his cronies tried to pacify in Nueva Galicia, those to the north-west, in that precipitous part of the Sierra Madre Occidental where the modern-day states of Nayarit, Durango, Zacatecas and Jalisco collide, proved impossible to conquer.

The tribes up here had remained well beyond the sphere of the Aztec, Purépecha or Otomí cultures. They led a primitive, semi-nomadic existence, hunting in the forests and criss-crossing the table lands and *barrancas*, tending their amaranth and maize crops with the seasons, and taking a variety of hallucinogens – including *peyotl*, the 'devil root' as the Spanish called it – to communicate with their gods. There were no great temples here; no dizzy stone staircases and terrifying blood-soaked priests; no cities – but a way of life that had persisted ever since the original hunter-gatherers had begun to settle here from North America at least a thousand years before the birth of Christ.

The Tarahumara, Yaqui, Tepehuana, Cora and Huichol in this remote north-west corner of Mexico were part of the same tribal chain as the Utes in Western Colorado and Utah, the Hopi in Arizona, and the Papago, Paiute, Shoshoni and Pima in the southern United States. And they were also related to the Aztecs who, of all the 'Uto-Aztecan' tribes in the chain, had travelled the furthest south, eventually divorcing themselves from their nomadic roots when they settled in the hospitable Valley of Mexico.

While the Spanish swiped the Aztec Empire its famous death-blow in central Mexico in 1521 it was not until 1722, two hundred years later, that the mountainous fortress of the 'Sierra de Nayar', the region which sheltered the Huichol, the Cora and the Tepehu-ana, was finally brought under Spanish control.

By then most of the tribes in the area had been wiped out. They'd resisted conquest long and hard, escaped even the iron fist of Nuño de Guzmán, and at one point it had even looked like the odds were in their favour. The Mixton War of 1542, orchestrated by the warlike Chichimecas (the tribe who had so relentlessly harried the Franciscans around San Miguel) and their allies from Zacatecas, together with tribes in Jalisco (the province that had suffered most at the hands of Nuño de Guzmán) was the most dangerous rebellion the Spaniards had to face in their three hundred years of occupation and the closest the conquerors ever came to defeat.

Eventually, though – and inevitably – the Spaniards found reinforcements, equipping their Indian allies with guns and horses for the first time, and the rebel tribes were systematically driven from their rocky fortresses. Tens of thousands of Indians were enslaved as a consequence, sent off to dig themselves a fast grave in the silver-mine shafts of Zacatecas and Guanajuato; many others, driven to despair, committed suicide, throwing themselves down the precipices of their strongholds, rather than face capture.

Disease played its habitual pitiless role in the demise of the wild tribes of the north. When smallpox hit the region in 1545–8 it wiped out half the survivors from the Mixton War. The combined impact of Spanish reprisals, bloodlettings and the plague on the indigenous population was apocalyptic. According to one estimate, in just the *tierra caliente* region of coastal Nayarit, there were at least 320,000 Indians at the time of Nuño de Guzmán's *entrada*. Thirty years later there were fewer than 20,000.

Only the scorpion-infested sierra, with its steep *barrancas* and deep canyons remained a *zona de refugio*, way beyond the reach of the Spaniards and the jaws of assimilation.

Little is recorded about Huichols during the Mixton War and for the two centuries following it. This isn't simply because they withdrew into isolation. They still travelled to the coast to trade for salt and fish; they sold maize and copal and pitch-pine and gum in local markets around Zacatecas, presumably learning a great deal about the new white occupiers of their country in the process; and they still made their annual 300-mile pilgrimage to the deserts of San Luis Potosí to collect their sacred peyote.

Geography kept the Huichols apart, kept them invisible. They had a place to retreat to, a haven where their culture remained safe and unmolested. But they also had a remarkable spiritual strength that they carried with them wherever they went; a moral self-sufficiency, an integrity, that, in the years to come, preserved them from the enticements that seduced the Indians of central Mexico over to the Spanish side. The Huichol were not avaricious or materialistic, they were blissfully unaffected by the magnetism of

Malinchismo, and they did not fall for the new religion, either, with all its hellfire and brimstone and promises of redemption.

They were also reluctant to mix their blood. Even today, marrying outsiders means losing identity. Mixed offspring are rarely accepted because they can be a threat to the cohesion of the family clan. A persistent myth, conveyed in modern yarn-paintings, is that the soul of a Huichol who has sex with a non-Huichol will be corralled with mules and trampled until there is almost nothing left of it. The symbolism of the mule is double-barrelled since the creature is both foreign (it was introduced by the Spanish) and barren, as the Huichol are said to become, metaphorically speaking, if they have intimate relations with *téiwari*.

Though the Huichol supported tribes like the Chichimecas or the Coras, especially in the early years during the Mixton War when they raided Spanish garrisons and *encomiendas*, or colonial ranches, they rarely launched into open war themselves. They were happy to offer food and refuge and occasionally reinforcements in the general struggle against the Spaniards, but preferred the less direct approach of passive non-cooperation themselves.

It was a tactic that paid off when the Sierra finally fell within range of the missionaries in the 1720s. The Coras, with their bellicose reputation, were aggressively and, for the most part, successfully evangelized by Jesuits. But the Huichol were sent a more benign task-force in the form of Franciscan friars and were able, without much effort, to avoid church altogether (sometimes even forceably evicting the men of the cloth from their land) or simply to pay lip-service while conducting their own ceremonies in the village and making their sacrifices and offerings to the gods in caves, on top of mountains and in the forest as they had always done.

Gradually, as they became more familiar with Christianity, the Huichol incorporated some elements of the Catholic Church into their own rituals, their pantheon being just as elastic as that of the Aztecs or Maya or Zapotecs. But this was not a gesture of great symbolism. Christ was simply admitted to the Huichol Mount Olympus as cup-bearer to the more traditional deities. Even the Virgin of Guadalupe learnt to pay homage to the ancient gods.

The story of the Huichol reaction first to the conquistadors, then to the missionaries and *encomenderos*, then, in the nineteenth and early twentieth centuries, to mining companies and revolutionaries, immigrant mestizos and loggers, is one of sanguinity and wisdom. They kept their heads while all around could quite literally be losing theirs. But it's a story that persists, even more remarkably, to the present day, with the added onslaught of anthropologists, tourists, new-age Carlos Castañeda freaks and Protestant evangelists.

Not for a second have the Huichol let down their guard. They are as wary and defensive and on the ball as they ever were; and they are also, to the chagrin of the Mexican government, still not willing to change. They can claim, justifiably, to be the only tribe of Mexico never to have thrown in their lot with the Spanish or any of their descendants. More than this, they have defended their culture and way of life more completely than any other native people in the whole of North America.

They have allies, naturally, in the outside world, especially among ethnologists, environmentalists and human rights' activists, but outsiders are constantly surprised by the hostile reception they can get even after months working on concerted projects in the field. Western sensibilities are hurt when Huichol lie overtly to people who'd considered themselves to be friends. But the Huichol are deliberately, compulsively slippery. As part of their defence against an intolerant world, they are taught, from a very early age, to be flexible with the truth, especially where outsiders are concerned; even to lie for the fun of it. Little children will practise this art of deceit quite openly, insisting on the obverse of the most apparent reality, like the time of day. They will exaggerate relentlessly; fabricate and misinform; provide a mine of misinformation for anthropologists; do anything, in effect, to throw professional investigators and the just plain nosy, off the scent.

Relationships between Huichol and *téiwari* can turn sour, too, and at the slightest provocation. Stories abound of anthropologists who have lived happily for years in one community, being turned on and hounded out of the village when they overstepped the mark or 'stole' one secret too many. Tourists have had their cameras and video-recorders smashed; souvenir hunters and art collectors have been assaulted when a deal has misfired.

By way of a sobering reminder of these tendencies I carried in my rucksack the current edition of *Newsweek* that ran the story of John True – an American journalist from Mexico City who had, just four months earlier, ventured alone and uninvited into Huichol territory in search of a story. His decomposing body had recently been found stuffed inside his sleeping bag in a shallow grave at the bottom of a ravine. His notebook had been buried with him and his camera had disappeared.

The instant that Chucho changed from being passenger to back-seat driver was unequivocal. We were a day and a half's drive from Mexico City. We had cleared the colonial pink-stone city of Zacatecas with its famous silver mine – the engine that had consumed the lives of hundreds of thousands of Indians, fuelled the ascent of the Spanish Empire and filled the pockets of Weetman Pearson; passed the agricultural town of Fresnillo with its bizarre shrine to El Santo Niño de Atocha – an image of the infant Jesus dressed in doublet and hose and wearing a colonial pilgrim's feathered hat; passed the massive silos and steel chimneys of the Corona beer plant looking like a space station in the desert; and were finally winding our way up into the foothills of the sierra. We'd overtaken our last sixteen-wheel articulated truck and our first *vaqueros* on horseback.

Suddenly as we were drawing into a stretch of oak forest, Chucho leant forward. 'Stop the car,' he demanded. We looked at him in surprise, wondering if one of the children was about to be sick. 'The machine needs a rest,' he commanded, 'and we need to talk', and he slid open the door and got out. His wife flattened herself under a barbed-wire fence and disappeared into the bushes for a pee.

Chucho sneezed convulsively, blew snot into his fingers and flicked it on the ground. 'Uggh. DF! Pollution!' he muttered contemptuously. I felt the cogs of our short relationship slowly grind to a halt and begin to turn the other way. Chucho was scanning the view gubernatorially. The countryside was on the rack, tinder-dry and gasping. You could almost hear it crackling with aridity.

Skeletal trees stuck out on the horizon like crucifixes. The rocks billowed heat. Every living thing in those woods would be stretched to its limits by now. It would take nothing short of a miracle, it seemed, to make this a green and fertile place again when it was so far gone, at the very door of death.

'These are Huichol hunting grounds,' Chucho announced, projecting his voice like a tour-guide, 'this territory used to belong to the Huichol but it's been taken over – illegally – by mestizos.' One of the Huichols' main concerns, one of their biggest threats, is that their country is being swiftly eroded at the edges by settlers. Land that was originally granted them by the Spanish crown in the eighteenth century is being fenced off, appropriated, by immigrant mestizo smallholders, forcing the Huichol to retreat into an ever-decreasing area. Most of the Huichol clans or settlements have lost their precious title deed, or had it stolen from them. Only Chucho's people still had theirs – a vellum scroll in a florid Castilian hand, much bloodied from sacrificial annointings – and Humberto had been entrusted to make an exact facsimile of it for safe-keeping, so that when the time came, as come it would, they could make a legal stand against these territorial incursions.

'We still come here with our shotguns to hunt deer and wild boar and turkey and squirrels,' Chucho was saying, 'but we come on the bus. Then we take our quarry back again – meat, skin, blood and horns – back to the village on the bus.'

There were more than 18,000 Huichol Indians now living within 400,000 hectares of Sierra, an area possibly as much as half the size of the territory originally designated as theirs by the Spaniards. Even though the forest we were driving through was now beyond the official boundaries, Chucho knew the Huichol name for every rocky outcrop, every blip on the landscape. There was another three hours' drive ahead of us but Chucho, as far as he was concerned, was home.

It seemed an age before we heard the burros stumbling up the hill in the dusk. Someone sang out a greeting, calling Chucho not by his Christian name (an affectionate nickname for 'Jesús') but by one of his five Huichol names – 'A-comer-xiete' – a Spanish/

Huichol concoction meaning 'Let's eat honey'. A young man came forward out of the greyness grinning and took Chucho's hand, then ours, in a triple downtown-LA-style handshake. 'Kia'ko! Welcome!' His smile was, I realized with surprise, a relief.

A boy stood beside him, eyes popping as we unloaded two crates of oranges and vegetables, some bags of beans, rice, sugar, salt, biscuits and two bottles of Zacatecas mezcal from the van. 'Don't put the mezcal on the burros,' said Chucho's friend Pascual, 'or they'll find a way to swallow it and get drunk.' 'And don't put any cameras on the burros, either,' added Chucho. 'They'll think it's a new type of food and eat them.'

Chucho had an obvious dislike of cameras. He'd already refused to let me take his picture on one of our pit-stops and now the shutter on my Nikon had jammed. I was beginning to feel uneasy and superstitious and left most of my equipment in the car.

By now the sun had slid behind the mountains leaving cold, wet streaks across the sky and barely enough light for us to see by under the trees. But there was an air of brightness in Chucho's step and an almost drunken gaiety on the part of his friend that had us stumbling down the path singing like the seven dwarves, and diving after oranges and limes in the dark as they thudded off the jolting burros.

When we emerged at last at the bottom, the ridges we had left were crowned with stars and in their waxy light, the valley floor around us was liquid and rippling like a sea. Ahead of us were dry fields ploughed up for planting which, awed now by the open theatre of the cosmos, we crossed in silence, filing one by one after Chucho towards the silhouette of his village.

Chucho's family was sitting around a blazing open fire. Reposing in a high-backed ceremonial cane chair, august as any paterfamilias at his hearth, was Cacayari, the *kawitéro* – elder of the village. He stood slowly and greeted Chucho with a gentle handshake and then let Chucho pass on around the fire to greet everyone else.

When it came to our turn to present ourselves, Cacayari's face wrinkled up with amusement. We delicately touched fingertips and then he gestured to a couple of miniature wooden milking-stools nearby for us to sit on. A young girl brought up two heavy plastic containers and stood them under the eaves of the hut behind us. 'This water is for you,' Cacayari said, graciously fulfilling another obligation of Mexican hospitality, an offer that, out here in the wilderness in the dry season, was the difference between life or death.

Not until everyone had settled down again, fathers with babies in their laps, children nodding asleep, women shifting pots in the ashes, when the fire had resumed its mesmerism and all was nothing but crackle and spit, did Cacayari finally indulge his curiosity. 'Where have you come from?' he asked, disgorging Spanish words from his throat like an owl spitting out pellets of fur. 'From Mexico,' said Jessica. 'I'm from Inglaterra,' I added. Neither answer seemed to register. 'And today?' 'From Zacatecas. We had lunch on the way in Puente de Camotlán.'

At last the old man was impressed. 'Ahh. That's a long way – a very long way.' There was a pause. 'It's good to be here,' I said lamely. 'Oh, but it's not as good as Zacatecas,' Cacayari retaliated swiftly, 'no big buildings, no cars, there is nothing here.' I wasn't sure whether to take this seriously. 'Your first time in the Sierra Huichol?' he continued. 'Yes.' 'You're like a child, then.' And he laughed, engagingly, but beneath the tease I could sense there was a caveat. I was a newcomer to the ways of the Huichol and my blunders would be forgiven, up to a point. Like a child my behaviour would be tolerated but I was also, as an adult *téiwari*, eligible for censure.

Then, like a locomotive slowly gathering steam, Cacayari launched into his native tongue and settled into a Homeric mono-logue that stretched out for the best part of twenty minutes. As his soliloquy came to a close Chucho pitched in with a long chant of his own. Then it was Pascual's turn, and on it went from one to the other, a ball of unravelling discourse, a psalmic ritual – through the welcoming speeches, returning home speeches, introductions, explanations of who we were and why we were here, and all the stories of the intervening weeks – passed over and picked up and knitted together until Jessica and I were nodding off with boredom and exhaustion, hunching lower and lower, elbows on our knees, head in hands, bottoms rolling around achingly on our bonsai milking-stools.

Finally, on the verge of collapse for the sake of good manners, Chucho asked, 'Aren't you two going to bed? Are you going to stay up and watch the sun rise?' We took the hint and slunk off to our hut like ladies banished from the dining-room while the men passed the port.

I awoke to the sound of children and the metallic squeak of someone winding a handle to grind corn. Jessica's sleeping bag lay beside me collapsed like a snakeskin. I lay still, collecting myself. Tiny shafts of sunlight, filtering through a *tepári* – a flower-shaped stone amulet – in the wall, perforated the gloom. There were corncobs in the rafters in five different colours – yellow, white, blue, red and pinto – and some white deer-tails. Behind me, by my head, was a musty jumble of ritual paraphernalia – calabashes, gourd bowls inlaid with beads, bunches of long, wilting candles, little woven bags and reed boxes, a bunch of dead marigolds: an altar. And on a platform above it, a miniature chair like Cacayari's with a pair of antlers attached – the seat of the deer god, Kauyumari. I realized with a frisson of unease that we'd been sleeping in the *xiriki*, the family god-house.

Chucho was sitting in Cacayari's chair by the fire, now a pyramid of warm ashes, picking his teeth with a stem of grass. Cacayari had long since gone out to the fields to work, and Chucho was lolling about on his laurels, second in command. The chair, an *uwéni*, was deceptively simple-looking. The base was like an up-turned waste-paper basket with the bottom of it, the seat, trimmed with deer hide. It was made of two different strengths of wood to symbolize the balance between soft and hard, pliant and resolute. The high, curved backrest was made out of swirls of interlocking circles supposed to represent peyote and to protect the occupant, especially if he was chanting or singing against sorcerers' attacks from the rear. Even used casually, the seat conveyed authority.

'Did you have good dreams last night?' inquired Chucho nonchalantly as I set about restoring myself with some coffee. I'd had, as it happened, some of the most vivid and arresting dreams I could remember since San Miguel de Allende – only there I'd been in a light, agitated sleep; here I'd sunk deep and heavy into another world and awoken dazed. 'That is a good house for dreaming,'

Chucho said, and he explained how sometimes, in times of stress, he would bed down in the *xiriki* so the deities could talk to him in his sleep. While I often dismissed dreams, those that I could remember, as the inevitable debris of the day, to Chucho, dreams were as alive and real and important as waking life. Dreams, he said, were visitations. They would come and go through the tiny stone amulet in the wall of the *xiriki*.

I added a spoonful of powdered Nido milk to the Nescafé granules and tried to forget Jessica had mentioned it could be radioactive (Mexico had allegedly bought millions of gallons of cheap Chernobyl-contaminated milk in secret from the Soviet Union – much of it supposed to have been dried under the Nido label, still being sold in out-of-the-way stores). The cup I'd borrowed from the cookhouse sang 'Waltzing Matilda' every time I picked it up. When I swapped it, I got one that sang 'You Are My Sunshine'. There was a knack to getting the lid off the water pot without burning your hands or blowing ash into the water, and I hadn't got it. It didn't pour easily. I sensed I was providing Chucho with some entertaining *téiwari* slapstick and he wasn't in a hurry to help.

Chucho's wife, Julia, caught my eye though, and, laughing, demonstrated how to hold the pot handle with a stick and slip the lid back with the hem of my skirt. She was looking suddenly quite beautiful. She'd lost the pinched, evasive look she'd had on the journey and recovered a breezy serenity. She was wearing a fresh, red paisley headscarf bias-bound in green and a multicoloured skirt with polar bears, Father Christmases and snowmen cavorting all over it. I wondered if she knew what they were. There were three thick skeins of beads around her neck in blue, red and yellow, a blue bead bangle on her wrist and a silver lozenge on her middle finger. I felt jaded and dowdy by comparison, my hair stiff as a creosote bush from all the dust on the road.

Even without its men, and some of its older children away at school, the little compound, with its half-dozen huts arranged in a circle around the eternal log-fire, was bustling with life. There were pigs tossing over maize cobs, toddlers chasing chickens, the drone of a metal bucket being filled at the tap, birds scuffling in the mulberry tree, the distant hee-haw of a donkey. And then, bringing me sharply to my senses and the reason why we were here, a low moan of pain from the open doorway of the hut next to ours. Julia hurried over and disappeared inside to join her sisters at her mother's bedside.

Jessica and I had arrived in the village all gung-ho with heroic purpose, the cavalry to the rescue. Perhaps we should have known it couldn't be so simple. Julia's mother had become bedridden in the time Chucho and his family had been away, and though she was still adamant she had to get to San Blas, her other daughters insisted she couldn't be moved. Our arrival, instead of relieving the tension, had intensified it. There was a battle of wills being played out over the sickbed and our presence was forcing the issue. There was nothing we could do, it seemed, but sit and wait and try to appear relaxed about the outcome.

Jessica was proving an invaluable companion in these rather tense circumstances – light-hearted and relaxed and easy-going, happy to switch into Indian time and let the current of events carry us along. Her father, she told me, was a mad inventor and her mother a more down-to-earth trade exhibition organizer. She had British great-grandparents on her mother's side of the family, and her English was so perfect and so colloquial I found it slightly disorientating after all the American accents I was used to. She was studying the Cora Indians as the main subject of her anthropology degree and had visited Cora and Huichol villages in the sierra before as part of her research. She'd also travelled with Humberto and some of his Huichol *compañeros* on parts of the peyote trail. There were interesting correlations between the Cora and the Huichol, she told me. Though the Cora were more warlike and aggressive than the Huichol, they were generally less able to defend themselves against the outside world. The Huichol understood the world of the *teiwari* far better than the Cora – they were more politically aware, they were conscious of their rights and they could communicate more easily with local government. But when communities from either tribe – Cora or Huichol – lost their footing and were tumbled into the maelstrom of Christianity and mestizification, as they had been in towns that were on the coast or close to big cities, she'd observed, the result was the same: alcoholism, drug addiction, violence; the complete loss of dignity and direction, a bitter kind of hopelessness.

In her spare time Jessica played the *jarana*, a small guitar, and sang in a band; and spent weekends going to fandangos in Veracruz with her wild musician boyfriend. She was unfazed by the political gridlock in which we found ourselves, advocating the two trump cards of diplomacy: sit on the fence, and wait and see.

So we succumbed to the soporific pace of village life, watching people come and go, pulling our legs closer into the shade as the sun reached its peak. We played with the children; helped a little with the cooking – mashing up *refritos* (refried beans) with the bottom of an old Coke bottle, pounding chillies and *cilantro* (fresh coriander) in the granite mortar, chopping tomatoes, frying sausage; we did the washing-up in tablespoons of water as if it were liquid gold, sprinkling the dregs on the open ground to damp down the dust.

Occasionally we helped Julia with the endless labour of tortilla making: from husking and shucking the corn to boiling it soft to squeezing it achingly through the grinder (twice) to kneading it with powdered lime and just the right amount of water, patting it into ping-pong balls, pressing each one in the wooden tortilla press, then warming them three at a time on a flat pan on the fire. Making choux pastry was fast-food compared to this and the novelty soon faded.

But Julia went at the whole performance three times a day, religiously. To her it was more than a household chore, it was a sacred rite. As the ancient staple food, maize has a special resonance all over the country. It is still sacred among the Maya in Chiapas, and the Purépecha in Pátzcuaro; there are dozens of names for it in Zapotec, defining every stage of its growth from seed to shoot to cob. In indigenous communities everywhere, maize still connects man with the land, and so with the ancient gods.

But nowhere was maize so hallowed, so revered, so anthropomorphized as it was here among the Huichol. Here its ancient status had never been eroded. The cobs Julia turned in her hands were the deity itself. The plant, she told us as she worked, was female; the ear was male. It was closely connected to the deer: the mature plant stood tall and proud and majestic, its leaves like the antlers of a stag; while the first shoots were like the short spikes on the head of a fawn.

Women and maize had parallel lives, she said; they were intertwined like sisters. Little girls were often named after the different words for maize in different stages of growth. When maize was planted there was a ceremony similar to the one that marked the act of conception; when it first showed itself above the earth, it was greeted like the birth of a child; when it was cut down, it was mourned. The life cycle of maize and of humans was reciprocal, mutually indistinguishable.

The Huichol tell a story about five divine maize girls – the five different colours of corn – who were descended from the great rain-mother of the Pacific Ocean. Blue maize, Yoa'wima, was the most sacred. It was she who had once been abused by an ungrateful mother-in-law, who had put her to work grinding maize on a stone *metate*. As Yoa'wima ground, her arms became a bloody pulp because she was, in effect, grinding herself. Because of this, people could never take maize for granted again. In his anger Yoa'wima's father had decreed that the cycle of maize propagation would be a long and complex one, physically exhausting and requiring many rituals to make it grow. Never again would maize sprout from the ground to fill the bellies of men, willingly and abundantly, in a matter of days. She must be coaxed and worshipped each year, instead, until she could be satisfied that the people knew the value of her bounty.

At least, it seemed the Huichol had learnt their lesson, unlike the rest of Mexico. Another Huichol story related how 'Jesucristo' had originally taught both the Huichol and the Mexicans the art of cultivation and maize rituals. But the Mexicans forgot to observe the proper ceremonies. Agriculture, and the fundamental pleasures of eating and drinking, became secular and mundane. They were no longer part of the magic of life. So Jesucristo punished them by giving them inferior maize which is why Mexicans today are forced to supplement their diet with foreign crops like oats and wheat.

The Mexican government's interference in traditional farming methods only served to bolster the conviction among Huichols that the *téiwari* have lost their special relationship with maize. The one time Chucho was persuaded to try out a new all-singing, all-dancing variety of corn from the States, he told me, he was rewarded with a bumper crop and then complete failure the following year. The seed was infertile, he said – what kind of maize is that? He was forced to buy in maize from outside to feed his family and animals, and more seed for the following year. Humbled and out of pocket, he returned to the traditional, time-honoured variety and apologized to the gods for his stupidity.

If only more of the Mexican *campesinos* had trusted their instincts instead of the great US-inspired agronomical campaigns of the 1970s, Mexico might be a very different place today. The so-called 'Green Revolution', funded largely by US fertilizer, seed and pesticide companies, had swept the country into a vortex of agricultural decimation and decline. In what seemed at first an unbelievable about-turn of generosity on the part of the Mexican government, farmers were given new seeds and bags of free fertil-izer to use on their maize fields. It was a godsend. The maize grew miraculously, luxuriantly, faster than ever before.

But then, as little as three years later, the farmers began to notice yields were dropping to their original levels; and soon they found that if they didn't add the new fertilizer the corn wouldn't grow at all. By now the fertilizer was no longer free and hundreds of thousands of farmers, trapped in the system like addicts or alco-holics, borrowed money from the banks – at incentivized rates – to buy more chemicals.

Eventually, in many regions the cost of the fertilizer needed to produce a marginal crop exceeded the value of the maize itself. It became cheaper for farmers to buy corn than to grow it. For the first time ever, Mexico began to import maize from the United States. Farming communities across the country collapsed and families fled in desperation – are still fleeing – to the barrios of the cities to find food and work.

There was another unforeseen effect of the chemical-fertilizer programme. Because the fertilizer was advertised as the miracle to end all miracles, farmers gave up adding compost and dung to their fields. In a country where most of the land is so close to being desert anyway, erosion was precipitously swift. The thin topsoil was washed away by the rains or blew away in the wind. The process the Spaniards had started in Mexico nearly five centuries ago, was suddenly given extra impetus by the most technologically advanced nation in the world – the United States. Nearly a third of Mexico's 50 million acres of farmland is now severely damaged by erosion. Michoacán, Hidalgo and Jalisco have been badly hit, but the states of Tlaxcala and highland Oaxaca have suffered the worst, with over 70 per cent of old arable land destroyed. Ironically, it is from these states that most of the migrants to the United States come – to work as cheap labour on the vast Californian farms. Only in places like the silt-rich Isthmus of Tehuantepec whose natural fertility remained unaffected by these new methods, did agricultural communities continue to prosper.

A morning in the village became a day; one day, two days, three; and still there was no sign of a resolution from the hut of the ailing woman-shaman. Tensions were mounting. Jessica and I lapsed uneasily into a routine. Lunch at eleven or thereabouts, sitting on the floor of the *xiriki* in the darkness with Chucho, Julia and the children, each of us reaching by turn into a handkerchief for warm blue tortillas to scoop up *refritos* and salsa. A candle was lit at the altar at midday and left to burn down. There was no conversational banter over meals. 'Why do you people ask so many questions,' snapped Chucho when I asked about some of the things on the altar, or tried to find out more about his life – 'always talking, even when you're eating.'

Outside the *xiriki* Chucho was more communicative and relaxed. He even began to make jokes. Laughter was one of the most conspicuous things about the Huichol. They always seemed in high spirits. If they were sad, they cried easily and profusely, an emotional thunderstorm that brought instant relief and cleared the skies. By contrast we appeared permanently *triste* to them; a smile, if it came, looked a struggle. Sometimes they'd become so concerned by our lack of gaiety that they'd come up and ask if we were all right.

Chucho, however, had a burden of responsibility on his shoulders and was beginning to feel doubtful about having brought us here. We were forbidden to wander beyond the small family compound among the other houses, or to stray anywhere near the ceremonial centre with its great round temple, the *tuki*, or to climb any of the peaks, or walk anywhere in the valley except up towards the ridge we had come from. When I made notes in my book Chucho told me I would become sick if I was writing about the Huichol.

The outside world, perhaps because it had entered the village so conspicuously with us, was a constant threat. 'Look at the children,' he complained, 'they have no self-respect nowadays. Plastic toys and ugly Western clothes (he himself was wearing a Halls T-shirt under his tunic, a *sombrero de caballero* – a cowboy hat – and some new sandals that had given him a blister). They are like tourists.' When Jessica enquired about a child with blond hair, Chucho answered slyly, 'I don't know how it happened. He probably bought a pill from a gringo doctor.' We thought it would amuse him to hear about Michael Jackson, a black man in the States who was turning himself white using pills and skin dye and plastic surgery. 'Who is he and what does he think he's doing?' asked Chucho, genuinely appalled. Jessica's rendition of 'I'm Bad' and a dusty imitation of break-dancing failed to lighten his mood.

As midday honed its knife it became too irritating to read or write or talk. Jessica and I lay about, taking turns in a hammock under the mulberry tree and being splatted by overripe berries and bird shit. White light seared into our shade. Tiny biting flies – *animalitos* Jessica called them – interrupted the luxury of a snooze. Noises – the human voice, neighing burros – jarred the nerves. The cockerels fell silent, smothered by the heat, but up in the desiccated forest on the hillsides, birds twittered interminably.

Then gradually, surreptitiously, the day went into decline. Children ran about again. The men came home. Cacayari, always jovial and friendly, came over to touch fingertips. 'Kia'ko!' Then he'd saunter towards his wife's bedside and come out again, crying. Sometime later, his violin could be heard, playing a tune like an Irish jig, from inside the *xiriki*.

We'd eat again. And at last the sun would begin to dip, the sky dissolving into an umbrageous Tiepolo ceiling. The village would breathe deeply once more and irritations melt into the mellowness of dusk. The evening star would burst out of nowhere; logs would be shifted back on to the ashes. Slowly the village reconvened around the flames and, once again, the planets blazed out pink and green and blue among the galaxies, and the odd satellite would plough its trajectory straight through them all.

Despite the magical evenings and the soporific days, Jessica and I were becoming increasingly worried about Chucho's family's diminishing goodwill and our dwindling supplies – factors that, it seemed, were intimately connected with each other. We'd planned for a generous week's stay but constant raids on our store boxes had meant almost everything had disappeared in the first few days. The Huichol have no concept of individual ownership as such and helped themselves freely to biscuits, chocolate, oranges, apples, slices of cheese and sausage whenever they fancied. I found it galling at first to find some grubby child rummaging around in my bag and pulling out an oat-bar I'd been saving for myself; until now, of course, when the tables had turned, and I was relying on Julia's goodwill for the odd tortilla and tomato from her stores.

With the disappearance of our food went the irritation of being plundered and a lot of the tension of disparity but now, we realized, we had nothing material to contribute to our stay here other than a little help with the chores. We were fast becoming a burden on the community, instead of a boon.

Then suddenly, just as we were thinking of abandoning ship, a decision was made to consult Juancho – a respected elder, village councillor and *mara'akáme* – on the subject of moving *La Inválida*. It was a galvanizing move. Juancho would be invited over to Chucho's to do an all-night chant so he could divine the right course of action. Juancho, however, was in the middle of a three-day ceremony to inaugurate a new *xiriki* in a village on top of the ridge on the other side of the valley. He might be too exhausted – and too drunk – to consent. A lift back to the village in our combi might be enough of an inducement, it was generally thought, for the shaman to come with us and we were dispatched with Chucho and Pascual to extricate the venerable sage from his hangover.

*

278

The fiesta was nearing its end when we arrived dust-encrusted and exhilarated to be back on the flight path and out of the clear-air turbulence of the village. It was Tuesday the 13th, an unlucky day for the rest of Mexico, but here the jokers fell from a different pack. To the people of Santa Isabel on a windy ridge among the pines, the day was propitious and they were propitiously drunk.

The village was not much larger than Chucho's – the same bracelet of huts around a similar open fire. But it reverberated drama as if the very walls of adobe, the fronds of thatch, the beaten earth in the middle had been stirred by the force of human energy that had hit it over the past few days. It was like walking into the last scene of a play. The protagonists staggered around or lolled about caught up in an inexorable performance, somewhere near the resolution of an incomprehensible plot.

Our entrance seemed to go unnoticed. An old man wearing ragged Western clothes like a bum sat in a ceremonial chair by the fire in the scorching sun, rocking. There were tears pouring down his cheeks. A couple of teenagers, red-eyed and dressed to kill, swayed across the ground, arms around each others' shoulders like blood-brothers. Their Huichol costumes boiled with visions – scorpions, deer, flowers, peyote, cats, embroidered Virgin of Guadalupes surrounded by angels. The words *Eres mi ilusión* – 'You are my dream' – were stitched up the side of one trouser leg; *Mi amor* on another. And across the back of one of their tunics was the national emblem – the eagle on a cactus with a snake in its talons and the exclamation *Viva México*; only here it seemed suddenly pagan, a symbol of Indianness. There was nothing Hapsburg or revolutionary or governmental about it at all.

Chucho ushered us into some shade under the eaves of a hut a stone's throw from the *xiriki* and then disappeared with Pascual. People were emerging and disappearing through the *xiriki* doorway like bees at a hive. Its walls were new and smooth, the colour of honey. From inside came the hum of a violin and a guitar, and a long, low buzz of chanting.

We were approached by a middle-aged woman carrying two bowls of deer soup. She was Juancho's wife, a princess of a woman, proud and composed with a face of moulded beeswax. Only a fractional over-deliberation in her movements betrayed her impressive consumption of alcohol over the past two days. She smiled warmly at Jessica, whom she'd met before, and gently patted her arm. 'Drink up,' she gestured.

The soup was blood temperature from its incubation in the sun. The beast it was derived from had probably been killed at least ten days before the ceremony began, in a distant part of the forest beyond Huichol boundaries where deer stocks were still high, completing its final journey in a sweltering bus. Every step of its transformation from quarry to corpse to cooking-pot would have been attended by complicated and emotional rituals. The resulting soup contained the essence of its spirit. Drinking it was like taking communion. I raised the bowl to my lips with irreverent but instinctive hesitation. Blobs of fat interrupted the flow when I finally let the soup into my mouth. Its smell fled up my nose and lodged somewhere deep inside the cortex. The liquid was pure animal – musky, pungent, foxy – and fizzed gently on the tongue. It tasted alive.

Scarcely had we put down our bowls than Juancho himself emerged from the *xiriki* and beckoned us inside. The deference with which people spoke of the *mara'akáme* had led me to expect someone showy and commandeering – an amplification of Chucho perhaps. But Juancho was small and unobtrusive, a tortoise of a man, a little stooped and wizened with skin like Spanish vellum. His age was incalculable. There were wispy rogue hairs on his chin and he had a way of moving his face that reminded me of a camel I had once seen in Morocco drinking a bottle of Coke. It was later that I began to notice his tungsten resolve, the depth of focus, the methodical, sequestered energy that would keep him chanting all night long, going from one ceremony to the next on just a few hours' sleep and a couple of tamales.

In Humberto's eyes he was one of the most powerful of all the Huichol shamans. He had twice saved Humberto's life Humberto had told me late one evening in Mexico City after showing me a slide show of the Sierra. Once, when Humberto was new to the ways of the Huichol, after a particularly long and disorientating peyote-taking ceremony, he'd fallen desperately ill. He had literally crawled away into a corner to die, he said. He was overcome by a horrific sinking sensation as if his spirit was suddenly ebbing away and a dreadful conviction that he would never make it back out of the Sierra alive.

No one seemed to have noticed his condition, or his terror, except for Juancho. Until the moment Juancho came over to Humberto to offer his help, Humberto hadn't noticed Juancho either. He had seemed to slip into the background, a steady beam eclipsed by the floor show of the flashier apprentice *mara'akámes*. He had taken Humberto to a river, along with a Huichol woman and her sick baby, and performed some kind of exorcism on them both. The baby had died. But Humberto was convinced Juancho had saved him.

A few years later, sometime into Humberto's campaign to protect the peyote valley of Huiricuta from the new highway, he was taking his leave of the *mara'akámes* and villagers he'd been visiting. Juancho had approached him agitated. 'Don't get into that truck,' he said, 'it will kill you.' Humberto had pressing business in Mexico City and diplomatically tried to reassure the shaman he would drive carefully. Juancho shook his head but went several times around the car, muttering oaths of protection and flicking sacred spring water on to the bonnet as if he were trying to build some sort of a force field around it. That night, ten hours into his drive and tunnelling against the strobelights of the motorway at high speed, Humberto fell asleep at the wheel. He was lucky to escape the wreckage with compacted vertebrae, a broken leg and six months in hospital.

It was cool inside the *xiriki* despite the jostle for body space. Barely 15 feet by 12 feet, the room was even smaller than the one we'd been sleeping in but had a very similar ceremonial altar with a platform above it. There were chains of toasted mauve tortillas strung across the altar. In the middle of all the traditional paraphernalia there was a Catholic crucifix but instead of Christ, there was a little stuffed doll wearing Huichol clothes attached to it. There was also a framed image of the Virgin of Guadalupe, bleached to a spectre from days of ceremony out in the sun, with blood smeared on the corners. Next to this was the rifle that had dispatched the latest sacrifices. Two tired musicians plodded on with the music while the congregation hopped about murmuring a refrain, kicking up spirals of dust towards the rafters.

Scarcely had we squeezed in the door than *teguino* – home-brewed maize beer – was pressed upon us in staggering quantities. We had a lot of catching up to do. Buckets came forward out of nowhere, gourds and tin cups were dunked and pressed dripping into our hands until we held three or four at a time and, sloshing them up to our lips, knocking them back, one by one, until the beer began to spill down our necks, still more came on – thick, sludgy yeasty beer; thin, fizzy beer; strong, malty beer – punctuated, like mortars among fireworks, with the odd thundery shot of mezcal.

A drunk in our corner began pestering us to dance, leering into our faces with breath by now only a little beerier than ours, and nuzzling uncomfortably against us in the crush. In our defence we began to hop – Jessica deftly, and in time; me next to her scuffling about like a jackdaw in quicklime. As the alcohol began to take hold, sloshing about in the stomach as if it were attempting a second fermentation, the muse began to reach my feet and I found myself doing a passable 1920s soft shoe shuffle.

Juancho was back in the centre, chanting and blessing people with his *muviéris* – sacred wands with feathers or deer-tails attached – which he dipped into gourds of sacred water and flicked on to the waiting communicants. He was attended by two *angelitos*, a little girl and a boy, symbols of purity, who stood patiently by holding their bundles of sacred objects like wise men in a nativity play.

At last the ceremonial chair for the deer god Kauyumári was brought before Juancho for the penultimate blessing. Juancho's chanting, husky with exertion, cranked up a notch. The horns of a recently sacrificed steer were already roped to the back of the chair, along with a bloody, feathery mass that I took to be the head of a cockerel. The little girl placed her bundle on the seat. The music and singing intensified. Then a man came forward and bound the antlers of the deer to the crest of the chairback. He was wearing a Chicago Bulls baseball cap. In the exultant confusion of religious symbolism the familiar bulls' horn logo had taken on new and mystic meaning. Juancho's voice cracked with emotion. People began to cry.

Finally the little boy climbed up on to the platform and the deer throne was handed up to him and installed dead centre. The billows of emotion began to subside. Bundles of candles were propped up on the seat and a few vital adjustments made to the position of the chair. Wiping his eyes matter-of-factly on his sleeves, Juancho pronounced the completion of his task. 'Everything is done,' he said in Huichol, 'nothing is missing. All is as it should be.' And he staggered outside.

Unsteady on our feet and now unsteady of resolve, we followed. Juancho was seated once again in his *uweni* by the fire, his two drunken attendants almost comatose in similar chairs by his side. At his feet were crates of Coke and beer – part payment for conducting the ceremony – and as he called up the villagers, one by one, he pressed a bottle or two into their hands along with some tamales and a benediction. He beckoned to Jessica and me as the villagers began to disperse and, handing us a Coke each, said, 'Tell Humberto he has offerings to make. I am taking my family to the sacred cave of Uramaka. You can meet me in Puente de Camotlán on Saturday morning. We go together.'

It was not the outcome we'd been expecting. Having struggled for a week in the net that inveigled the dying woman, it was exhilarating to be, suddenly, free. Juancho was not going to sing for her. He knew without visiting that she was too ill to make the journey. She might die on a dirt road in the back of our car or, worse, end up in some mestizo hospital, isolated from the Sierra and the consolations of ritual and family, the earth and the open air. The decision, now he had made it, seemed simple and inevitable; our involvement an inappropriate diversion.

Juancho had other priorities, too. It was the end of the dry season and the countryside was cracking up. Everyone's nerves were on edge. If the correct rituals were not performed, if the gods were not propitiated, then the rains might not come. There were a number of different deities to appeal to, not least of them the five water goddesses who assemble around the Uramaka Cave and in the nearby springs and cliffs and mountains every May. The cave was also the home of the spirit of the Kieri plant (*solandra brevicalix*), a powerful hallucinogen which, as Juancho's principal patron-spirit and power-ally, was specially close to his heart. As usual, Juancho had several strings to his bow and the forthcoming pilgrimage would also be a chance for him to help members of his family fulfil personal obligations.

If Jessica and I were relieved to be liberated from thoughts of painkillers and extra mattresses, sumps breaking, suspension cracking up, arrest for body-snatching or possessing illegal cacti, Chucho was positively uplifted. Back in the village he took Jessica and me aside into his hut, and affectionately bestowed us with gifts – beautiful bead necklaces for us both and for me a woven shoulder bag with a quadruple star-burst design of lime-green peyotes, and an exquisite black, pink and turquoise bead bracelet that he'd made himself.

'I'm sorry I persuaded you to come all the way to the Sierra,' he said disarmingly, 'but now I know it is not for nothing. It is best that La Inválida stays here, and it is best that you go now with Juancho. We will meet again – in Mexico City, perhaps, with Humberto. I will make a yarn-painting for you. I will not forget what you were willing to do for my family.'

Only now did I fully realize the dichotomy that had had Chucho cannoned like a Maya rubber ball between his family and us, between the will of his gods and the wishes of *téiwari*. He had found himself cornered, immobilized, as the situation in the village crept nearer boiling-point. It was an impasse that fuelled a kind of defensive aggression; a warm-weather low incubating a storm. I felt we'd brushed up against the temperament that had steel-coated the Huichol for centuries.

But Chucho was not a shaman. His were feet of clay to Juancho's winged heels. Chucho's strength lay in obeisance to the customs of the Huichol, whereas Juancho's authority came from the ancestors themselves. While Chucho had done his utmost to protect the secrets of his race, loyally distracting us like a mother hen when we strayed too close to his nest, Juancho took flight like an eagle and offered us a place on his back for a bird's-eye view.

Intuitively, even in his tequinoed condition, Juancho must have trusted us. Perhaps he saw an opportunity to open the eyes of another couple of fumbling, well-meaning *téiwari*; to cultivate more allies in the battle to protect his culture from digestion by the outside world. But it was a chance, too, to induct his *téiwari* protégées into another sacred mystery, and for Humberto to fulfil another in a series of offerings he'd promised the gods, to thank them for opening their doors to him.

We left Chucho to his familial duties, in the orbit of his own *xiriki*, to the pathetic groans of his mother-in-law and the endless squeaking of the maize grinder, and hightailed it to the nearest public telephone.

Humberto was characteristically pleased to be summoned away from his computer for a few days. We met him off the evening flight to Zacatecas and celebrated with a bottle of mezcal. He'd been missing the Sierra.

'Hell, I feel like I've done nothing but number-crunching and data processing for weeks. I've swallowed so much information it's given me indigestion.'

Humberto had been working on his most ambitious project to date: to map the entire 300-mile pilgrimage route from the Sierra Huichol to the peyote valley of Huiricuta, including all the sacred sites – hundreds of them – along the way, and to catalogue all the relevant fauna and flora along this, one of the most diverse, specialized and biologically rich areas of Mexico. He was trying to build up an argument for conservation of the route, both as a sacred site in its entirety, and as a wildlife corridor. His aim was to convince the Mexican government of the crucial role of the pilgrimage in Huichol culture. The journey, he was trying to illustrate, was far more than a simple cactus-collecting trip. It was, in Humberto's words, a 'nomadic university': a means of instructing *peyoteros* (as young as nine years old) in the mysteries of their religion, renewing the community's contact with the spirits and providing them with propitious energy for the coming year. It was, in a sense, a Huichol songline, a cultural 'dreaming'. Every landmark on the way was a mythic signpost, a message from the gods. For a Huichol to reach the status of a *mara'akáme* he or she must undertake five of these pilgrimages. Villagers left at home participate, too, empathetically following the *peyoteros* through rituals and ceremonies that connect them to every landmark as the *peyoteros* encounter it. In this way, each year, the Huichol tribes embark on the adventure together and the community renews itself, passing beyond the limits of geographical time and location, and into the continuous regions of the psyche. It was an inward as much as an external journey, guided and inspired by a considerable intake of peyote.

In recent years it had become increasingly difficult for the Huichol to follow their path. Across much of the route there were now barbed-wire cattle- and deer-fences. Land that had once belonged to the ancient denizens of Mexico was being parcelled up and handed over to rancheros or logging companies, or simply surreptitiously nibbled away at the edges by mestizo immigrants. Sacred sites were being exorcized, drained, levelled, absorbed amoeba-like into the profanity of the outside world.

In Huiricuta itself, it was becoming more and more difficult to find peyote as New Agers – Mexicans as well as gringos – were harvesting them for their own mystical Carlos Castañeda experiences. The 60s Californian cult-hero had a lot to answer for. Unlike the Huichol, these *locos*, as Juancho called them, were ignorant: they dug up the peyote disrespectfully, roots and all. Only the Huichol knew how to cut the peyote kindly, without harming the mother plant, in a way that would encourage even more bulbs to grow.

In addition to these difficulties, the Huichol *peyoteros* were hounded by the police and the military – for trespassing, for hunting on private property, for not using the roads, for being Indian, for simply existing in an age when only lunatics or hobos preferred to walk, when anyone involved in taking hallucinogenic drugs was a danger to society, the state and, it was argued, to themselves. When seven Huichol were detained by a military battalion and thrown in jail for possession of peyote the previous year, one of them made a statement: 'If the government and military are going to end our way of life by confiscating our religious items and putting us in jail for completing our spiritual obligations, then they might just as well kill us all right now and get it over with quicker.'

Humberto had been asked to fight for the Huichols' right to follow the ancient pilgrimage route and for dispensations that would allow them to harvest and use peyote for their own private, ritual purposes – dispensations that would at the same time protect the peyote from predation by outsiders. 'For the Huichol, the journey to Huiricuta is a magical journey, as inspirational as a pilgrimage to the Virgin of Guadalupe, or any of the other Catholic sites in Mexico,' Humberto railed over our fourth or fifth mezcal in a crowded bar in Zacatecas, 'yet the Huichol have fewer rights than wildebeest migrating across the Serengeti.'

Suddenly, though, Humberto seemed to be making headway. Both the World Wildlife Fund and UNESCO had backed the idea. The project, having once fizzled wearily, struggling to take off, had now rocketed into orbit and Humberto was finding the new perspective a trifle dizzying. He was not only swamped by raw data and GPS coordinates that he and his colleagues now had to organize and absorb, and by a barrage of administrative and secretarial work, but excited by suggestions from like-minded campaigners all over the world. The ten days since I'd seen him had worn him down. 'It's good to be back,' he sighed, leaning back into a Gauloise, 'Goodbye computers. Hello Sierra.'

Humberto, Jessica and I waited for Juancho in a brand-new restaurant in the one-horse town of Puente de Comotlán all morning and all afternoon. We waited and waited, while uneasiness turned to doubt and then despair. Only Humberto remained quietly confident. Occasionally he'd saunter down to the main square, just to check Juancho wasn't waiting for us there, but mostly he sat, happily contemplating another 'Vicky' – a Victoria beer – entirely unruffled. Just as I'd given up all thought of seeing him again, Juancho slipped into the restaurant. He grasped Humberto by the hand, laughing, a bubble of intimacy and understanding exploding between them. There was no need for courtesies. We were straight back to business. A truck was waiting outside with twenty of Juancho's family – men, women and children – standing up in the back, a riot of colour, in holiday mood.

Juancho and his wife, intentionally or subconsciously, were colour coordinated for the trip in a symphony of apple-green and scarlet. Julia was wearing a skirt covered in Christmas presents and holly; Juancho a green, checked tunic dotted with cherries. It was all I would have noticed if I'd seen them together in the street. There was more to their attire at close range, though. Juancho, in particular, was a walking display of shamanic curiosities. Under the paisley bandanna, and the three bead skeins (white, purple and yellow) that he wore around his neck, was a cowrie shell on a leather thong; and each wrist sported a blue and white bead bracelet like the one Chucho had given me.

On one hip, strapped to an embossed leather belt trimmed with red woollen tassels, was a Swiss-army knife in a sheath. On the other, a small gourd slung inside a deer's scrotum containing *makutse*, a native variety of tobacco with the highest nicotine content known to man. It is cultivated specially by the Huichol for ritual use and can be rolled up into corn-husk cigarettes or smoked in clay pipes during ceremonies that revolve around deer hunting and the peyote pilgrimage. Miniature *makutse* cigarettes would be tied to toy rattles during a ceremony in which Juancho, through his chanting and the rhythmic beating of a drum, would lead Huichol children on a metaphysical journey to the peyote desert.

Juancho's hat, broad and flat like one of a pair of cymbals, had two red pom-poms dangling either side of his ears, four on the brim and a fifth on the crown in the centre. It was trimmed with cockerel and eagle feathers, and a red plastic camellia Jessica had given him the previous year. This had been added to the assembly not simply because it was attractive – the Huichol wear nothing casually; every garment, every accessory has some religious purpose – but because flowers, like the plumes of birds, are prayers for rain and for life; even if they happen to be made in Taiwan.

Over Juancho's shoulder was slung a small, scarlet, pink and lime-green embroidered bag with a pattern of hearts and crosses and a safety pin stuck through the middle of it. In a larger bag, which he carried slung on his back, were the bulkier of his sacred power-objects: his magic *muviéri* in a long, lidded basket; the antlers of Kauyumári; a *xikiri*, or magical mirror, through which the deities would reveal themselves to him; some *urutexi*, or votive arrows; a gourd bottle containing sacred water; and a piece of yellow root from a desert shrub known as *uxa* which he would use to paint the faces of his companions. And last, but by no means least, it contained five large, gnarly bulbs of the famous cactus *lophophora williamsii*, collected on his latest trip to Huiricuta with Humberto.

I felt a knot tighten in my stomach when I knew peyote taking was on the agenda. And Humberto must have noticed the colour draining from my face. He started singing the opening bars of *The Twilight Zone*. 'The time has come,' he said in a voice like Vincent Price, 'for your journey into The Unknown.'

The truck sped along in front of us trailing clouds of dust. We lingered behind out of its way. On either side raw monoliths, jagged cliffs, chimneys and buttes, powered out of the wasteland. As the sun fell towards the horizon they cast colder, deeper shadows across the desert, filling gullies and ingesting the ocotillo and mesquite scrub, the yuccas and chaparral, like aprons of lava. We were winding through a Daliesque fantasy, a valley of sculpture and monuments, as if the landscape itself were intent on expanding the imagination for what was to come.

Juancho had opted for the relative comfort of our combi over a dusty ride in the truck. Occasionally he would lean forward to point out a sacred site, a pinnacle of rock, some petrified, dactyloid figure, an eagle circling. But most of the time he canoodled with his wife in the back seat like a teenager.

At last we began to climb out of the valley back into familiar pine forest, and as darkness fell we pulled off the road behind the truck to camp for the night. A shrill wind had picked up and was gusting off the top of the cutting. It masked the approach of a convoy of juggernauts – the first vehicles we had seen all day – bearing down on us round a hairpin bend. They were pulling trailers loaded with timber. There was a sound of chains and air-brakes, and a whiff of fresh wood as they thundered past, and then nothing. Only the heaving, nonchalant wind again, and a vague, empty sensation of loss.

We lit three camp fires and everyone started cooking. Juancho and Julia came over and joined us. Juancho was in a feisty mood. Humberto had warned us about Juancho's penchant for what Humberto mischievously called the 'ancient methodology of bio-geography'. Juancho had once homed in on a Danish photographer friend of Humberto's, grabbing her breasts on the pretext of describing a pass through sacred mountains. Juancho was excited to learn that Jessica was twenty-five and unmarried. 'So you still have a tight pussy,' he leered, pumping the finger of one hand through a hole he made with the other. 'Come on, come to bed, marry me. Julia won't mind. I like to be squeezed. These women can't do it – they've gone all loose from having babies.'

In the refracted light from the fire he looked impish and protean – shades of Dionysus, Shiva, Shakespeare's Fool, conspicuously lewd but also disconcertingly charismatic and perspicacious; like Kauyumári himself, the divine deer god, messenger between the worlds of mortals and deities, whose reputation as a trickster and sexual clown was wedded to his role as guardian and spirit guide; whose excesses were natural and unquestionable – the overspill from a vessel brimming with inspirational energy. Juancho's wife, at any rate, accepted his behaviour, sometimes looking unmoved, sometimes smilingly amused. And if Jessica was put out, she didn't show it. No one wants to slap a shaman.

Early the next morning after cold tortillas we packed up again. The children, from the oldest to the smallest, pitched in, laughing and fooling and wanting to help. It occurred to me weeks later that I never saw a Huichol berate or strike a child. I saw them verbally admonished on occasions but there never seemed a need for the constant ratchet of threats and bribes and punishments resorted to in the West. Children were trusted from a tiny age and universally loved. A child, in the Huichols' eyes, was everyone's child. They were indulged and cherished, and grew up engagingly sociable and confident, capable and uncomplaining. A Huichol upbringing was the antithesis of the adult-orientated world of the West. It was a source of amazement among the Huichol that we divorced our-selves from our relatives and promoted the nuclear family, or preferred to live, childless, on our own; that we entrusted our children to strangers and the brutish psychology of the school playground – and then complained about the results.

The Huichol community itself was divided over the issue of sending their own children to school. Many felt that knowing how to read and write were crucial weapons of defence and would be needed if the next Huichol generation was to survive; others that this was no advantage, and that school only drove a wedge between children and their community at a vulnerable age. Because the Huichol villages are so remote, boarding school is the only option and many children – boys in particular – are sent away for months at a time, unable to afford the bus ride for interim visits home. Whatever their feelings about literacy, Huichols are unanimous in their resentment of school authorities, who often use the opportunity to try to turn the Huichol children against their own culture, and to convert them to Christianity. One of the Huichols' most pressing desires is for bilingual classes where their children can learn to read and write in Spanish without being force-fed the Hispanic world-view.

Before leaving the campsite we paid our respects to Tatewarí, Grandfather Fire, who had kept us company during the night. One fire was kept alive, each of us feeding it a twig by way of thanks. 'We owe our life to Tatewarí,' Juancho impressed upon me, 'he clears the ground for us so we can plant, and he cooks our food. Without him, meat and maize and beans would remain inedible. In the night, he is the one that gladdens our hearts. He is our comfort when we are cold; our light so we can see things in the dark.'

It felt recklessly imprudent, though, leaving a fire burning unattended in the middle of the pine forest in this of all seasons. The Sierra was on its last legs, panting for rain. Coyotes and wild turkeys, half-crazed with thirst and heat, were losing their sense of caution and wandering out in the open. The skies heaved with false contractions, sending out flickers of lightning now and again – warning shots – and rolls of thunder like a giant hacking cough. We'd passed a fire truck on a ridge the previous week. It had little by way of firefighting equipment beyond shovels and a chainsaw and a two-way radio. But Juancho was confident in his deferment to the gods. 'Tatewarí is our protector,' he insisted. And we were, after all, on a mission to pray for rain.

We stopped at a bend in the road on the lip of a canyon, overlooking the hazy blue mountains of Santa Bárbara. Juancho stood close to the edge and blew his cow horn. A tremulous, triumphant sound, the ancient bugle-call of man, the trumpet of high priests and warriors, it sent a shiver of recognition down the spine and a blast of optimism singing into space. 'He's telling the gods we're coming,' said Humberto. In the far distance at the base of a cliff, one of the escutcheons marking the ridge-line, was the long, dark shadow of our cave.

A few miles later we were in Tepehuano territory in a village of log cabins roofed in slates of pine where mestizos and Indians in dusty jeans and sombreros were milling around or trudging the chalky roads with the slouch of broken men. It was midday and no one was out at work. Until recently this had been a logging centre, but the saw mill had closed when the mature timber had gone. Pulling out the last remaining stands and trucking them out was barely worth the effort. Mestizos who had moved in for the work were stranded high and dry; the Tepehuanos clinging to the wreckage of their culture and their land. The Tepehuanos hadn't been as lucky – or as wily – as the Huichol. Though they'd survived successfully into the twentieth century, modern pressures had proved too much for them. The twenty-first century was heralding their demise. In Jessica's words, the Tepehuanos had 'lost it'.

We got out to buy *refrescos*, and some chocolate and mezcal for the ceremony. Juancho's family jumped down to stretch their legs. Never had the Huichol looked so dignified and self-assured as they did meandering silently among the human driftwood of that Tepehuano township.

Beyond the logging centre the road deteriorated into a bumpy track that would prove impassable in the rains. We wound vaguely downwards and came to a final stop by the side of the road where there was only a valley between us and the cliff-face we had seen from Juancho's lookout. From here the cave looked like a mouth, deeper and darker and more expressive; the cliff above it rising a dizzying, magnificent five hundred feet.

It was a disorienting trek through the *roble* forest to the cave. The incline towards the bottom of the ravine was as steep as a dry ski-slope and had us slipping and skidding and clinging to branches to avoid falling. Superficially the forest looked as benign as oak woods in England but Mexico had given it extra spice. Between the oaks, gnarled and twisted like Spanish cork trees, blackened with drought as if fire had already torn through them, were spiny agaves, some of them thrusting up flowers like giant asparagus, fifteen foot high. There were thorn bushes, too, and, near the gully bottom, a long, scything type of grass.

I spent less time judging handholds, though, than I did thinking about my feet. Beneath dry oak leaves as large and crunchy as toasted tortillas, scuttled scorpions and snakes the size of bootlaces. Jessica told me she'd decided not to bring scorpion antidote with her this time. It was too expensive and had a shelf-life of only six months. I asked her how much a dose of it cost. 'Two hundred pesos for one person,' she said. Extortionate though it seemed to her, $20 seemed cheap at the price to me, especially at this moment. We were going to have to rely instead on the traditional Huichol remedy: catch the offending scorpion and eat it. Even with the mitigating sweetness of revenge, this sounded a bitter pill to swallow and as I walked I decided to make enough noise to scare off every lurking arachnid in the Sierra.

I followed a little girl, valiantly trailblazing up the other side of the ravine with her baby brother and a large bag on her back, and offered her a shove when she got into difficulties. Every time I pushed, she laughed, and then I laughed, and we ended up making the baby laugh. We were taking a very different tack to the one taken by the Nahua civilizations of central Mexico in their quest to bring rain. The Aztec rain god, Tlaloc, would have been outraged by this little girl's gaiety. It was the pain and torment of children, rather than their laughter, that moved him, that won his mercy. Only their tears could bring the rain, could stir the clouds to break.

The Aztec approach was a far cry from this happy Huichol family mission to honour the rain gods. In Tenochtitlán priests would take selected children away from their parents, incarcerating them in misery for weeks; and then, in a climactic thunder-burst, herd them, magnificently dressed, up the steps of a pyramid, where their throats would be slit as they wept and they would be gifted to Tlaloc as 'bloodied flowers of maize'.

The child-offerings to the rain god were the only sacrificial victims to come from the Aztec people themselves, rather than from captives taken in war from hostile tribes. So important was this ceremony, so crucial was water for the continuation of human life, that the Aztecs gave Tlaloc the most terrible of all sacrifices – their own children. They did not do this lightly. The Aztecs were as tender towards their young as the Huichol. When a new baby was born, it was welcomed on to this earth by all the members of its family, men and women, who gently stroked the tiny naked body 'so that it should know it was loved'. The annual sacrifice to Tlaloc was clearly traumatic. Onlookers wept as the litters with the weeping children were carried past them towards the temple-pyramid; they wept when the children's terrified wailing choked and stopped, their tears accumulating in a ghastly black storm cloud of death and rebirth.

Polarized as the Huichol and Aztec approach to gods seemed to be – one ecstatic and optimistic; the other fearful and doom-ridden – they were both tribes that had originated from the same 'Uto-Aztecan' rootstock. But circumstances and geography had changed them. The sacrifice of the sacred deer, shedding its blood for the Huichol to give life to the maize, to bring rain, to promote the harvest, to placate the gods, to bless the lives of men, was only one step away, albeit a giddy step, from the practice of putting human beings to the knife. The Aztecs, warlike, brutalized, imperial, obsessive, paranoid, desperate and afraid, had turned to the ultimate, most generous gift of all to please their deities enough to see them through another day. Perhaps this was inevitable, given the pressures building up in the cauldron of the valley of Mexico, between the vulcanic clashes of war and the demands of a burgeoning population, between the Scylla and Charybdis of famine and flood, and the endless intimations of impending doom, that the Aztecs should turn upon themselves like scorpions trapped beneath a glass. But it was clear they had broken their bond with

Nature. Somehow their world had flown out of kilter, defying the normal laws of humanity. Out here in the Sierra there was still comfort in the wilderness, reassurance in the sound of thunder, benevolence in the flowering ocotillo and the tracks of an armadillo. There were still pumas and, possibly, wolves out here. There was harmony in the universe. Man knew his place. And it was not at the top – or bottom – of a pyramid.

We stopped for a rest in a glade halfway up the slope to the cave and refreshed ourselves with spring water and tortillas. Juancho sat chatting for a while and then unpacked the *uxa* root and peyote from his bag and laid them on a rock as if giving them a chance to breathe. Then he took Jessica and Humberto and some of his family back down to the stream to make an offering.

The five peyote burned with intent on their stone in the dappled shade. They looked like scones, or rock-cakes, or some strange fibrous soufflé with skin like a celeriac. The top of them, the 'button', would have been flush with the surface of the desert and was a pattern of segments – solar panels, in effect – which were dotted with small white tufts. Peyote comes in five colours, like its sister, maize. These were of the blue, and supposedly most powerful, variety. All the colours, though, were virtually invisible to the untrained eye in the desert where they grew. Even here, exposed in full view, root and all, the peyote seemed to retreat metamorphically into the rock, folding in among the swirls of lichen.

Peyote is so difficult to see, even for experienced *peyoteros*, that the powers of Kauyumári are needed to find it. The deer god's affinity with peyote, like his affinity with maize, makes him almost interchangeable with it. In the Huichol creation story, when the gods and goddesses journeyed together to find light in this world, they were led through the darkness by Grandfather Fire, Tatewarí. At the end of their fabulous pilgrimage, they found the sun rising from a deep tunnel in a mountain to illuminate the world for the very first time. Kauyumári had been the last of the gods to arrive and, when the sun came up, the gods could see that Kauyumári had left round, luminous, disc-like tracks all over the desert. Tatewarí, who was also the first shaman, instructed the rest of the gods to eat Kauyumári's tracks because he realized they were sacred food. Now, when *peyoteros* look for peyote they summon up an image of the deer god, picturing him trotting across the landscape before them. Where they see his feet fall they find peyote.

For the Huichol, to eat peyote is, in effect, to walk in the footsteps of Kauyumári. Peyote is imbued with the characteristics of the deer god – tricky yet illuminating, laughter-producing yet also visionary, it is ally and protector, messenger and guide. It is 'hunted' not 'gathered', using ceremonial arrows as if it were animal. When it is cut, it is done ritually and with great care, leaving the rootstock – the 'bones' – behind so that another peyote will grow in its place. Sometimes this produces a clump of peyotes which are specially revered for the patterns they produce, often reminiscent of the shape of a deer. Little white tufts on the surface of the button are said to be deer tails.

When a deer is killed, its bond with peyote is given full recognition. It is laid out with great tenderness, its head facing east in the direction of Huiricuta, the land of the cactus. After the animal has been offered water and chocolate to sustain its soul on its journey back to the sacred desert, two peyotes are placed over the eyes, and the muzzle, horns, ears, everything by which it lived, sensed, and knew, are rubbed with peyote. Its mouth receives particular attention so that its breath can reinforce the power of the peyote; and the cactus can, in turn, propel its soul on its great journey.

The Huichol regard peyote as the key to the metaphysical world. Children as young as five years old are given little tastes of it so they can learn its magic at an early age. But the plant has physical properties, too, long familiar to the Huichol and yet only just becoming known to science. While the Huichol regard the medicinal aspects of peyote as secondary to its spiritual purpose – almost as a side-effect of its spectacular transcendental powers – the Western world has been going into a head-spin over 'its' biological discoveries.

Peyote is used by the Huichol as a general panacea, but it's known to be particularly effective applied topically to infected wounds and a certain type of scorpion sting and, swallowed in an infusion, it can kill intestinal worms and salve other problems of the gut. Western scientists have recently proved its antibiotic activity against a wide spectrum of bacteria and fungi, including – they were excited to find – strains of the deadly and robust *staphylococcus aureus* – a bacterium responsible for some pneumonias and for blood poisoning in surgical wounds and which has become increasingly resilient to antibiotics. According to recent reports from the United States 40 per cent of 'staph' infections in hospitals are resistant to every antibiotic except one – vancomycin – but it is generally thought to be only a matter of time before this antibiotic, too, becomes ineffective and mortality rates return to the levels of the 1950s and 60s when 80 per cent of people with this particular infection died. Not for the first time, indigenous knowledge has come galloping to the rescue of Western medicine. But there is clearly more to peyote than meets the eye of the lab technician.

I tried to follow the others' example and have a snooze while we waited for Juancho, but the presence of the cactus beside me was too distracting. I felt like a spear carrier waiting in the wings while the maestro limbered up for a gala performance.

By the time we reached it the cliff-face had assumed gigantic proportions. The path winding up to the cave at its base was so steep that at times I found myself crawling. There were boulders strewn about the slope, like crumbs brushed off a table, that had somehow come to a standstill. But there was the vertiginous feeling that the ground could give way at any moment or a rock come crashing down from above and knock us all unconscious. When we finally stood on the cave-ledge, dizzy from the climb, it was as if we were hovering in mid-air.

Opposite, in the distance, through the tops of the trees, was another sacred mountain, with a cliff like a nipple on the top of it. Another fortress of the gods. It drew one's gaze towards it mesmerically, like a mirror.

The cave itself, when we turned inside, was an alcove cleft in the rock with a high, jagged, double arcade that accentuated the impression of a temple. Along the wall at the back fell a shaggy curtain of fern and moss, fed by spring water – little more than a leak in this season – perspiring from the rock face.

Sticking out among the ferns, and on a spongy shelf like an altar at the bottom, were old offerings: *urutexi*, or votive arrows; gourd bowls; candles; a bead painting of deer; and the little woven nets like spiders' webs called *niérika*, which are used as magic portals for seeing into the other world. These were miniature replicas, Humberto said, of the snares which the Huichol used to make to catch deer before the advent of the shotgun.

'What do you think of this place?' Juancho asked me, 'does it make you afraid?' I wasn't sure how to answer, if Juancho might think me too afraid or not afraid enough. 'It's extraordinary – very striking. And beautiful,' I said, which I knew wasn't committing much but seemed enough to satisfy the *mara'akáme*.

There was definitely something unusual, something magical about this spot, though, something that seemed to add up to more than just the blessed feeling of moisture in the air, the miracle of water coming from dry rock. There was an aura of ancestral history, of ancient communications, a vague intimation of spirit, perhaps, or life, as if the cave were, somehow, occupied. Next door there was a smaller cave with no water but a sandy floor where we threw down our bags. It felt desolate by comparison.

Juancho's cave was not, in the strictest sense, frightening or awe-inspiring. There was none of that feeling of dread or fear that had struck me when I wandered around the Nuremberg citadels of Teotihuacán outside Mexico City, or the imposing temples of the Maya in Chiapas. But there was that same frisson I felt standing on the site of an Iron Age hillfort in Britain; that naked, elemental sense of possession.

The Huichol seemed oblivious, or at least unconcerned for the moment, about the spiritual occupants of the cave and bustled about with practicalities – gathering wood, sweeping the floor, placing *ollas* (pots) on the mossy bank to catch drips. A fire was lit near the mouth of the cave, each of us contributing a piece of wood to Tatewarí to request him to look after us during the coming night.

The scene devolved into one of domesticity – everyone began to relax, lying around chatting, shelling peanuts, picking at *tostadas*. Children clambered over the dank moss of the shrine. Some of the boys went off to collect more firewood and special herbs for tea. At Juancho's instruction, Jessica and I made a large pot of packet soup and noodles and handed it around. The women brought out their sewing. The *ting-ting-ting* of drips hitting tin pots mingled with the sound of talking and occasional bursts of laughter. A young man cradled his wife in his arms as their baby fell asleep at her breast. After another hot-blooded attempt to get Jessica to lie down with him, Juancho covered his face with a handkerchief and began to snore.

Gradually, as the day closed, the light grew dimmer in the cave and Juancho began to stir. He tied on his *mara'akáme* headband and began to daub the rocks with yellow spots from a paste made with the *uxa* root. Then he laid out a ground-cloth for the altar on a flattish piece of rock midway between the fire and the sacred spring. With no perceptible change of mood, no ominous announcement or deliberate change of gear, the secular shifted to the ceremonial. Sacred objects began to materialize from Juancho's bags: a yarn painting; bundles of candles; maize cobs in the five sacred colours; *jícara* containing a sacred crystal, the 'singing stone of the deer'; other gourds containing water and chocolate for the deer god; the plaited oblong baskets – or *takwátsi* – containing the shamanic *muv-iéris* and other power-objects. Out came the little mirror, a symbol that brought me back momentarily to the Mayan church of San Juan Chamula, to the Purépecha burial chambers in Tzintzuntzan, to the Toltec god 'Smoking Mirror' and Quetzalcoatl's expulsion from Mexico. Finally, in the centre, in pride of place, Juancho installed the head of the deer, its brow and antlers crowned with flowers. Gradually everyone came up to add their offerings – circular *tablas* of dancing deer; votive gourds and arrows; coins bearing the national emblem, that powerful talisman of the Mexican eagle and snake; colourful woven shoulder bags; bracelets and necklaces; necker-chiefs – things they were asking to be blessed and empowered by the gods.

Even now, there was no self-consciousness, no sepulchral hush. For the Huichol there was no separation between daily and spiritual life, between the sacred and profane; only degrees of religious intensity. There was no church door, no cut-off point, no time or place for stifling a laugh or talking in whispers. Humour and irreverence would not offend the gods or make light of the cere-mony. It was, in contrast to the dirge-like, Latinate communions of the Catholics, the sombre remembrances of the Purépecha, or even the shamanic rituals of the Zapotecs or the Maya, a natural component of the occasion. Someone had placed a tiny represen-tation of Christ on the cross on the altar, beside a picture of the Virgin of Guadalupe. 'Separate that man and that woman,' Juancho commanded, 'or they're going to fuck each other.'

It was time for the peyote. Juancho took out his Swiss-army knife and ceremoniously dissected a couple of the bulbs, cutting off the tough outer skin like a pineapple and pulling out the tufts. Then one by one, the men, several of the women, one or two of the younger boys, and lastly the *téiwaris* came forward and stood before him to be blessed. Shaking his deer-tail-eagle-feather wand with its tiny bell, he lightly touched the hands, feet, head and heart of each person, before placing a chunk of the cactus in their mouths. When it came to my turn, I had to suppress a desire to say 'Amen'.

The cactus was instantaneously bitter and seemed to suck my mouth dry. It was strangely cold on the tongue, like a sliver of ice. I hadn't yet dared to swallow any of it when I felt my stomach begin to heave. 'Chew it slowly,' said Humberto. 'If you swallow it in one go you'll be sick.'

Juancho had warned us not to grimace – to try to look like we were enjoying it. We should be grateful, he said: this was a gift from the gods. But it was virtually impossible, as I tried to smooth the furrows from my brow, not to look as if someone had slapped me across the face. I could feel my eyes starting out of their sockets and a sneer of offence twisting my lips. As I chewed, desperately trying to befriend the acrid taste, the fibres of the root seemed to warm up and swell on my tongue. My mouth, as dry as the desert a second ago, was now awash with saliva and the piece of cactus began to take on the disturbing consistency of raw flesh.

Juancho blessed himself and popped some peyote into his mouth. 'Uggh!' he exclaimed, screwing up his face, 'It's disgusting. I don't like this.' He pretended to spit it out. We laughed, but didn't feel it was quite our place to agree.

Juancho took the *uxa* root and ground some more of it to a paste with a little sacred water. Then he applied a dozen or so yellow spots to our cheeks. Holding his special religious mirror he carefully dotted paint on his own.

The world I have come from is beginning, imperceptibly, to go into retreat. Here in this cave we are *compañeros*, bound together on a collective journey. The *uxa* spots tighten the skin as they begin to dry. We look like reflections of each other. Juancho takes a phial of deer-blood, empties it into a gourd and places it on the altar. Then he pulls up a small rock and takes his place, with his back to the opening of the cave, facing south towards his homeland, the altar in front of him, the fire on his right. Someone gestures to me and I give Juancho my padded 'Therm-o-rest' to make his seat more comfortable. It's going to be a long night. Juancho begins to chant.

Outside the sun surrenders a few last rays and the cumulonimbi take a final, fiery curtain call. As dusk intensifies our fire springs to life, throwing the faces of the gathering into sharp relief. We could be sitting here at any moment in time. We've been lifted into eternity. My eyes are drawn to the fantastic colours dancing in the skirts and headscarves of the women, the acrobatic detail of the men's tunics and beads. My own clothes seem dowdy and joyless by comparison. I begin to consider it a metaphor.

Suddenly I notice the *uxa* spots on our cheeks. They look like raindrops on the white skin of my *téiwari* companions; but on the dark skin of the Indians they jump out, fluorescent and alive, ready to speak. Juancho is introducing us to the deities, singing in Huichol, explaining who we are and why we're here. His voice is steady, beseeching, rhythmic, softly rasping, mesmerizing. The youngest children settle down in a tent to sleep.

Everyone else sits around, as before, gazing into the flames, occasionally chatting, or passing the bottle of mezcal. The peyote, flower of the desert, doesn't react well with water, I've been told. It foams in the stomach like cappuccino, bucking and resisting the aquatic forces. It finds the distillation of agave, its biological *compañero*, much more compatible so we drink *tepe* – a kind of cactus moonshine we bought in the Tepehuano village – from old plastic Sprite bottles. It's fiery but comforting and acts as a much-needed *digestivo*.

Bats return to the cave, no doubt astounded at what they find, and a night chill sets in. Jessica notices me beginning to shiver. 'Try not to focus on the cold or it'll start to possess you,' she advises me gently. 'The peyote will warm you if you let it. Concentrate on the heat from the fire.'

Beyond the fire, on the other side of the cave, Juancho's assistant, a tall young man with a bright, lively face, leaps up and dances a jig. He is the son of Cacayari, the old man in Chucho's village and, though he was pointed out to me earlier, this is the first time I've really taken him in. He's wearing a sky-blue tunic and scarlet neckerchief. He wears a watch and has a camera with him. He even knows a few words of English which he speaks with an American accent. But he is, I am told, a true Huichol, a *mara'akáme* in the making. His Christian name is Raphael but here he is known as Cumanama. He is excited by the growing effect of the peyote. 'I love it,' he says, laughing, 'but it makes me talk too much, like you *téiwaris* when you get drunk.'

He's talking in fluent Spanish, translating the gist of Juancho's orations, but he also unburdens himself of some musings on the gulf between the West and the Huichol. 'You know, people look at us – in Zacatecas, in Mexico City – and they say "poor Indians, they have nothing". But we earn money selling our artefacts. It's just that we spend it all on making offerings and ceremonies for the gods like this. It's a big sacrifice to come here: it costs money to hire the truck, to buy the petrol; it's a hard walk; it's uncomfortable; we can't bring proper food with us. It's a sacrifice we make for the deities. That's what Juancho is telling them now: that we've come here to call upon them and give offerings, to meet with them and talk with them; but we don't do it lightly, without hardship and the right preparation.'

He lets out a large belch and laughs as if taken by surprise. 'They don't understand – the people in their offices and their businesses in the city,' he continues, firmly but amiably, 'that we do these things not for ourselves, but for the earth. Because the earth needs it. Now more than ever. The Huichol are one of the few peoples left who still listen, who know how to do the things the earth asks of us. It's very important we do this. We must struggle with every effort we are capable of to preserve the balance, to keep the worlds of the gods and men in harmony, to help the forces of nature, to keep everything we know in order. Our happiness, our whole existence, depends on these things.'

His speech is calm but impassioned and I find it deeply moving. I know I'll remember his words; they seem to have attached themselves to my soul and I don't feel the usual urge to reach for my notebook. I'm not sure my fingers would remember how to hold a pen anyway. My mind trails off, trying to follow Cumanama. This is what the outside world has forgotten, I consider, losing myself so completely in the fire that I forget to blink and my eyes begin to water – we're all in this together; everything is connected. A phrase of Cumanama's, a phrase I've also heard Juancho use, keeps returning: *todos unidos*. So far, I reflect, my travels have been characterized by separateness, by victories of diversity and regionalism, by the splintering of the country as it frees itself from seventy years of revolutionary nationalism. Everyone I had met seems to have been battling their corner, fighting for cultural recognition and independence, like ships scattering across the sea.

I'd been struck, of course, by obvious threads of Mexicanness, by forces that persisted despite four centuries of ethnic cleansing and colonial brainwashing. Indigenous Mexico seemed to hold the key to the *Mexicanidad* that Senator Zinser was so eager to see resuscitated in order to keep the country from blowing apart like a bomb. Among all the people I'd visited, there had been always that extraordinary, fearless, typically Mexican attitude towards death – something that went beyond a casual *indifferentia mortis* and reached deeper into a different understanding of life and time. There was a profound sense of community, something that bound individuals irrevocably to family, and to tribe, and most importantly, to the land; something we urban, egotistical gringos were so poor at imitating. And there was that exultant spiritual fecundity, that ritual intensity – even among people as openly disrespectful as the Juchitecos – for which Christianity in all its fundamentalist forms had been unable, in the end, to stand as substitute.

But there'd always been a consciousness, sometimes a deliberate striving for, regional recognition, for cultural or religious or political independence. Despite the ancient ties that bound them deep below the surface, all these different communities seemed to be trying to wrestle away from each other, and out from under the blanket of nationhood that had suffocated them for so long.

Only here, now, among the most marginalized and isolated group of Mexicans I've so far encountered, do I find myself unexpectedly challenged by the bigger picture. But it's not a picture of *Mexicanidad*, as such, that I'm confronted with. This is a perspective that's bigger than national boundaries, bigger even than continents, bigger than the here and now. It's a blast from the furnace of human evolution, from a memory the modern world has long forgotten; it's a vision of timeless, composite universality; an omneity of cause and effect.

Fragmentation, I begin to surmise, is a sign of the times; it's the natural process when one world of the sun is ending and another is due to begin. It's happening not only in Mexico, but in the post-communist bloc, across the whole of Asia, Indonesia, Africa and India; it's happening the world over as walls come down and empires breathe their dying last. Perhaps, I reflect, this is what globalization is about. Not politics or economics, free trade or democracy, squabbling between monkeys, elephants sneezing the mice out of their kingsize beds, but a greater, mightier perception – a notion of spiritual kinship and global empathy, of joint relationship: the realization that man, beast, bird, insect, tree, singing stones and Singer sewing machines, we're in this together; we're from the same root-stock and we're headed, come what may, for the same destination. This is the song of every animate and inanimate object; this is the hymn of the earth.

I feel the almost imperceptible flurry of air as a moth brushes past my face. Its wingbeats send shivers into the fire, fanning the flames. My heart is quivering like a bird in a cage. The peyote seems to be singing, trying to burst from my chest. The Spaniards toppled the Aztec idols, smashed the gods of the Maya, the Zapotecs, the Purépecha, the Inca and every other race in the Americas, north and south, in turn; they erased centuries of native learning – of astronomy, geometry, mathematics; they eradicated native writing: poetry, history, literature (the library of Netzahualcóyotl – 'Hungry Coyote', the King of Texcoco, the Aztecs' ally in the Valley of Mexico – took three days to burn); and art – plastic, sculptural and architectural; they overruled tested formulae of husbandry and agriculture; deforested and desertified the land; but in all this cultural decimation, this bonfire of knowledge, there was nothing in the Western world that could replace the indigenous Americans' unique use of hallucinogens and what they represented; there was no substitute for this sense of mystery, this vision of the beyond, this conversation with the soul. The channel through which the indigenous Mexican communicated with his universe, an information super-highway of a sort, was deliberately blocked so he would be starved of spiritual sustenance, his lifeline severed, so he would float for ever, aimlessly, in a void. It's nothing short of a miracle, I see, that out here, in the blazing Sierra, where there are no libraries to burn, a small band of Indians are living that ancient world-vision, keeping the channel open for the spiritual survival of the modern world.

Occasionally, overcome by tiredness I allow my head to drop into my arms and close my eyes. But I can't sleep. The waking dream has possessed me and images tumble on against my eyelids until, still exhausted, I have to open my eyes and direct them back into the fire.

Now people are taking it in turns to address themselves to the gods, to explain why they've come. They talk in eloquent, flowing monologues, breaking into tears as they recount their needs and fears and gratitude. One woman has come to give thanks to the deities of the cave for curing her son who was desperately ill as a boy. They brought him here several times and he lived. Now he has a girlfriend he's about to marry and it's time for his mother to surrender him and let him go on his way. That, she says, is why she's crying – for love and gratitude and the sweet pain of separation. For her, this is a ritual of transition. Her son is in the cave, too, to pay his due. Another woman is from the family that sponsored the ceremony at Santa Isabel. She's here to ask a blessing for the new *xiriki*. Another, tubby woman, has a stomach illness and is asking to be cured. And so it goes on.

I begin to see that this is what the new evangelism movement I'd encountered in Chiapas was trying to provide: a framework for emotional release, for self-empowerment, for spiritual and moral support. But from here the Protestant structure looks as lopsided and unnatural as its Catholic adversary. The Huichol ceremony is emotional, to be sure, but there's nothing hysterical, obsessive or fanatical about it. Its purpose is to illuminate life, not smother it; it's awe-inspiring but not intimidating; you can eat, drink and be merry with it – you can even take the piss. The Huichol religion is as generous and balanced and human and enjoyable as Catholicism and new wave evangelism are embattled and obsessive and pur-itanical, fighting with ultimatums and their backs against the wall. Protestantism is just building another, slightly more comfortable, cell for people to live in.

Juancho is cutting more peyote. He looks questioningly at me for a moment, perhaps trying to judge whether to give me any more. I try to look grateful as I receive the second slice. It's far more difficult to eat than the first. My whole body seems to resist, my stomach wrenching and shaking as if trying to release itself from the peyote's grip. Again I chew the cactus slowly, waiting for it to come alive in my mouth, trying to conquer my instincts, to calm myself, to meet its challenge. 'The first time you take peyote,' Cumanama tells us, 'is very important. Since I had no fear, the peyote became my friend. Now, when I take it, I know it will be my guide. It will not try to trick me or frighten me.'

The flames of the fire begin to judder as if they're being filmed on Super 8. Juancho is invoking the deities from all their secret places. He has hardly moved from his rock. The Therm-o-rest has slipped ineffectively to one side. And, though he is barely four feet from the flames, he doesn't shrink from the heat. Occasionally he raises a hand to cool his cheek. He's been chanting now for several hours. He's in a trance-like state yet he doesn't forget a single detail of the proceedings. He's aware of every individual in the cave and what they've come for. I can see how his energy, his *kúpúri*, must be channelled from somewhere deep and unfathomable, perhaps from Tatewarí himself, blazing beside him.

One of the Huichol takes some agave stems out of the hot coals. He slices off the blackened skin with a machete. Each stroke leaves a dozen images in the air like the arms of Shiva. I think of Indians on another continent, of gurus and saddhus, and then ascetics and mystics all over the world, striving in the same Sisyphean attempt to keep our world on its course. The agave is sweet and woody like sugarcane with a hint of roasted chestnuts.

Juancho is moving on to the fourth phase of his incantion preparing for the arrival of the gods. He asks his wife to pass him his ceremonial hat. She looks at him nonplussed. 'There, beside you,' he points. She looks at it in amazement and bursts out laughing. 'Aaieee!' she exclaims, 'I thought it was a turtle!'

The women gather themselves together and begin to light the candles. Juancho's voice becomes keener. All around the cave, people stir from semi-sleep and collect around the altar. The chanting gains purpose. The atmosphere becomes powerfully charged and the women begin to weep. Their tears fall generously, profusely, with the occasional wracking sob. They wipe their eyes with their scarves without, somehow, disturbing the paint on their cheeks. The *uxa* spots have begun to have a life of their own, rising out of their faces like glowing yellow pimples.

There are complicated rituals going on now that I find difficult to follow. But then, in one dramatic moment, Juancho raises the deer's head and seems to become Kauyumári himself. Remotely, I find tears in my eyes. One by one we go forward to receive his blessing, bowing our heads as if locking antlers with the god. When I return to my seat I notice the stars outside piercing the sky like *uxa* spots.

Sometime later we get up to be blessed again. The men are anointed with holy water gathered on Juancho's recent trip to Huiricuta with Humberto, using an eagle feather. For the women, Juancho dips a tiny pink flower into the gourd, shaking the drops over us, before touching it to our lips so that we can suck the moisture from it. Lastly we each bless the altar, using the feather or the flower to anoint it with water in the five sacred directions: East, West, North, South and Centre.

When I look into the fire now I feel heat where my heart is, as if part of the sun is burning in there and I wonder what genius called this part of the anatomy the 'solar plexus' because that's obviously what it is. My mind wanders back to the ancient Aztecs, making human sacrifices, tearing out human hearts, in their desperation to guarantee the rising of the sun. How they described their own predicament in the legend of Quetzocóatl – the Christ-like Redeemer, the Merciful One, who had fled from them, insulted and outraged, without doing his job. How they had lived in hope of his return. And mistook Cortés, of all people, as the answer to their prayers. Perhaps, I thought, they'd rolled out the red carpet in the wrong direction. Perhaps they should have looked to where they came from, to the aboriginal cultures flowering in their wake in the mesas of the Sierra; where east was the heartland of Huiricuta, not the seaport of Veracruz.

My meanderings are interrupted by a resounding, rumbling fart from the other side of the cave. Cumanama jumps and pretends it had nothing to do with him. 'Sun's coming up,' he jokes, 'I can hear it.'

It reminds me that I'm beginning to lose track of my own physical sensations and I think, but can't be sure, that I need to pee. Putting thoughts of snakes and scorpions to one side I slide off into the undergrowth on the hill, taking special care with my footing. The cave is spectacular from the outside – a Sibyllic yawn venting smoke and flames and incantations. It's still pitch-dark and from my precarious squatting position the cave hovers miraculously, a gateway to the unknowable, to the mysteries of the universe, a portal to the awe-inspiring energies of the spirit. I realize how lucky I am to see this. The Huichol use this portal as blithely as a turnstile but most of us in the West barely know of its existence. Occasionally in my lifetime I'd felt it open a crack – in the presence of extraordinary beauty, say, or at the birth of my children, or holding my father's hand across the frontier of death – but then it had closed again with a resounding bang and life returned to 'normal' and that indescribable awe, that sense of transcendence and of peace, had slipped through my fingers like sand and I'd returned useless and empty-handed to the frenetic business of the melting-pot. How ignorant and impoverished we must seem to people like the Huichol, we *téiwari* who believe ourselves so superior. I know, now, that I'm still – in Cacayari's words – a child. I pull up my trousers and head back to the cave.

Epilogue
Mexican Miracles

It would be a miracle, for example, if I dropped a stone and it rose upwards. But is it no miracle that it falls to the ground?

Alfred Polgar (1873–1955)

All miracles are magical mirrors;
never can we see our faces in them.

Logan Pearsall Smith (1865–1946)

On my last day in Mexico City I saw butterflies floating through the toxic haze in the Alameda outside the monolithic Bellas Artes palace.

Talk in the city was dominated by the forthcoming presidential elections in July. People were beginning to think the impossible. For the first time in seventy years the electorate were doubting whether the PRI contender, Francisco Labastida, would simply canter past the winning post like all official PRI Presidential candidates before him. For the first time in its history the election was beginning to look anything but a foregone conclusion.

Labastida's main challenger was the candidate for the conservative National Action Party (PAN). Vicente Fox was a Mexican of Spanish and Irish extraction, a devout Catholic from Guanajuato – the silver-mining town near San Miguel de Allende and source of the Independence movement, where the heads of the Independence heroes Hidalgo and Allende had once been hung up on display.

Vicente Fox was ex-chief executive of Coca-Cola's subsidiary in Mexico and used to hot competition. It was Fox who put Pepsi to

309

rout and turned Mexico into the biggest per capita consumers of
'The Real Thing' on the planet. Fifty-eight years old and six feet
six in height, he's a self-styled tough-talking *ranchero*. Pictures of
Fox on the campaign trail showed him not in the Preppy Ivy League
blazer and brogues of previous contenders and PRI apparatchiks,
but in jeans and cowboy boots and a thick belt with his name
carved on the buckle. He was galloping round the political ring
waving his sombrero like the Marlboro Man of the Mexican
opposition.

Fox had also taken to carrying the standard of the Virgin of
Guadalupe on his rallies – an action that drew cries of outrage
from PRI supporters. But Fox's admirers saw the gesture as justified: once again the Virgin was being called upon to stand up for
the Mexican in the street, to blow open the doors of power for
him.

There was an air of incredulity and tension in the press as the
race began to gather momentum. Could this really be the man who
would knock the PRI off its perch? My friend Senator Zinser
had clearly decided he would be. Along with other greens and
conservationists, with women's groups and student groups, and a
host of special interest groups, he was rallying support for the
outsider, Vicente Fox.

On the afternoon of my flight home Laurence and Humberto gave
me a goodbye lunch that I thought would literally be my last. Laurence had accidentally left a kilo of raw prawns sweltering in the boot
of her car for a day and a half but as there was nothing else in the
fridge, she decided to cook them anyway and serve them with plenty
of chilli and lime and shots of tequila to kill off the bugs.

We sat on their roof terrace in the hazy sunshine, surrounded by
pots of cacti, and toasted the Presidential elections, the future
of Mexico, and Juancho's dream to make a traditional Huichol
sacrifice to the ancient earth goddess Tonantzin on the Cerro de
Tepeyac. '¡Híjole! Hell! Imagine how it would wind up those
Católicos and animal rights people!' roared Humberto, 'killing a
bull, or better, a deer, in the middle of Mexico City, next to the
Basílica of the Virgin of Guadalupe!'

*

The view from the plane isn't nearly as daunting as when I'd first arrived. Mexico City no longer looks so alien and vast and uncompromising. Somewhere in the grey expanse beneath me are restaurants that I know, parks and houses and living-rooms and friends. If someone had suggested two years ago, before I came to Mexico, that I might grow fond of this place – this stifling, polluted, concrete disaster – I would have thought them mad. But Mexico City has transformed itself, and me. It is no longer simply the capital of misery; I've come to see it as a city of miracles, too.

Almost exactly a year before my British Airways flight took me away from Mexico for the last time, Pope John Paul II had taken off from the same airport on an AeroMexico flight, his plane swinging up and over a city that had been emotionally galvanized by his visit. His presence had sparked off the usual controversies in the press and the odd, fiery demonstration. There were volleys of criticism from intellectuals and atheists, liberals and radicals and New Age evangelists, indigenous rights protesters, feminists and family planners and pro-abortionists.

But these were eddies in an overwhelming tide of public euphoria. Young and old, the faithful flocked in their thousands to hear him say mass at the Basilica of Our Lady of Guadalupe on Tepeyac Hill. They pushed past police cordons to catch a passing glimpse of the bulletproof Pope-mobile; crammed into cafés and road stalls to see his address to the people on TV. A brand of crisps was released called *Papas* (a play on the word for Pope and potatoes) with John Paul's face smiling benevolently from the packet.

As the engines of the Pope's plane roared up on the runway, millions of Mexican *chilangos* were moved to express their devotion and a fond farewell. In a spontaneous gesture, reminiscent of the original Mexican wave, people all over the city rushed to find mirrors. Instinctively reaching, perhaps, for that ancient symbol of sanctified magic, they grabbed hand-mirrors, car wing-mirrors, mirrors off the bathroom wall, any mirror they could get their hands on – and scrambled with them to the tops of buildings – to the roof-terraces of hotels, the top-floors of office-blocks, the top-levels of carparks, on to the corrugated iron roofs of shacks in the barrios, and as the hour struck for the plane's departure, they angled their mirrors up towards the sun. Suddenly, like sunlight emerging from behind a cloud, a million shards of light came piercing through the *niebla tóxica*. For several minutes, the city of Mexico was bathed in a dazzling halo.

Six months after I left Mexico I awoke to the results of the Presidential election. 'Mexico's seven decades of single-party rule are washed away with a swig of champagne' ran the feature in the *Independent*. There was a picture of Fox chugging a bottle of Moët like a Formula 500 champion. 'I would have preferred tequila!' he'd cried seconds later over the microphone, to cheers from the crowd.

The result had confounded the polls, which had been predicting a slim victory for the PRI. But now it was clear what had happened. In many areas turnout had been a staggering 80 per cent. Thousands of polling stations had run out of ballots by late afternoon and had to rush in more to deal with the volume of voters. Queues had stretched for blocks. *Campesinos* and factory workers, mothers with babies, students, even the odd nonagenarian who could remember the Revolution, had stood doggedly for hours in the blazing sun. Thousands of migrants living in the States had flown back south, hitched rides across the border, or taken the bus, in order to vote. I learnt with amusement from mexicanwave.com, that 2,414 voters carried the name Juan Hernández Hernández, the same as the Chamulan Protestant evangelist I'd met in San Cristóbal. I hoped he'd been one of them.

But the victory, it was now clear, had been clinched by the votes of women and the young. Almost 52 per cent of the country's 59.5 million eligible voters were women, 2 million more than men. A few weeks before the election the *Financial Times* had reported Cecilia Loria, head of a national pressure group called 'Milenio Feminista' – Feminist Millennium – making the Juchiteca-style pronouncement that 'Women between eighteen and forty are going to define who wins this election'. I wasn't sure if Comandante Ramona would have made it to the ballot-box – there were rumours that she was in hiding in the Lacandón rainforest and very sick;

but I felt sure the sturdy little Mayan doll-seller I'd met in San Cristóbal would have voted for the first time in her life.

The PRI, rattled by this sudden uprising of woman-power, had evolved last-minute tactics to try to hold on to their votes – the only way they could think how. They'd started hosting huge fiestas in the poor neighbourhoods of Mexico City, featuring a male striptease act called 'The Sexy Boys'. Only now was it apparent that Mexico's answer to the Full Monty had failed miserably to impress the girls.

Half of Mexico's electorate was also under thirty-five and this, too, had had a huge impact on the outcome. Mexico was buzzing with a new generation of optimistic twenty-somethings; kids who'd been raised on city streets, on television and the internet. They weren't afraid of the PRI, by the roars of the old dinosaur that had once feasted on the life-blood of their country. They had fewer ties to bind them to the old web of bribery, intimidation and corruption. They'd been born in a world where the ancient feudal system of *caciquismo*, the curse that extended through colonial times back to the Aztecs and beyond, was losing its grip. To this new, bullish generation, anything was possible.

In his victory speech the '21st Century Fox' related his triumph to 'Mexico's marvellous women', acknowledging that 'the youth of Mexico imposed a tone of happiness and hope on my campaign. It was contagious. For them and with them, we will be able to govern.' The world of the sixth sun had begun. I opened an e-mail from Humberto labelled 'Mexican Berlin Wall' and noticed the first word – '*¡Híjole!*'

A few months later, Humberto sent me another e-mail. Just days after the swearing in of Mexico's new President, for the first time since its momentous eruption in 1994, Mt Popo – that magma-filled champagne bottle – had blown its top.

About 12,000 feet up in the mountains of Michoacán, three hours' drive from Mexico City, a miracle is happening. It is 3 January 2000. I'm with almost my entire immediate family – my children, husband, my mother and parents-in-law – to celebrate the turn of the millennium. We're standing in a clearing in a forest of oyamel fir trees. The Latin name for the trees is *abies religiosa* and this seems apt, although it's not the trees we've come to see, but what's in them.

The spectacle is as dramatic and arresting, as beautiful, as I could ever have imagined. It's so overwhelming it's almost too much to take in at first. It's easier, somehow, if you close your eyes. You can get some sense of presence, then, of the sheer volume of life presenting itself around you. You can hear the whisper of their wings, feel the thousands of bodies fluttering past like curtains of silk. One butterfly makes no sound. But a hundred million sounds like a distant wind.

The children take the manifestation in their stride, as if they've been covered in butterflies all their lives, as if these swathes of palpitating orange are as normal as sunrise. They hop over butterfly puddles, searching for dead ones.

Thousands of butterflies lie dying on the forest floor. Their tiny struggles mock the enormity of what their bodies have just achieved. These are monarch butterflies and they've flown all the way to Mexico, to this one forest in Michoacán, from as far north as the Great Lakes in Canada, over 3000 miles away. It's taken them two months. Fluttering along at an average speed of 7.5 miles an hour, they've crossed prairies and motorways, negotiated mountain ranges and cities, weathered rain and wind and blazing deserts, and relentless expanses of inhospitable mono-crops. Somehow, in the vast North American continent, they've managed to find sustenance when they needed it, alighting here and there in some remnant of wilderness – a vacant lot or a piece of wasteland untouched by pesticide and herbicide – laying their eggs in a patch of milkweed, the monarch caterpillars' principal source of food. No one knows why or how they make this mammoth expedition. The monarch butterfly migration is one of the last great unexplained wonders of nature.

Of course millions of monarchs fail to make it as far as Mexico, their tiny half-a-gram bodies are buffeted by every imaginable fate: splattered on windscreens, tumbled into the slipstream of juggernauts, singed in bush-fires and barbecues, waterlogged by sudden downpours, pulled apart by a cat in some back garden.

And for all those that ended their lives dramatically, by accident, there were as many that gave up the ghost through starvation and exhaustion, leaving a Hansel and Gretel trail of wing litter radiating tiny particles of magnetite down the length of North America.

'The Aztecs used to believe that the souls of dead warriors return to this earth not only as hummingbirds but as butterflies, also,' says Luis, staring up into the clouds of insects whirling in front of the sun. 'They called them the "Eternal Sun-dancers".'

Luis has been organizing this trip for us since I last saw him in Pátzcuaro for the Day of the Dead. 'You can't leave Mexico behind you without seeing this. Let me take you,' he'd begged last year, 'it's something incredible, something that will sing in your soul for ever.' The tape he'd given me then in Pátzcuaro included a song called 'Monarca'. 'See,' he'd said, playing the track three times on the trot as we drove back to Morelia, 'that little guitar sound in the background is a *charango* – made from the shell of an armadillo. It makes the sound like the wings of the butterflies. *Caramba!* But it's a beautiful song. If I'd heard this when I was in Chicago, I think my heart would have broken.'

Since then, when I thought of Luis I heard him singing along to this song – *Mariposas de Michoacán, Abre tus alas en par, llévame a soñar, enséñame la libertad* (Butterflies of Michoacán, open your wings, lift me up so I can dream, teach me freedom) – and the image of monarch butterflies had merged in my mind with the thought of hundreds of thousands of migrants like Luis crossing the border to and from the United States.

Luis has met us with a sedan chair that he's had made for my mother who, in her seventies and afflicted by chronic arthritis, won't be able to walk up the mountain. There's been a flurry of excited telephone calls from Luis over the past few weeks as the chair neared completion – it has clearly become a local legend – but nothing that could have suggested the throne that awaited us. Whole treetrunks have gone into its construction. It's more sofa than chair with a thick padded seat and heavy armrests. It would look perfect in a middle-class living-room in Morelia, a whole family piled on to it watching TV. Chiselled into the solid pine back is the outline of a butterfly. A great deal of thought has gone into the comfort of the passenger; very little to the poor souls who are expected to carry her. Even without my mother in it, the four porters struggle to get it off the ground. My mother was dismayed by the effort it was clearly going to be for them and suggested staying behind. Luis would have none of it. But didn't object when we doubled the porters' wages.

Now, triumphant, Luis is lying back in the chair while my mother has taken off on her crutches to photograph the butterflies. The porters have collapsed in the shade, oblivious to the clouds of orange alighting on their sweat-stained shirts and falling from the brims of their sombreros. 'It's a miracle,' sighs Luis. But I can't be sure if he's referring to the monarchs or the fact that my mother and the famous chair have made it to the top.

The champagne we've brought with us seems superfluous, now, and it's warm anyway. The butterflies are putting on the performance of a lifetime. The trees are coated as if by some fantastic lichen. They're dripping from the branches, thick as fur on the trunks. As the sun intensifies and warms their bodies, they begin to whirl up into the air like autumn leaves in suspension, moving in clouds – almost, one begins to sense, in formation, as if they're of a single mind, not separate, random millions but one, single, cooperative, sentient being. *Todos unidos* – the Butterfly Effect. But if the draught from one butterfly's wings can give rise to a hurricane, I wonder, what effect are these millions of monarchs going to have on the world?

In a few weeks' time the butterflies will start flying back to the States – the females at least. The males will all die here, extinguished by their final effort to mate. The pregnant females will lay their eggs somewhere in northern Mexico or Texas, leaving it to the next generation to continue the arduous flight north. They will also lay their eggs and die. Only their offspring, the third generation, will make it to Canada. Then the next generation – the fourth – will make the epic journey back to Mexico, doubling their natural butterfly lifespan in order to make it in one go, flying back to a place only their great-grandparents have ever been. Generations on generations, a myth in the mind's eye.

The children find a dead butterfly with a tiny white sticker under its wing. The sticker has coded numbers on it – like a price tag. Luis gives it to one of the porters. He'll get a hundred pesos when he presents it to the park warden. Like a balloon, or a message in a bottle. Perhaps this monarch will fly back to the States by airmail, in a plane, so a gringo lepidopterist of Mexican descent can marvel at it in a laboratory.

I realize the reality of the American/Mexican border has begun to blur. What started out in my imagination as a thick black wavy line, an insurmountable barrier, along the Río Grande (or Río Bravo) is now smudged and indiscernible, rubbed out by millions of wingbeats and the passage of human feet, by the ancestors of the Hopi, the Papago and Shoshoni; the Cora, Tarahumara and Huichol; the Chichimeca, Purépecha and Otomí; the Aztecs and Toltecs and Zapotecs and Olmecs; the Maya; by all the tribes of North America whose peregrinations backward and forward, up and down the continent over tens of thousands of years have set in motion the endless process of osmosis, the whorl of energy that continues to this day (despite the superficial efforts of border patrols and customs officials) in the migrations of Mexican labourers, New Age travellers and gringo OAPs and American stewardesses in need of a nose-job.

My concept of Mexico has expanded out of all proportion since my travels began. It's become a collage of contradictions and extremes and metamorphoses. Now it's outgrowing even the confines of national boundaries. It's sliding, like a sheet of tinted glass, over the surface of the United States. Mexico, to me, is where the continent begins. This is where the continent settled, grew up, and developed some of the greatest civilizations the world has ever known. This is where her natural orientation lies. Mexico is the heart and guts of North America, its anchor, its solar plexus. This is where the butterflies winter.